# PURCHASING

**Brad Matthews**
**Thomas Schneller**

Join us on the web at

**culinary.delmar.com**

THE CULINARY INSTITUTE OF AMERICA®

# PURCHASING

**Brad Matthews**
**Thomas Schneller**

## DELMAR
CENGAGE Learning™

Australia • Brazil • Japan • Korea • Mexico • Singapore • Spain • United Kingdom • United States

KITCHEN PRO SERIES

**KitchenPro Series: Guide to Purchasing**
Brad Matthews, Thomas Schneller

President: Dr. Tim Ryan '77

Vice-President, Continuing Education:
Mark Erickson '77

Senior Director, Continuing Education:
Susan Cussen

Director of Publishing: Nathalie Fischer

Editorial Project Manager: Margaret
Wheeler '00

Editorial Assistant: Shelly Malgee '08

Editorial Assistant: Erin Jeanne McDowell '08

Photography: Keith Ferris, Photographer
Ben Fink, Photographer

Vice President, Career and Professional
Editorial: Dave Garza

Director of Learning Solutions: Sandy Clark

Senior Acquisitions Editor: James Gish

Managing Editor: Larry Main

Product Manager: Nicole Calisi

Editorial Assistant: Sarah L. Timm

Vice President, Career and Professional
Marketing:  Jennifer Baker

Marketing Director: Wendy E. Mapstone

Senior Marketing Manager: Kristin McNary

Associate Marketing Manager: Jonathan
Sheehan

Senior Production Director: Wendy Troeger

Senior Content Project Manager: Glenn Castle

Senior Art Director: Casey Kirchmayer

Technology Product Manager: Christopher
Catalina

Production Technology Analyst: Thomas Stover

Library of Congress Control Number: 2010940044

ISBN-13: 978-1-4283-1988-2

ISBN-10: 1-4283-1988-3

**Delmar**
5 Maxwell Drive
Clifton Park, NY 12065-2919
USA

Cengage Learning is a leading provider of customized learning solutions with office locations around the globe, including Singapore, the United Kingdom, Australia, Mexico, Brazil, and Japan. Locate your local office at:
**international.cengage.com/region**

Cengage Learning products are represented in Canada by Nelson Education, Ltd.

For your lifelong learning solutions, visit **delmar.cengage.com**

Visit our corporate website at **www.cengage.com**

**Notice to the Reader**
Publisher does not warrant or guarantee any of the products described herein or perform any independent analysis in connection with any of the product information contained herein. Publisher does not assume, and expressly disclaims, any obligation to obtain and include information other than that provided to it by the manufacturer. The reader is expressly warned to consider and adopt all safety precautions that might be indicated by the activities described herein and to avoid all potential hazards. By following the instructions contained herein, the reader willingly assumes all risks in connection with such instructions. The publisher makes no representations or warranties of any kind, including but not limited to, the warranties of fitness for particular purpose or merchantability, nor are any such representations implied with respect to the material set forth herein, and the publisher takes no responsibility with respect to such material. The publisher shall not be liable for any special, consequential, or exemplary damages resulting, in whole or part, from the readers' use of, or reliance upon, this material.

Printed in China
2  3  4  5  6  7  18 17 16 15

# Contents

ABOUT THE CIA   vii

AUTHOR BIOGRAPHY   x

ACKNOWLEDGMENTS   xi

INTRODUCTION   1

## 1 HISTORY OF FOOD PURCHASING   3

Neolithic Era in the Middle East, Asia, and Europe   3
Mesopotamia   5
North Africa   6
Greece   7
Rome   9
Asia   11
Middle Ages   12
The New World   14
Industrial Age   18
Purchasing for Different Modes of Transportation   21
Modern Era Begins   23

## 2 DEALING WITH PURVEYORS AND ESTABLISHING A VENDOR RELATIONSHIP   29

Establishing a Relationship   31
Service Considerations   35
Financial Considerations: Minimum Deliveries
   and Payment Schedules   36
A Win-Win Philosophy   37
Keeping Relationships Viable   41
Legal Considerations   46
Basics of a Contract   48

## 3 DEVELOPING FOOD ORDERS   53

Recommended Skills for Buyers   54

# 4 PURCHASING FOR MEAT, POULTRY, AND FISH 91

Meat Purchasing 92
Options in Purchasing 93
Quality and Yield Grading 95
Shipping Condition and Packaging 101
Market Forms 101
Where to Buy Meats? 103
Purchasing Specs 105

# 5 INVENTORY MANAGEMENT AND THE STOREROOM 199

The Storeroom Function 199
Storeroom and Receiving Facility Layout 201
Sanitation 211
Inventory Management 213

# 6 SMALL AND LARGE EQUIPMENT PURCHASING 245

Small Equipment 246
Large Equipment 252

# 7 TRENDS IN THE INDUSTRY 261

Buying Local 262
Farm-to-Fork Initiatives 263
Seasonality 269
Reducing Carbon Footprint 270
Sustainability 271
The Slow Food Movement 274
Nose-to-Tail Menu Creation 275
Organic Products 276
Thinking Greener 277
Organizational Consultants 278

**READINGS AND RESOURCES LIST 282**

**PHOTO CREDITS 282**

**GLOSSARY 283**

**APPENDIX A 289**

**APPENDIX B 301**

**INDEX 304**

# ABOUT THE CIA

## THE WORLD'S PREMIER CULINARY COLLEGE

The Culinary Institute of America (CIA) is the recognized leader in culinary education for undergraduate students, foodservice and hospitality professionals, and food enthusiasts. The college awards bachelor's and associate degrees, as well as certificates and continuing education units, and is accredited by the prestigious Middle States Commission on Higher Education.

Founded in 1946 in downtown New Haven, CT to provide culinary training for World War II veterans, the college moved to its present location in Hyde Park, NY in 1972. In 1995, the CIA added a branch campus in the heart of California's Napa Valley—The Culinary Institute of America at Greystone. The CIA continued to grow and, in 2008, established a second branch campus, this time in San Antonio, TX. And in 2011, the college added its first international location with the opening of the CIA, Singapore.

From its humble beginnings more than 60 years ago with just 50 students, the CIA today enrolls more than 2,800 students in its degree programs, approximately 3,000 in its programs for foodservice and hospitality industry professionals, and more than 3,500 in its courses for food enthusiasts.

## LEADING THE WAY

Throughout its history, The Culinary Institute of America has played a pivotal role in shaping the future of foodservice and hospitality. This is due in large part to the caliber of people who make up the CIA community—its faculty, staff, students, and alumni—as well as their passion for the culinary arts and dedication to the advancement of the profession.

Headed by the visionary leadership of President Tim Ryan '77, The Culinary Institute of America faculty brings a vast breadth and depth of foodservice industry experience and insight to the CIA kitchens, classrooms, and research facilities. The faculty's more than 140 members have worked in some of the world's finest establishments, earned industry awards and professional certifications, and emerged victorious from countless international culinary competitions. And they continue to make their mark on the industry, through the students they teach, books they author, and leadership initiatives they champion.

The influence of the CIA in the food world can also be attributed to the efforts and achievements of our more than 40,000 successful alumni. Our graduates are leaders in virtually every segment of the industry and bring the professionalism and commitment to excellence they learned at the CIA to bear in everything they do.

# UNPARALLELED EDUCATION

## DEGREE PROGRAMS

The CIA's bachelor's and associate degree programs in culinary arts and baking and pastry arts feature more than 1,300 hours of hands-on learning in the college's kitchens, bakeshops, and student-staffed restaurants, along with an 18-week externship at one of more than 1,200 top restaurant, hotel, and resort locations around the world. The bachelor's degree programs, offered at the Hyde Park, NY campus, also include a broad range of liberal arts and business management courses to prepare students for future leadership positions, as well as a Food, Wine, and (Agri)culture travel experience in one of the world's top culinary regions.

In addition, in collaboration with the Singapore Institute of Technology and Temasek Polytechnic, the CIA offers a bachelor's degree program in culinary arts management at its Singapore campus for graduates of Polytechnic institutions as well as graduates of other hospitality, tourism, and culinary diploma programs.

## CERTIFICATE PROGRAMS

The college's culinary arts certificate program is designed for students interested in an entry-level position in the food world and those already working in the foodservice industry who want to advance their careers. The CIA also offers an Accelerated Culinary Arts Certificate Program (ACAP), which provides graduates of baccalaureate programs in hospitality management, food science, nutrition, and closely related fields with a solid foundation in the culinary arts and the career advancement opportunities that go along with that skill base. And the Accelerated Wine and Beverage Certificate Program (AWBP) gives students an in-depth, multisensory understanding of the beverage world and prepares them for a variety of careers in this important area of the hospitality industry.

## PROFESSIONAL DEVELOPMENT PROGRAMS AND CONSULTING

The CIA offers food and wine professionals a variety of programs to help them keep their skills sharp and stay abreast of industry trends. Courses in cooking, baking, pastry, wine, and management are complemented by stimulating conferences and seminars, online culinary R&D courses, and multimedia training materials. Industry professionals can also deepen their knowledge and earn valuable ProChef® Certification and Certified Wine Professional™ credentials at several levels of proficiency.

In addition, the college offers expert culinary consulting to the industry through its CIA Consulting group. Headed by a seasoned team of Certified Master Chefs and supported by the college's acclaimed international faculty, CIA Consulting offers foodservice businesses a rich menu of custom consulting services in areas such as product innovation, menu R&D, restaurant strategy and design, and culinary training.

## FOOD ENTHUSIAST PROGRAMS

Food enthusiasts can get a taste of the CIA educational experience during the college's popular Boot Camp intensives and Weekends at the CIA courses. In addition, CIA Sophisticated Palate programs at the California campus offer the very best of the Napa Valley food and wine scene, including exclusive visits to area growers, vintners, and purveyors. Enthusiasts who are considering turning their passion for cooking, baking, or wine into their livelihood can explore opportunities in the foodservice and hospitality industry through the CIA's Career Discovery programs.

# CIA LOCATIONS

## MAIN CAMPUS—HYDE PARK, NY

*Bachelor's and associate degree programs, professional development programs, food enthusiast programs*

The CIA's main campus in New York's scenic Hudson River Valley offers everything an aspiring or professional culinarian could want. Students benefit from truly exceptional facilities that include 41 professionally equipped kitchens and bakeshops; five award-winning, student-staffed restaurants; culinary demonstration theaters; a dedicated wine lecture hall; a center for the study of Italian food and wine; a library with nearly 84,000 volumes; and a storeroom filled to brimming with the finest ingredients, including many sourced from the bounty of the Hudson Valley.

## THE CIA AT GREYSTONE—ST. HELENA, CA

*Associate degree programs, certificate programs, professional development program, food enthusiast programs*

Rich with legendary vineyards and renowned restaurants, California's Napa Valley offers students a truly inspiring culinary learning environment. At the center of it all is the CIA at Greystone—a campus like no other, with dedicated centers for flavor development, professional wine studies, and menu research and development; a 15,000-square-foot teaching kitchen space; demonstration theaters; and the award-winning Wine Spectator Greystone Restaurant.

## THE CIA, SAN ANTONIO—SAN ANTONIO, TX

*Certificate program, professional development programs, food enthusiast programs*

Created to advance the appreciation of Latin American cuisines and the careers of the culinarians who prepare them, the CIA, San Antonio offers a variety of education programs and is home to the Center for Foods of the Americas research initiative. The campus includes three teaching kitchens, two skills kitchens, a bakeshop, demonstration theaters, and a unique Latin Kitchen that features both indoor and outdoor professional cooking facilities.

## THE CIA, SINGAPORE—SINGAPORE

*Bachelor's degree program*

Thanks to the CIA's historic partnership with the Singapore Institute of Technology, the college is offering its renowned degree program in Asia for the first time. With state-of-the-art facilities on the campus at Temasek Polytechnic and world-renowned CIA faculty, The Culinary Institute of America, Singapore provides a unique educational experience. Located on the banks of the Bedok Reservoir, the campus offers learning opportunities in the teaching kitchens, classrooms, and student-staffed Top Table Restaurant. CIA, Singapore students also have access to more than 140,000 volumes of texts and e-resources in the Temasek library, as well as meeting rooms and computer labs.

# AUTHOR BIOGRAPHY

Chef Schneller started working with meat at the age of 14 in his family's business. He is by all definitions of the word a "butcher." With over 30 years of meat cutting experience and having taught the meat class at the acclaimed Culinary Institute of America for the past 10 years, Chef Schneller brings a high level of understanding to this book. Chef Schneller also owned and operated his own restaurant and catering business for 11 years, has worked in a variety of restaurant positions including back and front of the house, and has an understanding of foodservice. As Chef Schneller continues teaching at the Institute, he is focused on acquiring more knowledge in all aspects of the meat industry.

Brad Matthews is director of purchasing and storeroom operations at The Culinary Institute of America (CIA). Directing a storeroom staff of more than two dozen, Mr. Matthews is responsible for all purchases on the college's Hyde Park, NY campus, including more than $8 million of food products for the college each year. Mr. Matthews and his staff must assure the value of those purchases through proper receipt, evaluation, storage, and timeliness of deliveries. He also oversees the distribution to the 41 kitchens and bakeshops of all food coming into the CIA campus.

Mr. Matthews is a 1974 CIA graduate. Before joining the staff of his alma mater in 1989 as manager of food purchasing and storeroom operations, he cooked at various restaurants in the Hudson Valley, managed an independent catering business, and ran the foodservice operation at Mount St. Alphonsus Seminary in Esopus, NY.

In addition to his CIA degree, Mr. Matthews holds a Bachelor's degree in organizational communications, which he earned from the State University of New York, Empire State College in 1991.

In 1990, Brad began a program of working with local farmers to ensure a steady supply of quality fresh local products for the CIA and to foster stronger ties with the college's neighbors. The CIA now purchases of locally grown or produced products now exceed $700,000. Purchases from all local merchants exceed 2.5 million. Matthews won the Glynwood Harvest Good Neighbor Award in 2006 for his efforts in supporting local agriculture.

# ACKNOWLEDGMENTS

I was practically born with an interest in food and cooking. That love for the aromas and flavors of food, and the joy of making people happy by my efforts at the stove, drove me into the kitchen from early childhood. My training began in my mother's kitchen and took form as a career option in my aunt and uncle's restaurants in my teens. During those years, we often shopped for great cuts of meat and specialty foods at Schneller's Butcher Shop on John St. in Kingston, New York. The quality, smells, and friendly knowledgeable staff made shopping there a wonderful experience; my coauthor Tom's dad owned that fine store.

My enjoyment of the kitchen led me to follow my uncle's advice and enroll in The Culinary Institute of America when it moved to Hyde Park, New York. When I graduated from the CIA and went to work in the field, I found my ability in sourcing ingredients and working with purveyors to be a very advantageous part of my skill set; so did most of my employers, who delegated much of those job duties to me. Life has a way of changing the choices you make; about 12 years after graduating from the CIA, circumstances dictated I give up cooking as a profession and find another way to make a living. I went back to college, got my four-year degree, and then was fortunate enough to come full circle and gained employment at the Culinary Institute of America as the manager of food purchasing and storeroom operations.

There will always be a part of me that misses working in the kitchen, but the past 20 years have been exceedingly rewarding in playing a role within an organization that trains people for the profession that I love. I have had the opportunity to learn much about what vendors and buyers should and should not do in building mutually beneficial working relationships. Many of these relationships have thrived over many years due to the professionalism, work ethic, integrity, intelligence, and character of many of the vendors I have been fortunate enough to work with, especially Suzanne Racjzi, now the COO of Ginsberg's Foods in Hudson, New York.

My tenure here at the CIA has also given me the privilege of striving to meet the high standards and demand of the faculty here at the CIA so they can ensure our students are exposed to the proper quality at all times. It has also given me the opportunity to work with Maggie Wheeler, Erin McDowell, and Nathalie Fischer in publishing, and I am grateful to them for their help and this opportunity. I have also learned much more about business, controls, and the value of integrity in business from my friend and boss, Charlie O'Mara. It's the confidence and trust he has placed in me that brought me to this place, that fostered my long tenure here, and that this book is dedicated to.

—*Brad Matthews*

On some mornings, when I arrive at the Culinary Institute of America, there are trucks waiting for a spot on our loading dock. These trucks are laden with goods that our students will use to gain their knowledge for a successful career in foodservice. The amount of work it takes to get that truck to the dock is amazing. I would like to acknowledge the CIA's storeroom staff, who work to make the job of the teaching faculty possible. Their patience and care in procuring and handling products from both local sources and around the world are appreciated. It is not uncommon to overhear staff talk about the quality of a certain cheese or fruit with a level of understanding that can only be described as "expert." At the helm of this busy department is my coauthor, Brad Matthews, who can often be seen in his office on the phone with a purveyor asking questions not only about price or quality but also about source and locale. Without him, this book would not be possible. He lives purchasing!

I would like to thank Nathalie Fischer for working with our publisher, Delmar Cengage Learning, to allow for the creation of this project.

Writing this book is only part of the process; editing, putting together the art, and arranging the document to make sense are as much a part as the written word. I would like to thank my editor, Maggie Wheeler, for her tireless work on this project. Her suggestions and ideas were appreciated, and without them this book wouldn't be the quality publication it has become. Erin McDowell was also extremely helpful in doing research and procuring art to enhance this project. The publishing team at the CIA continues to create opportunities and provide encouragement to faculty and staff, allowing their knowledge to be shared with the world.

Over my years as a butcher and chef, I have known countless salespeople. Some were aggravating, showing up at the wrong time of day or sending the wrong item; others became friends that knew my business as well as I did, and they were helpful in its success. Many enjoyed a good joke or a sample of my food, occasionally having a lunch or dinner. In a time where purchasing can be done by a click on a Blackberry in the middle of the night, a buyer can lose track of the importance of the lessons a good salesperson can provide. There is a relationship between buyers and sellers in foodservice, and I would like to thank all of those who taught me the art of purchasing.

—*Thomas K. Schneller*

# INTRODUCTION

The foodservice industry is an exciting, creative, and thoroughly challenging profession. Those who choose this line of work generally have a passion for the creative challenge it affords and an appreciation for fine food and/or drink, and take pleasure in creating dishes that nourish and please people. They also own or work in a business that needs to remain financially viable to survive and flourish. The reality is that no matter what aspect of the food business you are in, or how talented the chef is, your business will not survive if you cannot properly purchase the needs of that business in a manner that will ensure its profitability.

This book is meant to give people entering the foodservice industry, who will either be responsible for the purchase of goods or work with someone who does, a broad view of the needs and challenges inherent to that work. Much of the book is devoted to the various food groupings and the need for clear, articulate specifications. This is to ensure that vendors have a clear picture of an operation's needs and the ability to submit a competitive bid on the exact products required. This is the heart of food purchasing and where product knowledge is crucial. The book also covers the history of the practice of purchasing and the equipment, facilities, and people required to accomplish this function correctly.

We also look at trends in foodservice today; these include trends such as "farm to fork," seasonality, buying local, sustainability, organics, and aquaculture. Some of these trends were simply common business practice before advanced transportation and storage, chemical fertilizers, huge corporate farming, and a fast-food culture changed the landscape. However, recently we have learned that some of these modern changes can have a negative impact on our environment and health; this is why what was old is new again, as people have a growing respect for food that is grown well, and good for their health and that of the environment.

The names and places in the case studies have been changed.

1

# HISTORY OF FOOD PURCHASING

To understand food purchasing today, it is our goal to first explore the history of this subject. Looking back to earlier times allows us to fully understand the relationship between the foodservice purchaser and the various sources from which their food and supplies are coming today. The myriad of choices offered to the modern chef all have some connection to the past, and many of the food procurement systems that we use today are anchored in age-old market relationships. Today we find a chef examining produce during a delivery just as we would find a buyer in an early market square doing the same thousands of years ago. Being able to determine acceptable quality and identify a fair price is a skill that needs to be honed for a business to become successful. Building a relationship between the buyer and seller is also a part of the task and it has changed over many years. In this first chapter, we will take a look at how we got to where we are today.

## NEOLITHIC ERA IN THE MIDDLE EAST, ASIA, AND EUROPE

The earliest financial transactions between peoples were related to food. Even before humans started growing their own foods, tribes engaged in trading. Hunters and gatherers harvested the natural bounty and bartered with neighbors for other items. Along with the actual foods were the tools and storage vessels that were used to create and preserve the meals. These tools were the first rudimentary kitchen appliances, which were often traded and bartered as were the actual food items. Archeologists have pieced together the early diets of humans by examining the tools used and the remnants of early campfires. Evidence shows that humans began

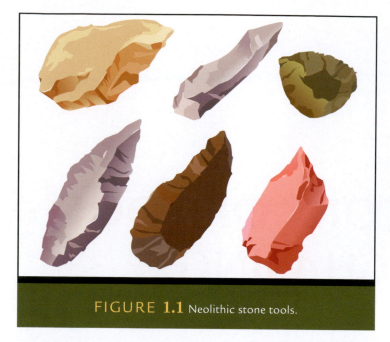

FIGURE **1.1** Neolithic stone tools.

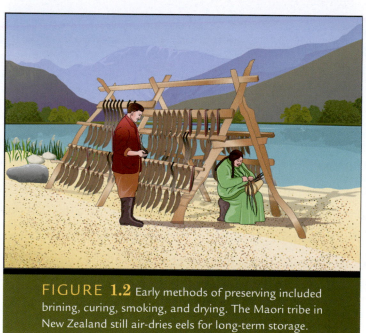

FIGURE **1.2** Early methods of preserving included brining, curing, smoking, and drying. The Maori tribe in New Zealand still air-dries eels for long-term storage.

agricultural practices around 11,000 years ago, and trading surpluses followed as technology improved.

The seasons played a major role in what a human's diet consisted of and how much food was available. Harsh times such as winter snows or summer droughts would force the community to learn how to preserve and ration foods. The well-being of a tribe often depended on the food source, and the need for food was often the cause for migrations and conflicts. Preservation methods, such as salting and fermenting, were developed so food could be carried or stored for months.

As humans progressed into agricultural societies and food was now grown instead of simply gathered, the overproduction of food that resulted became commodities that were traded. During the Neolithic era, trading centers where early tribes would congregate became the early villages. By 8,000 BCE, we find the beginnings of early cities such as Jericho, where salt was mined and traded. Markets and the rules that were created to run them became the first mercantile laws.

Over time, as many people were still focused on subsistence farming, some farms began to grow and produce much more food than needed for one family or clan. This allowed for food to be sold to those who did not engage in farming. Specializations within the economy began to take hold. Instead of everyone farming, traders or craftsmen focused on a single valuable skill such as fishing, pottery, carpentry, baking, brewing, metal working, butchery, and more. All of these workers needed food and bartered or bought foods from marketplaces. Even farmers themselves became more specialized by growing specific crops such as grains, fruits, or certain meat animals. Trading became more widespread as shipping and transportation methods improved.

## MESOPOTAMIA

The first large cities such as Babylon, found in ancient Mesopotamian, had marketplaces that were governed by the leaders such as Hammurabi. His rules were laid out partly to protect fairness in markets and to insure taxes were collected on commerce. Early capitalism was born. Mesopotamia was a valuable agricultural region, included within the Fertile Crescent, the area where agriculture began due to the ability of the land to support rich agricultural crops but was void of timber and many metals; trading with other sources was inevitable. The earliest forms of credit were arranged with contracts and agreement letters drawn up and enforced between trading partners. Documents discovered from over 4,000 years ago show

**Timeline for Mercantile Law**

- 7500 BCE—Middle East

  Early accounting methods using "tokens" or clay shapes were used to represent traded commodities such as grain and cattle.

- 3200 BCE—Sumeria

  Cuneiform writing is first used to create accounting records for trading agricultural products, textiles, and pottery.

- 3000 BCE—China

  The abacus is developed for computing value.

- 2200 BCE—Middle East

  The Code of Hammurabi is developed as the first uniform law for commerce, including standardizations for weights and measures, penalties, and contracts.

- 600 BCE—Greece

  Formal banking and the minting of coins by the state for business transactions are created.

- 50 BCE—Rome

  Roman banking systems are well established, and laws now include credit systems, strict record keeping, contract enforcement, coinage, and regulations for all sorts of business activities.

- 1 CE—Rome

  Basic sales tax law is formed, and records are checked by the state.

- 410 CE—Rome

  The fall of the Roman Empire results in fragmentation throughout Europe and the beginnings of the feudal system.

- 1000–1300 CE—Europe

  European trading systems are set up to trade with Eastern countries. Italian trading ports establish trade codes. The Medieval Merchant Laws were established and enforced by peer merchant judges.

- 1066 CE—England

  William the Conqueror invades England, and the formation of modern English law is completed by 1086.

*(continues)*

the receipts and ledgers that were in use at the time. Trade between the merchants was written on clay tablets, giving modern historians a glimpse into what was traded and its value. These systems laid the groundwork for those that followed up to our modern time.

# NORTH AFRICA

The Egyptian model was different. The markets and everything that was produced for them were under the control of the government. The godlike Pharaohs controlled all commerce and taxation. Wealth was distributed by the central government, and the economy depended partially on slave labor. Artisans and craftspeople were compensated more than farmers, and there was a clear class system that maintained the power in the hands of the central government, primarily the Pharaoh.

Ancient Egyptian history is divided into many dynastic periods that lasted for hundreds of years, starting around 3150 BCE and extending until the Romans conquered in 51 BCE. Egypt and its people experienced many downfalls and resurgences of power through the nearly

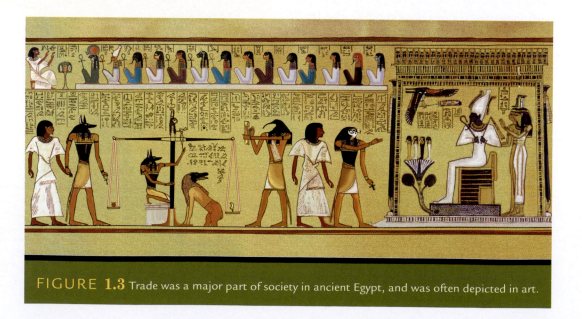

FIGURE **1.3** Trade was a major part of society in ancient Egypt, and was often depicted in art.

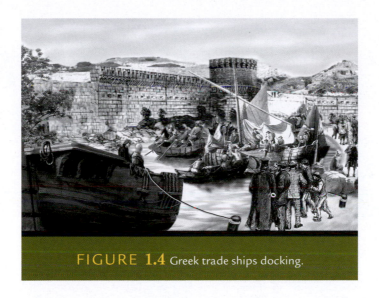

FIGURE **1.4** Greek trade ships docking.

3,000 years of Pharaonic rule. Ancient Egyptian commerce, for the average citizen, consisted primarily of bartering. Basic food necessities were traded by farmer's wives and there was no merchant class. Farmers provided all manner of grains, meats, fruits, and vegetables. Garlic, leeks, and onions were part of the regular diet as well as many green vegetables grown by irrigating harsh desert lands. The Nile, which was the basic life-blood of Egypt, provided the water needed for irrigation but was also a good source for fish, which was a mainstay of the diet. Meats were salted and preserved, and assorted fowl were captured and fattened, including ducks and geese, forming early versions of foie gras or fattened liver. Grain was traded like currency; a certain type of work, such as digging or masonry, would be rewarded with a specific weight of grain. Then that grain could be traded for clothing or other necessities. The grain, typically barley, was used to make the two staple foods, bread and beer. Coins were not used until the Late Period, which started around the fifth century BCE. Before that, all foreign trade was controlled by the state and was limited to obtaining wealth for the Pharaohs. In the Egyptian society, when the economy was good, the wealth was spread throughout the land.

# GREECE

Greek society brought a much more advanced system of food distribution. Greek city-states had bustling marketplaces filled with a variety of nutritious foods and kitchen wares. Fresh vegetables were only found seasonally and were sometimes expensive, but staples such as lentils, barley, beans, and other grains and legumes were consistently found in the market. Olives and olive oil as well as vinegar and wine were common. Assorted utensils were used during meals and banquets: knives for cutting meats, ornamental spoons for soups, and a variety of bowls and plates. Forks were not yet invented; therefore, foods were eaten by hand using flat breads. Bread was often eaten with olive oil and herbs.

The market, known as the *agora*, was the center of activity in the Greek city-states. It was where most government buildings were located, and politicians could be seen expressing their views to the public. Markets were the social centers, and religious temples

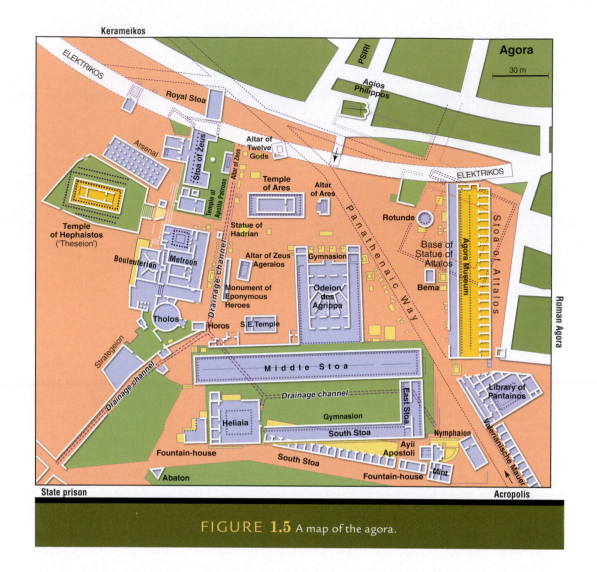

FIGURE 1.5 A map of the agora.

were often located there. The markets were bustling and filled with all of the bounty available from the surrounding farms, but there were also prepared foods to eat on the go, similar to modern fast food. Businessmen and politicians would come to the markets to discuss their dealings and enjoy a lunch of baked bread and olives and some cooling drinks such as wine or fruit juices. Meats and fish were laid out on chilled marble slabs to keep the meats cool during the heat of the day. Foods were only part of the market; all manner of goods could be found there. Clothing, bowls, baskets, artworks, candles and oils, and metals and precious stones all were sold in booths; this meant many of these merchants would also buy food for themselves. These markets became the foundations for what we consider modern marketing, with people explaining and representing their goods as superior over others, or downplaying their competitors' products.

This was a time of many great thinkers such as Socrates, Plato, Pythagoras, and Epicurus, who used the agora as their stage to present new ideas to the masses. Orators would stand and deliver speeches to the public and were considered part of the market scene. It was an open time where new concepts were embraced such as the idea of democracy, where the masses would have a say in how the government was formed. It was also a time of laws and fairness in the market place. Trade in these markets was regulated by three entities. *Metronomoi* checked weights and measures, *agronomoi* checked the quality of goods including foods, and *sitophylakes* checked the quality and wholesomeness of grain. These first regulators of markets were the precursors of modern merchant laws, and we find their influence in the modern grading and inspection services found in many modern agricultural nations.

Wine was the festive beverage of choice, and it was consumed in copious quantities. Wine was stored in large urns and transported throughout the islands. Wine was so revered that the Greeks devoted a god, Bacchus or Dionysus, to it. Tangy cheeses such as Feta, made from sheep milk, were used in recipes and salads. Food was, and is to this day, a major part of Greek culture, and many feasts and celebrations mark the calendar. The feast celebrating the birth of the god Dionysus was celebrated in the spring, known as the Great Dionasia, and was focused on dramatic theater and wine. Feasts celebrating gods or acts of gods were typically multiple-day affairs, and food and drink were always part of it. Another festival celebrating the vine and devoted to Dionysus was a celebration of the "new" wine in the fall, similar to the French celebrating the opening of the first Beaujolais Nouveau of the year.

The procurement of foods for the large extravagant feasts meant buying from numerous farmers and traders. Being surrounded by the ocean and having many islands, the Greeks were heavily engaged in trading with kingdoms farther east and west. They traded from North Africa and southern Italy in the west to India and beyond in the east. This brought exotic foods and spices back to add to the menus. The Greek food culture also included the bounty of the sea. Fish was and is a staple protein, and favorites would have included the Mediterranean sea bass and other fin fish that were caught by netting. Greece was not able to raise large herds of cattle, and both meat and fish were relatively expensive. Meat was considered a "relish," or a treat on the plate. The Greek menu and dining were divided into three categories: *sitos* was considered the staple of barley grain, usually in the form of porridge, mash, or flat bread; *opson* was the fish, meat, vegetables, olives, or olive oil; and *oinos* referred to wine, which was of course a staple. The primary grain of Greece was barley, but proper bread wheat grains were bought from North Africa and Sicily. The culinary world owes a lot to the ancient Greeks and their wine, breads, and olive oil. But more than products, the Greeks gave us the beginnings of the modern market system with controls over merchants and democratic decisions over how regulations were enforced. The Greek market system was mimicked by the later Romans and adopted by many nations indirectly to this day.

# ROME

After the Greeks were conquered by the Romans, Rome became the center of a huge empire, and the food of the Roman Empire paved the way to our modern food culture. Markets in the many Roman cities were bustling centers of commerce, with foods of all sorts available. Like the Greek *agoras*, Roman markets were also the centers of activities and politics. The gigantic Roman Forum was known for its fanfares and parades, but first and foremost it was the marketplace for Rome. There were different sectors of the market: civilian food markets for the average Roman to buy their food needs and wares, grain markets for large-volume dealers, cloth markets, all mixed with religious temples and government buildings. The food markets consisted of covered stalls that were semipermanent structures where merchants often lived in the back in small apartments. Cleanliness and quality were checked by the market authorities. Punishments for violations were severe and may have been public and humiliating by nature. Floggings and worse were common for repeat offenders.

The Roman Empire grew to an expansive boundary and at its peak encompassed large portions of Europe, North Africa, and the Middle East. As the empire spread and built cities, the model of the Forum was recreated in smaller form. Each province brought unique foods to the marketplace, and many were in turn traded in Rome itself. Beyond the boundaries of the empire, Rome traded with neighboring kingdoms, which resulted in a market filled with exotic spices, fruits, meats, and fish. Spices included cumin, coriander, fennel, mint, various peppers, celery seed, dill, lovage, and lots of other seeds and herbs. The Romans traded with Persia and in turn with India and, even farther, East Asia. The Roman diet was varied but similar to that of the Greeks, with olives and olive oil playing major parts.

Vegetables of all sorts were consumed; baked goods, honey pastries, porridge, and many varieties of rice and grains were part of their diet. Wine, as in Greece, was very important, and the varieties of grapes grown in the northern climates expanded their palates. The wines were categorized by color and also age. *Albus* (young, light white wine), *Fulvus* (older, rich white wine), *Sanguineus* (light mild red wine), and *Niger* (deep, older, rich red wine) were the main categories. Many other wines and alcoholic fermentations existed too. Wine was often flavored with herbs and honey. Rough beer was brewed from grain but was considered a poor person's drink.

Roman ideas about curing meats and sausages, especially pork, gave birth to the modern salumi that we find today. The preservation of meats allowed merchants to sell their wares over greater distances and allowed Roman armies to be self-sustaining and more mobile. Animals were raised and slaughtered for both meat and sacrifice to gods, and early meat inspections were established probably to examine organs to see if offerings were fit for the sacrificial purposes.

As with the Greeks, Romans were a seafaring people and fishing was a major occupation. Fish was an important part of the Roman diet, and many varieties were sold in markets, especially in seaport cities. All varieties of Mediterranean fish were available, including sea bass, tuna, squid, mollusks, and snails. The seafood was bountiful along coastal cities and, as in many ancient cultures, buying and selling fish were part of the outdoor markets. The Romans also liberally used a fermented fish sauce, *garum*, as a flavor enhancer. It was a staple in many recipes and used widely by rich and poor.

Seasonal feasts would feature a huge variety of foods for the wealthy in Rome, and the procurement, purchase, and preparation of all these items were arduous tasks for early cooks. Recipes created by the Roman chef/epicure Marcus Gavius Apicius, who was a prominent gourmet of the time, included such a variety of ingredients that they could be used today. He wrote 10 cookbooks in a series that highlighted ingredients and described flavors. During the age of Tiberius, in the first century CE, Roman high society was treated to a vast array of decadent and exotic foods, and Apicius was a part of this.

The ancient Roman Empire had a huge influence on our modern diet and the foods we often find appealing. The Romans, unlike many other conquering nations that came before and after, adopted foods from those they conquered instead of rejecting them. Foods from all over the Empire were included in the Roman diet, and often an early sort of "fusion" cooking was accomplished by applying Roman cooking methods to the new ingredients. These influences are seen today, and many Italian recipes still reflect some of the Roman cooking styles in the use of olive oil and wine in cooking. In the time that Rome ruled the Mediterranean rim, food and cooking were changed forever.

## ASIA

Another culture that influenced modern cooking and food purchasing was that of ancient China. During the conquests of Alexander the Great, around 300 BCE, we find trade routes extending from the Middle East through Persia and east toward India. The Greeks at this time had also established routes east, and trade began to influence the diet of the western kingdoms. By the time Rome had established itself as an empire, the routes east had become established trading corridors and extended from Rome to what are now Japan and Korea. During the Han Dynasty in China, which ruled starting in 220 BCE, trade between China and the West was established with the "Silk Routes," a series of dangerous roads that crossed many mountains in Tibet, the high Steppes of eastern Asia, and thousands of miles of desert. These routes were responsible for bringing more than silk, which was popular in Rome; they also brought exotic spices and foods from the Orient for the first time. During the first century CE, the Chinese general Pan Ch'ao secured the routes to the West by defeating the Huns, and trade was now temporarily secure with Rome.

Over the many years following, control over these trade routes was contested by many kingdoms. Rome eventually fell to the barbarians, China was fragmented and conquered by the Huns, and the Middle East changed and trade slowed. Europe fell into the "Dark Ages" after the Roman Empire collapsed, and the Silk Roads were often used by invading armies rather than for trade. By 1200 CE, things began to change again. The famous explorer Marco Polo traveled to China, recording all he saw and creating interest in the Asian trade again. Europe was in the grips of the terrible Black Plague and trade slowed, but in China trade was expanding.

In the early 1400s, China was a trading giant. The early Ming Dynasty was trading with Persia and India as well as all the way to Africa. They traded food items with Korea, Japan, Southeast Asia, and many of the smaller island nations of the South Pacific. Like the Romans, this era infused new foods into Chinese culture. They traded for spices and medicinal plants and brought back exotic game. The Chinese sent out huge armadas that sailed for many months to reach the far corners of the Indian Ocean and beyond. These ships carried their own gardens and food sources but also had the ability to bring back foods and treasures. The treasure ships were enormous with the ability to carry up to 2,000 tons of cargo, and this was in a time before Columbus when the Europeans were just beginning to enter the more modern trading era. The great distances the fleet traveled meant the Chinese almost reached the trading ports on the other side of the world. The fleets traveled on basic currents and seasonal trade winds so they would have had to sail around the bottom of Africa to reach trading ports in Europe. Some historians believe the Chinese actually discovered the Americas long before Columbus. But, the Ming Dynasty decided to curtail all trade and become reclusive during the 1400s for fear of losing power to the Uyghurs of western Asia. The Manchurian Chinese halted almost all trade, which was unfortunate for they had begun what the Europeans would finish, the circumnavigation and exploration of the world.

Chinese, Japanese, Indian, Southeast Asian, and Korean food cultures were all unique, and their markets reflected foods that were not seen in Europe until much later. Market places in Chinese cities were, as in Rome and Greece, the centers of commerce with assorted vegetables, meats, teas, and spices. Markets were regulated by law; the central governments established rules of fairness and meted out strict punishments for selling adulterated foods. Unlike the Greeks, most Asian markets were regulated by their governments without much input by democratic means, which meant merchants had to adhere to the law. In China there were two basic schools of thought: Confucianism and Legalism. Confucius believed that people were inherently good and wished to trade fairly and that leaders needed to simply guide their people by example, whereas Legalists believed most people were greedy and therefore strict rules and punishments had to be in place to control markets.

In China, food was also part of medicinal treatments, where specific foods were given to treat ailments. Teas, mushrooms, animal bone powders, herbs, spices, and fermentations of grains and roots were all prescribed for treatments. The fermentation of soybeans was developed to enhance flavor and create *umami*, or the taste of savory. The modern uses of ginger, cinnamon, star anise, fennel, a variety of peppercorns, cardamom, and clove, to name just a few, all stem from trade with the East. Spices, especially from India, were prized and traded like gold. Today India produces over 1.6 million tons of spices annually, over 80 percent of the world's spices, while China, Bangladesh, Nepal, Turkey, and Pakistan combined produce about 17 percent. The Asian spice markets were the primary reason for global exploration by the Europeans in the late 1400s and early 1500s.

## MIDDLE AGES

The many kingdoms of Europe were supplied with goods by their taxed subjects. Farmers grew crops to feed themselves and to pay for the lands they worked. Farming and the breeding of animals evolved as Europe came out of the Dark Ages into the modern era. Monarchs were provided a wide variety of foods. For example, in 1359, King Richard of England was served a menu including venison, boars' heads, boiled meats and stews, roasted swan, chickens, pheasants, herons, peacocks, and cranes for a feast. Accompanying this was jellied meat and fish, roast pork, fish, tarts, meat served in pieces, roasted rabbit, clear broth, spiced pudding of pork, dried fruits and eggs in a sauce of almond milk or wine, meat in puff pastry, and a rice pudding dish. The excess was beyond imagination.

By the 1400s, cities began to grow and markets such as the Smithfield market in London expanded. This huge market was a scene of much of the livestock commerce for London and was the center of selling meat for hundreds of years. Much of the commerce was controlled by the butcher's guilds, which dictated the prices of live cattle for slaughter. Charles Dickens describes the scene of Smithfield in his classic *Oliver Twist*:

> Countrymen, butchers, drovers, hawkers, boys, thieves, idlers, and vagabonds of every low grade, were mingled together in a dense mass: the whistling of drovers, the barking of dogs, the bellowing and plunging of beasts, the bleating of sheep, and the grunting and squealing of pigs; the cries of hawkers, the shouts, oaths,

and quarrelling on all sides, the ringing of bells, and the roar of voices that issued from every public house; the crowding, pushing, driving, beating, whooping and yelling; the hideous and discordant din that resounded from every corner of the market; and the unwashed, unshaven, squalid, and dirty figures constantly running to and fro, and bursting in and out of the throng, rendered it a stunning and bewildering scene which quite confused the senses.

Market towns were established throughout the countryside of continental Europe. All of the larger cities of the kingdoms in Germany, France, and Italy had active markets where food was traded and regulated. Seasonality played a part, and the summer months saw a huge assortment of fruits, vegetables, meats, and fish come to the market. Farmers and foragers from outlying regions would herd their animals or haul their fruits, vegetables, and grains in slow-moving carts. This required roadhouses to be set up for overnight stays. These roadhouse taverns traded for food and purchased provisions from the traveling farmers. These early taverns were basically lodging with complimentary foodservice. Price would include a night's stay plus a hearty meal. Menus were basic and seasonal and were served family style.

In Europe the winds of trade were blowing by the end of the 15th century. The explorers of the time had discovered new lands to the west. The Portuguese began fishing for cod off the shores of Newfoundland. Explorers brought back new vegetables and fruits such as the tomato. The turkey was introduced to the European diet and became an instant success because of its capability for fast growing and large size. Potatoes, tomatoes, maize, and cocoa were imported as new exotic foods from the Americas. Explorers began to circumnavigate the globe, bringing back exotic spices from the Far East.

The Islamic nations of the Middle East had very strict regulations for measurements and trading. The use of specific containers and scales for weighing teas, grains, salt, and more was part of trading with these nations. The Europeans adopted many of these measurements for trading among kingdoms.

As the English became the dominant power in trade and colonialism, they implemented their systems of measurement. The English had established standard measurements for volume, weights, and lengths after the signing of the Magna Carta in 1215 by King John. This document was the basis for English law and set guidelines by the barons of England so that there would be fair trade between markets and cities. Measurement standards were updated through the 1400s, and we find standards for the English pound, ounce, quart, inch, yard, and more. Many of these measurements were based on the physical features of kings and became known as the "Imperial" system. The United States, in defiance to English rule, developed its own system based on the English but differing just enough to make trade difficult. The English adopted the metric system to adhere to international standards for trade reasons.

The metric system was developed in the 1700s in France. This simpler system based on multiples of ten became the world standard, and by 1998 every country except the United States, Liberia, and Burma used the metric system as the standard for weights and measures. Today the United States now uses the metric and English systems for many products, and it is common to find liquids measured in both liters and quarts, with weights in pounds and kilos listed on boxes, making it confusing for some international chefs dealing with purchasing here in the United States.

## THE NEW WORLD

By the late 1500s, the numerous colonies were sending back a large variety of new foods and beginning to establish farms and creating the economy of the future. Products such as sugar cane and tobacco required intensive hand labor. This labor was provided by slaves, and the slave trade and provisioning for slaves became an industry unto itself. Cod fish purchased from New England fisherman was dried and sold to island sugar plantations. Sugar was traded back to New England to be made into rum. *Bacalao* or saltfish was a staple food for many slaves and later became part of the Caribbean food culture.

Along with the new settlements came economic opportunities. Port cities such as Montreal, Boston, New Amsterdam (New York), and Charleston became trading hubs. Purchasing companies were set up to provide a steady flow of goods back and forth. The East India Company was a major trading force in Boston and eventually became a focal point for the unjust taxation of tea, resulting in the Boston Tea Party. In New Amsterdam (early New York), the Dutch East India Company established settlements up and down the Hudson River, creating trading outposts up to Albany. These Dutch settlements cleared land and planted the early orchards and crop fields that would later feed the teeming metropolis of New York. Trading with local indigenous peoples introduced the Europeans to a wider selection of berries, fruits, grains, and wild game. As settlements grew, taverns and public houses were set up primarily to sell alcohol but they also sold basic food to travelers. These taverns became the meeting places for politics and the ideas of dissent toward English rule. Eventually the new world broke with its English and European rulers, and new governments were formed. Early taverns or public houses or "pubs" were the only form of low-priced

commercial foodservice. Below is an excerpt of an article written about the foods of the time. This shows that the types of foods were varied and quality was high at the end of the 17th century. Food was part of what made the United States a world trading power.

The foods served in Thomas Allen's tavern demonstrates the variety of foodstuffs available in agrarian America; the types of foods used, the kinds of dishes prepared and served at the City Coffee House and other taverns in urbanized areas did not vary significantly from what might have been found in a private home. Between January 9 and March 16, 1774, Allen purchased locally, and subsequently served to his customers, beef once, veal seven times, fowl and turkey five times, mutton twice, and lobsters, salmon, eels, oysters, duck, and other fish caught in nearby Long Island Sound at least once. He kept stores of gammons (smoked ham or bacon), smoked and pickled tongue and beef, salt pork, crackers, butter, coffee, apples, and sugar on hand. Meat, heavily salted for preservation, was the mainstay of the 18th-century diet.... In addition, Allen regularly served bread and a potpourri of vegetables: potatoes, carrots, peas, beans, beets, onions, cabbages, turnips, squashes, and cucumbers for pickling. He bought several types of English cheeses and imported lemons and limes for punch. In 1790 Allen ordered four tin plates "to Bake Gingerbread."

—From *Early American Taverns*

## UNITED STATES

As the population of the new United States grew, a wealthy business class grew along with it. Upscale establishments that catered to the very wealthy were found in most of the larger cities. These exclusive hotels focused on catering to well-to-do patrons and had huge kitchens to produce large banquets and balls. City Hotel in New York City was one of the first established in 1794. Other upscale establishments followed in the prosperous cities of Boston, Washington, Philadelphia, and beyond. The Tremont of Boston began serving French cuisine, and every new hotel had its attractions.

Beyond the cities, resorts for wealthy customers were established to allow an escape from the hectic new urban life. An example is the Catskill Mountain House perched high above the Hudson River near Haines Falls, New York. This grand hotel, built in 1824, was known for serving fine food and provided a cool atmosphere in hot summer months. Local foods from Hudson Valley farms provided fine fresh summer meals, and foraged blueberries were featured on the dessert menu. Other areas such as beach resorts along the East Coast and the mountain resorts of West Virginia had grand hotels that have long since faded into the past.

Many wealthy city dwellers had private country estates such as those found along the Hudson River. Often chefs and cooks were hired to work in the seasonal dwellings when large banquets would occur. Entertaining, especially with lavish food and drink, was a status symbol, and families such as the Vanderbilts, Carnegies, and Astors would spare no expense to entertain their guests.

Not just the rich needed to escape the city life, especially during the summer, resulting in a large resort industry later in U.S. history. Businessmen in cities would send their families away for the entire summer to small boardinghouse resorts, many of which were semi-self-provisioned by growing large gardens and raising chickens. These small resorts, many run by recent immigrants, featured family-style dining and hearty menus.

Feeding the growing cities became a profitable business. The Erie Canal opened in 1823, and it brought goods from the West Coast to the East Coast cities. Rochester, New York, was known as the "Flour City" due to its numerous flour mills on the Genesee River. By 1834 it was producing over 500,000 barrels (40,000 tons) of flour annually, and by 1838 it produced the most flour of any city in the world! The dairy industry grew, and milk cows were a common site on the rural byways of the new country. Cheese, butter, and cultured milk products such as buttermilk were sent to the cities via train or boat. Cows raised in the cities were fed slop leftover from distilleries of liquor. These city milkers produced very poor-quality milk and were often diseased, leading to some of the early milk regulations. Pasteurization began in the late 1800s, and this increased the safety and consequently the consumption of milk. In the early days, milk was sold by "milkmaids" who sold the fermented "butter" milk in the streets by calling out in the early morning hours.

In the United States, the California gold rush and the new immigrant populations began pushing west. In the mid-1800s, thousands of travelers set out from St. Louis to travel by wagon train. This required outfitters to supply travelers and work crews with provisions that would last, such as salted pork, flour, grains, dried beans, and rice. It took a skilled purchaser to understand the quantities required for the journey.

FIGURE **1.8** Early pasteurization equipment.

The loads needed to be light enough to not overload the wagons yet full enough so travelers wouldn't starve. Trading posts were set along the way to help feed both travelers and their animals. Cattle ranching began in order to raise large herds and drive them toward the cities. The "chuck wagon" with its cook was a fixture on these drives. The cooks had to provision the outfit with enough food to keep the hardworking cowboys satisfied. Understanding proper ordering of food stocks as well as basic butchery was essential to the success of the drive. Once the West became more established and the railroads began connecting towns and cities, the flow of goods expanded. Railroads became the primary movers of cattle, and trains brought live cattle into the huge stockyards of Kansas City and Chicago. Here is a provisioner's price list from the mid-1800s in San Antonio, Texas:

*Pork, 11 cents/lb*
*Bacon, 12 1/2-15 cents/lb*
*Salt beef, 8 1/2-9 cents/lb*
*Fresh beef, 4 1/2-5 cents/lb*
*Flour, 4/14 cents (superfine)-5 cents (extra fine)/lb*
*Hard bread, 9-10 cents/lb*
*Beans, 10 1/2cents/quart*
*Rice, 8-10 cents/lb*
*Coffee, 12 1/2 (Rio) to 18 (Java) cents/lb*
*Sugar, 7 1/2-8 cents for "Louisiana brown"/lb*
*Vinegar, 6 1/4 cents/quart"*

—*The Southwestern Historical Quarterly*

The Civil War of the 1860s created the need for soldiers' rations to be purchased. Huge amounts of salted meats, grains, sugar, beans, and coffee were sold to the governments of both armies. Private companies made many thousands of dollars supplying the army with food. The Commissary Departments were assigned the difficult tasks of procuring enough food and then distributing it to the soldiers. The Northern soldiers were given "hardtack," a stiff basic biscuit that was extremely stale. In the South, they made "Johnnie Cakes" from corn meal. Both sides did better nutritionally in the summer months, when fresh fruits and vegetables were available and wild berries could be foraged along the way. All in all, the food rations during the war were pretty monotonous and unexciting.

# INDUSTRIAL AGE

After the Civil War, the United States expanded and modernized. No longer was it necessary to work on the farm for subsistence. People began migrating to the cities, and huge immigrant populations came to work in factories. Industrial output soared, and with it came the beginnings of the middle class. Labor unions fought for better wages and more free time, and, once this was achieved, people had a little disposable income. The idea of eating out in a restaurant was more accepted, and small and large establishments sprang up in the cities. Here is an example of a summer menu circa 1900 in New York City.

Eating establishments from the entire spectrum of the economy were buying foods from provisioners and grocers. Each food item had its own vendor. Meat was bought from the butcher or packer, fish from the fishmonger or fishing docks, oysters from the oystermen, vegetables from the green grocer, breads and pastries

| Appetizers | Main Course | Vegetables | Dessert |
|---|---|---|---|
| Half of a | Channel Catfish | Corn on the | Lemon Layer Cake 5¢ |
| Cantaloupe 10¢ | 20¢ | Cob 10¢ | Ice Cream 10¢ |
| Sliced Orange 10¢ | Pork Tenderloins | Buttered Beets | Ice Cream and Cake |
| Young Onions 5¢ | 20¢ | 5¢ | 15¢ |
| Sliced Tomatoes 10¢ | Omelet with Jelly | Mashed Potatoes | Raspberries and Cream |
| New Radishes 5¢ | 15¢ | 5¢ | 10¢ |
| Sliced Cucumbers 10¢ | Roast Pork with | Pickled Beets 5¢ | Rhubarb Pie 5¢ |
|  | Applesauce | Cole Slaw 5¢ | Green Apple Pie 5¢ |
| **Soup** | 20¢ | Salad 10¢ |  |
| Old Fashion Navy Bean | Chicken Fricassee |  | **Drinks** |
| 10¢ | 20¢ |  | Coffee 5¢ |
|  | Roast Beef |  | Milk 5¢ |
|  | 15¢ |  | Tea 5¢ |
|  | Pork and Beans |  | Buttermilk 5¢ |
|  | 15¢ |  |  |

Source: *A Cultural History of the United States: The 1900s.*

**FIGURE 1.9** Summer menu from 1900.

from the baker, and dry goods and cereals from a staples provisioner or miller. The connection between the actual producer and farmer of the food and the end consumer began to slowly unhitch. Especially in the cities, farmers no longer were the only source for goods. Now the purveyor was the source of goods for most food establishments. Large hotels such as the original Waldorf began serving high-quality meals to their upscale guests, and the purchasers for this type of establishment had to find the finest ingredients. By 1900, over 700 hotels were located in New York City, and the task of supplying them became enormous. Fine china, linens, and fancy flatware were required, and business for supplying these products flourished.

The Gansevoort Meat Market district near 14th Street began by the mid-1800s. At first the district was a combination of foods, including fresh vegetables, and then the city purchased the property to consolidate most of New York's food market booths. It gradually became focused on meat sales, and by 1900 the meat market had over 250 slaughter and packing houses. Quality-hotel customers were highly sought after, and the competition between vendors was robust. Today the famous Waldorf-Astoria Hotel still buys meat from the district. The wealthy Astor and Roosevelt families invested in the market to cash in on the meat industry that they saw growing at the time. By the 1930s, an elevated railroad was built through the district to supply meat from the Midwest. Another market, the Fulton Fish Market at the South Street Seaport, became the hub for seafood sales. It too started as

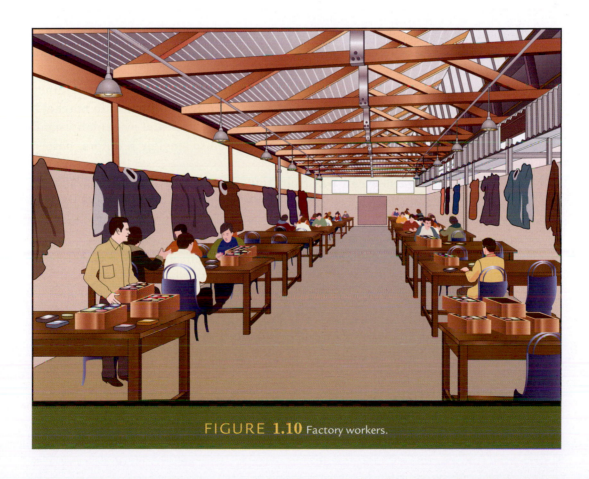

FIGURE **1.10** Factory workers.

FIGURE **1.11** Gansevoort Meat Market.

a multiproduct market featuring fruits and vegetables brought in by boat, but soon fish became the focus. Started in 1822, it rapidly grew to become the largest fish market in the nation.

Many other cities had specific market districts. Boston had the thriving Quincy Market, Philadelphia had its Market Street and Third Street wholesale markets, and Washington, DC, had the Eastern Market. All larger cities and even many small towns had a market area where wholesalers would sell to smaller retailers, hotels, and restaurants.

During the Spanish-American War from 1898 to 1901, the U.S. Army was sent to Cuba to fight. One of the provisions purchased for the Army was canned beef. It was discovered that much of this meat was treated with formaldehyde! This poisoned thousands of soldiers and led to government regulation of the meat industry. The angry public demanded action, but the government and the powerful meat lobby delayed regulations. In 1906 Upton Sinclair wrote the disturbing book *The Jungle* about the horrible working conditions of the Chicago meat-packing industry. This finally got the public angry enough for regulation. The Food and Drug Law was implemented in 1906 and then amended in 1912 and 1930. This law regulated the food industry and guaranteed truth in packaging. In 1938 the Food and Drug Administration was established to further regulate contents, packaging, and now also quality. Regulations have changed and been implemented up to the present day. All of these laws affected distribution, packaging, and commerce for foodservice. Distributors now had to follow the newer regulations or else pay fines, which meant losing customers.

**FIGURE 1.12** An early menu from the Happy Days Diner.

# PURCHASING FOR DIFFERENT MODES OF TRANSPORTATION

From the 1800s to the 1940s, the train was the primary method of long-distance transportation, and to travel between coasts took a few days. This meant railroads developed large dining cars for their patrons. The Santa Fe line was the first long-distance carrier to offer dining on board. First-class passengers were treated to fine foods equal to those found in superior hotels. Railroad operators demanded a more consistent quality of meat for their train dining cars, leading to the meat quality grading system performed by the U.S. Department of Agriculture. Lower-class passengers would eat in "grill" cars where food was prepared in front of them. Many old dining grill cars were transformed into stationary "diners," and some can still be found today as historic landmarks.

Supplying trains with food was a lucrative business. Depots were placed along routes, and clerks would arrange the purchases according to the passenger lists that were telegraphed ahead. Most meals were prepared on board, and chefs would make everything from steaks, roasts, chops, and fish to desserts including cakes and pies. Three meals a day were served, and multiple seatings had to be coordinated. Food supplies were stored on board, and everything had to be carefully prepared and portioned to be sure all patrons were fed. All of this occurred while the train was speeding along, rocking back and forth.

Also along the railroads were numerous hotels. The Harvey House chain owned by entrepreneur Fred Harvey was set up along the Santa Fe Line to accommodate long-distance passengers that needed a layover. They all offered food and drink. Here is an excerpt from a memoir of a Harvey House worker, D. K. Spencer:

> I worked in the storeroom, receiving the necessary supplies to run a hotel and eating establishment. It was a two man operation, and I was the low man. I did the manual labor of receiving, storing and distributing all inbound items such as produce; fresh meat in quarters; bakery flour in 100 lb sacks; canned goods and alcoholic beverages by the case; fresh trout in iced containers from Frantz Hatchery at Salida; and whatever else came in for the hotel operation.
>
> The storeroom was actually two rooms. One was like a grocery store, with canned goods on shelves. The other room contained refrigerated coolers, one for fresh meat which was hung on hooks from the ceiling; one for produce; and a third for storage of liquor kept locked with access only by the hotel manager.

This was also the era of luxury steamship travel. The enormous cruise lines that crossed the Atlantic were known for their superior dining and exclusive customer service. Lines such as the White Star needed to purchase very large quantities of raw foods, wine, liquor, dry goods, china, linens, and kitchen supplies. The journey would last over a week, so purchasing had to be done accurately on both sides of the Atlantic. Purchasing clerks needed to procure these items and have the products in warehouses at the docks when the boats landed. Loading and checking in food were huge undertakings. Today we find cruise lines buying tractor trailer loads of food that are then loaded into on-board warehouses and coolers. The boats are like floating cities, with the kitchen resembling the type that would be run in a large casino. Systems of requisitions for food would be issued out to the many stations. The contracts for supplying a cruise line are complicated documents with insurance and guarantees of wholesomeness embedded in the contract. A cruise line must be extremely careful about food buying due to the fact that the clients are a captive audience and an outbreak of foodborne illness while out at sea could be disastrous.

On land, restaurants, hotels, and nightclubs prospered into the 1920s, and providing food and supplies to their patrons was an ever important part of their growth. For large operations, there were no computers, and ordering was done by clerical workers who would inventory goods and communicate with chefs, bar managers, and head waitstaff about what was needed. Handwritten lists were given to suppliers, and there was a lot of hard work involved in receiving. Often items were sent in returnable containers such as milk and beer bottles, wooden vegetable crates, barrels, boxes, and tubs of all sorts. All of this meant a lot of storage and handling on loading docks.

In smaller operations the chef or owner might be in charge of all the ordering. Often small operations were family-run, and husbands, wives, children, and grandparents all had a part in operating the restaurant. These typically ethnic establishments developed tight bonds with their vendors, who were sometimes extended family members also. Ordering was done by a variety of homegrown systems but often simply by understanding the business and knowing their weekly needs. The owner would have their finger on the pulse of the restaurant and know, almost by instinct, how much to order. They would be so familiar with prices they would know immediately if a price was fair or not. Many small restaurants are still run this way, which, although not very high tech, can be effective. But the owner-chef must be there at all times to have this sort of insight.

## MODERN ERA BEGINS

The beginning of the 20th century saw the invention of many modern products and convenience foods that allowed foodservice establishments to change the way they ordered. Refrigeration became available for commercial use around 1914. This allowed the purchase of meat, fish, and vegetables to be done in larger quantities at lower prices. Refrigerated boxcars brought meats from the western plains to the eastern metropolis markets. Fresh fruits and vegetables from California and Florida were now available year-round. Between the years 1910 and 1920, all of the following products and companies were established: Morton's Salt, Kellogg's Corn Flakes, Aunt Jemima Pancake Flour, Ocean Spray Cranberry Juice, Hellman's Mayonnaise, Birds Eye Frozen Foods, Domino Sugar, and many more. It was a time of innovation, and foodservice began to speed up in urban settings.

The era of Prohibition began in 1920 and devastated many hotel restaurants and bars. Many restaurants had fake walls and back rooms for patrons to use for illegal drinking. Chefs could no longer use alcohol for cooking, and cooking wine was salted to make it unpalatable. The age of the grand hotels came to an end, and then the Great Depression of 1929 really put a damper on the business.

During the 1930s through the 1960s, purchasing for restaurants and hotels was primarily considered clerical work. Inventory counting, recording, and forecasting were done by many hands and lots of paperwork. Salesmen for vendors were an integral part of the relationship, sometimes knowing the customers' business as well as the operators. When most restaurants and hotels received goods, they were given a bill of sale. Handwritten invoices were tallied using old-style mechanical adding machines or added by the purveyor using a basic pen and ink. There were no computers or calculators. Receiving and bookkeeping were full-time jobs. Most purchasing and receiving were done by clerks who were given orders from stewards in the kitchens and front of the house. Clerks might give orders to buyers, who would drive to the marketplace early in the morning to get the best produce, meat, and fish. Being a buyer for a prestigious hotel or restaurant was considered a quality job. They had to understand quality and price plus be able to haggle with the seller to get the best price.

In the 1940s, the restaurant business started changing for some establishments. Early casual-dining restaurants, such as the Krystal hamburger restaurant found in the South, offered burgers for 5 cents.

With many women working during the World War II, families began eating out at casual establishments as opposed to dining for an occasion. In the 1950s and 1960s, we find the beginnings of the chain-type fast-food establishments. McDonalds, Burger King, and Kentucky Fried Chicken all began in the 1950s. Once established and popular, they sold franchises to expand. Each establishment had to follow the company guidelines to be able to recreate the exact same meal anywhere. With the growth of volume in business came a much larger purchasing power. No longer did each restaurant depend on local purveyors. Now large companies were formed to supply the growing chains. Ordering specifications had to be followed to insure the same tastes could be recreated. Distribution systems were set up, and prices were similar no matter where the restaurant.

The late 1950s and early 1960s found restaurants buying from more wholesalers that offered more than just one food or product. Restaurant purveyors started "associations" to discuss business and combine forces when buying. Some restaurants also formed associations and groups to increase buying power. Larger food corporations began changing the way things were packaged, stored, and handled. Meat companies, Iowa Beef Processors (IBP) in particular, began placing precut meats into vacuum-sealed bags. This changed the way meat could be stored. No longer were whole sides shipped to large city marketplaces; now "boxed beef" could be purchased and resold directly to the kitchen without a butcher's skill to break it down. The North American Meat Processors Association developed the NAMP Meat Buyer's Guide. This guide gave consistent names to each cut so both purveyors and their customers could develop specs for orders.

Frozen and canned foods became more typical, and vacuum-sealing technology allowed for more precooked foods to be sold to high-volume restaurants and institutions. The use of blast-freezing technology changed the way many items were sold. Fishing boats would arrive on the dock and unload to large packing plants, where fish was processed and frozen. Frozen products could now be warehoused and shipped out on pallets. The connection between the actual producer-farmer and the foodservice establishment was completely severed.

In 1969 nine separate food distribution companies united to form Systems and Services Company, also known as SYSCO. SYSCO's member companies were strategically located throughout the United States. Through the 1970s the company grew rapidly, developing what were very modern warehouses and multi–temperature zone delivery trucks. Their products focused on prices and convenience for the restaurant. By 1979 sales surpassed $1 billion. Today SYSCO's sales are over $200 billion annually, and they are the dominant foodservice distributor.

For restaurants in the 1970s and 1980s, choices and selections grew dramatically. Now foods from around the world were available throughout the year. Fruits and vegetables were no longer out of season. Imports of fancy foods increased. Fine cheeses from France and Italy were now more commonplace. Specialty distributors were formed that focused on very expensive specialties such as truffles and foie gras. Wines from all over the world became more common on menus. Fancy imported beers were first found in the 1970s, and the imported beverage business boomed.

Another change in purchasing also took place. A buyer could now pick products according to the capabilities of the kitchen crew. No longer was purchasing a simple task of inventory and forecasting. Now purchases were made with labor in mind. Could the kitchen eliminate prep staff? Before, the kitchen needed to hire and train large crews to put out the same food that a much more condensed operation could now do. For instance, a chef could now order precut portion steaks, premade sauces, prepared vegetable dishes, and much more. Instead of estimating the yield of a product, the buyer could simply conduct an inventory of available portions.

In the 1980s, the larger distributors first started to use computers for inventory. Digital adding machines and scales improved accuracy, and new labeling cut down on mislabeled items and sped up deliveries. Early computers were used minimally and a lot of hand counting still took place. But innovations in software were developed throughout the 1990s. Ordering and delivery became much more frequent. In the 1950s and 1960s orders were delivered once a week, and in the 1970s and 1980s some vendors started two deliveries per week. Today we find some companies with daily deliveries, though this can get expensive. Many vendors began charging delivery fees and making deliveries only after a certain dollar amount of goods was ordered. Salespeople would call on the establishment once a week but would also be in contact by phone for additions or emergency orders. The phone became more popular, and many restaurants would simply phone in their weekly order. The invention of two machines changed ordering dramatically, the phone answering machine and the fax machine. The invention of the fax machine allowed for ordering over the phone at times when it was convenient for the buyer-chef. Now the chef could order at any time of day, and bids could be sent to the restaurant by the purveyor easily. Inventory was still hand-counted, and the purchaser still needed all the old skills of forecasting their business, but the times were changing. By the 1990s, the computer began to take over as the ordering system.

Many hotels and restaurants used bid systems for ordering to get the best possible price. The purchaser would establish specifics or "specs," which would include everything from size to count, grade, appearance, package quantity, and more. These specs were then sent to the vendor, and they would in turn return the list with prices for the week or month. Today we find this practice still viable, and developing proper specs is crucial when ordering.

By the turn of the 21st century, internet ordering was established and e-mail became a dominant sales and purchasing tool. Orders and specs can now be checked from mobile computers and cell phones, delivery times can be fine tuned, and sales staff can now promote items almost instantly. A purchaser has the ability to compare prices from other vendors in just seconds.

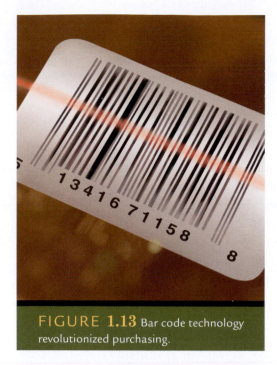

The computer bar code system revolutionized receiving and inventory. The invention was used first for identifying railcars in the 1950s, and then in 1974 Kroger Supermarkets introduced it to rapidly check out customers. Soon the technology expanded into foodservice. Large processors used bar codes to code all meat items, dry goods, vegetables, and fruits, and this meant they could capture instant data on product use. For the vendor, bar codes meant rapid picking of orders and much tighter inventory control. For the restaurant, the bar code meant inventory control and traceability. A large hotel or casino could now conduct inventory almost daily. Pilfering could be minimized, and managers could now know how much should be in house at any time. Data were collected, and forecasting became easier.

The invention of point-of-sale (POS), touch screen, meal-ordering systems in the mid-1990s meant that ordering could be streamlined and somewhat automated. No more monthly hand counts and discrepancies. At first it was only fast food that used the technology, but then many fine dining establishments realized the advantage of POS systems.

FIGURE **1.14** Touch screen point-of-sale system.

Today we find chefs and managers ordering; checking inventory; redoing menus; scheduling staff; talking with salespeople, staff, and customers; checking cash reserves; and even checking the temperatures and humidity levels of their coolers all from their phones on their way to work. Monitoring systems can keep track of all parts of the restaurant. But, make no mistake about it, the highest-quality purchasing is still done by those who are constantly involved in their business, and, just like a great palate, purchasing instincts take time to develop.

Purchasing has moved from the clerical position, where the purchaser simply restocked the pantry, to a valuable position that can influence the profitability of the foodservice establishment. The modern purchaser must have many skills, including a full understanding of product specs, a good working relationship with the chef and cooks using the products, the ability to operate computer inventory and tracking systems, an understanding of market trends, and a basic understanding of laws and regulations affecting their buying. Today's purchasers control more "spend" of a company; they are more involved in the decision-making process over food products, dry goods, cleaning supplies, equipment, and even in some cases services. Purchasers may be asked to shop around for better insurance and advertising rates in some establishments. Communication with the front- and back-of-the-house managers is key to successful purchasing. Ultimately the purchaser connects, through their choices, to the customer. A good purchaser knows the business and what works and what does not. With all of the new technologies, in some ways purchasing has gotten easier, but in other ways, due to all of the choices, purchasing has become more complicated. The fiscal well-being of a foodservice operation depends on effective purchasing.

# DEALING WITH PURVEYORS AND ESTABLISHING A VENDOR RELATIONSHIP

Two of the most crucial abilities one can have to be successful in purchasing are the ability to first determine the optimal vendors for your company's needs and then the ability to establish good working relationships with these vendors, especially those purveyors that you will be working with on a consistent basis. The nature, frequency, and the volume of the product that are required will likely have a significant influence on the nature of the relationship. Also, whether the product is a commonly found commodity or a unique item that is proprietary to that vendor will have a significant role in how that vendor relationship is formed and conducted.

This is especially true within the foodservice industry, where you may be dealing with a wide variety of purveyors. They can range from a large national, broad-line distributor such as SYSCO and U.S. Foodservice; a smaller regional broad-line company such as Ginsberg's Foods, where the buyer's intent is to obtain a wide range of commodity goods for the least cost; or a small local grower of a specialty produce, meat, poultry, or seafood item desired by the chef when in season.

FIGURE **2.1a** Small purveyors offer fresh, local products, but often operate in smaller quantities and have less flexible delivery hours.

FIGURE **2.1b** Larger purveyors often have a large selection and can take larger, more frequent orders.

Many circumstances can dictate the best approach to take in dealing with a vendor, but the key is to always be respectful, professional, and trustworthy in those dealings. That and, of course, to find purveyors that are willing to work with your company in the same manner. This is true if you are making a single large purchase where the main focus needs to be driven by cost or if you and the vendor sense the opportunity to develop a long-term relationship that will grow and improve over a sustained period of time. The best specific method of conducting business can vary greatly, but trust and proper ethics should always be observed and there must be an understanding that all parties need to profit in some way from the transaction.

# ESTABLISHING A RELATIONSHIP

The first step in establishing a relationship with a vendor requires a clear sense of what matters most in your business model. Determine what types of products are required to meet those business needs, and then seek out companies that can best provide those needs. This, on the surface, sounds quite elemental, but the more clarity you have and can share with prospective vendors about your business philosophy, and exactly what your needs are, the better and easier it is for both parties to determine if it is feasible to develop a relationship.

There is considerably more detail required here than simply ascertaining who carries what product line. Many other factors, such as exact specifications, quality, brand, point of origin, the raising methods used by farmers for vegetable and proteins, and more, will all play a role. Other factors will include frequency of delivery, minimum required order size, vendor location and reputation, payment method, and the purveyor's ability to purchase at a good price and rapidly turn over inventory; these are also crucial considerations to make when determining who can best meet your needs. When buying from local producers or growers, you need to know about their ability to fulfill your needs, if their delivery times are reliable, how they pack, that proper cooling and HAACP controls are adhered to, if they require a quicker payment schedule, and how they can be reached during business hours. With small local vendors, you also need to consider the length of the season that certain products will be available, whether their products can meet your exact specification, and if your specifications are reasonable in the market. You should also ascertain if their price will represent a good value to you in terms of quality, shelf life, and yield. You may find from time to time that your expectations are not readily available in your market and need to rethink your specification rather than place impractical expectations on your vendor.

The initial stage of any relationship can basically be seen as getting to know one another. With any prospective vendor, it is critical at the initial meeting stage for all parties to be completely frank and clear as to what is required and expected in a relationship. No one benefits from entering into a business relationship that will not allow both parties to satisfy their needs in an efficient and profitable manner. It is also important to do your due diligence in verifying a vendor's financial position; they will certainly look at your credit history. Also, plan to do on-site inspections of their place of business early into a relationship; look at the size of the operation and volume of inventory held, examine the quality of the product, and signs of how and how long it has been held in inventory, and be aware of the overall cleanliness and signs of pest infestation in the facility. When visiting vendors, talk to other employees besides the sales team; ask how long they have worked there, about the company's history, and who their other customers are. If they are proud of their company, they won't have any trouble answering your questions and you will get a clear sense as to that purveyor's culture.

Today many products and businesses may be found online, and transactions are done by fax or e-procurement. You lose the human touch and much of the ability to interact with such companies, but at least they can still be checked for reviews of performance and inquiries made as to the nature and origin of what is being purchased.

| VENDOR EVALUATION FORM | | |
|---|---|---|
| **VENDOR:** | | **DATE:** |
| Rating: Excellent = 4, Satisfactory = 2, Poor = 0 | | |
| **CRITERIA** | | **SCORE** |
| Product | Quality | |
| | Consistency | |
| | Price | |
| | Availability | |
| Service | Timely delivery | |
| | Delivery frequency | |
| | Condition of product | |
| | Delivery accuracy | |
| | Handling of complaints | |
| | Attitude of delivery personnel | |
| | Ability to handle emergency deliveries | |
| Company | Size | |
| | Selection | |
| | Location | |
| | Management policies | |
| | Accuracy of invoices | |
| | Credits handled in timely manner | |
| Sales Personnel | Knowledge of company policies and procedures | |
| | Product line knowledge | |
| | Willingness to provide information about products | |
| | Accuracy and timeliness of price quotes | |
| | Schedules sales calls | |
| | Handles complaints | |
| | **TOTAL** | |

**FIGURE 2.2** Sample Vendor Evaluation Form

Finding the right vendors may take some work and time, so it is important, whenever possible, to start the process well before you require the product in house. Word-of-mouth references from other professionals in your business community are always a good start in identifying which companies have good fill rates, make timely deliveries, and are easy to deal with. Most broad-line distributors and other large wholesale companies usually have sales representatives with established territories that will likely seek you out. Local chambers of commerce, trade publications, the internet, and yellow pages as well as national trade directories such as the Thomas Register are all good sources of information.

## CONSIDERATIONS FOR SPECIALTY PRODUCT VENDORS

Perishables require a high level of quality in both product and purveyor due to their high cost, yield factors, short shelf life, and product knowledge. Seek out those vendors that will best meet these more stringent quality and service needs. Produce is best when in season and found as local as your location permits. When seeking a local farm or rancher, the local green market is a great place to start or an agricultural grange if you are in a rural setting. For farm products not found locally or not in season in your area, seek out a produce vendor that has the selection required, but also has the volume to buy well and to rapidly turn over inventory and help insure the freshness.

Proteins such as fish and meat can often be a bigger challenge depending on your location and needs. Broad-line distributors carry many common cuts of boxed meat in specific grades and trim specifications, and it is important to understand if these will satisfy your needs. Such vendors also carry a limited range of the more commonly called-for species of fish, much of them in fillet form. However, if, your business requires a niche market to obtain custom cuts, heritage breeds, grass-fed specialty game, or extreme-quality meat products, you will need to find a specialty meat vendor in your area or one online that can ship to you for the price and quality you can be satisfied with. Fish, with its exacting need for quality and freshness due to its high perishability and cost, and the seasonality of many species, requires an excellent and trustworthy fishmonger to properly service a demanding clientele. The best vendors for meat or fish generally specialize in that one line because of the extraordinary efforts it requires to market such pricey and perishable product well.

You will also want to know how long a specialty protein vendor has been in business and whom their client base is to be certain they can meet your demands over the long term. Your location will likely dictate if such a purveyor can be found locally or if it will be necessary to find a quality firm in a distant location that can properly ship the quality seafood or meat desired for an appropriate price. In recent years, there have also been a growing number of firms on the internet that can supply quality (if potentially expensive) varieties of meat and fish by shipping them overnight to your door. This can give you direct access to a specific region or rancher's lamb, pork, or grass-fed beef as well as wild king salmon, spotted prawns from Alaska, or Wahoo from the Caribbean that are only a day or two out of the water, no matter where you are located. Naturally, such products have a higher price point than the more limited selection of fresh or frozen product available from your broad-line vendor; again, the nature of your business will drive which product you need to pursue.

Some foodservice companies seriously consider their impact in regard to social responsibility; this creates definite value judgments on the type of product they will purchase. These buyers must be sure that the vendor has the means to deliver what they specify and understands why it is important and that these values are surely being conveyed to their customers. These standards can include requiring sustainable or organic rather than commercially grown product, local rather than global produce, grass-fed rather than corn- and grain-fed animals that meet Certified Humane handling practices, fair trade practices, and other distinctions that promote

FIGURE **2.3a** A large purveyor's warehouse.

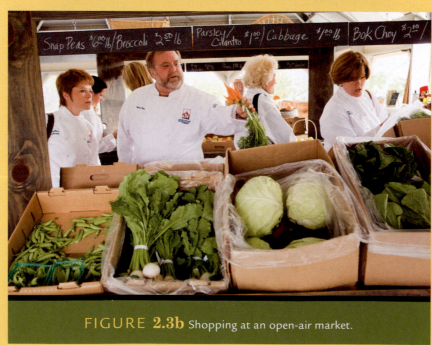

FIGURE **2.3b** Shopping at an open-air market.

your business's standpoint. You may also define the product's point of origin if health codes, carbon footprint, or environmental impact is integral to your purchasing philosophy. There are vendors that are geared to meet these requirements and those that cannot.

## SERVICE CONSIDERATIONS

Once you have determined the vendor(s) that can provide you with the selection and quality you seek for a price you can work with, their ability to properly service your account and other terms need to be ascertained. The greatest ingredients, even at a great price, are of no value if they are not available to you when and as often as they are needed. In the foodservice profession, with everything predicated on menu, timing, and shelf life, service is absolutely essential in determining the company with which a purchaser should establish a relationship.

There are several service factors to consider in opting for a vendor to develop a business relationship. The company's fill rate indicates the percentage of items ordered that are filled on time without shortages or back orders out of each scheduled delivery. Vendors should be able to supply that information so you can identify what company will appear best able to meet your demands. The purchaser should also track that company's track record over time to assure that the required level of service remains consistent. Purchasers should also demand that vendors alert them in advance if ordered items will not be available so that alternative sources or recipes can be developed in time. Larger firms allow purchasing agents to buy through an online procurement system that should indicate if sufficient inventory exists in stock when the order is placed. With smaller firms, it is incumbent on the salesperson or customer representative to supply this information in a timely enough manner for it to be of use.

Delivery days and times are also factors that need to be negotiated and then adhered to. Purveyors should provide a window of time during which the buyer can expect to take a delivery of merchandise ordered, and that time frame requires strict adherence. A time that can work for both vendor and client can usually be negotiated to everyone's satisfaction. Production in foodservice kitchens is very time bound, and delayed or late orders can make

FIGURE **2.4** Purveyors must provide a window of time in which they will make their deliveries, so that the purchaser has time to properly receive the order and put it away.

it extremely difficult for cooks and prep staff to assure their customer's needs and timelines are met. Weather, mechanical failure, or traffic can occasionally create unavoidable delivery delays, but at such rare times it is essential that the vendor advise the customer of the delay and offer some notion of when delivery can be expected. Service should also work both ways; buyers can ask their vendors what they can do to help them service their account better. Flexible delivery dates or times, an extra day's lead time and cutoff times, and using item code numbers when placing orders are some examples of things you can do for your vendor to ensure you get the service and product needed.

# FINANCIAL CONSIDERATIONS: MINIMUM DELIVERIES AND PAYMENT SCHEDULES

Purveyors generally establish minimum dollar values for orders to guarantee that all deliveries will generate some margin of profit, or at least insure against loss. Purchasing agents must be sure their company's volume of business can support such minimums and in doing so insure a high enough frequency of deliveries to allow for optimum product freshness. For example, it would not be acceptable to receive fresh fish just once a week as the quality and flavor of fresh product will certainly diminish or decay by week's end. When establishing a relationship with a vendor, always be clear that the company can deliver as often as required, that you can live with the minimum order requirements, and if delivery or fuel surcharges are assessed.

Satisfactory payment terms are an important factor to be considered, and negotiated if possible, when determining what vendor to do business with. The size of your business and your business's credit history will have a direct bearing on what terms can be agreed on. The chef or buyer in most foodservice operations will not likely dictate these terms, but must be part of the discussion to insure that all arrangements can be adhered to. As a rule, the customer should ideally hold onto his money for as long as possible, usually 30 days. However, some vendors will offer discounts to companies that pay off their invoices on the first day. These discounts can usually offer better savings than the interest that can be gained by holding payment for the 30-day period. Obviously, the foodservice establishment's financial condition will dictate whether this is possible. Sufficient cash reserves should be maintained for unexpected expenditures, such as when the ice machine dies before a busy weekend. When working with small family farms or other boutique producers, it may be necessary to work on a tighter payment schedule such as 10 days from delivery as such small growers may not have sufficient cash reserves or operating funds to accept a 30-day window. Cash on delivery would likely be very welcome by many boutique growers and distributors, but may lack the tight controls desired by many firms' financial management. Paying cash may also complicate the ability to manage later credits or debits if further controls are needed. Again, a buyer's willingness to accommodate these needs is based on the perceived value of buying that local product.

Late payment will also create difficulties between a customer and the vendor. Late payments can cause a company to be put on a COD (cash on delivery) basis, ruin their reputation with other firms, and drive up interest rates or retract discounts from purchase prices, and may make it necessary for purchasers to lower standards and buy from vendors of lesser quality. Too many late payments can also result in legal troubles and costs. All these problems obviously should be avoided if at all possible. This problem may not influence your choice of a vendor, but it may well determine their desire to maintain or initiate a business relationship with your firm.

When looking for vendors and working to establish a relationship with them, an essential step is clear communication between both parties. There should be indisputable specifications and standards, and when in doubt, sample products will need to be cut to insure all quality standards are met. Purchasers must be assured that the vendor can also supply them with the appropriate service in sales information, fill rates, and delivery needs. All this is needed to establish a good working relationship with a vendor. If this company is expected to be a regular and essential part of a buyer's purchasing needs, then the trick is to grow the relationship and foster regular communication to insure not only that the company's needs are met but also that the relationship continues to grow. In an age of e-procurement, faxed invoices, and email, it is easy to lose the human contact often needed to further a business relationship. Make time whenever possible to schedule times for face-to-face meetings to further these relationships so that new and other profitable ways of dealing with each other can be found and relationships can be improved.

## A WIN-WIN PHILOSOPHY

Purchasing personnel have various approaches in the tone they wish to set when dealing with a vendor. There is the philosophy that your vendor is your adversary and only wishes to encourage his clients to buy more than needed and at too high a cost. The response to this type of thinking is to try to beat them at their own game and pay as little as possible while demanding unrealistic service expectations or to threaten to take your business elsewhere. Such an adversarial approach to selling or buying is very untenable in the long run; it is what could be termed a win-lose situation. In any transaction where one party must "lose," that party will likely find a way to recoup their losses by another means. The alternative is that the "losing party" will either take their business elsewhere or chance going out of business.

The "winner" in these arrangements may find that the company that can best meet their specific needs will no longer be able or willing to work with them. In the long run, there is clearly no gain, no winner. Even when a purchase is for a product required only once, it is always better to conduct any transaction in a reasonable manner. The keys in such a transaction are in understanding the true value of the product, being willing to insure that the purchase price asked is of a proper value, and having the ability to negotiate a price that is fair to both parties. Your reputation and that of the firm you represent are in part dictated by the manner in which you negotiate and deal with your vendors. You also never know for sure when you will need to work with them again. Obviously, this is not to say that negotiating for the very best price for your company is not required and essential; it simply means that the negotiation should be managed honorably, professionally, and with realistic demands.

When vendors and buyers work together to establish a working relationship that meets the needs of both parties in that the buyers get the quality and service they need for an appropriate cost and vendors gain a customer they can move merchandise with profitably, this is known as a win-win relationship. This can also be termed as a sustainable business relationship as it allows all parties to continue to work together in a manner beneficial to both. Win-win relationships can take a variety of forms, but however they are done, the results will be mutually satisfactory on the whole. No one party may see the arrangements as completely ideal in every aspect, but their overall needs are still satisfied.

## OPERATIONAL CONSULTANTS

Some companies now employ the services of what can be termed as operational or buying consultants to act as liaisons or agents in determining what vendors to use while ensuring a mutually acceptable, but narrow, margin of profit. In such a relationship the consultant generally represents a group of high-volume accounts, which allows the consultant to leverage a great deal of buying power to drive these agreed-upon narrow margins. The system requires that the client purchase within a sole vendor model utilizing one vendor in each major product line. In other words, the client will give each "program vendor" an agreed-upon high percentage of all purchases made in that particular vendor's line (such as 80% of all produce purchases to vendor A, 75% of all seafood purchases to vendor B, etc.). The vendor makes less on each dollar of product sold, but has the guarantee of much higher volume.

In doing this, the consultant will have thoroughly investigated each vendor and assured the client that the vendor is also buying correctly at the best price to ensure that they can charge the client a very competitive price. Once established, the consultant will review what the vendor paid for the relevant product on a monthly basis and verify that the price charged by the vendor is within the appropriate margin. Discrepancies, if any, are identified, and the correct dollar variance is paid through the use of a credit or debit. Large or frequent discrepancies may also require that the vendor be assessed a penalty on top of the required credit. Often, depending on volume, there is also a small percentage of total sales issued to the client by the vendor(s) as a rebate at the end of each annual audit by the consultant. If all works as it should, the initial and annual fees for the consultant are considerably less than the savings realized from the aggressive pricing and the annual rebate.

The client benefits from the improved price savings and recoups the time required to conduct repetitive competitive bidding among several vendors as well as other improved administrative costs realized when dealing with fewer vendors. However, there is some loss in options in where and what specific brands will be available. The vendor has a guaranteed increased volume of business for a specific length of time, but must work on tighter margins and supply the agreed-upon portion of the client's needs in close adherence to the client's specifications. It is a win-win scenario, but within narrow margins, and this format is usually only effective for high-volume clients.

Purchasing a wide range of items using a sole vendor model can potentially yield savings without the use of an outside consultant. However, without another means of verifying costs on a regular basis, you put your company at risk for dramatically overpaying. Vendors may start out working on very tight margins to win an account and build favor, but without an ongoing method of monitoring price against the market, it is likely that over time your margins and prices will increase to an untenable margin. The ability to verify the proper market price is always a requisite.

## SUPPORTING LOCAL BUSINESSES

Another model of a win-win relationship can exist when your business model dictates that you buy as many products grown or produced locally as possible. Such small growers, ranchers, or producers will not likely be able to meet the prices of product that are mass produced in other parts of the world and distributed through huge international corporations. Also, the buyers need to provide the farmer with sufficient lead time to meet their needs, adapt their menus to what is currently in season and weather permitting, and pay their bills promptly.

However, the offset is a pronounced gain in quality, the ability to have some product grown to the chef's exact specifications, a reduced carbon footprint in sourcing locally, improved yield because the product came out of the field that day and has not spent days or weeks in transit and cold storage before arriving at your door, and that amazing farm-fresh flavor. Some growers and ranchers will offer a discount of a small percentage of the sale price if their farm or company name is noted on the restaurant's written menu. Plus, there is the public approval and appreciation gained from your local community when your business is known to go out of its way to support its neighbors.

In order for this to work for the buyers and chefs, farmers and growers need to understand that these folks are in business and need to turn a profit on what is purchased. Quality product can carry a premium but only within workable limitations. Farmers also need to appreciate that they need to be accessible to buyers during

working hours, pack in standard case sizes, meet the agreed-upon quality standards, and arrive at the chef-buyer's place of business at the agreed-upon time. For this added effort, the farmer will gain a known and agreed-upon source for the products grown, at a reasonable price, and therefore an assured amount of income. It is also critical for the farmer and buyer to meet periodically throughout the year. They should meet in the winter to discuss what the buyer's projected needs will be; in the spring, the buyer and/or chef should visit the farm and allow the farmer to bring them into the field so they can be very specific about their needs; later in the season, the farmer could be invited for a meal in the restaurant or foodservice operation to fully appreciate how the crops were utilized. Such closely interconnected relationships are a bit more work, but the results are well worth the effort and create a true win-win relationship between buyer and producer.

## COMPETITIVE BIDDING

When not looking for small local producers for niche product or taking part in a sole or primary vendor program, purchasers will generally use a bidding system from a small group of approved vendors. The buyer and chef first need to develop clear specifications for each product needed and share these with the approved vendors so it is very clear to all what the required expectations are. The type of product will likely dictate the timing and duration of the bid. Produce, meat, and fish bids are generally done each week, if not daily. Dairy and most dry goods bids are most frequently done on a monthly basis. Given the volatility of the food market and all the external factors that can impact price, this is generally about as far out as many vendors will commit to price.

Ethics dictate that buyers are respectful of a purveyor's confidence and never share one company's pricing with another firm to drive down their bid price. Buyers must also understand that, as previously noted, vendors will still need to achieve minimum orders for them to benefit from the sale. If a vendor only successfully bids on a relatively few number of items or those with a low purchase volume, it may be necessary and reasonable to either place fewer orders or drop that vendor and use the next closest bidder on those few items. This will also save the purchasing firm administrative costs in receiving and billing for a relatively minor savings in price. Relationships that utilize bid systems can also be win-win scenarios provided that each participant delivers what is promised in a fair and ethical manner. Whatever the style of purchasing dictated by the purchasing organization—multiple vendor bidding, an intermediary such as an outside consultant, or the close interaction between chef and farmer—a win-win relationship is possible and essential if you are looking to build a strong and enduring working bond.

## KEEPING RELATIONSHIPS VIABLE

Once a purchasing agent or chef-buyer identifies those companies that best suit the firm's needs, and has established a relationship, it benefits both parties over the long term to identify other needs that can be satisfied. Both sides should continue to find ways to grow the relationship and seek ways to maximize each other's benefit. However, over the long run, buyers also need to remain vigilant and not become complacent due to feelings of trust or because they have come to like doing business with a vendor or their sales representative. Liking a company and the people that represent them is a beneficial result of a business relationship, provided that the feeling of affection does not become the motive behind making purchases. Likewise, buyers can get into a "comfort zone" with certain vendors and lose their focus on ensuring their purchasing dollars are being put to the best use. A good vendor–client relationship should be seen in many ways as a partnership, but not to the extent that proper controls are no longer exercised. A feeling of uncertainty about the unknown can prevent an inexperienced buyer from exploring new and potentially better avenues for procurement. Buyers should also be wary of unethical dealings if key personnel in their company are demanding a specific vendor be chosen over others without a clear and rational motive. All purchases must be driven for the company's benefit only.

Similarly, buyers may trust a vendor too quickly to always do what is in their best interest because they have gotten a good feeling about their salesperson, or just like how that vendor does business or what they market. Trust in a business relationship is a crucial aspect of any relationship but should not immediately be given. Trust comes over time when both sides have shown that they can deliver as promised, work to find ways to benefit each other, supply and purchase as obligated, and simply do what is ethically obligated without duress. This requires a track record that is built over time and should not be given for reasons more emotional than cognitive. The relationship can never be what drives the purchase; if a vendor is unable to supply your needs or act honorably, it is best to cease relations and find a new vendor that will meet your needs, even if this will cause some temporary confusion and shortages. A business relationship built on trust and conducted by people who like to work together is something to strive for, but it cannot be rushed or taken for granted. Nor can it be assumed that everyone employed by a vendor is as trustworthy as the sales representative.

# ACCURATE BIDDING

This study illustrates the consequences of not maintaining current bid sheets with thorough and up-to-date product specifications. Any bid requires fully detailed information in order to have any real validity. It also makes it clear that complacency in any business relationship, whether exhibited by vendor or client, is simply bad business. Developing excellent long-term and trusting relationships in business requires work; staffing and ownership will change, and buyers must always be sure to verify that trust. Vendors also must remember that long-term customers should be treated with respect and given attention to ensure the relationship does not deteriorate as trust is replaced by skepticism.

Chancellorville Tech is a small New England college with about 1,800 full-time students. The school's purchasing program is fairly centralized, with limited exceptions for specialized IT and some construction needs. This includes supplying the needs of the campus' classrooms, housekeeping, dormitory, and foodservice departments.

The purchasing program utilized at Chancellorville is not a single or primary vendor system. However, almost all of the school's needs for paper and cleaning supplies had long been supplied by one excellent regional vendor, St. George Paper Supply. This company had provided for the school's needs in a most proactive manner. In order to secure a broad range of products, the vendor operated on a very slim profit margin and was constantly looking for ways to secure better pricing from the manufacturers with whom they did business in order to drive better value to the school. Whenever a manufacturer failed to provide Chancellorville with what they believed was a strong buying program, St. George would contact other manufacturers to see if a better option could be provided.

Buyers at the college responded in kind by ordering a broad range of items from St. George Paper each week, ensuring each delivery was profitable. Periodically, to be safe, a request for prices on a sampling of these products was sent to other competitive vendors to guarantee that Chancellorville was still getting an optimal price to complement the excellent service they received. Over many years, no competing company was willing to afford Chancellorville the combined value of price and service offered by St. George Paper Supply. It was an ideal business relationship for all parties, and after a time, in some ways, the buying team at the college became complacent. Spec sheets and full competitive bidding sheets were not maintained and updated because the two operations functioned like a partnership, each looking out for the other's needs.

Then one day the college's sales rep from St. George came in to see the college's buyers with some devastating news; their company had been sold to a much larger national paper company. The owners were getting old, and the buyout afforded them a lucrative way out of business. Chancellorville's buyers were told not to worry; the new firm was promising to provide them the same kind of service to which they had become accustomed. Plus, the new company's size and product range would likely afford the college greater savings and an even wider array of products to choose from. As sad as they felt in losing their old partner, the purchasing team realized there were possible advantages here, and continued as before, only with the new owners.

However, over time it became evident that the new vendor's priorities were different and the rules were changing. Sales calls diminished, and most business was conducted by fax. Products went up in price, or changed in quality, or became more difficult to get, and little was offered in the way of suggestions to obtain better value. Delivery days were dropped, the formerly early delivery time came later in the day, and a fuel surcharge was added to each invoice. The buyers at Chancellorville Tech finally understood it was time to conduct a full-inventory competitive bid with other available firms to be certain that they were still at least getting a fair price along with the diminished service. The college's purchasing manager identified two competitive firms and instructed the paper buyer to send out bids as soon as possible. The buyer in this line was relatively new to the college and had never purchased these products from another company, nor did he have any proper bid sheets on file.

In order to expedite the process, the buyer sent out copies of his current product inventory and asked these competing firms to simply add their pricing to those sheets. These sheets were sorely lacking in the information required to obtain a proper bid; all required specifications and product codes were not updated, the projected volume of purchase was not included for each item, nor was there a due date and time frame for the bid. What the buyer thought would enable him to most quickly access the desired information became the cause of much consternation, uncertainly, miscommunication, and loss of time. The two new companies were eager to get their foot in the door and therefore worked hard at getting all the information they needed that was not immediately offered on the bid sheet. This resulted in many phone calls, and return calls, and double checking to assure all required information was obtained and accurate. The current vendor, relying on what they thought was a guaranteed sale due to many years of business, gave the bid request very little thought and simply treated it as a request for current pricing.

When the bids were finally received and compared, another two months had transpired. The buyers at Chancellorville found that they were currently overpaying, at least to some degree, for roughly 85% of their purchased paper and cleaning supply inventory; they consequently moved all of their purchases to the other two firms. This, as you can expect, caused great acrimony with St. George Paper Supply's new owner.

They claimed that the fact that this was a competitive bid had never been made clear. They thought that loyalty required they get another shot at the bid and that the buyers were either incompetent or possibly in cahoots with the new companies. The fact that the other companies took the time to get all the necessary information and St. George Paper had merely taken the college for granted was lost on them. Obviously, this process had been poorly managed by both the vendor and the client. The relationship had been abused by the seller, and the buyer had been asleep at the wheel and was not properly prepared to proceed with this bid in a professional manner.

The transition from St. George to the new vendors had the expected hurdles. Pack sizes changed, some specifications had not been clear despite all the interaction beforehand, and internal customers at Chancellorville were upset when products they had used for years were substituted with new options, even when there was a savings exhibited. Yet in time all these difficulties were overcome and a thorough bid was conducted quarterly with all of the required information available to assure that the vendors exactly understood all of the college's needs fully. Both vendors are still with the school, even though the product mix has adjusted over time. The lessons from that first botched bid were well learned.

People filling the orders and drivers can often short-weight cases or substitute inferior product in order to make cash sales or pilfer items for their own use. It always pays to be wary and exercise the proper controls in purchasing and when receiving product.

## VENDOR ASSESSMENT CHECKLIST

The following is a brief list of things to seek out in a purchasing relationship and things best to avoid. Your standards may expand upon this, but this will give you a good place to start.

Look for vendors with the following characteristics:

- A willingness for on-site inspections and access to personnel
- A sound financial footing
- Knowledgeable and direct sales personnel, both territory and in-house representatives
- Transparency in business dealings
- Sufficient inventory to meet needs (good fill rate) and volume to quickly turn over inventory

FIGURE **2.5** Choose a vendor that is knowledgeable, can meet your purchasing needs, and is punctual with deliveries.

- The ability to purchase well and a consistency in inventory selection
- Friendly, courteous, knowledgeable, and punctual delivery personnel

Avoid vendors that do the following:

- Make offers that are too good to be true; they usually are.
- Ask what you are currently paying for bid items.
- Promise they can meet every request.
- Do not take the time to understand your business' needs before seeking to make a sale.
- Have "hidden" charges such as fuel and destination fees, charges for packing crates, or both handling and shipping fees.
- Cannot demonstrate proper temperature retention in delivery vehicles.
- Ship in trimmed produce or in repackaged cases.

## IN-HOUSE RELATIONSHIPS

A buyer in a foodservice establishment is the customer of the various companies and farms that sell to their place of employment. In that role, they need to assure their employer's business needs are well tended by ensuring that all controls are intact and that they purchase with the best product value in mind. It is equally true that this position acts as the vendor for the various other positions within that establishment that count on the buyer for the quality products they need to perform their job function.

This will likely include the various chefs and cooks requiring raw food ingredients. It will also include the service personnel that manage the dining rooms and the liquor service for the operation, and the maintenance and stewarding teams that maintain and clean the facility and its wares. In some establishments, it will also include procuring products such as information technology and point-of-sale (IT/POS) equipment, furnishings, utilities, insurance, and services such as waste management and landscaping. Wearing this many hats can be a trying experience, and it is imperative that the purchasers develop excellent working relationships not only with the vendors of these various products but also with their fellow employees. These people not only have the need for these items, but also likely have more expertise with them.

Many times, these various customers will assume that the buyer is merely there to provide whatever is demanded and, if they feel they have the budget to support those decisions, that it is their call to determine what gets bought and where. The buyer's main concern must be with the financial well-being of the employer, and meeting their customers' various demands must be done only within that context. It is imperative for these buyers to understand a product's true value and not just consider price or brand name. This requires some finesse in achieving customer satisfaction and support without losing sight of the fiscal realities of the business.

In foodservice, it is likely that the most challenging and time-consuming relationship a buyer will have in house is with the food preparation staff. Chefs and cooks will have very definitive ideas and opinions on the nature and the quality of the food products they require, including being brand specific. The purchasing agent's job is to find a reliable source for these items at a cost that will allow the company to meet their food cost percentages with a menu cost that is acceptable to the public, or to find an alternative product that will meet the price criteria and still meet the chef's standards. This also requires having these products in house just prior to when the cooking team requires these items for their mise en place and being able to replenish inventory quickly if demand outpaces forecasted need.

Buyers must be knowledgeable, or have quick access to knowledge, in terms of the seasonality, the effects of weather, market conditions, or anything else that will dramatically affect their ability to meet the product needs of the chefs, and be able to advise them if a menu choice is untenable. This especially applies to any perishable and fresh items such as meat, fish, fresh produce, dairy, and cheese. Buyers will also need to insure that the vendors they utilize can meet the delivery schedule required by their chefs. The key here is to be the liaison between the chefs and the producers and growers in the industry.

In many smaller restaurants, the chefs themselves act as the food-purchasing person for that operation. This means they must juggle the demands and focus required to prepare high-quality food for service with the fluctuations and competition of the market place. Also, these chef-buyers are equally responsible to buy properly and ensure they meet the menu food cost percentages dictated by management.

Buyers in foodservice will also need to forge a good relationship with the bar and beverage personnel in their establishment to ensure the brands and quality meet the demands of their customer base. With alcoholic beverages, most name brands are sold by specific vendors with little negotiation allowed on price unless volume discounts can be managed. Wines require more knowledge and specificity to purchase well and will likely require a very close relationship with the sommelier or manager and some training for the buyer in this area. Proper storage for these beverages is also a must if the product will be held for any period of time. Coffee and tea can also encompass a great deal of knowledge in the various types sold and the different brewing and service techniques popular with today's consumer. Issues of fair trade and organically raised products figure prominently with these beverages, and the establishment's culture will dictate whether these should be sought out.

# LEGAL CONSIDERATIONS

Basic purchasing contracts are legally binding, and even simple food purchases have legal implications. When a foodservice establishment orders from a purveyor, there are many legal issues that can take place. There are many varieties of contracts that can relate to purchasing, but one is most common: the purchase agreement. What is a purchase agreement? State laws govern what is considered a contract, but there is a nationwide document that unifies the states. The Uniform Commercial Code (UCC) is the group of articles that insures uniformity and consistency throughout the states so contracts can be enforceable across state lines. Business contracts fall under the UCC, which gives certain protections to buyers and sellers. Any company that conducts business in the United States should be familiar with the Code.

The UCC consists of the following:

Article 1: General Provisions—Interprets the document and explains its intentions
Article 2: Sales Contracts—Regulates the sale of goods
Article 2a: Leases—Regulates leasing of goods

Article 3: Commercial Paper—Negotiable instruments, promissory notes
Article 4: Bank Deposits, Collections—Regulates collection practices
Article 4a: Fund transfers—Transfers of money between banks
Article 5: Letters of Credit—Defines credit terms
Article 6: Bulk Transfers—Auctions and liquidation of assets
Article 7: Warehouse Receipts, Bills of Lading, Documents of Title
Article 8: Investment Securities—Financial assets
Article 9: Secured Transactions—Sales of accounts, collateral

The UCC governs many aspects of purchasing, and a buyer must understand their responsibilities and rights under the code. The term *caveat emptor*, meaning "buyer beware," implies that the burden of determining the quality, condition, and price of the item is on the purchaser, not on the seller. There are certain regulations in the Code that define when caveat emptor is enforceable and when the seller is obliged to uphold implied conditions. For instance, the seller is obliged to provide goods that are free of defects and meet the terms of the contract. The buyer is obliged to inspect the goods and inform the seller of any problems immediately.

Purchasing agreements would be covered under Article 2. A contract is simply an agreement made between two or more parties that are enforceable by law. There are two basic types of contracts, verbal and written. Purchases of over $500 must be in writing to be enforceable. Written contracts are preferred over verbal to ensure clarity and alleviate the conflict if one or both parties forget the terms. But the fact of the matter is that we often enter contracts verbally whenever we order food over the phone or with a salesperson. For instance, a chef calls the purveyor and orders some goods, a price is discussed, quantity is arranged, specs are given, and delivery time is agreed upon. If the goods arrive and an authorized person signs for the item, the contract is now enforceable. The "Bill of Sale" or invoice represents the contract.

A Bill of Sale should always have the following:

- Buyer's name and address
- Seller's name and address
- Price or consideration
- Description of property
- Date of sale and items received
- Date order was placed
- Terms of payment

But what if everything is not as agreed upon? What if the goods are not up to specification, the items are spoiled, or the food's temperature is too high? It is up to the buyer to immediately check all products before signing. Once signed, the terms of invoice are enforceable, so be sure to be diligent. There may be some recourse if there is deception involved. Maybe the vendor places some fresh product over the top of some that is spoiling. The Uniform Commercial Code Article 2-315 states,

> Implied Warranty: Where the seller at the time of contracting has reason to know any particular purpose for which the goods are required and that the buyer is relying on the seller's skill or judgment to select or furnish suitable goods, there unless excluded or modified under the next section an implied warranty that the goods shall be fit for that purpose.

Implied warranties are enforceable when noticed soon after the product has been received. If the buyer waits until the bill is due and then claims, "That stuff was rotten, I'm not paying!" the seller may be able to collect legally despite the actual quality of the goods. The best solution is to check over products carefully.

Another legally tricky situation is when a chef continually orders products but then rejects part or all of the order upon delivery for no other reason other than error in ordering or financial inability to pay. The vendor may then refuse to send products, or written contracts might be in order to allow the vendor some recourse, but typically the buyer is not liable until the bill is signed. However, a chef who continually acts this way may be considered acting in bad faith and may be legally responsible at some point.

In foodservice, there are numerous types of purchases including provisions such as foods, beverages, dry goods, and cleaning supplies; sale of durable goods such as large kitchen equipment, furnishings, and vehicles; and services such as pest control, laundry, cleaning, landscaping, legal, and accounting. All of these purchases require different types of contracts. Be sure to read the fine print on all contracts, bills of sale, invoices, and even emails. Whenever entering into verbal contracts, be sure to take notes.

It is bad policy by the seller to practice deception, and it is also poor for the buyer to behave irrationally. Contracts and lawsuits are part of business, and both parties should know their rights.

# BASICS OF A CONTRACT

What makes a contract enforceable? Each contract must have certain components to make them enforceable. There are four basic components of a contract: *legality*, *offer*, *acceptance*, and *consideration*.

## LEGALITY

Before any part of the contract can be agreed upon, the parties involved must be legally valid. Are they of legal age or able to enter contracts? Minors typically are not able to enter certain contracts without a guardian. Also, parties that do not have mental capacity or are inebriated might be considered incapable of understanding the terms of the contract.

Is the property legally transferable? An example would be stolen property, contraband alcohol, or noninspected meats. Any contract for illegal property is immediately void.

Is the buyer or seller authorized by the company? An unauthorized person in the kitchen might decide the restaurant needs more cleaning supplies and order them from a company without the management's knowledge. This may render the contract invalid.

## OFFER

Once legality of the parties has been determined, the buyer can offer to purchase products advertised by the seller. Offers are where all product specs, prices, delivery times and places, and terms and responsibilities of all parties are discussed and negotiated.

## CONSIDERATION

Consideration is the amount of money, property, services, or action that is transferred. In a basic food purchase, the buyer offers a certain amount of money for the goods to be delivered by a certain time. The consideration for the seller is the payment; the consideration for the buyer is the product delivered by the time agreed.

## ACCEPTANCE

Acceptance is simply the agreement by one party of the contract to accept the offer put forth by the other. There are various types of acceptance:

- Verbal or nonverbal: Saying "yes" to a price or term is considered an agreement; also a nod or handshake might be acceptance. Voicemail can be considered a verbal acceptance.
- Written: The terms and price are clearly written and summarized. Written acceptance can be in the form of a mailed document or fax; an email and text message can be considered an acceptance tool today. The acceptance of a bid sheet is another form.
- Accepting a deposit or partial payment: If one party accepts an agreed-upon partial payment or deposit, the contract is considered accepted.

## BREACH OF CONTRACT

When one or both parties of a contract do not keep the promises of the agreement, it is then a *breach of contract*. There are two basic types of breach of contract: willing and unwilling. An example of an unwilling breach would be an accident where a delivery is held up. Some causes for nonperformance are reasons for the contract to be considered void, such as natural disasters, acts of war, government intervention, strikes, and civil disorder, but these are exceptional cases. There are many causes for one party not performing as agreed upon, but most are still considered a breach of contract even if the party at fault has no control over the situation. A breach of contract is considered when either party fails to act on time, does not act or provide services within the terms of the contract, or does not act or perform at all. An example would be a restaurant that has a contract with a linen service to deliver 50 table cloths by Friday. The service brings them on Saturday, too late for the Friday dinner time. Another scenario would be if the service brings them on Friday but only delivers 35 cloths. Both of these would be partial breaches and not providing within the terms. The last situation would be that the service never shows at all yet bills the restaurant anyway. This would be a total breach.

When a contract is breached and a party seeks compensation or *damages*, there are certain levels of *remedy* that can be obtained. The remedy is the final legal solution of the breach. The remedy may simply be to fulfill the terms of the contract as stated or to compensate for financial loss. This is when there may have been harm caused by the breach of contract. A court may need to decide whether the breach was *material* or *immaterial*. An immaterial breach is one where no real harm came from changing the terms of the contract. If we look back to the linen service example, if the linens weren't needed until Sunday and the service brought them on Saturday instead of Friday, the breach of contract may be deemed immaterial and no compensation would be due. But if the linens were needed that Friday and customers had to be seated at dirty tables, then the breach would be considered material especially if it was clearly stated they were required by that specific time.

So how does the harmed party seek compensation when a breach of contract occurs? If the contract is deemed legally enforceable, the damaged party can sue in court. Each state has certain thresholds for compensation. Typically if the contract is for less than $3,000 to $7,500, depending on which state, the harmed party can sue in a small claims court. The party that has been harmed and brings the lawsuit is known as the "plaintiff," and the breaching party is then known as the "defendant." It is up to the plaintiff to state their case in a way that shows they were legally harmed by the breach of contract. Any lawsuit is time consuming and can be expensive, but sometimes it is necessary.

## DAMAGES

Compensatory damages: This compensation simply returns the harmed party to their financial situation before the act occurred or finishes the terms of the contract.

Nominal damages: A token damage paid to the nonbreaching party to state who won or lost. This is when no real financial harm came from the breach.

Punitive damages: A lawyer may seek further compensation, beyond the simple remedy of the terms of the contract, to punish the defaulting party. This is not typical in contract law but may apply when there is a repeat offender.

Liquidated damages: Damages that are specified in the language of the original contract and are a reasonable compensation in the case that the contract is breached. In other words, the contract tells both parties what the remedy is if one party defaults on the contract.

Specific performance: This is a remedy where the court will order a specific performance or action to be completed by the breaching party for remedy. This occurs when a remedy proposed by that party is considered inadequate. If a company states they will compensate with money but the injured party needed a specific task done that only the breaching party can do, then a specific performance may be ordered.

Cancellation and restitution: When a contract is breached, the damaged party can cancel the contract and sue for "restitution." This is when a party has given something out in advance such as a deposit or goods and then the contract is not fulfilled, so the harmed party is given enough compensation to return them to their precontract financial condition and the contract is then voided, releasing all parties from future obligation.

Be sure that all contracts are accurate and enforceable before even considering a court action. If necessary, have your lawyer read over all parts of the contract and consider alternatives to court action. Realize also that there are "statutes of limitations" meaning there may only be a certain amount of time for action on a breach to take place. If no action takes place in the set amount of time, then the contract may be voided. Each state sets statutes of limitations on a variety of contracts. Act quickly if a serious breach has occurred.

Settling contract disputes is frequently done outside the court system. Often parties want to avoid expensive court action and may even wish to continue doing business together. One party may not even realize they are in breach and will quickly remedy the situation once it is brought to light. Referring back to our previous example, the linen service may not realize that the restaurant needed 50 tablecloths but would certainly bring them with the next order or will gladly show up on Friday earlier if required.

Other situations may require action by lawyers threatening a suit, which may quickly result in the breaching party delivering on the terms of the contract. But there may be times when a third party is appointed by the parties or the court to settle the dispute. This is known as arbitration or mediation. Some contracts disallow a court action and allow only for "binding" arbitration where the parties agree beforehand, in the language of the contract, to abide by whatever the arbitrator deems fair for compensation. Mediation is similar in that a mediator helps the parties come to a mutual agreement to settle the dispute. Neither party is bound by what the mediator comes up with, but this method often results in the parties resolving the dispute equitably.

To avoid all of this litigation and dispute, be sure to know your business parties and get clearly written agreements that are signed by all involved. Contract law can be tricky, and there are often clauses within contracts that can result in the agreement being disallowed and void. Read through all contracts, and have a lawyer look them over if needed. Have an understanding of who you are dealing with. Well-established distributors and vendors are much less likely to breach a contract than a fly-by-night operation. Organize all of your contracts, bills, and invoices, and keep them until the statute of limitations expires. Keep all warrantees and paperwork in files, and save related emails and text messages. When developing a contract, look over the capabilities of the company you are dealing with. If a company bids on a deal but they look too small to handle the job, be frank about your concerns. Ask how they will handle unforeseen situations and problems. Also realize large corporations have entire legal teams to enforce their contracts so don't go above your head when dealing with them as well. Always think of both sides of a contract and be sure all is equitable. Contracts and purchasing agreements are a necessary part of business and take many forms, so think about each agreement and how it can affect your operation.

The key in these critical relationships and in supplying the needs of any other position in house is to get a clear grasp of what that person wants. Then compare those wants with the realities of the marketplace to ascertain what will best meet the client's needs while still representing the best value to the business. Decisions need to be based on the best business solution and not be about personal preferences or ego. Buyers need to have the product knowledge and people skills required to find these solutions while retaining a good professional relationship with all relevant in-house customers.

# DEVELOPING FOOD ORDERS

When buying food products, the buyer will need to work with the chef and other relevant members of the food production staff and develop the ability to properly select those food items that will meet the quality standards and specifications required. The buyer must also insure that these present a good value to the company in that their quality needs are met at a price that will allow them to generate a profit. Therefore, the ability to make the correct selection of product is a key component of the purchasing agent's job. The product must satisfy both the chef and the end customer; and it must also be viable in cost.

Procurement is simply the exchange of payment for the goods desired. The trick is assuring that the goods received present the best value to the business. When purchasing proteins, specifying the right grade, yield, and freshness, ask yourself: is the produce fresh, grown properly, and sized appropriately? Do research to see if there is another cut of meat or type of fish that will yield an equally desirable end product for less cost. Does every ingredient have the right flavor profile—does it taste good? Also, is the product readily available if it will be required on a regular basis? In order for these questions to be answered, the business management and chefs need to determine the type of menu that will be served. This will include the price point and region of origin of that menu and the specific quality and range of ingredients needed to produce that style of menu. This information then needs to be provided to the buyer(s) well enough in advance to verify that these needs can be met before the menu is formalized.

Once the menu needs are determined, the buyers and chefs must determine the exact specifications of the items required. Specifications must be appropriately detailed so the vendors chosen know exactly what the buyer requires and a standard is set that must be met when delivering the goods. How to write specifications and examples of appropriate specification sheets will be discussed later in this chapter. Once these exact standards are set, it is the buyer's job to find the appropriate vendors that are able to consistently meet the needs stated in these specifications while maintaining the required service levels and a workable price. Price must always be a primary concern for the foodservice operation to survive, but before that the required quality standards and the ability for the vendor to meet the service needs of the business must be met.

# RECOMMENDED SKILLS FOR BUYERS

In order for a buyer to do this job successfully, there are specific abilities and assets that buyers should obtain or have. The first is very high ethical standards; the Institute for Supply Management (ISM), formerly the National Association of Purchasing Management (NAPM), defines their standards as follows:

## NAPM PRINCIPLES AND STANDARDS OF PURCHASING PRACTICE

### Principles

- Loyalty to your organization
- Justice to those with whom you deal
- Faith in your profession

From these principles are derived the domestic and international NAPM standards of purchasing practice, which are as follows:

Standards of Purchasing Practice

1. **Perceived Impropriety.** Prevent the intent and appearance of unethical or compromising conduct in relationships, actions, and communications.

2. **Conflicts of Interest.** Ensure that any personal, business, or other activity does not conflict with the lawful interests of your employer.

3. **Issues of Influence.** Avoid behaviors or actions that may negatively influence, or appear to influence, supply management decisions.

4. **Responsibilities to Your Employer.** Uphold fiduciary and other responsibilities using reasonable care and granted authority to deliver value to your employer.

5. **Supplier and Customer Relationships.** Promote positive supplier and customer relationships.

6. **Sustainability and Social Responsibility.** Champion social responsibility and sustainability practices in supply management.

7. **Confidential and Proprietary Information.** Protect confidential and proprietary information.

8. **Reciprocity.** Avoid improper reciprocal agreements.

9. **Applicable Laws, Regulations, and Trade Agreements.** Know and obey the letter and spirit of laws, regulations, and trade agreements applicable to supply management.

10. **Professional Competence.** Develop skills, expand knowledge, and conduct business that demonstrates competence and promotes the supply management profession.

*Source:* Institute for Supply Management.

The buyer must always put the needs of the business before personal desires and gain. This requires the integrity to resist temptations because salespeople and brokers will often make tempting offers to curry a buyer's loyalty and favoritism. These can range from seemingly benign favors to larger gifts and perks that could be considered bribery. The buyer's concern and actions must always follow the direction and needs of the employer, providing these too are in meeting with all legal and ethical standards.

Besides high standards in ethics and honesty, there are other traits important to being a successful buyer. Initiative is important; the buyer must be self-motivated to constantly examine and reexamine the choices made in terms of product selection and vendor choices. Initiative is required in seeking out better ingredients or sources when there may be nothing apparently at issue with the status quo. It is very easy to become complacent about product choice even though the fresh food market can be a very volatile place and what was once a good product choice can become untenable quickly. Complacency and comfort in set relationships can also drive a buyer to stop looking at other sources in the marketplace that may be a better option for the business. Chefs may also have a comfort level with specific vendors or products, and buyers need to have the initiative to challenge these loyalties if new options will best serve the needs of the operation.

This leads to three other attributes of a good buyer. Teamwork is required as the buyer must work to meet the needs of internal customers, management, and outside vendors. It is imperative that middle ground can always be found to meet the needs of all members of the team. Communication skills, therefore, become important in order to convey all pertinent information and assure that all relevant parties' needs are understood clearly and can be met. Common sense then comes into play because the buyers must be sure that the various demands from these diverse groups simply make sense. Demanding product from a vendor simply because the internal customer wants it, even when this item is not in season or available for a workable price, does not make sense, and a more reasonable option needs to be given to the buyer. Meeting vendor demands for high minimums, infrequent deliveries, or lowered quality standards may also not make good business sense; if vendors cannot be reasonable, then other sources will need to be determined. The buyer must learn how to temper unrealistic desires with common sense based on real-life market conditions and still meet the needs of the operation.

Excellent product knowledge of the items purchased is also a required skill and one that needs to constantly grow and adapt with both the marketplace and the inevitable evolution of the business. This is especially important when buying and receiving perishables; the quality and specifications of poultry, meat, and fish must be known and met when ordering and receiving product. Purchasing cheese also requires a good knowledge of the proper appearance, texture, flavor, and aroma of the many various types that are often demanded in the foodservice industry. The buyer should also know what will serve as a close substitute should the originally requested product become unavailable. Produce requires a thorough knowledge of the many types and seasons of fresh fruits and vegetables and the ability to judge if product is ripe and has been properly stored. Having a thorough knowledge also enables the buyer to ascertain a suitable substitute when a desired produce item is unavailable. Market conditions need to be consistently monitored as well to assess if availability or seasonal quality will be affected. This product knowledge is essential for one to be able to write the required detailed specifications for products sought and to determine the best choices when developing a menu and purchasing to meet those needs. There will be more on this later in this chapter.

A buyer also requires some basic conceptual skills to grasp how their business is perceived by other businesses and in the local community as well. Working in a way that supports local business and is fair to others in the community makes good business sense. Understanding the laws of commerce in that community or state is also important in order to avoid any complications.

Basic math skills in determining cost, yield, and menu pricing are also a key attribute. One must be able to determine the final plated cost of an item to properly determine its value. Computer literacy is essential in these times. E-procurement platforms, spreadsheets, and the ability to communicate and, often, purchase properly online are all part of the daily function in today's purchasing office.

Management also has a role in defining the purchaser's responsibilities. There should be defined rules and roles assigned to this function. It should be clearly stated in writing who is authorized to both buy and receive merchandise and, if necessary, a written policy stating the required procedures and authorizations of the position. This should include the dollar level of the purchase allowed without management approval and define specific areas of authorization (e.g., food, alcohol, equipment, or contracted services), if relevant. The chain of command must also be defined so that it is clear whether the buyer is answerable to the executive chef or the financial management. Management may also opt to have the operation join in a cooperative purchasing group or to work with an operational consultant (see Chapter 2, page 38) that will set more defined rules for the buyer to work within, but can wield that person much more buying power and drive far better pricing.

Generally, the larger the firm and the amount of dollars spent, the more formalized these rules regarding hierarchy and accountability become necessary due to the chance of more significant error. For example, contracted services alone for a large firm can encompass payroll, pest control, waste management, grounds and snow removal, equipment maintenance or rental, linen, insurance, law services, vending, and horticultural services. Firms with the need for these kinds of services need to clearly define the levels of responsibility for the purchasing function.

## MENU PLANNING

A foodservice company's buyer is rarely responsible for determining the firm's menu style or menu choices. However, the buyer should take an active role in helping the chefs and management determine these choices to assure their viability in that market. The buyer should have "a seat at the table" in all menu development meetings and have the opportunity to thoroughly evaluate the ingredient choices being made.

At the earliest stages of menu development, buyers can consult with vendors for help in gauging the level of competition in the immediate area for a specific style of menu or use of key ingredients. Even popular menu themes can be unprofitable if there is a great deal of direct competition, unless a way to differentiate the planned menu can be determined and publicized. Vendors may also have clues as to what is growing in demand but not yet widely sold in that area. This gives the buyers the ability to give their operation a step ahead of the local competition.

Buyers can also work with vendors and seasonal charts to identify to the chef and/ or management what menu options or ingredients are a wise choice at certain times of the year. Buyers should be able to identify what produce items or species of fish are just coming into season or fading in availability. Also, due to market demand, certain cuts of meat will be more expensive at certain times of the year, while others will carry a lesser price tag. Buyers can provide this information so management will know how to plan menu options with an optimal profit margin. There is nothing more frustrating than having popular featured items that require frequent substitution or finding that those menu items that are selling well are no longer at a profitable margin.

Buyers also need to understand the cost of labor as well as the skill level of the production staff when identifying the proper ingredients to purchase. With ample skilled labor, it may prove more profitable to utilize primal cuts of meat or whole fish if the restaurant has the facility to both fabricate these products and thoroughly utilize all of the byproducts. Equally, the buyer should know when it is more advantageous to buy portion cuts of proteins or peeled and cut raw vegetables. Making the availability and cost of these value-added ingredients known to the chef and management will help them determine how best to plan the menu items. Limitations on prep space in confined but busy establishments are also a factor in determining menu choices. All these types of considerations identify why it is wiser to include the buyer in the planning process rather than simply letting that person know what is required once the menu is fully determined.

Once the menu is developed and rolled out to the public, the buyer's responsibilities still extend beyond the daily purchase of the required ingredients. The buyer should monitor the sales volume of an item to evaluate if it makes a sufficient contribution to total sales and if inventory levels turn over rapidly enough to insure that the product's quality and condition are maintained. Be vigilant when monitoring price to ensure the menu continues at a profitable level. Changing market conditions in supply and demand can quickly affect the cost and availability of certain products. However, if an item must be kept on the menu to satisfy the customer base but can no longer be sold for a profit, then the menu needs to feature enough items with a low enough food cost to offset that poor margin. Obviously, items with low customer demand and a high food cost need to be rethought and changed as they add no value to the sales mix.

In regard to fresh produce items, seasons are more dictated by actual weather conditions than the calendar. A sudden change in the weather can dramatically alter a key product's availability or price in the market, and it is incumbent upon the buyer to advise the chef when a menu item needs to be changed due to seasonal adjustments. Certain seafood items have seasonal quotas placed on them to help assure their continued sustainability; this can be done by setting a specific length of time when the species can be fished, which is easy to plan for, or by issuing a set number of tags to account for the number of fish which can legally be taken. These numerical quotas can run out with little notice, and the buyers must be alert to the need for immediate adjustment in the menu item selection should a quota be reached before a menu change has been determined.

Ensuring all items required for a daily or special event menu are in inventory just prior to production needs and procuring them for a workable price are vital components in a buyer's job description. However, as described here, there are a variety of other duties and services a good buyer can provide to the chefs and management of their particular business; this adds much more value to that person's position.

## DETERMINING PRODUCT SPECIFICATIONS

Once all parties involved are in agreement on the menu and the products required for that menu as well as in the dining room and bar, the buyer must then formulate the product specifications. These specifications are crucial to the buyer in guaranteeing the exact nature of the ingredients ordered and received. Specifications also assure that any bids received pertain to equivalent products, which provide an accurate comparison and notifies the vendor of the exact nature of what the customer needs. No aspect in purchasing is more critical than an accurate specification sheet.

Prior to the final development of a list of specifications for the vendor (external specifications), the buyer and chef will develop an internal specification list relevant to the menu. This should detail each dish that will be made, the portion size of the ingredients needed, and how that ingredient will be cooked and presented. This will allow the buyer to determine how much raw ingredient is needed to meet the demand for the number of dishes forecasted for sale. It also allows the buyer to identify an ingredient that will make a suitable substitute if the desired item is unavailable.

The specifications developed for purchasing from the vendors will include the product's name, a product code if relevant (such as from the Meat Buyer's Guide), the desired size or weight, the trim level, and the pack size for each ingredient.

| Lamb Shoulder | 3 8266 | Square cut, single shoulder. MBG #207. Foreshank and brisket portion of breast and neck removed |
|---|---|---|

When appropriate, government grades (AA, USDA Choice) should also be indicated. Also, when required, brand names (Hellman's, Heinz) or packer grades (blue label) should be indicated. Be careful when specifying a brand name as sometimes that name will drive costs higher than using other packer label products that have the same quality inside; it pays to compare thoroughly. These specifications must be quite detailed and explicit to insure your vendors will bid on and supply products that meet the needs of your customers.

When requesting bids on products from your vendors, other non-product-related specifications may be required. These may have an effect on what the vendor needs to charge for the items you require and could include delivery days, delivery times, and billing instructions. Again, the clearer the needs are presented, the more accurate the response will be.

Dry goods specifications are the cleanest and easiest to write in that there is no subjectivity in quality to assess once any required cutting has been accomplished. The name, brand (if specified), and pack size may be sufficient; for example:

| ITEM | PACK | CODE | VENDOR |
|------|------|------|--------|
| 5314 Clams, chopped Ocean | 12 case/#5 | | Gins |

**FIGURE 3.1** Dry goods specifications.

As discussed, other specifications for meat, fish, dairy, and produce may require significantly more detail.

| ITEM | CODE | REQUIRED SPECS | PACK |
|------|------|----------------|------|
| Eggplant | 1116 | Heavy, dark purple to black in color, green top intact, no scarring, pear shaped. | 25#/cs |
| Eggplant, Chinese | 1118 | 8 to 10 inches long, thinner shape, light purple in color, thin skin. | 10# bx |
| Eggplant, Holland | 1117 | Baby eggplant, 4 to 6 inches long, Heavy, unscarred, tight green top. | 11# bx |
| Eggplant, Thai | 1119 | Golf ball sized, green to green and white in color, tight shiny skin, heavy for size. | 10# bx |
| Endive, Belgian | 1122 | Creamy white to pale yellow green at tips, firm, unblemished tight heads. | 10# bx |
| Endive, red | 1121 | White stem with deep claret red leaf, unblemished, tight head. | 8# bx |
| Escarole | 1124 | Dark green loose outer leaves, bleached center. Slightly bitter taste, no brown spots or slime. | 18#/cs |
| Emmentaler | 1 2144 | Imported Swiss Cheese, whole cow's milk. Hard, smooth, shiny rind with pale gold springy paste. Faintly sweet aroma and nutty flavor. | 10# print |
| Asiago d'Allevo | 1 2144 | Imported Italian cheese. Aged, graded stravecchio. Reddish brown rind, firm and granular paste. | 30# whl |

**FIGURE 3.2** Perishable food specifications. (*continues*)

| ITEM | CODE | REQUIRED SPECS | PACK |
|------|------|----------------|------|
| Parmigiano-Reggiano | 1 2120 | Imported aged Italian cheese from partially skimmed cow's milk. Closely textured granular paste with a smooth oily rind. Aged 2 years (stravecchio). | 70# whl |
| Romano, Pecorino | 1 2136 | Aged imported Italian cheese from Lazio. Made from ewe's milk. Pale to white in color with sharp flavor and aftertaste. Smooth dark rind. | 40# wheel |
| Taleggio | 1 2150 | Cave ripened imported Italian cheese. Soft cow's milk cheese from the Stacchino family. Cooked curd variety with a gray rind. | 4# |
| Ricotta Salata | 1 2126 | Ewe's milk imported Italian cheese. From whey with snow white color. | 5# wheel |
| Fish, Wild Striped Bass | 20013 | Size may vary, but large is preferred. Tagged only, firm, fresh, good gills and eyes. | 8–12# |
| Fish, Bluefish | 20016 | Small size is better, relatively firm, No belly burn, good eyes and gills. | 2.5–4.5# |
| Fish, Catfish Fillet | 20023 | Firm texture, not frozen or flaking, white to pink color, clean smell. | 7–9 oz |
| Clams, Manila | 20026 | Tight, clean smell, substitute cockles. | 10# bag—split if necessary |
| Clams, Littleneck | 20028 | Tightly closed, no mahoganys, evenly sized, approx. 10 per pound, clean odor. Minimal breakage. | 400 ct bag, or by 100 ct. |
| Clams, Topneck | 20024 | Mid-range in size, approx. 4–5 per pound. Closed, clean smell. Minimal breakage. | 200 ct bag, or by 100 ct. |
| Fish, Market Cod | 20036 | Head on, good firm white flesh, clean belly, good clear eyes, and red gills. Steak cod is acceptable. | 4–6# avg. Larger is acceptable |

**FIGURE 3.2** (*Continued*)

Following is a breakdown of two of the various product lines a foodservice establishment may require and the general considerations that need to be taken into account in each area. This is not a detailed description of all foodservice items available, just a quick overview of the various product types. Additional specific purchasing information can be found in Chapter 4 on page 41.

## FRESH PRODUCE

There is a great variety of produce items of which a foodservice operation can avail themselves. Some operators will utilize many types of these ingredients and rotate their choices to reflect the best season in which to offer them. Others may use a more limited approach and want the same items year-round regardless of season, due to the confines of their menu or their kitchen staff. In either case, there should be clear standards for the specifications to insure that everything received meets the level of quality determined for that style of operation. Following will be brief descriptors of the various classifications of produce available in today's market and some factors for

a buyer to consider when determining the best choices for their business to utilize. The best value for almost any produce item is found when sourcing these items in season, during which time that produce item will be of the best quality and at the best prices as it is more available. Improved quality for less cost is the definition of obtaining value in purchasing. For more information about specific storage information for produce, see page 207 in Chapter 5.

## GREENS

Greens are wonderfully flavorful, varied, and nutritious ingredients. They are also relatively easy to prepare and adaptable to many dishes and cuisines. In general, these vegetables are fairly inexpensive, making them a good nutritional value for your dollar.

Thorough cleaning is essential due to the large amounts of sand and grit that collect in the leaves. This may require several washings to manage. This added labor is usually more than offset by the economical nature of the product. However, many value-added products are now available that have been washed and trimmed if labor and time are of greater concern.

Some greens can be large and tough and lend themselves well to low, slow cooking, whereas others are very tender and can be cooked quickly or simply dressed and served raw. Because of the range in sizes and textures and the culinary applications that suit them, they are usually classified as either salad or cooking greens.

Salad greens are an excellent nutrition source, are low in calories, and come in a myriad of colors, textures, and flavors to challenge the chef and delight the diner. The key, which holds true for all fresh produce, is to utilize what is fresh and best in that season and, when possible, what is grown locally. Salad greens can be mild and silky

FIGURE **3.3** Red Leaf Lettuce.

FIGURE **3.4** Mache.

in texture and flavor, such as the butter head lettuces; crunchy with a spicy bite, like arugula or baby mustard greens; and everything in between. Salad greens can also be utilized in various combinations to afford the diner a contrast of flavors and textures.

The range of flavors and textures of salad greens means that almost every choice will have two or three others that may work well as a substitute. The key then is to shop and construct the salad according to what is best and freshest in the marketplace that day. This will yield better results than developing your menu and trying to source what is required; this will often yield better financial benefits as well. Using local sources, and especially working directly with local growers, is critical to finding the best and freshest ingredients. Interacting with local growers in the off-season can yield chef-buyers exactly the type and size of product desired once the season begins. This aids the chef-buyer and the farmer in planning ahead and guarantees one a source and the other a market. Urban-area chef-buyers can seek out local greenmarkets to source fresh products and to cultivate relationships with the growers that come there. Once again, a willingness to adapt and create according to the market will provide the best results and a living menu that reflects the season, the location, and the personality and skill of the chef.

## COOKING GREENS

This category of greens is often associated with southern cooking in the United States, but it is integral to the cuisines of many cultures. This grouping consists of a wide variety of greens from the loose-leaf cabbage family such as collards and kale to the pungent mustards to the softer and rich-flavored chards. Historically, many

FIGURE **3.5** Red Chard.

FIGURE **3.6** Kale.

of these were trimmed and cooked slowly with a piece of pork, but they can be cut finely and cooked relatively quickly to add a more pungent jolt of flavor to many dishes. These greens lend themselves to a variety of strong seasonings and marry well with beans, potatoes, pastas, soups, and various meats.

Heartier greens such as kale and collards are best in late fall and early winter, but can be found year-round. The best quality and selection will be found at the local greenmarket and farm stands, but these greens can usually be found in reasonable quality from your produce wholesaler or retail market. Always look for cool and moist greens with a rich green color and no dryness, yellowing, or wilted edges.

## CABBAGE

There are two main types of cabbages in this category: head-forming cabbages and non-head-forming or stalk-forming cabbages. Head-forming cabbage grows into a dense, firm, rounded bolting head or a dense, squat, barrel shape. These would include red and white (or green) and Savoy cabbage as well as Napa cabbages The non-head-forming cabbages, including broccoli, rapini, cauliflower, broccoflower, bok choy, and kohlrabi, grow on stalks of varying thickness. Some of these stalks are edible, whereas others are not. Brussels sprouts seem to fit both categories because each sprout looks like a tiny red or green head of cabbage. These "little cabbages" are really the buds of the plant that grow on long stalks.

Kale and collard greens are technically classified as members of the cabbage family and are very green and leafy with tough, thin stalks. However, they are more often thought of as a cooking green.

There are a great number of different horticultural and culinary items that fall in the cabbage family. They are nutritious, and most are relatively inexpensive. They have culinary applications to suit most every taste and season, and they are present

FIGURE **3.7** Savoy Cabbage.

FIGURE **3.8** Brussels Sprouts.

in almost every ethnic cuisine. Many can be served hot or cold, raw or cooked, utilizing many different methods of preparation, and seasoned mildly or in a very assertive manner. Whatever your culinary plans are, it is likely some member of the Brassica family would be a good fit.

## MUSHROOMS

Edible mushrooms comprise only a few percent of the many types of mushrooms and fungi that exist, but offer many options for buyers to source for their chefs. Most mushrooms, by volume, used for culinary purposes are now cultivated. There are also a wonderful and delicious variety of wild mushrooms prized by chefs in foodservice. Wild mushrooms should never be foraged by or purchased from anyone other than a certified expert. Buyers must be aware that there are far more wild mushrooms that are poisonous than those that are edible, and some look strikingly similar. The need to be cautious and knowledgeable in the use of wild mushrooms cannot be stressed enough. Buyers should also advise their chefs that wild mushrooms should always be thoroughly cooked to prevent allergic reactions as well.

The types of mushrooms available in foodservice come in a broad array of appearances, flavors, shapes, sizes, consistencies, and textures. They offer the chef-buyer a great selection when choosing which one will best complement the other foods being prepared. However, due to this wide range, one mushroom will not necessarily substitute well for another in a particular dish. This is especially true with the wild varieties, but common sense needs to play a role in the selection of the commercially grown types as well. A good rule of thumb is to know that the bigger and darker a mushroom gets, the more pronounced and assertive the flavor will be. European, Asian, and American cuisines all take strong advantage of the culinary possibilities provided by mushrooms, and each prizes certain varieties over others.

FIGURE **3.9** Cremini Mushrooms.

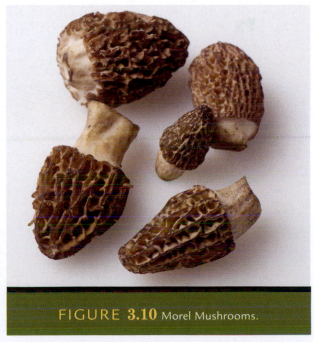

FIGURE **3.10** Morel Mushrooms.

Commercially grown mushrooms are available year-round; these include whites, cremini, shiitake, portabellos, and enokis. These are grown in large commercial farms and smaller boutique operations. Those grown in factory-like settings, most commonly in Pennsylvania and second most commonly in California, will be more homogeneous in flavor and appearance. Those grown in smaller operations will have a more pronounced flavor and reflect the growing style and medium used by that grower; these will also come with a higher price point.

Wild mushrooms are available fresh only in the appropriate season and are products of nature and its variables. These mushrooms will be more varied in size and flavor, and more expensive, and availability will be driven by the season and the weather. Still, these are delicious items and highly prized. Commonly used wild mushrooms include morels, porcinis, chanterelle, hedgehog, lobster, and trumpets. Many of these wild varieties are available in dried form year round. Mushrooms can be expensive and perishable, and lose moisture content when held in coolers too long; buyers should try to buy and hold only what is required and replenish supply often.

## STALKS AND OTHER VEGETABLES

There is a small group of vegetables that in some way defy classification in other categories or culinary applications. Stalks refer to those vegetables that grow heavy, fibrous, and edible stalks. Celery is the most obvious and commonly used member of this group. Rhubarb is similar in appearance to celery stalks that have been removed from the bunch, except for its bright red color, but its applications are completely different. Fennel has long stalks and frilly fronds on a heavy bulb, and is nearly 100 percent edible.

Also included in this grouping is asparagus. Artichokes are in the thistle family and have no culinary equal or relative other than the cardoon, which has not yet gained popularity in the United States. Fiddlehead ferns are a wild and foraged item that come into season for only a few weeks each spring and, again, have no similarity to other culinary vegetables, although some compare the flavor to that of asparagus.

However varied these vegetables are, you could say they all do have a common thread; all of these are wonderful, delicious, nutritious, and unique.

## ONIONS

Onions are divided into two main categories, dry and green. Dry onions are the round or flat bulbs of the *Allium cepa* species. These are the mature bulb of the onion with tight layers of flesh and a dry, papery skin that can be white, red, or yellow. Dry onions are purchased from two categories: sweet (spring/summer) and storage (fall/winter). The storage onion is not as sweet, with a stronger, more pungent aroma and

FIGURE **3.11** Rhubarb.

FIGURE **3.12** Asparagus.

FIGURE **3.13** Onions.

flavor. As their name indicates, these onions will keep for long periods of time when properly stored. Commonly available varieties of the storage onion include yellow or Spanish, white, boiling, shallots, and red onions.

Sweet onions are generally flatter in shape and have a much milder and sweeter flavor. Sweet onions typically have a much shorter shelf life and need to be utilized quickly. Vidalia, Maui, Texas 1015s, and Walla Walla are all well-known sweet onions; they are named for their growing region but are available nationally depending on the season. The varieties of sweet onions being developed and coming into the market continue to expand.

A green onion is simply an onion that has been pulled from the ground when the shoots are still vibrant and green and before the bulb has begun to fully develop. Green onions are separated into three categories, but each is very similar and can be interchangeable with the other. A scallion is considered to be youngest of the three classes because they should only have a short white tip with no bulb growth at all. A green onion has started to mature further and the bulb is just beginning to become more pronounced. The spring onion has developed a small bulb, approximately 1 inch/2.5 centimeters in diameter. Scallions are available year-round from commercial produce vendors; green and spring onions are more generally found from spring into summer.

The entirety of the onion is edible except the root. Green onions are most commonly eaten raw but are excellent sautéed or grilled. Grilled spring onions make an outstanding accompaniment to grilled poultry and steaks. The green shoots of these onions have a delightful, mild, grassy flavor that is a terrific addition to the salsas and relishes that are used as delicious garnishes for many dishes. Scallions are also stir-fried with pork and chicken in spicy Asian preparations.

Because the green shoots are what are most often prized with green onions, be sure to only accept those with vibrant, brightly colored greens. Avoid those that are slimy, shriveled, or wilted and very dark or coarse, indicating dehydration. The tips or bulbs should be clean and white with no browning, slime, or mold. Green onions are sold in bunches by the count per case.

Leeks appear to be a type of green onion, but are not. The leek is related botanically to both the onion and garlic. Unlike green onions, only the white part is desired, so buyers should spec this product to indicate a sufficient yield. (The green parts can be used to flavor stocks). Those grown using the hydroponic method are more expensive, but that is often offset by a much better yield in the preferred white portion.

FIGURE **3.14** Scallions.

The leek's rich flavor is highly prized by many chefs and can be used in soups, braised, or fried.

Garlic is the most pungent member of this family and is available in either hard or soft neck varieties. Hard necks are usually easier to peel and has a bright intense flavor that is prized but often more expensive. Buyers should accept only rock-hard bulbs with no bitter green sprouting. Also beware of shriveled or strongly sour-smelling product.

## ROOTS AND TUBERS

Both roots and tubers grow underground and are frequently referred to as root vegetables. A true root is the actual root portion of a plant that stores the plant's nutrition in a swollen bulb. Often, the tops or greens of these roots, such as beet greens, are also a valuable food source that buyers should ensure are used. True root vegetables include carrots, beets, celery knob, parsnips, turnips, salsify, and radishes. A tuber is the stem of the plant that grows underground and swells as that plant's means to store nutrition. Potatoes are tubers, as are jícama, cassava, ginger, and galangel. Roots and tubers have good nutritional value, varied flavors and textures, a traditional role in many food cultures, and relatively low food costs, which are why they play such an important role in foodservice today.

FIGURE **3.15** Round Carrots.

## BEANS AND PODS

In each of the bean or legume families, the seed of the vegetable is enclosed in a pod; some pods are tender and edible, and others require the seed to be shelled from their tough inedible pod casing. We include corn and okra here because they have many seeds that are encased by the outer covering of the plant. The common culinary factor between these vegetables for buyers to remember is that they should all be picked, purchased, and consumed when very young and while still very fresh. Corn and peas may be the most sensitive to this, but freshness is a key quality factor for all of these vegetables. You may be able to source fresh corn throughout much of the year, but it is only truly at its

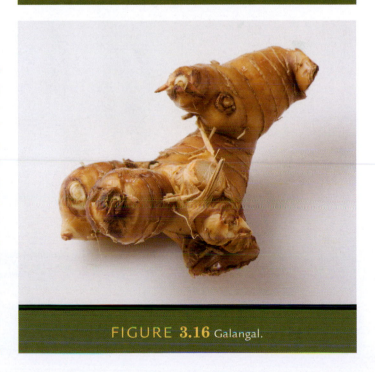

FIGURE **3.16** Galangal.

FIGURE **3.17** Potatoes.

FIGURE **3.18** Beans and Pods.

peak when grown close by, picked at its peak, and sold and consumed within a few days. Locally grown pod and seed vegetables will almost always be the best option.

Snap beans, shell beans, edible and nonedible pod peas, soybeans, and Chinese long beans are all included in this group as well as sweet corn and okra. As noted, freshness is the key, so carefully examine the pod or outer shell of each, even those that are inedible. They are often, but not always, an indicator of how these vegetables have been handled and how long they have been in transit or storage. When there is any doubt, open the pod and sample the seed or pea within, or snap and sample those with edible pods. They must be tender and sweet with good moisture content. Sweet corn kernels should be plump, bursting with juice, and very sweet. Poor product at this stage may improve when cooked, but will never achieve the quality desired. Buyers need to ensure that their receiving personnel are vigilant when checking in these items.

## Dried Legumes

Many beans are available year-round in their dried form. Worldwide these are used in most cultures and in a wide variety of forms and recipes. They are prized not only for the delicious contribution they make to many dishes but also because they provide an inexpensive source of nutrition that is very shelf stable. Care should be taken to sift through dried beans to remove pebbles and/or other foreign objects. Many dried beans benefit from presoaking to expedite cooking time and soften the texture. They should have a good color and no signs of dust or mold; always wash your beans prior to cooking or soaking to remove any dirt. These continue to dry and harden over time, so try to utilize your inventory within a few months of purchase.

### TABLE 3-1 COMMON DRIED LEGUMES

These beans are used in great numbers in many diverse cultures and cuisines, and are readily available. These represent an economical and diverse dietary staple.

| NAME | DESCRIPTION | CULINARY USES |
|------|-------------|---------------|
| Black beans, Turtle Beans | Medium sized and shiny black in color. Full earthy flavors that complement strong spices and aromatics. | Latin American dishes, sides, soups, refried, salsas. |
| Cannelini Bean | Elongated white bean. Smooth texture with a nutty flavor. | Works well in soups and salads, and braised with escarole. |
| Cranberry/ Borlotti Bean | Speckled purple, pink, and ivory colored. Medium-sized bean with Italian origin. | Nutty-flavored beans work well in soups and stews. |
| Fava/Haba Bean | Large, pale, pinkish brown bean with very meaty texture and assertive flavor. This bean is best when fresh. | Used as a side dish and for purées. |

*(continues)*

TABLE 3-1 COMMON DRIED LEGUMES (Continued)

| NAME | DESCRIPTION | CULINARY USES |
|------|-------------|---------------|
| Flagelot | Thin, oblong, greenish-white European bean. Very creamy in texture. | Excellent braised with aromatics and herbs; complements lamb very well. |
| Garbanzo/Chick Pea | Round, tan colored bean with a nutty flavor. Also can be found in red, white, and green hues. | Heavily used in Middle Eastern cuisine such as hummus and falafel. Also delicious with garlic and pasta. |
| Great Northern | Fat oblong white bean. Very mild in flavor. | Works well in soups, paste, or cassoulet. |
| Kidney/Red Kidney | Found in varying sizes and shades of red. | Popular bean used for chili, refried, and salad. |
| Lentils | Very small commonly used bean found in shades of brown, green, red, yellow, and black, depending on European or Egyptian origins. Rich earthy flavors. | Common in Northern European and Middle Eastern cuisines. Well used in soups, purees, dals, and salads. |
| Lima/Butter Bean | Large white bean with a prized buttery texture and flavor. | Used in soups and stews or as a stand-alone side dish. |
| Navy/Yankee Bean | Small, white, but hard-to-digest bean that is very mild in flavor. | Popular in baked beans, soups, and bean paste. |
| Pinto Bean | Fat speckled pale brown to dark red bean that cooks to a pale pink color. | Popular in Southwestern American dishes. Used commonly for refried beans and chili. |
| Rice Bean | Very small thin white bean that resembles pasta. | Cooks quickly and used in soups or instead of a starch like rice. |
| Black-Eyed Peas | Small kidney-shaped tan bean with black ring on concave hollow. | Mild earthy flavor popular in southern cooking such as Hoppin' John. |
| Pigeon Peas | Small round beige and orange-colored bean. | Very popular in Caribbean and African cuisines. |
| Split Peas | Small round peas in shades of dull green or yellow. Rich, strong earthy flavor. | Popular in soups with smoked pork. |

| TABLE 3-2 HEIRLOOM DRIED LEGUMES | | |
|---|---|---|
| These varieties are not as commonly found in the market as the preceding types. However, their unique appearance and fine texture and flavor make them worth looking for and justify the additional cost. | | |
| **NAME** | **DESCRIPTION** | **CULINARY USES** |
| Anasazi | Oblong, red and white colored, with a smooth creamy texture. | Mexican dishes. |
| Appaloosa | Slender, curved, purple and white bean with an herbal flavor. | Good used in Southwestern dishes such as refried beans. |
| Christmas Limas | Large burgundy/brown and white bean with a meaty texture and nutty flavor. | Good in soups or as a side simply dressed. |
| Corona (Sweet White Runner) | Large, white, half-moon-shaped bean. | Roast, or marinate in oil vinegar and garlic. |
| Marrow | Round plump white bean. | Purées smoothly, good for baking, bacon-like flavor. |
| Mark | Unusual speckled black and purple to lavender in color with a rich flavor. | Use in salads or bake them. They are very versatile in use. |
| Peruano | Oblong shape, yellow color. Holds shape in cooking. | Works great in spicy Latin stews and soups as they absorb flavor of cooking liquid very well. |
| Rattlesnake | Slender oval shape with a light and dark brown in color. Tastes like a pinto but more robust. | Great in stews and chilies. |
| Scarlet Runners | Beautiful large purple and black to lilac color beans. They are European in origin. | Good with roast root vegetables and aromatics. |
| Tiger Eye | Unusual light and dark orange/brown hues with a smooth texture. | Works well in baked dishes such as cassoulet. |
| Tongues of Fire | Similar in heritage and appearance to the Cranberry/Borlotti bean. Attractive speckled purple. | Bakes well with pork or sausages. |
| Vaquero | Interesting black and white mottled look. Related to the Anasazi. Mild in flavor. | Good in chilis and stews. |

## TOMATOES

There are literally hundreds of varieties of tomatoes, and few things in the culinary world spark as much passionate discourse. Tomatoes are baked, stuffed, fried green, puréed, juiced, concentrated—you name it. They are sliced raw for sandwiches, diced in salad, concassed, chopped into salsa cruda, sliced with fresh mozzarella and basil, and so on.

Sadly, the passion for this fruit isn't justly addressed or satisfied during the proper season, when tomatoes are in plentiful and varied supply and really taste bright and sharp with acidic flavor. They are still consumed by the tons year-round even though the only true similarity to tomatoes in season is a paler color. This challenges the buyer's ability to get a reasonably good product for a workable price.

For many years in the foodservice industry, there were three basic tomatoes: the slicing tomato, the plum tomato, and the cherry tomato. In today's market those still represent the general categories, but a multitude of variations, flavors, and colors challenge the chef-buyer and the palate and enhance presentation. Commercially, outside of certain heirlooms, tomatoes are not sold by the specific variety but rather the type, separated into these three basic categories: round, plum, and small (which include cherry, grape, currant, and pear). Now there is popular demand for tastier, but more fragile, heirloom varieties, which gain more recognition each year. There are literally hundreds of heirloom varieties; some of the most common are Brandywine, German Red and Green, Black Krim, Green Zebras, and Cherokee Purple. To some extent,

FIGURE **3.19** Tomatoes.

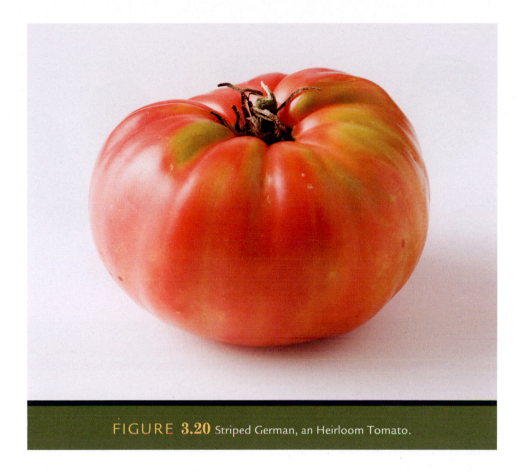

FIGURE **3.20** Striped German, an Heirloom Tomato.

these too can now be found year-round, but the quality and price are best when truly in season.

## PEPPERS

Peppers are members of the Capsicum genus and provide a good deal of sweetness as well as heat in cooking. They provide bright color in the dishes they are part of and come in vibrantly colored hues of green, red, white, yellow, orange, brown, and purple. There are an enormous number of members in this family, but in foodservice they are divided into two main groups: sweet peppers and chile peppers. Sweet peppers, mostly of the bell variety, can provide sweet to somewhat tart flavors to a recipe. Chile peppers provide the heat in many recipes; depending on which chile pepper is used, such as Anaheims, Fresnos, Jalapenos, Serranos, or Habaneros, they can give anything from a mild touch of heat to a very fiery burn. Generally, the rule of thumb is that the smaller the pepper, the higher the heat. The broader the shoulder, the sweeter the pepper will be. Capsaicin, the chemical that creates the level of heat in peppers, is genetically nullified in the sweet or bell varieties.

Most every pepper starts off green in color and ripens into the other shades seen in the market. Peppers are prized in both stages of maturity. The flavor generally gets more complex and sweeter as it ripens. Look for peppers that have a clean, full color and shiny rind. They should be firm, full, and heavy for their size, with a clean aroma. Avoid peppers with a shriveled appearance, soft spots, or signs of mold. Regardless of

FIGURE **3.21** Peppers.

choice, buyers need to advise their chefs to taste test peppers to gauge their heat level before adding them to a dish.

## SQUASH

The family of squashes is a large and varied group that is broken down into the hard skin, or winter squash, category and the soft skin category, which consists of summer squash, cucumbers, and eggplant. The latter category is not generally thought of as squash, but it does fall into this grouping.

The winter and summer designation came from a time when those were the only seasons that such squash were available. Winter squashes, including Butternut, Acorn, Spaghetti, Hubbard, and Carnival squashes as well as pumpkins, grow into the autumn of the year and, with their hard shells, last far into the year if stored properly. Summer squash, such as zucchini, crookneck, and patty pan squashes as well as cucumbers and the various eggplants, only grew in the warmer months and had a very short shelf life. Now these summer squashes are in the market year-round, although the quality is not the same as when they are in season.

FIGURE **3.22** Carnival Squash.

FIGURE **3.23** Green and Yellow Zucchini.

FIGURE **3.24** Purple Basil.

FIGURE **3.25** Oregano.

## HERBS

Herbs are the fragrant leafy parts of certain plants that have nonwoody stems. They are prized for the aroma and flavor they impart to the food we cook. These differ from spices in that the latter comes from the plant's bark, roots, fruits, or seeds as opposed to the leaves and foliage. Herbs have been cultivated for nearly all of recorded history and have always been held in high esteem for their aroma, flavor, and medicinal properties.

Fresh herbs are very fragile, have a short shelf life, and should be utilized quickly before they lose their essential oils and begin to wither or mold. Typically only the delicate leaves are utilized in final cooking, but the stems will supply excellent flavor to stocks, sauces, and broths and are simply strained out before service or final use.

Herbs were once only found fresh at certain times of the season. However, due to the hydroponic growing method and the ability to fly in imported product quickly, herbs are now found year-round. Those commonly found in the market today include various basils, mint, marjoram, thyme, chives, tarragon, and oregano. As noted, these are highly perishable, so choose herbs carefully when buying; they should be clean, look vibrant, and carry a full, strong aroma. When rubbed between finger and thumb, they should release their oils and the aroma should be more pronounced.

Avoid anything that is wilted, turning black, and/or exhibiting an off or sour aroma. Having little or no aroma at all is a sign that an herb is past its prime, even if the appearance seems acceptable.

## APPLES AND PEARS

The apple and pear are members of the *Rosacea* family and are tree fruit. They are both referred to as "pomes," which means they have a paper-like core surrounded by flesh and covered with a thin skin. The flesh in each is white or pale yellow and crisp and juicy, although the pear is generally juicier and the flesh usually softens when ripe. The flavor of the apple can range from very sweet to quite tart, whereas the pear is generally sweet. The apple varies in size but is always round in shape, whereas the pear can be round but usually has either an elongated or squat teardrop shape. Both fruits have some year-round availability due to improved controlled atmosphere storage techniques, but apples and pears are truly best in the fall and winter when they first come into season. Look for a designation on the case to ensure the product has been properly stored over the winter.

Avoid fruit that is shriveled, washed out in color, or pitted, or that has soft brown bruising. Apples and pears should be heavy for their size to ensure high moisture content. Russeting on the skin is not an indication of poor quality unless the fruit is being used only for presentation.

A whole book could be written about apples, given their popularity, their great variety, and the number of countries where they are enjoyed. Worldwide, over 80 percent of all apple varieties are used commercially (cooked into other forms), but in the United States over half of all apples grown are consumed raw. There are literally hundreds of varieties of apples grown worldwide; many are almost exclusively grown in certain regions, while others are very widely grown. The most popular eating and culinary apples appreciated in this country include Delicious, Macintosh, Granny Smith, Gala, Braeburn, and Fuji.

FIGURE **3.26** Braeburn Apple.

FIGURE **3.27** Comice Pear.

| | Snacking | Salads | Pies | Souce | Baking | Freezing |
|---|---|---|---|---|---|---|
| Braeburn | E | G | G | G | G | G |
| Cameo | E | E | E | E | E | G |
| Cortland | E | E | E | E | E | G |
| Empire | E | E | G | G | G | G |
| Fuji | E | E | G | G | G | E |
| Gala | E | E | G | E | G | E |
| Ginger Gold | E | E | G | G | G | N |
| Golden Delicious | E | E | E | E | E | E |
| Granny Smith | E | E | E | E | E | E |
| Honeycrisp | E | E | E | E | G | E |
| Ida Red | G | G | E | E | E | G |
| Jonagold | E | E | G | E | E | G |
| Jonathan | G | G | E | G | E | G |
| McIntosh | E | G | E | E | N | G |
| Newtown Pippin | G | G | E | E | G | G |
| Cripps Pink | E | E | E | E | G | G |
| Red Delicious | E | E | N | N | N | N |
| Rome Beauty | G | G | E | E | E | G |

U.S. Government Apple Usage Chart.

*Source:* Unites States Apple Association.

The pear comes from the same genetic family as the apple but is not known to have the great number of varieties as the apple. In the United States, pears are too often consumed when still quite firm before the sweetness and silkiness of the flesh develop. Buyers should try waiting to find pears that look about ready to turn too soft in order to taste the best flavor when eating them raw or purchase early enough for the fruit to ripen. For poaching or baking, you will likely require the fruit to still have some firmness to it. Popular varieties of pears include Bartlett, Bosc, Anjou, Comice, Forelle, and Asian.

## CITRUS FRUIT

All members of the citrus family are noted and prized for their acidity, which provides food and beverages with a brightness and balance to other flavors. The rinds come in bright and easily recognizable colors that also add to the visual presentation of the plate. The zest of the rind is the thin outer coating which has the distinctive bright

FIGURE **3.28** Blood Orange.

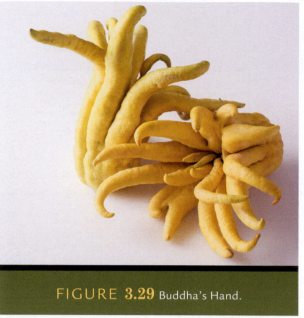

FIGURE **3.29** Buddha's Hand.

orange, yellow, red, or green color; this zest also contains the oils that energize dishes with their fragrance and bright, sweet, or tart flavor. The flesh of the fruits is formed in segments circling the fruit's core; these segments will either be seedless or carry several seeds each, depending on the specific fruit.

Nearly every citrus fruit utilized today in foodservice, oranges, lemons, limes, and grapefruit, is a hybrid or cultivar of other fruits. As noted, these fruits are widely used in foodservice due to their acid content, color, and aroma. It should also be noted that these fruits are very nutritious; rich in vitamins, fiber, and flavonoids; and low in calories.

Many of these fruits are equally, or more so, valued for the juice they provide. These juices, when used as a dietary supplement, provide the nutritional content of the fruit in a more easily accessible manner. Due to their tartness, many of these juices, such as lemon and lime, require a good deal of sweetening to be palatable. The juice in its unsweetened form is utilized in many different recipes to provide the acidic kick desired as well as a bright flavor. When receiving citrus, look for fruit that is heavy for its size, which indicates that it is not dehydrated; it should also be firm and unblemished with no signs of mold.

## GRAPES AND BERRIES

Grapes and berries are not botanically related, but both supply small, bite-size packages of delicious fruit that can be utilized in pies, jams, jellies, sauces, or salads, or eaten out of hand. They supply color, sweetness, and an acidic bite to many dishes. Berries kick off the U.S. growing season in the spring and come back toward the end of the growing season. Imported product is available year-round, but the higher price and diminished flavor can bring their value into question at these times. Grapes, of one type or another, are almost always available, but sample when buying to ensure they are sufficiently sweet to meet your needs.

In the United States, grapes are grown in many locations, but the bulk of commercial production is focused in California. These many varieties can be separated into two types: white grapes, which are actually pale green, and red grapes, which can vary in shade from a medium red to what is referred to as a black grape. Seedless grapes now account for the overwhelming percentage of world production in table grapes simply because they are easier to prepare and cook and less messy to eat. All of the varieties of seedless grapes available today in the United States originated from three sources: the Thompson green grape, the Russian red seedless, and the Black Monukka. These are all native to the western United States. Eastern varieties are bred to be heartier due to the less favorable weather and have a much smaller market; such varieties include the Reliance and Venus varieties. When purchasing, avoid anything pale or washed out in color, shrunken or shriveled, or showing any signs of mold where the grape met the vine. The vine, or stem, will also be a quality check; it should be green and pliable and hold firmly to the grapes. Grapes should hold tight to their stems and not show any discoloration of shriveling.

FIGURE **3.30** Green Grapes.

Berry is the name for any of a number of small edible fruits. Botanically, a true berry is different from many of the fruits considered or named as berries in the food-service industry. True berries are fruits that have seeds surrounded by pulp and that

FIGURE **3.31** Berries.

come from a single ovary. In foodservice, true berries would include the huckleberry and currants. Most "berries" favored in foodservice are false berries that come from a part of the plant that does not include the ovary; this group would include the blueberry and strawberry. Others are aggregate fruits or those where multiple tiny fruits all spring from a single flower gathered into a single cluster; these include raspberries and blackberries.

Look for berries that are dry, plump, and full colored; be sure they exhibit no soft spots or signs of mold.

## STONE FRUIT

The term "stone fruit" in the foodservice industry generally signifies nectarines, peaches, plums, cherries, and a few hybrid or specialty fruits such as pluots and apriums. These fruits are usually divided into either "freestone" or "clingstone" varieties. In a freestone fruit, as their name suggests, the seed, or stone, more easily separates itself from the flesh, whereas the clingstone pit more tightly adheres to the flesh of the fruit. Because of their ease of use, freestone varieties are more frequently utilized for cooking purposes that requires the removal of the stone. This ease of use translates to a higher consumption of raw freestones as well. Consequently, due to this trend, the freestone variety has become nearly the total focus of the marketplace and in retail markets. Clingstone varieties are rarely seen outside of farm markets and stands these days.

Stone fruits are generally only available in the summer months, except for some imports from South America. Most domestic peaches are from California, Georgia, South Carolina, and Michigan. They will soften once picked but not gain any sweetness. Therefore, the fruit generally found in the marketplace will have been picked while still very firm or hard to facilitate shipping without incurring damage to the soft, fully ripened fruit. Color is the best indicator of a fruit that is fully matured before picking;

FIGURE **3.32** Saturn Peaches.

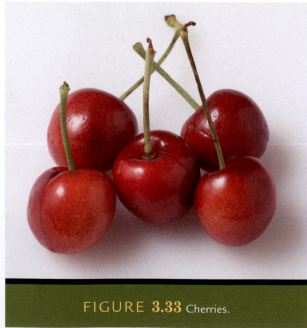

FIGURE **3.33** Cherries.

look for full and vibrantly colored fruit with no hint of green. There should also be a full, sweet aroma indicative of the flavor when the fruit is softened.

When allowing stone fruits to soften, it is important to not refrigerate them. Spread the fruit out in single layer to prevent the weight of the fruit from flattening and bruising each other. If the fruit must be refrigerated prior to use, storing the fruit in colder conditions (below 35°F/1.6°C but above freezing or 32°F/0°C) is much better. Storing stone fruits between 36° and 50°F/2.2° and 10°C can actually hasten their decay.

## MELONS

Melons are divided into two main categories, those of muskmelon and watermelon. Under these two headings, a surprisingly varied array of types, colors, flavors, and levels of sweetness can be found. This gives way to a wonderful array of options for service; serving a wedge for breakfast or putting diced melon into a fruit salad is no longer a sufficient use of this wonderful sweet fruit. Melons can be used in salads married with savory and acidic ingredients, puréed into a refreshing cold soup, served in unusually delightful cocktails, paired with cheese, spiced with pepper, or chilled into a sorbet.

Muskmelons can have netted veins covering their rind as found on the cantaloupe, or smooth waxy rinds like the honeydew. Muskmelon varieties can have orange, green, golden, or pale yellow to white flesh with all their seeds held in a stringy wet mass

FIGURE **3.34** Melons.

located in the center of each melon. Watermelons come in a variety of sizes with the typical red or bright yellow flesh and with or without seeds.

Most melons are best in the summer months, when they are grown domestically and are at their sweetest; warm days and nights are required for maximum sweetness. Melons grown in South America definitely extend availability well into or through the winter, but take care when selecting them in order to find good sweetness. Two muskmelon varieties, the Christmas and Santa Claus melons, are available from early fall into December.

Choosing and receiving a good melon require experience and a good sense of smell. In foodservice, try to actually cut and taste melons when receiving. In general, look for melons that have the appropriate color, that are heavy for their size, and that have a "full slip" at the stem end. The latter indicates that the melon was fully ripe and fell easily from its stem. Melons with a jagged piece of stem still attached or a flat cut at the stem should be avoided as they were prematurely harvested. Some muskmelons will have a slight give at the blossom end and give off a sweet aroma indicating good sugar content. Another ripeness test is to listen for the sounds of seeds rattling inside when the melon is shook, but this often does not work. When ripe, watermelons should sound hollow if lightly thumped. Watermelons may have a pale area on one side where they lay on the ground; look for those with a yellow cast in that area over a pale or dull white shade.

Selection is not always simple and requires some practice; melons should feel heavy for their size, and muskmelons should exhibit a sweet aroma at the stem end. Learning how to select a ripe melon is important because melons will not ripen further once picked. They will soften further as if ripening, but the sugar content and flavor will not improve. As with most fruits and vegetables, melons are best enjoyed in season and grown locally whenever possible.

## TROPICAL FRUITS

Tropical fruits as a group have little in common botanically or from a culinary perspective. What unites them all is the inability to survive a frost; in fact, most will not grow in temperatures below 50°F/10°C.

Other similarities within this classification of fruits are that they are delicate in nature and taste much better if allowed to fully ripen before being consumed just after picking. This is why only a percentage of the hundreds of fruits that exist in these specialized climates make it to a broad commercial market. Also, in order for them to be hardy enough to survive transport undamaged, these fruits are picked before their time and are ripened during transit, often by gassing with ethylene. The flavor of these fruits that most people know is actually much less pronounced and sweet than that appreciated by people who consume them locally. However, the steadily improving means of harvesting and transporting these fruits in a very short period of time have dramatically improved both the variety and the quality of these fruits in the marketplace. Currently over half of the world's production of tropical fruits comes from the Asian and Pacific growing regions. Another 30 percent or so grows in the Caribbean and Latin American countries, with the remainder coming from Africa (mostly dates) and only a few percent from the rest of the world. Tropical fruits most popular in the United States are bananas and

FIGURE **3.35** Tropical Fruit.

plantains, avocados, figs, papaya, mangos, kiwi, pineapples, pomegranates, and star fruit (carambola).

## CHEESE

Cheese, depending on the type of foodservice operation, can be either a very simple purchasing issue for a buyer, or one that is very complex and can take years to fully master. Cheese is considered a living thing because the aging process transforms its shape, texture, flavor, and aroma. To develop a variety of cheeses, cheesemakers will use bacteria to transform the rind or encourage the formation of the bleu mold running through the paste, or interior, of the product. Cheese commonly comes from cow's, sheep's, and goat's milk and is sometimes made with buffalo's milk. Different milks are more prevalent in some cultures than others.

FIGURE **3.36** Black Mission Figs.

If your type of operation is utilizing mainly processed commercial cheeses such as American, Swiss, and Provolone or bagged bleu cheese crumbles and shredded mozzarella, then writing your specifications and purchasing these items are very easy to do. Like any other commodity or dry good, these can be bid on and purchased through your full-line distributor. However, if you purchase for an operation that needs a variety of cheeses with specific flavor profiles or an evolving cheese course selection, there is much more to learn. It is crucial to find a cheese purveyor that is knowledgeable and will work

FIGURE **3.37** Cheese aging room.

FIGURE **3.38** Cheese aging room.

with you to convey what is the best they have in selection at any given time. Such a vendor can provide invaluable information and guidance. For the purposes of this chapter, we will only cover the various rind types and styles of cheese available. For more information about specific storage information for cheese, see page 207 in Chapter 5.

## TYPES OF RIND

### Fresh Cheese

This denotes the absence of any sort of rind; the outer surface is the same as the paste. The exterior of the cheese will be same as its inside unless it has been brined.

### Natural Rind

As the name indicates, these cheeses form a natural rind as they age. These cheeses maybe be brined to act as a preservative or regularly rubbed with an oiled cloth to abate the growth of mold.

### Bloomy Rinds

These cheeses have edible rinds that form as molds develop on the surface and create the familiar white bloom, a mold that most are familiar with on cheeses such as camembert and brie. These cheeses generally need to be utilized when young; buyers should avoid any that appear runny or smell ammoniated.

### Washed Rinds

These cheeses are often referred to as the "stinky" cheeses because the bacterial coating that forms on their skin is not as benign as that on the bloomy rind products. These "smear" types of bacteria form on the surface, which is often washed with brine during aging to encourage these types of bacteria to grow. The trick for buyers is to learn the difference between the funky aroma of a well-aged washed rind cheese and one that has gone bad. One is delicious, and the other is just awful.

## Artificial Rinds

These cheeses have rinds that have been added by a human being; they do not form naturally as the product ages. These rinds may be composed of ash from burned grapevines or dried herbs, or they can be made from wax, as is found on a wheel of Gouda. Generally these rinds are added to protect the product, but some are meant to impart some flavor.

## CHEESE CATEGORIES

Cheeses are identified by their flavor profile. Each of the following groupings is organized by when the cheese's flavor should be at its peak or as it is intended to be eaten. Some varieties may be enjoyed at several stages of the aging process, but they are usually identified in only the category when the cheese is considered to be at its best state.

### Fresh and Young Cheeses

These cheeses are consumed when very young and have a milky, uncomplicated flavor. The type of milk used will obviously have a significant impact on that flavor. These cheeses have very high moisture content and will deteriorate quickly; most are soft and creamy, but there are those that can be quite crumbly. Examples of these cheeses are mascarpone, cottage or farmer's cheese, fromage blanc, queso blanco or fresco, chevre, ricotta, and domestic provolone. Be sure these cheeses have a clean dairy aroma and show no sign of mold.

FIGURE **3.39** Queso Fresco.

### Mild Aged Cheeses

The cheeses in this class have not been aged for long, but they have aged long enough to be identified more as a cheese than a solidified milk product; they are also aged to reach the desired flavor and texture. These cheeses generally have mild, uncomplicated flavor profiles, as is expected with short aging, but there can be a range of intensities in flavor in the various types within this category. Their texture can range from chalky to buttery, and these cheeses will have higher moisture content than those that are aged longer.

Some mass-produced types of cheeses that fall within this category are brie, mild cheddar, fresh goat, Monterey jack, mozzarella, Muenster, and domestic Gouda. Popular but smaller production examples

FIGURE **3.40** Humboldt Fog.

FIGURE **3.41** Pierre Robert.

FIGURE **3.42** Garrotxa.

FIGURE **3.43** Mimolette.

FIGURE **3.44** Bobolink Cheddar.

include Robiola, ricotta salata, and various goat cheeses such as Humboldt Fog. Triple crème cheeses are rich, somewhat decadent varieties that include Explorateur, Pierre Robert, and camembert. Other types of mild aged cheeses that are a bit more assertive are Morbier, Garrotxa, and Tomme de Savoie.

## Medium-Strength and Nutty Cheeses

These types of cheeses have largely been affected by a longer aging process, which lessens the water content and increases the intensity of their flavor. The additional aging increases the amount of bacterial and fungal activity, making the flavors even more complex. The loss of moisture and time also hardens the paste, increases the shelf life of the product, and intensifies the flavor. Some of these are also stacked or weighted down by other means to further eliminate moisture from the paste.

Larger production examples of these cheeses include aged cheddars and domestic bleu cheeses. Other examples include Mimolette, Cotija, Idiazabal, Pecorino, Caciotta, and Cantal.

### Strong Stinky Cheeses

The flavors of some of these washed rind style of cheeses are generally, but not always, mild despite the strong aromas they come with. Also, these cheeses are often high in moisture content and should be consumed when relatively fresh. As noted earlier, buyers need to learn to identify those that are "good stinky" from those that are simply bad.

Still other cheeses in this category can have a very strong aroma and an assertive bite in the flavor. These varieties have aged longer, reducing their moisture content and allowing for a more in-depth, pronounced flavor. Buyers should remember that if the chef is looking for that savory rich *umami* flavor, cheeses in this category such as Parmigiano-Reggiano and Roquefort can supply that. Obviously, this category can have a wide range of textures and flavors for the buyer to choose from.

Examples of strong cheeses include Romano, aged Gouda, Manchego, Asiago, aged or cave-ripened Cheddars, Grana Padano, Parmigiano-Reggiano, and Sbrinz. Other varieties include Reblochon, Pont L'Eveque, Taleggio, and Appenzeller. Pungent bleu-veined varieties include Great Hill Blue, Stilton, Roquefort, Gorgonzola, and Cabrales.

There are some facts about how these cheeses react to heat and cooking that buyers should be aware of; this information will tell the buyer what to look for in order to obtain the desired end result. First, the higher a cheese's moisture content, the lower the melting point. Very soft cheese will melt thoroughly at temperatures as low as 130°F/54°C, while an aged Parmigiano won't melt until it reaches 180°F/82°C. Some cheeses that are overheated to any extent can melt and become oily looking on a dish. Younger cheeses, like mozzarella, will melt with a stringy consistency, while some aged cheddars may form granules as they melt. Salting cheeses or adding an acid to cheese will help the cheese to melt more smoothly. If the chef wants a cheese to get warm but still hold its shape, consider one curdled with an acid only as opposed to acid and rennet, such as Ricotta or Halloumi.

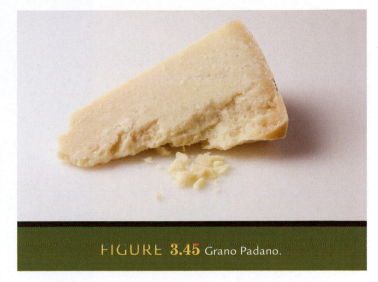

FIGURE **3.45** Grano Padano.

FIGURE **3.46** Canrales.

# PURCHASING FOR MEAT, POULTRY, AND FISH

When the waitstaff walks up to the table, they will often orally suggest that evening's special dishes. Items such as fresh wild-caught salmon, Colorado lamb chops, or a steak with an exotic mushroom sauce are explained with details to entice the customer. Meat and fish proteins are often the focal point of the sale. The goal of this chapter is to allow the purchaser to understand the many options to be considered when buying animal proteins. The text will go in depth with details about product specs, definitions of quality, freshness checks, packaging and storing techniques, and general information that will help the buyer considering proteins.

The cost of animal proteins is often higher than any other food cost, so this information will be extremely valuable when dealing with salespeople to ensure that the best price is paid for the best quality of goods. This chapter also discusses in-house fabrication versus buying portion cut products. The decision to buy larger cuts of meat or fish and process them in-house must be considered carefully so as to understand if the production was profitable or not. Included are charts that explain packaging styles, basic cooking uses, and accurate terminology so the buyer can create purchasing specs that can be given to the vendor so the products will be exactly what the buyer wants.

# MEAT PURCHASING

Meat is defined very basically as the parts of animals fit for human consumption. That general definition can be said to include any part of the animal that is served on the plate, which would include the lean muscle tissues or what most consider the "meat" such as a steak or cutlet, but also fats, connective tissues, bones, and the variety of organs that are edible. The cooking of meat changes its structures and flavors, creating the tastes that we describe as savory or *umami* and this taste is now included as one of the basic tastes our tongue senses along with sour, sweet, salty, and bitter.

Around 10,000 years ago, humans began a change from hunting and gathering to practicing basic agriculture, creating excesses of grain and crops, and this allowed for animals to be domesticated rather than hunted. Grazing animal herds that "raided" the human's crop fields were captured and kept. The role of the "butcher" became a necessity to properly fabricate animals into meat that the society could use. Along with the harvested meat, tools, clothing, and medicines were derived from the animal, and in early villages there was a group effort to create these, so butchery was known by all. As civilizations grew from small villages and camps to larger community centers and, later, cities, the craft of butchery was more specialized. As discussed in Chapter 1, each global area developed its own food culture and market systems, and part of that is the ways in which cultures bought, sold, cut, and used meats. During the medieval period in Europe, guild systems were formed to regulate trade and guarantee that skills were effectively passed on through generations. The butcher would start as an "apprentice" at around 10 or 12 years old and after a few years graduate to a "journeyman"; then, if their skill level showed a level of complete understanding of the craft, they would become a "master." The masters held great political power in a village or city-state and would help regulate trade with the local farmers.

For many years meat fabrication was done by hand, with the butchers improving their craft with the advent of higher quality metals, knives, and tools. With the coming of the Industrial Revolution in the mid-1800s, meat processing changed. Rather than a small local butcher working with the farmer on a one-to-one basis, modern transportation allowed for meat carcasses to be transported over greater distances. By the 1900s train carloads of animals could be brought to larger packinghouses of inner cities. The large stockyards formed in Chicago, Kansas City, and St. Louis were examples of how the meat industry became more centralized. Butchers no longer had to do the entire harvest from slaughter to final product. Assembly line–type fabrication took hold. Also at this time, farming technologies changed. The farmer could produce more plant food not only for human consumption but also for their farm animals. This "feeding" of animals led to higher quality products. The use of tractors and farm machinery meant that large animals were no longer needed to pull plows, clear land, or any other arduous task they were previously bred for. Now breeding could concentrate on meat production. Universities developed animal science programs devoted to the "meat breed" whether it was beef, pork, chicken, lamb, or another.

The growth of the meat industry changed the way meat is fabricated and purchased. No longer did a single butcher need to know the entire process of taking the animal from the farmer to the portioned cuts for customers. Nor did a restaurant or hotel feel the need to hire a "butcher" as was done for many years. Meats could now be purchased as individual cuts or portions, and the idea of meat processors having many "meat cutters" with a few particular skills increased the volume of what could be done. In 1960 the implementation of the vacuum-packaging system in the beef industry by Iowa Beef Processors (IBP) transformed the industry further, allowing meats to be processed and shipped with a much longer shelf life and no longer requiring the meats to be shipped as whole carcasses. Today modern meat-processing plants fabricate cuts in a huge variety of sizes, quality levels, trim specifications, styles, and price ranges, and an establishment that understands all of these specifications and has a trained employee with good fabrication skills enables the meat buyer to identify the most profitable way to buy.

Once a foodservice operation decides on a meat menu item, it has to purchase the cuts to create that dish. It is up to the purchaser to determine how the meat should be purchased depending on the ability of the kitchen staff. Some restaurants decide to forgo all fabrication and buy precut or even precooked portions. These cuts eliminate the labor and yield loss involved in producing the cut. The downside of this is that it limits the purchaser to those exacting cuts and does not allow for any flexibility on the menu. An example would be a restaurant that purchases an eight ounce striploin steak. That chef is stuck with the eight ounces, whereas a chef that purchases a full striploin can trim it to specs and cut an eight, ten, or twelve ounce steak from the same piece.

The goal of the purchaser, whether it is a chef, owner, purchasing agent, or anyone responsible for buying, is to produce the least expensive portion with the highest quality product and stay within the proper food cost for the establishment. Being able to analyze the fabrication skills of the kitchen staff and also the general quantity that will be used will be crucial when deciding how to buy. What may work for one establishment may not for another. The way to determine the best purchase is to weigh all options.

Developing proper meat specs for purchasing, even if for precut portions, is very important to the success of the establishment. The meat purveyor-vendor must understand clearly what is required by the restaurant so they can fill the order correctly. Also the restaurant must have a clear understanding of what is acceptable and what must be rejected. The purchaser and the meat purveyor must have a good understanding about all the products that might be ordered. Most meat purveyors will provide a list of all the products they can provide. A foodservice establishment should also create a list of every meat they might be ordering, with acceptable alternatives if possible. A comprehensive list of meat specifications is part of this chapter; see the "Purchasing Specs" section below.

# OPTIONS IN PURCHASING

When buying meat cuts, there are some basic market forms that should be defined before creating the specifications for purchasing. The most basic specification would be the class of market animal.

## MEAT CLASSIFICATIONS

### Beef

- Cow: Female mature beef animal, used for milk production, for reproduction, and as inexpensive ground meat products. These animals are much older than quality graded beef, and their meat is very lean and tough.

- Bull: male mature beef animal, used for genetics, reproduction, and inexpensive grind products, similar to cow meat.
- Bullock: A young noncastrated male. A rarity in today's market. Its meat can be off-colored or "dark cutter" caused by hormones. Some certified organic beef is from bullock.
- Heifer: Younger female beef animal used for quality meat, typically 16 to 22 months old. About 40% of graded beef is from heifer. Heifers tend to be slightly fattier than steer.
- Steer: Castrated male beef animal, used for quality beef, 16 to 22 months old. About 60% of beef is from steer. Fattened steer are considered the benchmark for the beef industry.

## Veal

- Bob Veal: Very young beef animal, under 10 days old, small with underdeveloped flavor, inexpensive, used for processed veal items, prebreaded cutlets, and grind.
- Formula Fed, Special Fed, Nature Veal: Typical veal raised to 5 to 6 months today on a milk-based formula feed, light in color, considered high quality, can be fed in tight stalls or group housed for more space. Formula fed is typically USDA graded and considered the benchmark standard.
- Milk-Fed Natural, Pasture Raised: Veal that is fed from its own mother or surrogate. Can be very expensive and not readily available from most purveyors, distinctive, richer flavor, 4 to 5 months old.
- Rose Veal, Calves: Older veal that has developed its ability to eat grass and grain, redder color, stronger flavor, larger than all other classes, 6 to 8 months old. Sometimes sold as "pasture raised" but beyond the milk-fed stage; can be tougher.

## Pork

- Suckling Pig: 18 to 35 lbs used for roasting whole, not much fat, can be expensive.
- Roasting Pig: 40 to 150 lbs (sold and priced in 20 lb increments) for roasting whole.
- Market-Style Hog: 180 to 200 lbs, 6 month old, male or female hog that is used for typical market cuts such as loins, hams, butts, etc.
- Sow: older female, about 2 to 3 years, used for reproduction, very large, meat used for processed items and cured products, tougher meat.
- Boar: older male used for reproduction, tough, very strong flavor due to boar "taint" caused by hormonal release into meat. Not typically found commercially.

## Lamb

- Hot-House Lamb: 20 lbs, young, very tender, milk-fed, specialty item used for roasting whole, expensive and must be ordered ahead of time.
- Spring Lamb: 30 to 40 lbs, under 6 months old, smallish market cuts, tender. Most New Zealand lamb is considered Spring Lamb.

- Market Lamb: 60 to 75 lbs if raised in United States, under 1 year old, typically 6 to 8 months, market-size cuts, high quality, USDA graded.
- Yearling: 70 to 85 lbs. over 1 year, up to 16 months. Large but still tender enough to be graded, can be fatty.
- Mutton- Older sheep used for reproduction, not often available in United States.

## Game

- Venison: Meat from deer, typically farm raised, cut similar to lamb.
- Bison: Meat from American Buffalo, cut similar to beef.
- Ostrich: Red meat from a large land bird, red meat tastes similar to beef
- Rabbit: Small, 3 to 5 lbs light-colored poultry-like meat.
- Wild Boar: Reddish meat from feral swine, stronger flavor than regular pork, smaller than market hog.

## POULTRY CLASSIFICATIONS

### Chicken

- Cornish Game Hen: 1 to 2 lbs
- Petite Poulet or Poussin: 1 to 2 lbs
- Broiler or Fryer: 2.5 to 4.5 lbs
- Roaster: 5 to 8 lbs
- Capon: 6 to 9 lbs (castrated male chicken)
- Stewing Hen or Fowl: 5 to 7 lbs, older laying hen

### Turkey

- Young
  - Tom: Male 16 to 30 lbs
  - Hen: Female 8 to 16 lbs
- Mature: Flder large birds 28 to 35 lbs

### Duck

- Young
  - Duckling: 3 to 5 lbs
  - Roasting: 5 to 8 lbs
- Mature: Moulard males from foie gras production

### Goose

- Young: 12 to 16 lbs
- Mature: 14 to 20 lbs

### Game Poultry

- Pheasant: 2 to 3.5 lbs
- Guinea Fowl: 2 to 3.5 lbs
- Quail: 1/2 lb each
- Squab: 1 lb

# QUALITY AND YIELD GRADING

Each meat has its own set of USDA-quality grades that should be considered when meat purchasing and creating ordering specs. Beef and lamb also have yield grades that may be added as additional specs. Grades are applied according to guidelines that the USDA has developed criteria to judge the palatability of each meat. Generally only higher quality meats are graded, increasing their value, and lower quality ungraded products are sold as ground burger or processed meats such as sausage, hot dogs, and the like.

The USDA has guidelines for grading that will include many of the following features depending on the animal:

- Size and weight of the animal
- Age or maturity of the animal
- The weight of the carcass
- Overall fullness or conformation (basic meat to bone ratio)
- The color of the lean muscle tissues
- Any defects in the lean muscle tissues
- Marbling scores (intramuscular fat)

## BEEF

Beef is quality graded at what is called the Rib Eye Area or REA, the spot between the 12th and 13th rib. This location will tell much of what is needed to judge the quality of the entire carcass.

Higher quality beef is typically used in steakhouses, where the flavor and texture are important to the sale. Choice beef has significant quality and can be used as a quality item, but the range within choice requires the purchaser to be aware of some lower end product that could represent a lesser quality dining experience. Select beef which has a lower marbling score usually requires some help. Select grade cuts are typically enhanced or tenderized to aid palatability. Marbling, although not the only factor in quality grading, substantially increases flavor.

- Prime
- Choice
- Select
- Standard
- Commercial
- Utility
- Cutter
- Canner

## VEAL

Veal has become a specialized meat in that growers are able to achieve a very specific quality score. This lack of diversity means that veal grading has narrowed. In 1977, 29.1% of veal graded as Prime, 44.7% as Choice, 22.8% as Good, and 3.4% as Standard. By 2006, only 3.7% graded as Prime, 94.9% as Choice, and 1.4% as Good. Choice graded veal has become the standard, and growers are consistently hitting the choice

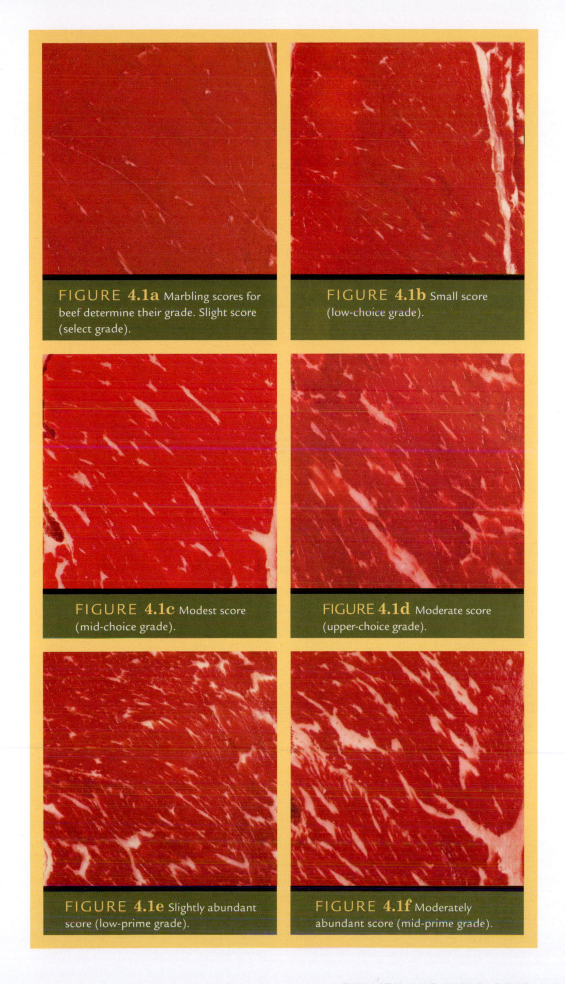

FIGURE **4.1a** Marbling scores for beef determine their grade. Slight score (select grade).

FIGURE **4.1b** Small score (low-choice grade).

FIGURE **4.1c** Modest score (mid-choice grade).

FIGURE **4.1d** Moderate score (upper-choice grade).

FIGURE **4.1e** Slightly abundant score (low-prime grade).

FIGURE **4.1f** Moderately abundant score (mid-prime grade).

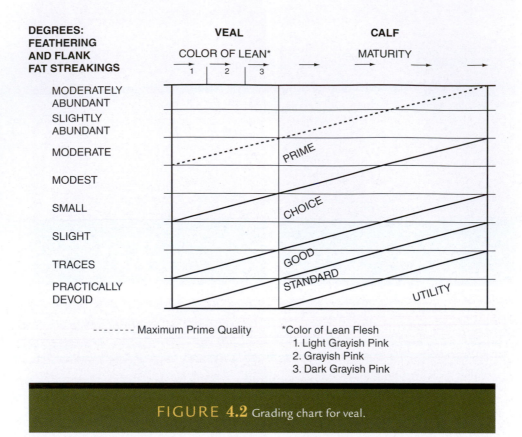

| DEGREES: FEATHERING AND FLANK FAT STREAKINGS | VEAL COLOR OF LEAN* | CALF MATURITY |

FIGURE **4.2** Grading chart for veal.

mark. Due to this, some veal-processing companies have opted not to USDA grade and simply apply a company name brand to their products. In these cases the company stamp or name brand can be used to establish a quality standard. There are also veal products that are not graded due to the fact that they are under- or oversized and therefore would achieve a low grade. Be sure to establish your color and weight specs with the purveyor or simply use the USDA grade as a guide.

- Prime
- Choice
- Good
- Standard
- Utility

## PORK

The evaluation of live hogs for today's commercial market depends on a few basic features, which include the thickness of the fatback, size and shape of the loin eye, length of the loin in general, width and muscling of the ham and shoulder, and width and thickness of the belly section. The USDA has a grading system for hogs that is based on these criteria. The USDA grade is not reflected in finished product as it is in beef, veal, or lamb. There is basically "Acceptable" and "Unacceptable" pork. The Unacceptable is basically used for processed products and not sold as whole muscle cuts. The Acceptable pork is divided according to yield on a 1–4 scale, with 1 being the leanest. Most pork processors will assess pork in-house, foregoing the USDA grading system and using guidelines set up by the National Pork Producers Council.

- Acceptable
  1
  2
  3
  4
- Utility

## LAMB

Lamb is evaluated on two basic factors, color and marbling scores of the lean muscle tissues and conformation of the carcass. Lamb is graded as a whole carcass, and evaluation is determined first by age. Age is judged by looking at the "breakjoint" at the end of the front trotter bones. A "crowned" breakjoint will indicate less bone ossification and therefore a younger animal. Marbling and color of the lean muscle are judged at the flank area just inside the carcass. Fatty streaks in the flank and a bright reddish color indicate high quality.

- Prime
- Choice
- Good
- Utility
- Cull

## POULTRY

Poultry are divided into classes. Classes will divide poultry by size, age, and sometimes gender and breed. Only certain classes, those that will result in a high value, are typically graded. Grading will consist of two types, ready-to-cook whole poultry carcasses or poultry products such as ready-to-cook legs or breasts. Typically the USDA will grade poultry for larger processors. Graders will judge the following:

- Conformation or meat-to-bone ratio
- Fleshing
- Fat covering
- Skin covering or exposed flesh
- Defeathering or pin bones
- Discolorations
- Disjointed or broken bones
- Missing parts
- Poultry Grades: A, B, C

## GAME

The USDA does not grade game animals, but most processors will have some criteria for what is considered marketable. Be sure to buy game from a reputable dealer.

## BEYOND QUALITY AND YIELD GRADING

The USDA provides the service of "certifying" a variety of meat products. Certification is generated by meat processors or private entities that want characteristics judged beyond normal quality and yield grading. The intention is to fine-tune the product and therefore be able to market it more specifically. An example of a typical certified product is "Certified Angus Beef." This item has a live animal requirement which guarantees the cattle will have some Angus characteristics. It also requires a marbling score of "modest," which eliminates the bottom third of Choice; a specific carcass weight of not more than 1,000 lbs; and a yield grade score of not more than 3.9, among other requirements.

The majority of USDA certifications are for the beef industry. There are numerous certified beef products available, and some will be helpful to ensure a higher level of quality, but the buyer needs to understand the differences between requirements so as not to purchase certain certified items that are no more than marketing. The USDA lists all of the requirements for certified products on their website, http://www.ams .usda.gov.

Before purchasing, especially at a higher price, the consumer needs to compare them to see the actual advantage of one over another.

Processors may also create "branded" products where beef is selected by in-house graders that can choose quality criteria and label it as a specific company brand name. These products may use the USDA to verify attributes but also may decide to verify things "in-house," which would not be restrained by the agency. A company may use a trim spec as a guideline to ensure a specific yield. Certain companies are separating beef that are achieving marbling scores that are above prime, such as those of the Wagyu cattle or Kobe-style beef.

Another form of USDA certification for meats are those identifying specific feeding or handling practices and branding these traits regardless of quality grading scores. The USDA National Organic Program (NOP) states animals must be raised on organically grown feeds, be allowed outdoors, and given no antibiotics or growth hormones. The NOP prohibits the use of genetically engineered feeds, and animals cannot be given a long list of prohibited medicines. Other certifications may include parts of the organic regulations but not all, singling out some specifics. "Grass-Fed," "All Vegetarian Diet," "Antibiotic Free," and "No Growth Promotants or Hormones" are examples of "process-verified" branded products. Another category is "Certified Humane Handling," which verifies the animal is allowed to engage in natural behavior; raised with sufficient space, where they are able to lie down; given shelter; handled gently to limit stress; and given ample fresh water and

FIGURE **4.3a** Certified label.

FIGURE **4.3b** USDA certification is another form of verification.

a healthy diet. These many market products may have an in-house certification process that guarantees the farmers are adhering to their specific guidelines as well. The goal of all certified and process-verified products is to differentiate them from standard products, giving the foodservice operator a way to market their beef products at a higher cost.

# SHIPPING CONDITION AND PACKAGING

Meats can be shipped in a variety of conditions, including fresh, frozen, raw, or vacuum packaged.

- Fresh: Chilled products that are not frozen or thawed, no odor, recent pack date, can be stored at 28 to 35°F (most fresh red meat will not freeze slightly below 32°F).
- Fresh: Topped with ice. Used for poultry; ice should be completely covering the product.
- Vacuum packaged: Tightly sealed heavy plastic bag providing an anaerobic environment, increases shelf life, typical brand name is Cryovac packaged. Can be for large subprimals or individual portion cuts. Most typical form of packaging meats sold to foodservice today.
- Frozen: temperature at or below 0°F, items should not be thawed and refrozen, no freezer burn, dry spots, large ice crystals or open packaging.
- IQF: Individually quick frozen, items are blast frozen, then packaged as individual portions.
- Irradiated: Meat is exposed to either an electronic beam or gamma radiation to destroy pathogens and extend shelf life, must be listed as an ingredient, also known as "cold pasteurized."
- MAP storage: Modified atmospheric packaging, similar to vacuum packaging but bag has a modified air content rather than a tight seal. Typically $CO_2$ or NO is used to help preserve meat.
- Hanging Meat: Large carcass, primal or subprimal cuts that are never stored in vacuum packaging, typical for dry aging. Be sure hanging meats are wrapped in paper or loose plastic when receiving. If aging hanging cuts, be sure allow for good air circulation.

# MARKET FORMS

## FULL CARCASS

A full carcass is not typically purchased by most restaurants today when considering beef, veal, lamb, or pork, but a full carcass may be considered by a restaurant that is buying from a local farmer or small processor who only sells the entire animal. It requires extreme skill to cut a large beef, veal, hog, or lamb carcass, and the whole carcass must be used in equal parts, which presents many challenges. In other words only about 15% of a lamb carcass is rack that can be served as chops; what does the establishment do with the rest? A restaurant that buys the whole carcass will often feature a menu that is changeable and allows for flexibility to sell all of the parts. Due to their size and usage, whole carcasses are not readily available from most restaurant purveyors today.

It is much more likely to see poultry sold as whole; these are small, manageable, and readily available from the purveyor. An example is a restaurant buying whole Cornish game hens to be served as an individual portion or ducks, splitting them for roasting. In both these and many other poultry applications, the whole bird is a common purchase and simple to fabricate.

## PRIMAL CUTS

Large portions of the whole carcass are called "primal" cuts. Depending on the size of the original carcass, primal cuts can be as unmanageable as a full carcass or a cut considered normal when purchasing meats. Beef primals, for example, are large, weighing over 100 lbs in some cases and difficult to fabricate, while lamb primals may weigh no more than 10 or 12 pounds, making them a viable purchase. Most restaurants have forgone the purchase of primal cuts and have opted for further fabricated cuts that are easier to use.

The advantages a primal could give a restaurant is that primals can be custom cut, outside the norm, to create unique presentations. An example would be the beef Tomahawk Chop with its unusual elongated bone structure, created from the primal beef rib. Primals might also give the buyer a price advantage such as the primal rack of lamb compared to a pre-frenched rack. The price difference may be significant, but yield testing and labor evaluation must be part of the decision. Primal cuts of beef, which are large and difficult to ship, have become much less available by most purveyors and would need to be ordered in advance.

### SUBPRIMAL OR HOTEL, RESTAURANT, AND INSTITUTION–STYLE (HRI) CUTS

Subprimals can best be described as the muscle divisions of the larger primal cuts. These are typically purchased by restaurants today but require some skill and fabrication. Hotel, Restaurant, and Institution–style (HRI) cuts are basically the same as subprimals but more accurately can be explained as the cuts typically purchased by foodservice establishments that have a specific trim or cut spec. An example would be a boneless beef striploin that has been trimmed to a 1/4 inch of fat. It still requires the kitchen to trim it and portion cut it into steaks, but this fabrication does not require as much skill as larger primal cuts. An HRI or subprimal cut can be custom cut to varying thickness and styles, giving the restaurant many options from one cut of meat and offering flexibility from one cut. There are hundreds of HRI cuts available today, and all have their own trim specifics. A trained chef or butcher will often buy HRI cuts to save money over the next category, and they can calculate the number of portions each cut can provide through experience and yield testing.

## PORTION CUTS

Portion cut items are those that require no fabrication and are ready to cook upon receiving. The advantage is no labor cost involved, with all of the work done off site, and portions are easy to inventory so the chef knows how many portions are on hand. Portion cuts can be more expensive, and the chef must do a cost analysis to judge if portions are the best option. A drawback of portion cuts is that they are inflexible, and a chef can only purchase one size for each dish. An example is that if a chef orders an eight ounce tenderloin steak, they cannot then sell a 12 or six ounce steak without ordering that cut separately.

Another subcategory of the portion cut would be the "reformulated" cut. These cuts refer to those which take pieces and meld them together by a chemical bonding process to create a "new" portion. Many restaurants are buying portion cuts today, and the purveyor will have a large assortment of specs, so be sure of your specs.

# WHERE TO BUY MEATS?
## MEAT VENDORS

When buying meat, first an establishment must decide who to buy from. As discussed in Chapter 2 on page 31, developing relationships between vendor and buyer is key to success in purchasing but especially for meat items due to the fact that they tend to be the most expensive portion of the dish. Meat and fish both present their own sets of shipping, storage, and spoilage issues that must be addressed. Meat spoils more rapidly than other foods; therefore, transportation must be well chilled and items might not be able to be shipped with other foods. An example would be poultry topped with ice, which will leach out juices that cannot come in contact with ready-to-eat foods such as salad greens.

The foodservice buyer may be purchasing for a variety of businesses, including restaurants, hotels, resorts, cruise ships, casinos, catering services, schools, institutions, military operations, and others, but no matter the size of the operation, the meat needs to end as plate portions. What we will attempt to do in this section is explain who different types of foodservice establishments will consider meat purchasing from and what factors should be considered.

As previously discussed when deciding on market forms, an establishment with a passionate, highly trained chef may be able to buy large primal cuts and fabricate all portions in-house and utilize everything that comes with the cut. This type of restaurant may be buying from a large meat market or from local farmers who sell only these large primal cuts. This restaurant may even include this fact on its menu, stating, "All meats butchered on the premises," and use it in advertising. There may be a hired "butcher" as in the style of years gone by, where a specialist fabricates the meats to the exacting specifics of the chef. Due to the labor expense, this is typically only done in very upscale establishments that can reflect the high cost of this labor on the menu.

On the other hand, this same establishment may choose to buy what are known as subprimal or HRI cuts. These cuts will require some fabrication but not the amount that a full primal would require, and kitchen staff can be trained to fabricate these in a short amount of time. These cuts are sold as whole muscle pieces and can be relatively easily cut into portions but may also yield some "usable trim" that can be used for side dishes, appetizers, sauces, and so on.

Another option is precut portions with a specific weight designation to free up time to do more complicated food items such as desserts or sauces. All of these options require proper purchasing specifications. There is also the option to mix and match depending on the need of the restaurant. Both HRI cuts and portions can be purchased from a number of different vendors, and the North American Meat Processors Association has developed a standard for each cut, including very distinct descriptions and a numbering system. It is common for a meat purchaser to use the NAMP numbers when describing a desired meat cut.

A high-volume restaurant that has a minimally trained crew, such as a chain-type restaurant, might not be able to fabricate in-house and would need all the meat cutting to be done off-site by the purveyor. These establishments will establish strict specs for their portions. Managers will need to check products to be sure specs are adhered to. Contracted purveyors would create a national spec that these high-volume restaurant chains would then receive, no matter the location, so that all of those meat menu items would taste the same.

## GENERAL FOODSERVICE PURVEYOR

This type of purveyor sells a huge variety of goods of which meat is just one part. Often the large purveyor has a large assortment of meat specs and quality grades. They feature most national brand name items and sell a large variety of pretrimmed HRI and portion cuts. They often have a knowledgeable sales staff that can be helpful in ordering products. Often the general food purveyor is regionally or nationally owned and is part of a larger corporation. This enables the large purveyor to purchase products in huge quantity, therefore offering the best prices.

There are a few drawbacks of purchasing from a large purveyor. It may be that they have a minimum order. In other words, the restaurant would need to buy a minimum dollar amount that might be difficult for a smaller establishment to meet, especially in slower times of the year.

Also a delivery surcharge may be included. Many companies now charge a fuel surcharge. If your establishment is off the beaten path, this charge may be substantial. Typically delivery will be once or twice a week by a large semi-trailer truck. Proper forecasting of usage is very important.

Large distributors use a catalog of items and often use the NAMP number system as well as their own in-house item numbers. It is very important for the purchaser to understand purchasing specs and check over orders as they delivered. There may be a charge for returned items.

## MEAT PURVEYOR

The meat purveyor is more regional than the large foodservice distributor. They are typically long-established smaller corporations, often second or third generation and family owned. They may still fabricate some meat from whole primals and often provide dry aged or specialty products. Often these establishments are USDA inspected and have their own brand names and labels that are not available anywhere else.

The true meat purveyor is focused on customer service. They will often deliver multiple times per week and will custom cut meat items outside the norm. If the restaurant has an emergency, the meat purveyor may be flexible enough to deliver on a weekend.

Many singular meat purveyors have come under pressure by the larger broad-scope vendors and are now often looking to sell exclusive items. These smaller companies will sometimes feature organic, naturally raised, fancy imported meats or meat products that the large company cannot deal with. Many meat purveyors are often a part of the restaurant community in that they support local ACF chapters or participate in food shows, fundraisers, and the like. They even may be on a level to help a struggling restaurant by allowing some extra time to pay the bill, whereas a larger establishment might be stricter.

## RETAIL DISCOUNT STORE

Today we find large "club" stores that are selling in bulk product to retail customers and also restaurants or caterers. These types of retail establishments offer a limited selection of HRI or subprimal type cuts at very reasonable prices. The chef can select the items by hand and pick through the stock to find the best quality. Quality levels can vary, but some very good deals can be found on occasion. The downside is that these stores offer no delivery, and all product must be hauled back to the restaurant by the purchaser. This may lead to improper transportation, especially in hot summer months. Another drawback is the payment, which is due at checkout. Purchasing from a discount retailer can be advantages but also presents difficulties.

## INTERNET

There are many mail-order distributors that send out specialty products that are found on the internet. Sometimes these are the only places where certain products can be found. An example would be a specific game bird from a company in Vermont that only sells a small amount per year. The product is limited, so the seller has no distributor and simply ships to orders placed on its website. This is good when buying very special meat items but can be very expensive. Shipping costs and packaging can sometimes exceed the price of the product, and returning product is very difficult due to the perishable nature of meats.

## FARMER

Some restaurants are looking to purchase meats directly from the farmer. The chef may have an established relationship with the farmer and want their specific animals because of feeding style or the quality and uniqueness of the meat. This presents a challenge due to the fact that all meat needs to be inspected, so the farmer cannot do a simple field dress and ship the carcass. Before the restaurant can get it, the animal would need to be trucked to a local slaughter facility, properly slaughtered, chilled, and inspected, then it can be delivered. The other part of buying this way is that the farmer typically wants to sell the entire carcass, so a restaurant would need to use all the parts of that carcass equally. That implies a lot of braising or lesser quality cuts that need to be sold and also requires a lot of butcher skill on the part of the kitchen staff or chef. This presents challenges to the menu, but some chefs view that challenge as part of the trade-off for selling local product.

# PURCHASING SPECS

## BEEF

The North American Beef Processors Association has developed a number system that identifies most of the beef cuts available today. Meat processors develop their own code numbers that may or may not incorporate the NAMP numbers, but meat purveyor salespeople are familiar with them. This book uses the NAMP numbers as a guide, but be sure to identify individual processor codes to receive the exacting specs you require. Some cuts may have multiple names, and listed below are the most typical.

### Primal Cuts

- Round
- Loin
- Rib
- Chuck

# Beef skeletal structure

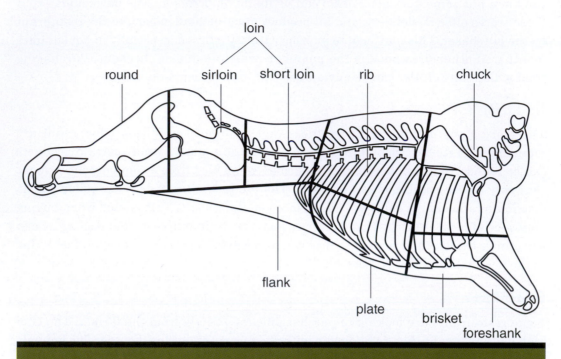

**FIGURE 4.4** Beef skeletal structure with primal divisions.

## Minor Primals or Market Forms

- Plate
- Brisket
- Foreshank

## ROUND

The beef round or back leg is generally the largest primal. It consists of large, lean muscles that have a high yield percentage. The cuts vary in quality and size. The largest and most tender is the top round. In foodservice, the "top round" is used most often as roasts, steaks, and various thin sliced items. Other round cuts are lean and do not have much connective tissue, but their muscle fibers tend to be slightly thick and therefore can be tough. Retail stores embrace the round cuts, selling them as roast for reasonable prices, but foodservice operations often struggle to create high-value cuts from most of the round. The classic buffet presentation of the "Steamship Roast" is the entire round with its shank bone frenched and trimmed to specific levels. This large (sometimes upwards of 65 lbs) roast can be an awe-inspiring carving station that still can be found at large functions and weddings.

## Subprimal Cuts

- Top or Inside Round
- Knuckle
- Bottom or Outside Round Flat
- Eye Round
- Shank
- Heel

## Breakdown of Beef Round

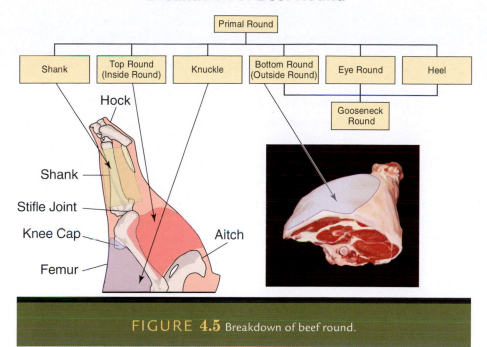

FIGURE 4.5 Breakdown of beef round.

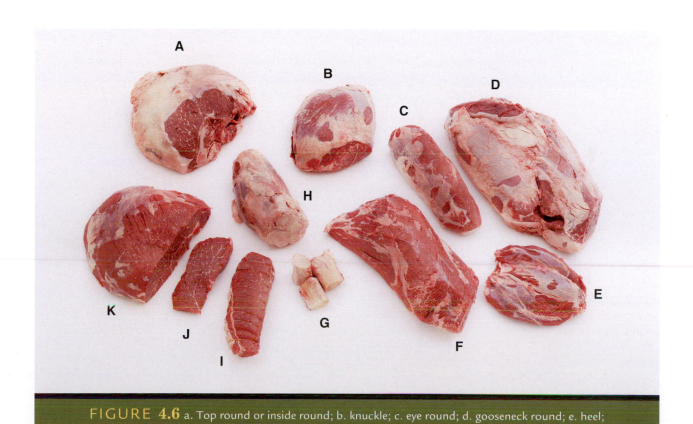

FIGURE 4.6 a. Top round or inside round; b. knuckle; c. eye round; d. gooseneck round; e. heel; f. bottom round or outside round; g. marrow bones; h. shank; i. top round roast; j. top round London broil; and k. top round, cap off.

| TABLE 4-1 NAMP HRI CHART FOR BEEF ROUND | | | | |
|---|---|---|---|---|
| **ITEM AND NAMP NUMBER** | **DESCRIPTION OR FABRICATION** | **SUGGESTED COOKING METHOD, OR APPLICATION** | **AVERAGE SUGGESTED WEIGHT IN POUNDS** | **TYPICAL PACKAGE SPECS** |
| 158 Round, primal | Large, full primal | Round cuts tend to be large, full-muscle cuts that can be slow roasted; some dry cooked as steaks, braised, or ground. | 70 to 100 | Sold individually |
| 166B Steamship round with handle | Full primal, trimmed for large roasting | Slow roasting, 8 or more hours; be sure to check temperature. Used for carving station, or catering. | 60 to 70 | Sold individually |
| 167 Knuckle | Untrimmed, requires fabrication; also known as *sirloin tip* | Roast, steak, braise, can be split; *tip side* is tender. | 10 to 14 | 4 per box |
| 167A Knuckle, peeled | Trimmed, may need some fabrication | Roast, steak, braise, can be split; *tip side* is tender. | 8 to 12 | |
| 168 Top / inside round | Untrimmed, needs fabrication; sold with various levels of fat trim | Roast beef, slicing steak, *London broil*, sliced thin for stuffing and rolling (roulade, braciole), thinner for quick cook. | 17 to 23 | 3 per box |
| 169A Top round, cap off | Trimmed, roast ready; can be purchased split | Same as above. | 16 to 19 | 4 per box |
| 171B Outside round flat | Trimmed or untrimmed | Braise, pot roast, sauerbraten; can be roasted and sliced thin; excellent for jerky, consommé. | 12 to 16 | 4 per case |
| 171C Eye round | Trimmed | Braise, pot roast, oven roast (sliced thin), inexpensive carpaccio or fondue (well trimmed). | 3 to 6 | 12 per case |
| Hind shank (no NAMP number) | Sold bone in or boneless | Braise, stew, grind, consommé, goulash, ragout (good flavor). | 7 to 9 | 2 per bag, 4 bags per case |

## TYPICAL FOODSERVICE PURCHASE CUTS

### Top Round

The top round is most often cooked as a large roast. It is excellent for slicing roast beef due to its large, collagen-free muscle structure. It can be used for large slicing steaks but is better if marinated or pinned (mechanically tenderized). The top round is also excellent for thin slicing as a stuffed and rolled braising cut (roulade, bracciole, paupiette, etc.) or even thinner as a quick sauté or stir fry.

### Beef Shank

The beef shank is one of the toughest muscles on the carcass but also one of the most flavorful. It is loaded with collagen, which adds a lot of flavor and protein to the dish. It is used for a superior stew or a flavorful grind.

Assembling grinder and grinding

### Beef Knuckle

Although the knuckle is not that well known with most chefs, it does present some inexpensive options for roasting, steak, or braise. It is sometimes known as the sirloin tip roast. The knuckle has collagen seams that lessen the quality of the cut. Steaks should be tenderized and seams removed.

### Beef Bottom and Eye Round

Also known as the Gooseneck when left as one piece, these cuts are best braised whole for pot roasts or sauerbraten-type dishes. Avoid these cuts as steak.

### Steamship Round

The "Steamship" is the entire round with the shank meat removed (frenched) from the shank bone and the top "hock" end of the bone cut off, exposing the end of the marrow. The Aitch bone was also removed, and the exterior fat trimmed to about a 1/8 thickness. This item would be roasted whole and, weighing about 60 to 80 lbs, is used as a carving station item for large parties. The cut is very large and may not fit into a conventional oven.

### Marrow Bones

The beef round contains the shank and femur bones, which are sold as cut portions that are full of fatty, rich marrow. Marrow bones can be expensive compared to regular beef bones. Marrow bones are sold as a type of garnish, roasted and served with grilled steaks, or can be used to bolster sauces such as sauce Bercy.

## BEEF PRIMAL LOIN

The beef loin holds more value than any other section. The HRI cuts are some of the most tender and expensive on the carcass and are generally dry cooked as quality steaks and roasts. The loin is fabricated two ways. First, the loin can be cut in a way to fabricate for large steaks such as the porterhouse and t-bone. These two steaks are standards on many steakhouse menus.

Second, the loin can be fabricated into individual subprimals, creating the beef tenderloin and striploin separately, which are often the marquee steaks on the menu demanding the highest prices. Beyond the exclusive cuts, the loin also holds a few cuts of lesser quality that are also very popular on a lesser expensive menu. The top

**Beef Loin**

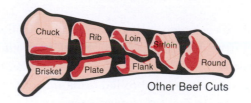

Other Beef Cuts

**Beef Loin Breakdown**

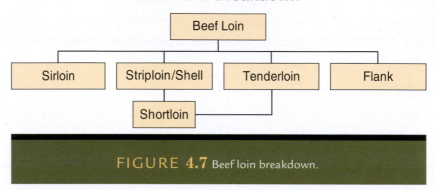

FIGURE **4.7** Beef loin breakdown.

sirloin is the largest section of the loin and offers a reasonable steak or roast with a lot of options when cutting. It is typically sold as a large steak for slicing or broken into its "eyes" or sections and individual portion cut. It is used in dishes such as the "Churasco," where it is cut into large chunks and grilled on large skewers. Bistro-style steaks from the tri tip, flank, and sirloin flap are flavorful and have unique textures that, if cut correctly, can offer a very satisfying dining experience.

## Subprimal Cuts

- Striploin
- Tenderloin
- Shortloin
- Sirloin
- Flank

### Beef Striploin, Bone In or Bone Out

The striploin is considered one of the premier steaks and is sought after by many chefs. This continues to keep its prices relatively high, but it is one of the best-tasting and -presenting steaks on the carcass. There are many specs that should be included when ordering this cut. Be sure to check the chart included in this chapter to create those specs.

The striploin can also be roasted whole or split lengthwise for a carving station item. The bone-in version can be dry aged for several weeks.

### Beef Tenderloin

Trimming a beef tenderloin

The beef tenderloin has the finest fibers of any cut in the carcass and therefore is very tender, highly prized, and the most expensive. The tenderloin is very popular on many menus and is served as many different dishes. Filet mignon, tournedos, and chateaubriand are just a few of the classics that are made from the tenderloin.

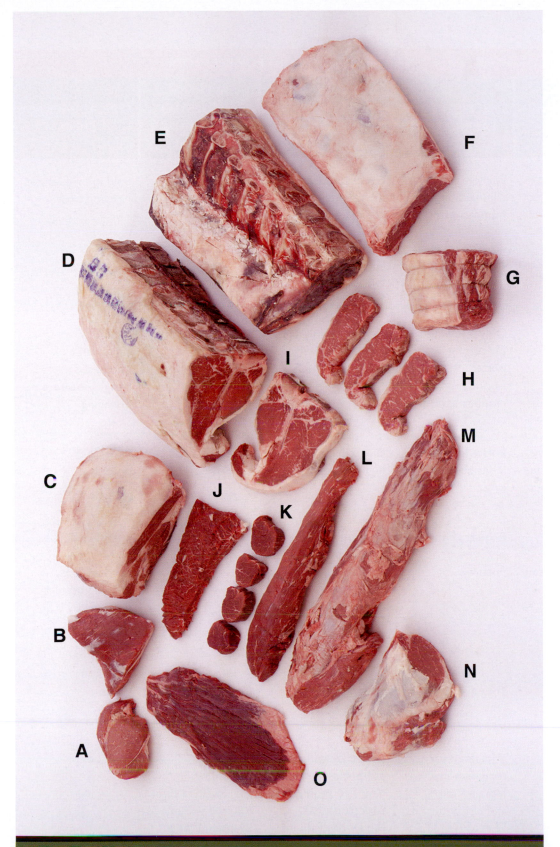

FIGURE 4.8 a. Beef ball tip; b. beef tri tip; c. top sirloin butt; d. beef shortloin; e. bone-in beef striploin; f. boneless beef strip loin; g. striploin roast; h. striploin steaks; i. porterhouse steaks; j. sirloin flap; k. tenderloin steaks or tournedos; l. beef tenderloin, denuded; m. beef tenderloin, peeled, side muscle on (PSMO); n. beef tenderloin butt; and o. beef flank steak.

| ITEM AND NAMP NUMBER | DESCRIPTION OR FABRICATION | SUGGESTED COOKING METHOD, OR APPLICATION | AVERAGE SUGGESTED WEIGHT IN POUNDS | TYPICAL PACKAGE SPECS |
|---|---|---|---|---|
| 172 Loin (primal) | Full loin, trimmed, requires fabrication | Cuts from the loin are generally dry cooked as steaks or roasts; many options exist from the many cuts created from the loin. | 55 to 80 | Sold individually as hanging beef |
| 174 Shortloin trim specs—0x1, 1x1, 2x3 | Only purchased for cutting porterhouse and t-bone steaks; requires band saw | Grill, char-grill, broil; high heat preferred; can be dry aged. | 22 to 28 (varies with trim specs) | 3 per box; can also be purchased as hanging beef for dry aging |
| 1174 Porterhouse / t-bone portion cuts | Porter house has larger tenderloin eye | Grill, char-grill, broil; high heat preferred. | Customer specified | Varies with processor |
| 175 Striploin, bone in trim specs—1x1, 2x3 tail measurements | Requires band saw; cut for portions | Grill, char-grill, broil as bone in steak, shell steak, top loin steak, New York strip, or Kansas City strip steak; can be dry aged. | 18 to 20 | 4 per box; can also be purchased as hanging beef for dry aging |
| 1179 Striploin portion cut | Trimmed | See above. | Customer specified | Varies |
| 180 Striploin, boneless trim specs—0x1, 1x1, 2x3 | Trim levels vary, requires some fabrication | Grill, char-grill, broil as boneless steak, pan sear, sauté, New York strip steak; can be divided into medallions. | 8 to 14, depending on trim level; be sure to order within a 21-pound range for consistent portion sizing | 6 per box |

*(continues)*

**TABLE 4-2 NAMP HRI CUTS CHART FOR BEEF LOIN**

| TABLE 4-2 NAMP HRI CUTS CHART FOR BEEF LOIN (Continued) | | | | |
|---|---|---|---|---|
| ITEM AND NAMP NUMBER | DESCRIPTION OR FABRICATION | SUGGESTED COOKING METHOD, OR APPLICATION | AVERAGE SUGGESTED WEIGHT IN POUNDS | TYPICAL PACKAGE SPECS |
| 1180 / 1180A Striploin portion cut | Trimmed, "A" is missing the vein steaks | See above. | Customer specified | Varies |
| 181 Sirloin | Large bone-in item, requires extensive fabrication | Very large bone-in steaks if crosscut on band saw, grill, broil. | 19 to 28 | Sold individually |
| 184 Top sirloin butt, boneless | Requires some fabrication; sold with varying amounts of trim | Grill, broil, pan sear, sauté, large slicing steaks, divided into portion steaks. | 12 to 15 | 6 per box |
| 1184 Top sirloin portion cut | Trimmed; a variety of specs available | Grill, broil, pan sear, sauté. | Customer specified | Varies |
| 185A Sirloin flap | Trimmed | Slicing steak, barbecue, grill, broil, excellent for marinating, may need tenderizing. | 3 to 4 | 6 per bag, 2 per box; packaging varies with processor |
| 185B Ball tip | Trimmed, may need trimming of collagen bands | Slicing steak, grill, broil. | 2 to 3 | 6 per bag, 3 per box |
| 185D Tri tip | Defatted, trimmed | Slicing steak, barbecue, grill, broil, excellent for marinating, may need tenderizing, carne asada. | 2 to 3 | 6 per bag, 3 per box |

*(continues)*

TABLE 4-2  NAMP HRI CUTS CHART FOR BEEF LOIN (Continued)

| ITEM AND NAMP NUMBER | DESCRIPTION OR FABRICATION | SUGGESTED COOKING METHOD, OR APPLICATION | AVERAGE SUGGESTED WEIGHT IN POUNDS | TYPICAL PACKAGE SPECS |
|---|---|---|---|---|
| 189 Tenderloin, full | Untrimmed, poor yield | For roasting whole if fat is desired. | 8 to 10 | 8 per case |
| 189A Tenderloin, peeled, side muscle on (PSMO) | Most typical purchase; requires trimming | Roasting whole, grill, broil, sauté, filet mignon, medallions, tournedos, served raw as carpaccio, steak tartare, brochette, kebab; trim can be dry cooked as well. | 4.5 to 6.5 | 12 per case |
| 190 Tenderloin, side muscle off | Requires some trimming | See above. | 4 to 5 | 12 per case |
| 190A Tenderloin, skinned, denuded | Trimmed | See above. | 3 to 4 | 12-14 per case |
| 1190 A / B Tenderloin portion cuts | Trimmed, "B" considered *barrel* cut without any gaps | Grill, broil, sauté, filet mignon, medallions, tournedos. | Varies | Varies with processor |
| 191 Tenderloin butt | Thick side or head of tenderloin; sold with varying trim levels | Can be used for all tenderloin applications; also used for the classic roast chateaubriand. | 2 to 4 | 2 per bag, 18 per box; packaging varies with processor |
| 193 Flank steak | Trimmed | Grill, broil, London broil, slicing steak, stuff, and braise. | 1 to 3 | 6 per bag, 4 per box; packaging varies with processor |

### Beef Shortloin

The beef shortloin is purchased primarily for cutting steaks, specifically the "porterhouse" and "t-bone" steaks. Cutting these steaks requires the use of a saw, preferably a band saw. The shortloin can be dry aged for weeks. Being a combination of tenderloin and striploin, the shortloin is an expensive cut. Trim specs are important when ordering.

### Beef Top Sirloin Butt

The top sirloin is a fairly tender steak or roast cut and is widely used in the foodservice industry. It is a flexible cut that can be used as a roast, a large slicing steak, or a small portion cut; cubed for skewers such as brochette, churasco, or kebob; or cut thin for quick grilling such as cheesesteak or satay. It is sold whole or sectioned.

### Beef Sirloin Tri-Tip and Flap

Both of these cuts are good for marinating and grilling whole and then creating sliced steak or London broil. They have an obvious grain and should always be cut across the fibers to ensure tenderness. Both marinate well and should be tenderized in some way. The tritip has a little higher quality and is better known.

### Beef Flank

Primarily a steak cut often used for marinated London broil, quick-grilling steaks, or stir fry or fajita. It should be cut across the grain and on a bias to insure tenderness. The flank can be butterflied and opened for stuffing.

## RIB

It is the smallest of all the primals, averaging only 30 to 40 lbs. The rib has one main section, the rib eye. Other than the rib eye, there are a few short ribs and a small cap of blade meat. The rib of beef is known for popular steak cuts such as the Delmonico and the cowboy steak. It is best known for the roast fabricated from the eye. The terms "standing rib" and "prime rib roast" are commonly seen on buffet menus, and the roast has been a customer favorite for many years. Even a lower-quality grade of rib eye can present fairly well due to the fact that the eye muscle has sections, and layers of fat form between them infusing the cut with extra flavor. Some chefs today are separating the rib eye into its individual layers. The top layer, sometimes known as the inner "deckle," is normally highly marbleized and considered one of the most flavorful cuts on the entire carcass.

### Subprimal Cuts

- Rib eye (Bone-in or boneless)
- Short ribs
- Blade meat

### Rib Eye

The rib eye is sold bone in or out and in a number of trim levels. Be sure to write very specific descriptions when giving your purveyor specs on this item. There is always a large section of intermuscular fat that is lodged in the eye muscle. There are two types of rib eye that are most typically sold commercially, the export style or bone-in rib eye and the boneless rib eye, both of which are sold with a two-inch fat lip left on. Both are good for steaks and roasts.

Using a band saw to cut porterhouse steaks or possibly marrow bones

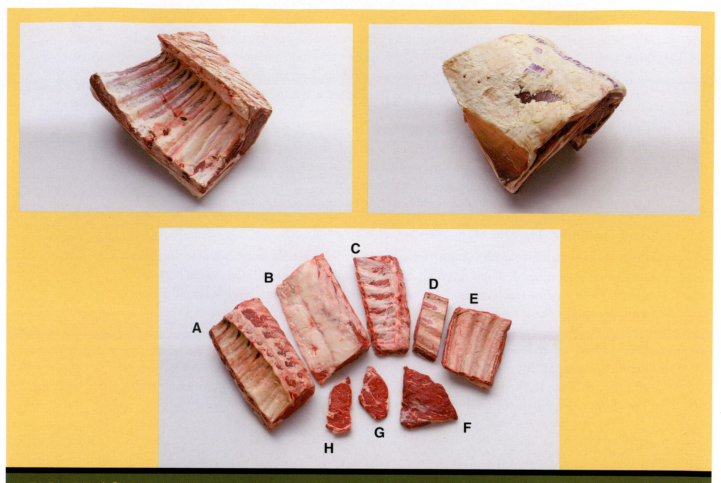

FIGURE 4.9 Beef rib breakdown: a. beef export rib; b. boneless rib eye lip on; c. beef back ribs; d. beef short ribs Korean-style short cut; e. beef short ribs; f. beef rib cap; g. beef rib steak boneless; and h. beef rib steak, boneless.

| TABLE 4-3  NAMP HRI CUTS FOR BEEF RIB | | | | |
|---|---|---|---|---|
| ITEM AND NAMP NUMBER | DESCRIPTION OR FABRICATION | SUGGESTED COOKING METHOD, OR APPLICATION | AVERAGE SUGGESTED WEIGHT IN POUNDS | TYPICAL PACKAGE SPECS |
| 103 Rib | Full primal | Multiple uses, purchased to dry age "tomahawk chop" portion cut. | 35 to 40 | Sold as individual item |
| 109 Rib, roast-ready | Large rib bone-in item with feather bones and thick cap fat included; poor yield | For roasting only; standing rib roast, prime rib. | 18 to 26 | 3 per case |

*(continues)*

| ITEM AND NAMP NUMBER | DESCRIPTION OR FABRICATION | SUGGESTED COOKING METHOD, OR APPLICATION | AVERAGE SUGGESTED WEIGHT IN POUNDS | TYPICAL PACKAGE SPECS |
|---|---|---|---|---|
| 109D Export style 109E | Rib bones in, fat cover off, short-cut, two-inch lip included | Standing rib roast, prime rib, bone-in rib eye steak, cowboy steak, frenched bones. | 16 to 20 | 4 per case |
| 1103 Rib steak portion cut, bone in | Trimmed | Bone-in rib eye steak, cowboy steak. | Customer specified | Varies |
| 112A Rib eye, lip on | Boneless, no cap, two-inch lip of fat included | Boneless rib roast, prime rib, boneless rib steak, Delmonico steak. | 11 to 14 | 6 per case |
| 112 Rib eye roll | Boneless, well trimmed | Well-trimmed boneless rib roast, boneless rib steak, Delmonico steak. | 8 to 10 | 6–8 per case |
| 1112 / 1112A Rib steak, portion cut, boneless | Trimmed, "A" has lip of fat on | Boneless rib steak, Delmonico steak. | Customer specified | Varies |
| 1103 Rib steak, portion cut, bone in | Has curved rib bone in | Bone-in rib steak, cowboy steak if frenched. | Customer specified | Varies |
| 123B Short ribs | Three bone sections, can be cut into Korean or flanken style | Braising, slow roasting, barbecue style. | 3 to 4 | 4 per bag, 4 bags per case |
| 124 Beef back ribs | Not as meaty as short ribs | Braising, slow roasting, barbecue. | As specified | |

**TABLE 4-3** NAMP HRI CUTS FOR BEEF RIB (Continued)

### Short Ribs

Beef short ribs are perfect for slow cooking such as a braise or barbeque. They are sold whole in about 10-inch long three- or four-rib sections or blocked into smaller portion cuts.

## CHUCK

The beef chuck contains muscles that experience more movement and range of motion than any of the other primal cuts. The result is some cuts being very tough and many cuts containing multiple muscle groups with connective tissues. These cuts have great flavor and are excellent for braising, stews, and grind. For years, the chuck was simply cut across all the muscle groups on the band saw, creating the "chuck steak." Today we see the chuck also being separated into individual muscle cuts. This has allowed for the discovery of some tender, deep-shoulder muscles that can be dry cooked and are excellent as steak items. The bone structure of the chuck is the most complex and requires a high skill level to fabricate it. The bones themselves, especially those from the neck, make a superior stock. They contain a lot of connective tissue and usually a fair amount of meat.

### Subprimal Cuts

- Shoulder clod (includes the top blade, teres major, and heart of the clod)
- Chuck roll (includes the chuck eye roll, and under blade)
- Chuck tender
- Short ribs

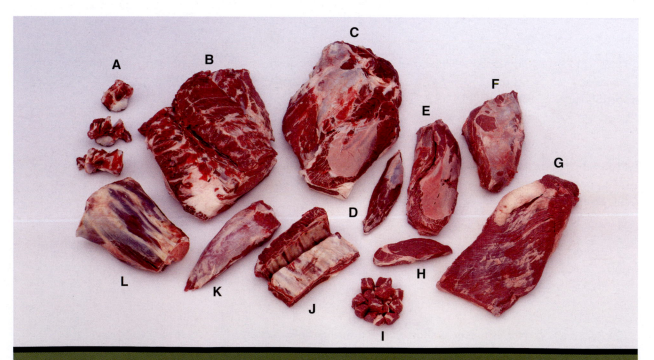

FIGURE 4.10 a. Beef neck bones; b. beef chuck roll; c. beef shoulder clod; d. beef teres major/shoulder tender; e. beef top blade; f. trimmed beef shoulder clod heart; g. beef brisket; h. beef shoulder London broil; i. beef chuck stew; j. beef short ribs/Korean or flanken style; k. beef scotch tender; and l. beef foreshank.

| | | TABLE 4-4 NAMP HRI CUTS FOR BEEF CHUCK | | |
|---|---|---|---|---|
| ITEM AND NAMP NUMBER | DESCRIPTION OR FABRICATION | SUGGESTED COOKING METHOD OR APPLICATION | AVERAGE SUGGESTED WEIGHT IN POUNDS | TYPICAL PACKAGE SPECS |
| 113 Chuck | Square-cut (primal) | Chuck cuts are flavorful but tend to be tougher; excellent for stewing, goulash, grinding, large braises, barbecue, slow roasting. | 79 to 106 | 1 per case |
| 114 Shoulder clod | Large, untrimmed, requires some fabrication | Braising, pot roast, stew, slow cooking, grind; can be dry cooked if trimmed correctly. | 15 to 21 | 3 per case |
| 114C Shoulder clod, trimmed | Large trimmed, requires some fabrication | Braising, pot roast, stew, slow cooking; can be dry cooked if trimmed correctly. | 13 to 18 | 3 per case |
| 114D Top Blade / flatiron | Defatted, silverskin and connective tissues on | Braising roast or steak; dry cook as flatiron steak if trimmed. | 5 to 6 | 1 per bag, 10 per case |
| 114E Shoulder roast / heart of clod | Trimmed center section of clod | Braising roast; dry cook as "shoulder London broil" if well trimmed. | 8 to 10 | 6 per case |
| Teres major, and shoulder tender | Small and very tender | Grill, broil, cut as medallions. | 1 to 2 | 6 per bag, 8 bag per case |
| 116A Chuck roll | Trimmed and tied | Slow roast, grill, barbeque, braise. | 15 to 21 | 3 per case |
| 116D Chuck eye roll | Center-cut portion cut of chuck roll, very flavorful | Slow roast, grill, barbeque, braise, chuck eye steak. | 5 to 7 | |
| 116B Chuck tender | Small, tough | Braise, stew, goulash, ragout, grind. | 2 to 3 | |

### Beef Shoulder Clod, Shoulder Tender, and Top Blade

Beef shoulder clod can be used as braising roasts or portion cut into steaks. The clod contains four basic sections: the top blade (also known as the flat iron), the heart of the clod, the shoulder tender (teres major), and a no-name trim section. Due to its current popularity, the shoulder tender is often removed from the clod and sold separately. The top blade is often split lengthwise to create the flat iron grilling steak. The heart of the clod can be cut for an inexpensive "London broil"–type steak.

### Beef Chuck Roll

The beef chuck roll is a large section containing many muscle pieces. It would be very time-consuming and unprofitable to isolate every single muscle. Some divisions can be done easily and can create some interesting, very flavorful dishes. The middle of the chuck roll contains the "chuck eye roll," which is an extension of the rib eye. While not as tender, the chuck eye roll offers a flavorful roast. The other main section is known as the "chuck flat," which is tougher but is excellent for stewing and braising. Its meat is similar to short ribs.

## PLATE, BRISKET, AND FORESHANK

These cuts in their rough form, as cut from the whole carcass, contain a lot of bone and waste fat. Being lower on the carcass, they tend to be tougher but very flavorful. The brisket is well-known for multiple uses. It is a mainstay of beef barbeque, being smoke roasted for hours. Brisket is also typically used for corned beef and pastrami, being cured and seasoned. It is a favorite as pot roast as well.

The plate contains short ribs and the skirt steak. The skirt is well known as the original "fajita" and is actually the diaphragm of the animal. The two sides of the diaphragm are connected in the middle of the carcass at the "hanger." The hanger is considered a high-flavor, quality steak known as the "Anglaise" in French cooking.

The foreshank contains some of the toughest muscles on the carcass. It is primarily used for grind and can make a quality broth or stock.

### Foodservice Cuts

- Plate
  - Short ribs
  - Skirt steak
  - Hanger steak
- Brisket
  - Fresh, cured
  - Whole or split

### Beef Skirt and Hanger Steaks

Both skirts and hangers are good for marinating and grilling. They have tough exterior membranes that must be removed, which can be done relatively easily in house. Both cuts can be purchased pretrimmed and portion cut also.

## BEEF OFFALS

Beef offals are generally reasonably priced and can offer some unique flavors and textures. Braised oxtail creates a rich full flavor; the cheeks also are presented as a

| TABLE 4-5 NAMP HRI CUTS FOR BEEF PLATE, BRISKET, AND FORESHANK | | | | |
|---|---|---|---|---|
| ITEM AND NAMP NUMBER | DESCRIPTION OR FABRICATION | SUGGESTED COOKING METHOD, OR APPLICATION | AVERAGE SUGGESTED WEIGHT IN POUNDS | TYPICAL PACKAGE SPECS |
| 120 Brisket 120 A / B (also purchased as corned beef if cured) | Boneless, deckle off; flat section (leaner), point section (fatty) | Braise, barbecue, slow cooking, can be purchased as corned beef and simmered. | 10 to 12 | 6 per case |
| 121c Plate, skirt steak (diaphragm), outside | Higher quality than inside skirt, needs to be peeled and defatted | Grill, broil, fajita, fan sear, cut across grain. | 2 to 3 | 4 per pack, 12 packs per case (packaging varies |
| 121d Plate, skirt steak, inside | Lesser quality, requires fabrication | Grill, broil, pan sear (may require tenderization before cooking), cut across grain. | 3 to 4 | 4 per pack |
| Hanger steak | Also known as the *steak Anglaise*. Requires peeling and removal of large collagen band | Very flavorful steak; grill, broil, sauté; may require marinade or tenderizing. | | 2 per bag, 6 per case |

very flavorful braise; the tripe is used in many classic dishes and needs a long cooking time. Beef tongue is often cured and smoked, which gives it a ham-like flavor.

- Beef liver
- Tripe
- Oxtail
- Tongue
- Cheeks

# VEAL

## VEAL CARCASS BREAKDOWN

The veal carcass is broken down differently than that of beef. A beef carcass is split immediately after slaughter, whereas the veal carcass is not. Veal is divided into hind and fore "saddles" traditionally between the 11th and 12th rib bones. The hind and fore saddles are divided further into the primal cuts. The primals can be purchased unsplit or untrimmed, but in most cases restaurants are not purchasing these primals in this unprocessed form. Cuts are normally split and trimmed into typical HRI or portion cuts.

Beyond the major primals, there are two minor primals or "market forms" that are not included in the major primal cuts.

### Primals

- Legs
- Loin
- Hotel rack
- Square cut chuck or shoulder

### Market Forms

- Breast
- Foreshank

Veal cuts fabricated from these primals are offered according to the NAMP Buyer's Guide using the number system aforementioned in this book. Many veal processors go outside the NAMP guidelines and customize cuts. Processors have created their own product code numbers and will sometimes custom fabricate cuts for large customers.

## LEGS

Veal legs could be purchased in pairs, but this is unlikely in today's market. The leg can be purchased whole and then fabricated in the restaurant. This requires a fair

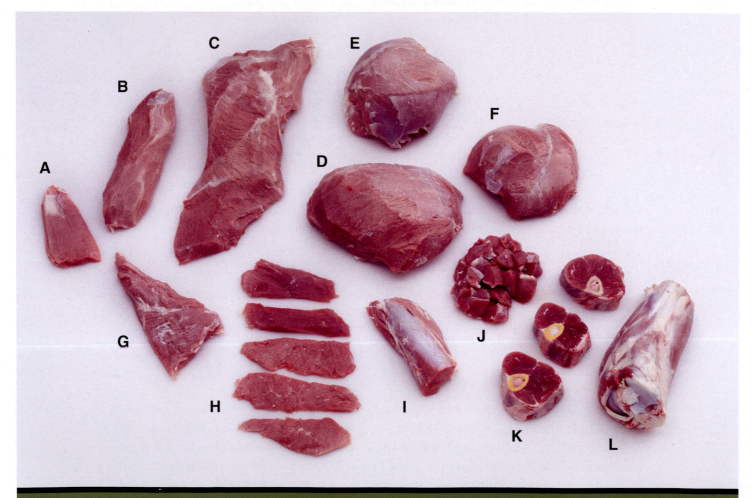

FIGURE **4.11** a. Veal flank; b. veal eye round; c. veal bottom round; d. veal top round cap off; e. veal knuckle, f. veal sirloin; g. veal tri-tip, h. veal portion cut leg cutlets; I. veal tenderloin butt; j. veal leg stew; k. veal osso buco; and l. veal hind shank.

amount of skill and time. Once boned, the leg is divided into subprimals. Each subprimal can then be trimmed completely and is typically cut for cutlets. Subprimals vary in tenderness, and it may be difficult for a restaurant to utilize all of the subprimals equally; therefore, it is common to buy each subprimal individually. Subprimals are often portion cut into exacting ounce portions, and many restaurants choose to purchase veal cutlets prefabricated. Some catering services use the leg as a "steamship" roast similar to that of beef. This impressive presentation requires the leg to be roasted whole and carved on a buffet line.

A whole leg of veal will also yield a fair amount of usable trim that can be used for grinding, stewing, or fortifying a stock. There is also a shank that is best known as a portion cut called osso buco. The entire veal leg will yield only three or four portions of osso buco. The bones from the veal leg are a good quality for stock.

### Subprimals or HRI Cuts

- Hind shank
- Top/inside round
- Bottom/outside round
- Eye round
- Heel

- Knuckle
- Sirloin or rump
- Tenderloin butt
- Flank

## Leg of Veal

- Top Round/(Inside)
  *Best for Cutlets*

- Knuckle—*Cutlets/Stew*

- Bottom Round (Outside)—
  *Cutlets, Roast, Braise*

- Eye Round—*Cutlets, Roast*

- Heel—*Stew, Braise, Grind*

- Sirloin/Tenderloin—
  *Cutlets, Medallion, Escalope*

- Hind shank—*Osso Buco,
  Braise*

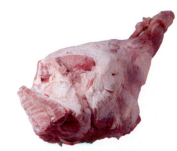

Top Round

Trim Bottom Round,
(Outside)

Trim Knuckle
(Sirloin Tip)

Hind Shank,
Center Cut

Trim Sirloin Butt (Hip)

FIGURE **4.12** Veal leg breakdown.

| TABLE 4-6 VEAL LEG HRI CUTS | | | | |
|---|---|---|---|---|
| **ITEM AND NAMP NUMBER** | **DESCRIPTION OR FABRICATION** | **SUGGESTED COOKING METHOD, OR APPLICATION** | **AVERAGE SUGGESTED WEIGHT IN POUNDS** | **TYPICAL PACKAGE SPECS** |
| 334 Veal leg primal/split | Whole primal leg; requires major fabrication and a high skill level; shank is typically cut off and packaged separately | Cutlets, roasts, usable trim for grind or stew, bones for stock. | 45 to 50 | 1 per box |
| Veal leg/ steamship | Shank bone exposed and cut as handle, pelvic bone removed, trimmed | Roast whole. | 30 to 35 | 1 per box |
| Veal leg TBS (top, bottom, sirloin) | Sectioned leg trimmed and divided into subprimals | Cutlets, roast. | 18 to 20 | 3 different sections per box |
| 349 Top round | Whole sub primal; requires fabrication; cap muscle removal | Large high-quality cutlets, cap for usable trim, emincé. | 7 to 9 | 3 per box |
| 349a Top round, cap off | Trimmed, ready to cut for cutlets | Large high-quality cutlets, sauté. | 6 to 8 | 3 per box |
| 1349a Top round cutlets | Ready to cook, large high-quality cutlets | Sauté. | 4 to 6 ounce cutlets | Varies |
| 350 Bottom round (gooseneck) | Sold as the entire gooseneck with bottom round flat, eye round, and heel; requires some sectioning | Lesser-quality cutlets, roast, braise. | 8 to 10 | 3 per box |
| Eye round | Trimmed and ready to roast or cut into cutlets | Roast whole, cutlets, medallions. | 2 | 2 per bag, 6 per box |

*(continues)*

| ITEM AND NAMP NUMBER | DESCRIPTION OR FABRICATION | SUGGESTED COOKING METHOD, OR APPLICATION | AVERAGE SUGGESTED WEIGHT IN POUNDS | TYPICAL PACKAGE SPECS |
|---|---|---|---|---|
| 351 Knuckle | Requires some fabrication; separate through natural seams | Cutlets, some trim for usable trim. | 3 to 4 each | 3 per box |
| 352 Sirloin hip (top sirloin butt) | Trim for cutlets | High-quality cutlets, medallions, sauté. | 4 to 5 lbs each | 3 per box |
| Flank steak (no NAMP number) | Minor trim required | Grilling, slice across grain; marinating. | 0.5 | Varies |
| 337 Hindshank | Sold whole or blocked | Braising whole or cut for osso buco. | 3 to 4 | 2 per bag, 6 bags per case |
| 1337 Hindshank, osso buco, portion cut | Ready to cook | Braised. | 2-inch typical; thickness specified by customer | 6 per bag, 4 bags per case |
| 1336 Veal leg cutlets | Ready to cook; full muscle cuts; not knitted together | Sauté. | 2- to 6-ounce portions, specified by customer | Varies; typically 12 per bag |
| 1302 Veal slices | Ready to cook; tougher sections mechanically tenderized; some fat or connectives may be present | Sauté. | 2 to 6 ounces | Varies |

TABLE 4-6 VEAL LEG HRI CUTS (Continued)

Seaming a veal top round and showing different grains

### Veal Leg Top Round

The top round is sold in two basic forms, cap on or off. The cap is easily removed, and fabrication is not difficult. The cap off has a better yield but tends to be more expensive. Many chefs prefer the top round because it is basically one large muscle without collagen bands. This popularity drives the price up.

### Veal Shank

The most common form of veal shank is portioned as osso buco. There are only three or four portions per shank, so the price remains high. They can be ordered in a variety of thicknesses. The "volcano" cut is a shank cut with the end frenched off.

### Veal Bottom and Eye Round, Knuckle

These cuts are tougher than the top round but can make good-quality cutlets if cut thinly and across the grain. They can also be roasted or even braised with good results. Some processors and kitchens will tenderize these cuts with a Jaccard or pinning system.

## LOIN

The loin or "saddle" consists of the longissimus and psoas major muscles (striploin and tenderloin, respectively). It has the distinctive t-bone structure, and the cuts from it are very tender and flavorful. It can be sold as an entire saddle, which is unsplit and connected at the spine. This purchase would require a band saw, so it is not typical for most restaurants. More typically, it is sold as a trimmed and split loin, or otherwise known as a "shortloin." Even this item presents problems for a restaurant that cannot cut their own portions because of the fact that there is no band saw. It is common to purchase the loin precut as chops. It can also be purchased as a boneless striploin with a variety of trim levels available.

### Subprimal/HRI Cuts

- Full loin/saddle unsplit
- Trimmed loin/split (shortloin)
- Striploin (bone in loin)
- Striploin boneless (boneless loin)
- Tenderloin

### Veal Shortloin or Loin Chops

The shortloin is purchased primarily for cutting into chops. The chops are divided into three categories, porterhouse, t-bone, and simply bone-in chops. The porterhouse chop will have a larger tenderloin section. All of these chops are high quality and can be grilled, broiled, or pan seared with great success.

### Veal Boneless Strip Loin

The veal striploin is often purchased trimmed and can be used for cutlets, medallions, or roasted whole. It is uniform in shape, making it a quality plate presentation, but can dry out if overcooked.

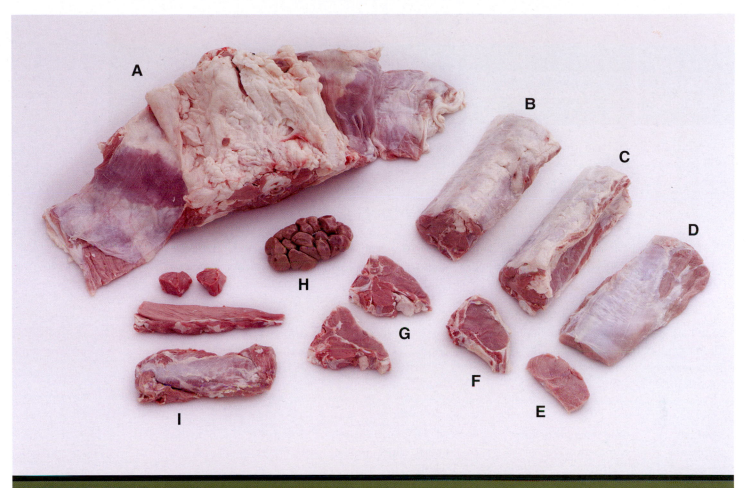

FIGURE **4.13** a. Veal loin primal or saddle; b. veal loin trimmed; c. veal loin trimmed, block ready; d. boneless veal loin trimmed to silver; e. veal loin medallion; f. veal loin chop rib end; g. veal porterhouse chops; h. veal kidney; and i. veal tenderloin and medallions.

### Veal Tenderloin

The veal tenderloin is sold as either the tenderloin butt or a full tenderloin. It can be cut into medallions or roasted whole. The veal tenderloin is extremely tender, and its medallions are often pan seared, almost like a scallop.

### VEAL HOTEL RACK

The veal hotel rack is often considered the finest cut for chops or roasting. It has a distinctive bone structure that adds to the look of the plate. Often "frenched" or trimmed, exposing the ends of the rib bones guarantees attention to the center of the plate. In its primal form it is also unsplit, attached at the spine. The rack, also known as the "rib of veal," is most often sold in a variety of trim levels, enabling the purchaser to consider which is most logical and/or profitable. Although often expensive to purchase, this cut can command a high price on menus. Traditionally the rack contains seven ribs but can be purchased as a six-rib rack. A few producers have defied traditional cutting and are now selling eight- and even nine-rib racks.

| TABLE 4-7 VEAL LOIN HRI CUTS | | | | |
|---|---|---|---|---|
| ITEM AND NAMP NUMBER | DESCRIPTION OR FABRICATION | SUGGESTED COOKING METHOD, OR APPLICATION | AVERAGE SUGGESTED WEIGHT IN POUNDS | TYPICAL PACKAGE SPECS |
| 331 Veal loin (full saddle) primal | Full loin unsplit; requires a band saw and trimming; may contain all of the kidney fat | High-quality, dry cook items. | 20 to 30 | 1 per box |
| 332 Loin trimmed/split (shortloin) | Trimmed to a 4″x4″ flank tail length; requires fabrication; band saw for chops | Roast whole, cut for chops. | 4 to 5 each; typically sold as pairs | 2 per box |
| 332a Loin trimmed/split/ block ready (shortloin) | Trimmed to 1x0 tail length; requires band saw to cut chops | Roast whole, cut for chops. | 3 to 4 each; typically sold as pairs | 4 per box |
| 344 Loin striploin/ boneless 1x1, 0x0, denuded | Sold partially or fully trimmed | Medallions, boneless chops, cutlets, roast whole. | 2 to 3 | 6 per box |
| 346/347 Tenderloin | Sold as butt end or whole 9 (peeled, side muscle on, or PSMO); may require trimming and silverskin removal | Medallions, roast whole. | 1 to 3 pounds each (varies) | 2 per bag, 6 bags per box; Can also be sold individually packaged |

## Subprimals or HRI Cuts

- Veal hotel rack, unsplit
- Veal hotel rack, split and chined
- Veal hotel rack, chop or roast ready
- Veal rack frenched
- Boneless veal rib eye

## Veal Rack

The rack is one of the most popular cuts of veal, and it continues to maintain a higher price than most other cuts. The chops, often frenched, present well and are tender if not overcooked. It can also be roasted similar to a beef rib roast. When purchasing, be

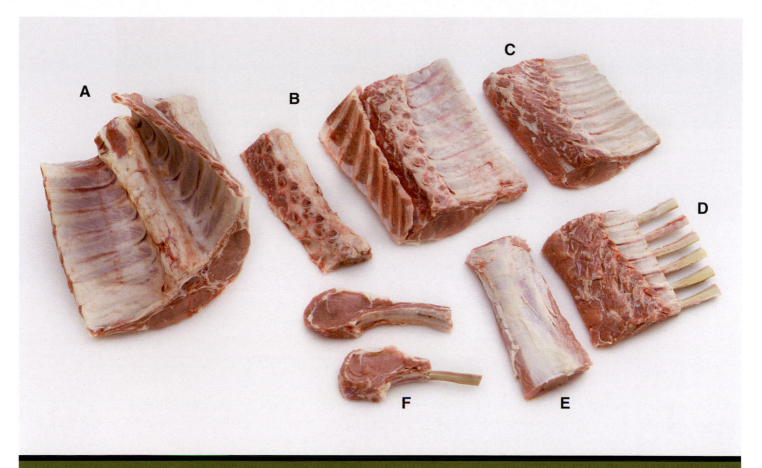

FIGURE **4.14** a. Veal hotel rack; b. veal hotel rack split and chined, with chine bone; c. veal rack chop ready; d. veal rack frenched; e. boneless veal rib eye; and f. veal rack chops.

sure to pay attention to the length of the bones; the rack is often sold in varying bone lengths, changing the value.

## VEAL SQUARE CUT SHOULDER

The veal shoulder, otherwise known as the chuck, is composed of a multitude of muscles that are all relatively active and therefore tend to be tougher but flavorful. The shoulder has a complicated bone structure; therefore, it is typically purchased boneless. Bone in cuts are still fabricated but are difficult to present as a portion. The cuts from the shoulder tend to be less expensive than other cuts and become affordable for a larger scope of foodservice operations. Traditionally the cuts from the shoulder require a slow-cook method such as braise, stew, or slow roasting.

As in beef, these complicated muscles can be separated and all of the connective tissues removed for use as dry cook items. The veal industry is currently contemplating separating the shoulder into untraditional cuts to realize more value and give chefs more dry cook options. As previously stated, the veal shoulder is purchased boneless but the neck bones, which can be purchased separately, are prized for their flavor when used in stocks.

| TABLE 4-8 VEAL HOTEL RACK HRI CUTS | | | | |
|---|---|---|---|---|
| **ITEM AND NAMP NUMBER** | **DESCRIPTION OR FABRICATION** | **SUGGESTED COOKING METHOD, OR APPLICATION** | **AVERAGE SUGGESTED WEIGHT IN POUNDS** | **TYPICAL PACKAGE SPECS** |
| 306 Veal hotel rack, split and chined, 6 or 7 ribs (some producers are now fabricating 8-rib racks) | Sold whole or split and chined; requires trimming and some bone removal, frenching the bone ends for presentation | Roasted whole, grill, broil, pan sear as chops. | 6 to 7 pounds single; 12 to 14 pounds pair | 6 per box |
| 306b Veal rack, chop or roast ready (sold as 6- or 7-rib rack) | Sold split and well trimmed, 4"×4" trim level; may require some minor fabrication, frenching the bone ends for presentation | Roasted whole, grill, broil, pan sear as chops. | 7-rib rack, 5-pound average; 6-rib rack, 4 to 5 pound average | 4 per case |
| 306c Veal Rack, frenched (6- or 7-rib rack) | Trimmed and frenched; may require cleaning of the frenched bones | Roast whole or chops. | 3 to 4 | 6 per case |
| 307 Veal rib eye | Boneless; sold with a variety of trim levels; tie as roast or cut into medallions or steaks | Roast whole, grill, broil, sauté, medallions, or steaks. | 2 to 3 | 6 per case |
| 1306b Veal rack chops | Chine off or cap off trimmed | Grill, broil, sauté. | 10 to 16 ounces, as specified | 12 per box; packaging can vary |
| 1306e Veal rack chops, Frenched | Cleaned, frenched | Grill, broil, sauté. | 10 to 14 oz as specified | 12 per box; packaging can vary |

## Subprimals or HRI Cuts

- Veal square cut shoulder (boneless)
- Veal shoulder clod (trimmed and untrimmed)
- Veal neck roast
- Veal chuck eye roll
- Veal chuck or scotch tender

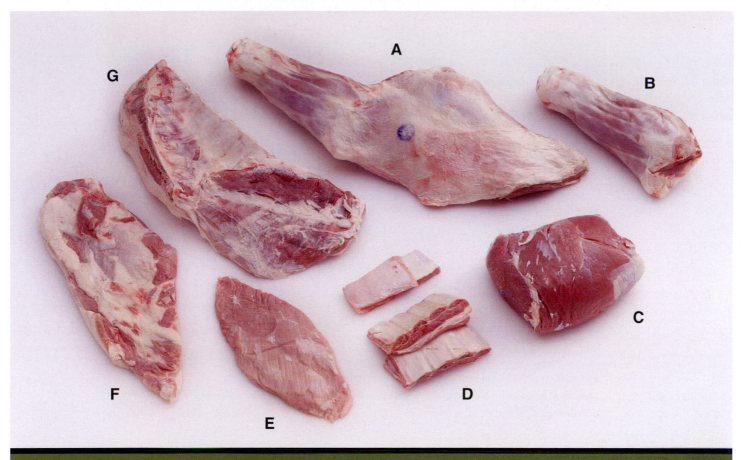

**FIGURE 4.15** a. Veal chuck outside arm; b. veal foreshank; c. veal shoulder clod trimmed; d. veal short ribs; e. veal brisket, trimmed; f. boneless veal breast; and g. bone-in veal breast.

## Veal Shoulder Clod

The shoulder is less expensive than many other cuts of veal. It is typically used for braising but can be roasted or possibly cut into an inexpensive cutlet. The cutlets will not be as tender as those from the leg or loin, but if tenderized they may work in a breaded form.

## Veal Breast and Veal Fore Shank

The veal breast represents the plate and brisket combined. It has thin layers of meat and fat on a rib bone structure. It is normally very reasonably priced and can have a remarkable profit margin. The breast can be opened and stuffed and roasted, braised, or poached. Some processors are now fabricating veal short ribs from the breast, which are sold as individual portion cuts. The breast can be boned, yielding a good-quality stew, usable trim for grinding, and quality bones for stock. Curing and smoking the boneless breast and serving it as "veal bacon," sliced and crisped like regular pork bacon, comprise an interesting alternative.

The veal foreshank is typically cut for portioned osso buco. The quality of the foreshank is not quite equal to the hindshank and therefore should be more reasonably priced. The foreshank has more connective tissues, and the bone structure has less

TABLE 4-9  VEAL SQUARE CUT SHOULDER HRI CUTS

| ITEM AND NAMP NUMBER | DESCRIPTION OR FABRICATION | SUGGESTED COOKING METHOD, OR APPLICATION | AVERAGE SUGGESTED WEIGHT IN POUNDS | TYPICAL PACKAGE SPECS |
|---|---|---|---|---|
| 309 Veal chuck, square cut | Whole primal cut, requires major fabrication and high skill level | Braise, grind, stew, slow roast. | 25 to 30 | 1 per box |
| 309b Veal chuck, square cut, boneless | Whole primal, boneless; contains many sections; requires a large amount of fabrication | Braise, grind, stew, slow roast. | 15 to 20 | 1 per box |
| 310 Outside shoulder | Large section includes clod, top blade, and chuck tender; requires trimming and fabrication | Braise, stew, slow roast. | 6 to 8 | 2 per box |
| 310 A or B shoulder clod | Includes the top blade and main section of the clod; sold untrimmed and trimmed, lean | Braise, stew, slow roast. | 5 to 6 | 3 per box |
| 310c Chuck tender | May need silverskin/collagen removed | Small braise, stew. | 1 to 3 | 12 per box |
| 311 Blade roast, neck off | Containing the chuck eye and flat underblade section; has some fat and may need trimming | Braise, stew, slow roast. | 12 to 14 | 2 per box |
| Veal neck meat (no NAMP number) | Some heavy connective tissues | Very flavorful braise; long, slow cooking. | 3 to 5 | 3 per box |

marrow; it also tends to fall apart when braised. It may make sense to tie the osso buco to maintain shape.

## VEAL OFFALS

Veal offals hold more value than most other species. Classic dishes such as sautéed "calves liver," poached sweetbreads, braised veal cheeks, and sautéed veal kidneys with cognac. The veal feet are used to make a stock that is very high in protein and can be clarified to make "aspic."

- Veal liver
- Veal sweetbread or thymus gland

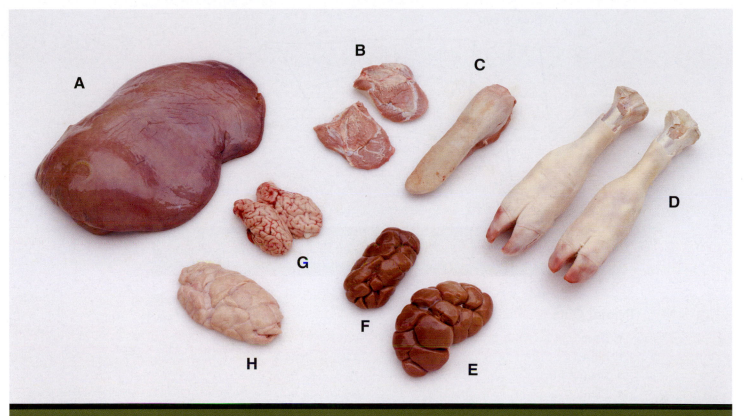

FIGURE **4.16** a. Veal liver; b. veal cheeks; c. veal tongue; d. calves feet; e. veal kidney; f. veal kidney; g. veal brains; and h. veal thymus or sweetbreads.

- Veal kidneys
- Veal cheeks
- Veal brains
- Veal feet

Preparing sweetbreads

## PORK

### PORK CARCASS BREAKDOWN

The whole market hog is split down the middle creating sides or halves. A typical half-hog weighs around 100 lbs and is about 5–6 feet long, making it a difficult but not entirely unmanageable for breakdown in a kitchen setting. The hog has an extremely high utilization rate, and all of it can be used in some way. Pork has a sort of dual personality in that it can be used as a fresh meat, like veal or beef, or it can be cured to make a multitude of hams, bacons, sausages, and literally hundreds of other products. A chef that wants to experiment in creating their own specialty cured meats can certainly utilize every portion of the hog.

As in other meats, pork can be purchased as pretrimmed fabricated cuts. A large variety of "specs" can be found for each specific pork cut. Pork producers develop trim levels and specific measurements for cuts depending on customers' needs and also profitability.

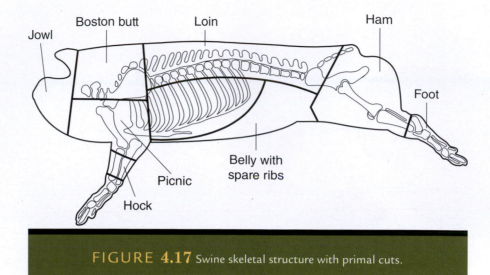

FIGURE 4.17 Swine skeletal structure with primal cuts.

## Primal Cuts

- Ham
- Loin
- Boston butt
- Picnic
- Belly with spare ribs

In this book, we will examine the pork cuts according to North American standards and cutting styles. Pork is fabricated differently in other sections of the world. Divisions of the carcass can vary depending on intended uses and cultural differences.

Traditionally most mammal meat carcasses have four primals, but due to the value of the belly section of pork, it too must be included as a primal.

## Market Forms

- Neck bones
- Hock
- Fatback
- Jowl

There are cuts that are not traditionally found attached to the primals. Certain sections are trimmed off and sold separately as market items.

## HAM

The pork ham or back leg is the largest muscle section of the hog. It contains the same basic muscle groups or subprimals as the round of beef, including the top round, bottom, eye, heel, knuckle, shank or hock, and a small section of the sirloin. It has four basic bones, the femur, the aitch, the kneecap, and a portion of the shank. The ham is sold skin on unless requested otherwise. It can be sold fresh or cured. Cured hams are sold in two basic forms, dry or brine cured.

Examples of dry-cured ham include "country-style" or "Smithfield" ham from Virginia, but other forms can be found throughout the southeastern United States.

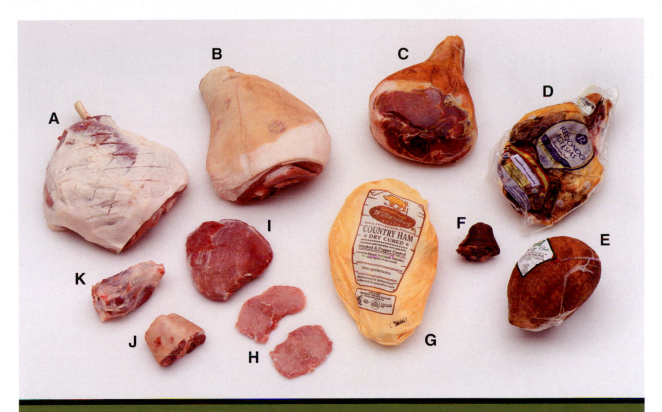

FIGURE 4.18 a. Fresh ham steamship; b. pork fresh ham; c. prosciutto ham; d. Serrano ham; e. smoked ham (ready to eat); f. smoked ham hock; g. smoked country ham/Smithfield ham; h. pork top round cutlets; i. pork inside ham/top round; j. fresh pork ham hock; and k. pork shank skinless.

Many are smoked or peppered and require soaking to release some of the heavy salt flavor before using. Other forms of dry-cured product include the Italian prosciutto-style ham. These hams require an exacting procedure of salting and storing for many months to create the delicate flavor of this specialty. The Spanish serrano ham is selected from specifically fed hogs and carefully salted and stored to create a fine and unique flavor. Other dry-cured hams include the French Jambon Bayonne, the heavily smoked German Bauernschinken, and the Chinese Yunnan Ham. Many dry-cured hams are sliced very thin and served as an appetizer or included as an ingredient in other dishes.

Wet or brine-cured hams are manufactured by taking a raw ham and injecting it with a brine solution or soaking it in a salt brine. This type of ham is mild in flavor and is often smoked and precooked. Typically sold as "deli"-style ham, it includes boiled ham, "pit" hams, bone-in spiral-cut hams, ham steaks, and a huge variety of smoked hams.

The ham can be separated into subprimals and sold as smaller cuts. The hock is sold alone as a flavoring agent for soups and stews. The top round, otherwise known as an "inside ham," is sold as a separate subprimal and is excellent for cutlets.

| ITEM AND NAMP NUMBER | DESCRIPTION OR FABRICATION | SUGGESTED COOKING METHOD, OR APPLICATION | AVERAGE SUGGESTED WEIGHT IN POUNDS | TYPICAL PACKAGE SPECS |
|---|---|---|---|---|
| 401 Fresh ham (primal) | May be trimmed and semiboned, boned, rolled and tied, or sectioned into subprimals. The ham can be cured and smoked. | Roast whole, roast as smaller sections, cutlets hock section braised. | 20 to 25 | 3 per case |
| 401a Fresh ham/short shank | Same as above. Tougher hock section removed. | Roast whole, roast as smaller sections, cutlets. | 18 to 20 | 3 per case |
| 402 Fresh ham skinned | Skin removed for easier carving. Sold with specific fat trim. | Roast whole, cutlets. | 14 to 16 | 3 per case |
| Fresh ham, steamship | Skinned, shank bone exposed, pelvic bone removed, for easy carving. | Roast whole, carving item. | 12 to 14 | 3 per case |
| 402c Fresh ham, boneless | Sold rolled and tied, can be further fabricated and trimmed. | Roast whole, roast as smaller sections, cutlets. | 10 to 12 | 3 per case |
| 402e Outside ham | Bottom and eye round subprimals sold trimmed and defatted. | Small inexpensive roast. | 4 to 5 | 2 per bag, 4 bags per box |
| 402f Inside ham | Inside/top round sold trimmed and defatted, may need to peel cap muscle off top. | Very good for cutlets, thin julienne slices, small roasts | 4 to 5 | 2 per bag, 4 bags per box |
| 417a Fresh ham Stock | Short shank section of ham. | Flavor agent for soups, vegetables, braise as osso buco | 1 to 2 | Varies |
| Fresh pork shank | Full shank of pork, sold skinless. | Braised whole, cut in half for osso buco–style braise | 1.5 to 2.5 | Varies |

TABLE 4-10 NAMP HRI CUTS FOR FRESH HAMS

## LOIN

The pork loin consists of the entire back of the hog containing both a rib end and a loin end. In other species, the two would be separated into two parts such as a rack and a loin as in veal. The pork loin is typically dry cooked and is generally the highest value of the primals. When fabricated or boned, the loin yields a loin eye muscle, a tenderloin, and baby back ribs, all of which are high-value items. The loin is sold as a "primal" or as a "center-cut." The primal has a section of sirloin on one end and a section of blade or shoulder on the other end. The center cut has those removed and is more uniform in shape. Those end pieces can be purchased separately and are generally inexpensive. The loin can be purchased precut as chops. Chops can vary in size and quality, so be sure to specify exactly what chops are desired. Center-cut chops are any chop that is cut from the center-cut loin. "Loin" or "porterhouse" chops are cut from the loin end and would contain a piece of the tenderloin and a t-bone structure. "Rib" or "rack" chops would have the curved rib bone structure and can be frenched. Sirloin and blade chops are cut from the end pieces and tend to be considered lesser quality.

The baby back ribs have become extremely popular in foodservice, and there are a large variety of specs to choose from when ordering. They are often sold by the count of ribs in the rack as well as the length of the rib. They can be purchased precooked and flavored and with a large variety of marinades.

## PORK PRIMAL LOIN

The primal loin is less expensive than the center cut but requires extra fabrication and creates some trim that needs to be used for the purchase to be profitable.

Boning a center-cut pork loin

### Pork Chops

Loin chops can be divided into subcategories, loin or rib chops. Loin end chops resemble the porterhouse or t-bone, while the rib chop can be frenched off as in veal. There are many purchasing specifications for loin chops, and each processor's specs may vary.

Trimming a center-cut pork loin

### Baby Back Ribs

Back ribs are cut from the rib end of the loin. They are the most popular rib and maintain a higher price. Baby backs come in varying rib counts and lengths, so be sure to compare products. There is a membrane on the inside of the ribs that should be removed, and they can be purchased pre-peeled.

Tying a center-cut pork roast

## PORK BOSTON BUTT

The front of the hog is known as the pork shoulder. It can be purchased whole, and some restaurants will buy it that way to cook it whole, typically as "barbeque." Traditionally it is broken into the Boston butt and the picnic. The Boston butt is the top section of the shoulder and therefore is the most tender of the two. It is sold skin and fatback off and can be purchased either bone in or boneless. It contains a blade bone and requires a relatively simple boning technique. There is a center section that is also known as the "cellar" or "cottage" butt, and this item is where the pork loin eye extends into the shoulder.

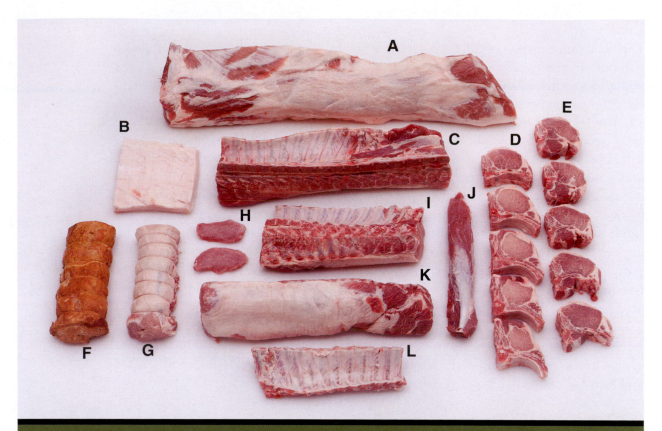

**FIGURE 4.19** a. Primal pork loin; b. pork fat back; c. center cut pork loin; d. rib end chops; e. pork loin chops; f. Canadian bacon; g. boneless loin roast; h. pork loin cutlets; i. pork rack; j. pork tenderloin; k. boneless center cut loin; and l. baby back ribs.

| | TABLE 4-11 HRI CUTS FOR PORK LOIN | | | |
|---|---|---|---|---|
| **ITEM AND NAMP NUMBER** | **DESCRIPTION OR FABRICATION** | **SUGGESTED COOKING METHOD, OR APPLICATION** | **AVERAGE SUGGESTED WEIGHT IN POUNDS** | **TYPICAL PACKAGE SPECS** |
| 410 Pork loin primal | Full primal cut, includes sirloin section and blade rib end section, some fat cover. Requires some fabrication, trimming. If boned, creates baby back ribs as a byproduct. | Roasting , chops, cutlets. | 18 to 22 | 2 per bag, 2 bags per box |
| 412 Pork loin, center cut, sold as 8–11 rib cut with varying trim levels | Center piece of loin without sirloin or blade ends, can be boned for roast or cutlets. | Roasting, center-cut chops (loin end and rib end chops). | 9 to 14 | 2 per bag, 2 per box |

*(continues)*

| TABLE 4-11 HRI CUTS FOR PORK LOIN (Continued) | | | | |
|---|---|---|---|---|
| ITEM AND NAMP NUMBER | DESCRIPTION OR FABRICATION | SUGGESTED COOKING METHOD, OR APPLICATION | AVERAGE SUGGESTED WEIGHT IN POUNDS | TYPICAL PACKAGE SPECS |
| 413/412 b/c Boneless pork loin, center cut boneless loin | Sold with varying trim levels, boneless, may be trimmed for cutlets, | Roast, cutlets, medallions, boneless chops. | 6 to 12 (Size varies with specs) | 1 per bag, 6 per box |
| 415 Pork tenderloin | Sold with side muscle on or off. May require membrane removal. Can be cut into medallions. | Medallions, pan-seared, roast, broiled whole. | 1 to 1.5 | 2 per bag, 6 per box |
| Pork rack / rib end loin | Contains 8–10 ribs (rib end only), chine bone removed, fat capped, trimmed. | Roast w/ frenched bones, chops, Cowboy chop. | 3 to 4 | 4 per box |
| 1410 Pork loin chops/ sold with varying specs | Full loin cut into chops; contains quality chops from center and some odd shaped chops from end pieces. | Grill, broil, pan-sear, sauté, breaded, stuffed. | Requested by purchaser | Varies |
| 1412 Pork loin center cut chops | Uniform center cut chops, can be sold bone in or boneless with varying trim levels. | Grill, broil, pan-sear, sauté, breaded, stuffed. | Requested by purchaser | Varies |
| Pork porterhouse | Contains a large piece of tenderloin with each t-bone-shaped chop, high quality. | Grill, broil, pan-sear, sauté, breaded, stuffed. | Requested by purchaser | Varies |
| Rib chops | Contains only rib cuts with curved rib bones. Can be frenched. | Frenched, chops, grill, broil, sauté, stuffed, breaded. | Requested by purchaser | Varies |

## TABLE 4-12 BOSTON BUTT HRI CUTS

| ITEM AND NAMP NUMBER | DESCRIPTION OR FABRICATION | SUGGESTED COOKING METHOD, OR APPLICATION | AVERAGE SUGGESTED WEIGHT IN POUNDS | TYPICAL PACKAGE SPECS |
|---|---|---|---|---|
| 406 Boston butt | Sold bone in, skinless; trim levels vary with processor's specs. Typically 75% lean, 25% fat. Super-trimmed versions available. | Slow roasting, barbecue, pulled pork, slow braising, stewing, grinding, forcemeats, sausage, kebab cubes | 6 to 8 | 2 per bag, 4 bags per box |
| 406a Boston butt, boneless | Boneless, with varying amounts of trim; sold rolled and tied also. | Slow roasting, barbecue, pulled pork, slow braising, stewing, grinding for sausage. | 5 to 7 | 2 per bag, 4 bags per box |

The Boston butt contains a fat ratio of about 70% lean to 30% fat depending on its trim spec. Much of the fat is internal, making the butt a moist and very flavorful roast, and it is typically used for slow-cooked barbeque and pulled pork. The fat-to-lean ratio also makes it a superior choice for sausage fabrication.

The "smoked pork butt" is also cured and smoked for a ham-like flavor. It is also cured and aged spiced to form the cappacola or coppa-style ham.

## PORK PICNIC

The picnic is the lower part of the shoulder. It is leaner than the Boston butt and is sold with the skin on. It is a lean cut and can be purchased boneless and skinless if required and can be sold as a boned, rolled, and tied (B.R.T.) roast. The price of the picnic tends to be very low, and therefore many pork processors will often use the picnic for lean to mix with fat when making sausage products. It can also be cured and smoked as a "picnic ham."

## BELLY AND SPARE RIBS

The belly is considered a commodity meat item, and prices of pork bellies are quoted daily in the *Wall Street Journal*. Traders will buy and sell futures of bellies on the Chicago Mercantile Market. Pork belly is used for a large variety of culinary applications. Number one on the list must be bacon. Smoked belly bacon, sliced and fried, has been a breakfast mainstay for many years. Bacon is used as an ingredient in many culinary favorites.

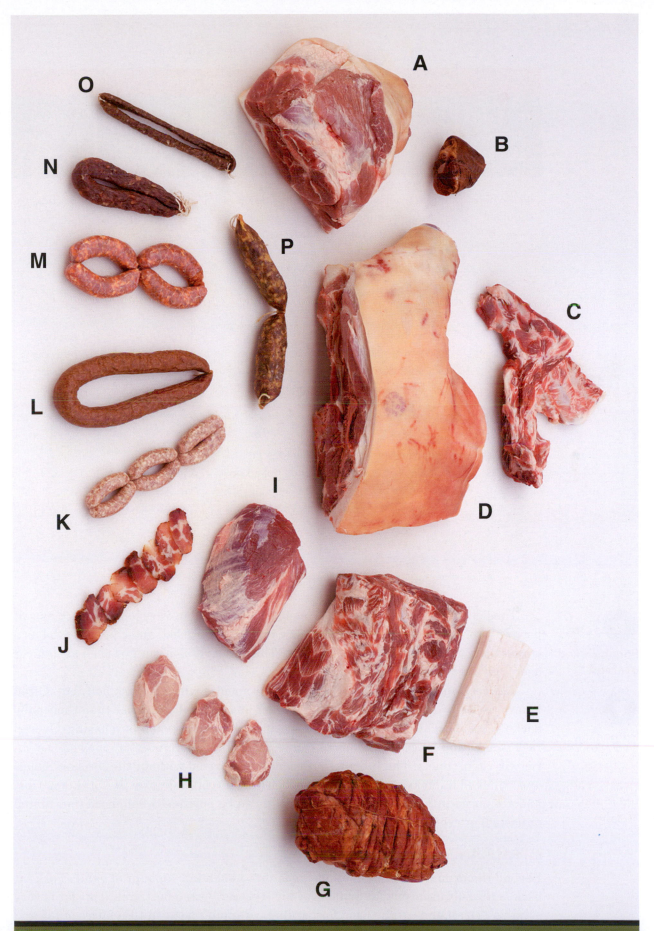

| TABLE 4-13 PORK PICNIC HRI CUTS | | | | |
|---|---|---|---|---|
| ITEM AND NAMP NUMBER | DESCRIPTION OR FABRICATION | SUGGESTED COOKING METHOD, OR APPLICATION | AVERAGE SUGGESTED WEIGHT IN POUNDS | TYPICAL PACKAGE SPECS |
| 403 Whole shoulder | Entire front section of hog; contains picnic and Boston butt; includes skin and heavy fat back and bones. | Used for slow-cooking barbecue, grinding for sausage, braising. | 16 to 20 | 2 per box |
| 405 Picnic | Leaner bottom section of the shoulder, sold skin on; can be boned for lean usable trim. | Slow roasting, barbeque, slow braising, stewing, grinding. | 8 to 10 | 2 per bag, 4 bags per box |
| 405a Picnic, boneless | Sold as whole, boneless section or as trimmed individual lean cushion meat. | Slow roasting, barbecue, pulled pork, slow braising, stewing, grinding. | 6 to 8; cushion is smaller, 2 to 3 pounds each | Varies |

Pork belly and pancetta

Portioning: beef tenderloin steaks, veal top round, and ribs

The belly can be purchased fresh, smoked, and cured in various ways such as salt pork or pancetta. Fresh belly is often slow roasted or braised, and can be served as a stand-alone main course or as a side dish. The cured versions can be used as a flavor agent, giving dishes a salty crispy boost.

The pork spare ribs are the rib cage that coincides with the pork belly cut. Often known as "belly" or "rack" ribs, they are wider and generally meatier than their baby back rib cousin. There are a variety of specifics to consider when purchasing. Overall rack weight and length of the bones can be requested, and processors may offer a variety of rib products. The full spare rib can be purchased without the "brisket" bones and trimmed to make a more uniform rib. These are often known as "St. Louis ribs" and are normally slightly higher priced. Ribs can be purchased enhanced (marinated or basted) or even precooked.

## OFFALS AND MARKET ITEMS

Beyond the primals, there are other items that hold a fair amount of value. Pork fat back is the subcutaneous fat found over the loin and Boston butt area. This fat is very solid and clean and can be used for barding, wrapping meat in thin slices of fat and larding, threading fat through meat. The "leaf lard" is the lumbar fat found on the

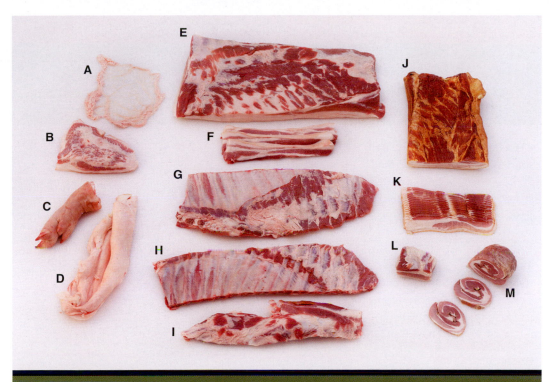

FIGURE **4.21** a. Caul fat; b. fresh jowl; c. pig's foot; d. leaf lard; e. fresh pork belly; f. fresh belly slices; g. spare ribs; h. St. Louis–style ribs; i. pork brisket bones; j. slab bacon; k. sliced bacon; l. salt pork; and m. pancetta.

| ITEM AND NAMP NUMBER | DESCRIPTION OR FABRICATION | SUGGESTED COOKING METHOD, OR APPLICATION | AVERAGE SUGGESTED WEIGHT IN POUNDS | TYPICAL PACKAGE SPECS |
|---|---|---|---|---|
| 422 Baby back ribs | Contains at least 8 ribs; result of boning the pork loin; may need to be peeled; sold with varying bone lengths. | Slow cooked as barbecue racks; sectioned and coated and cooked individually; can be steamed first to tenderize. | 1.5 to 2 | 2 per bag, 6 per box; packaging varies with company |
| 416 Pork Spareribs | 11–13 ribs from belly region; may need breast bone removed or notched. | Slow-cooked barbecue; can be steamed or simmered to tenderize. | 3 to 5 | 2 to 3 per bag, 3 per box; packaging can vary with processor |

TABLE 4-14 title: **TABLE 4-14  PORK BELLY AND SPARE RIBS HRI CUTS**

*(continues)*

TABLE 4-14  PORK BELLY AND SPARE RIBS HRI CUTS (Continued)

| ITEM AND NAMP NUMBER | DESCRIPTION OR FABRICATION | SUGGESTED COOKING METHOD, OR APPLICATION | AVERAGE SUGGESTED WEIGHT IN POUNDS | TYPICAL PACKAGE SPECS |
|---|---|---|---|---|
| 416a Pork spare ribs, St. Louis style/Chinese style | Trimmed belly ribs; blocked and trimmed for consistent shape and size. | Slow-cooked barbecue; can be steamed or simmered to tenderize. | 2 to 4 | 3 per bag, 4 per box; packaging can vary |
| 423 Country-style ribs | Butterflied; 3–4-rib end piece of loin; very meaty; chine bone must be cut, can be pounded flat. | Grill, slow-cooked barbecue. | 2 to 4 | 2 per bag |
| 408 Pork belly | Large, rectangular, flat side of the hog; traditionally sold with skin on but can be purchased trimmed and skin off. Thickness can be specified. | Typically cured for bacon; can be slow roasted or braised as a fresh belly; very flavorful. | 12 to 18 | 1 per bag; 60 pound box |
| 416b Brisket bones 412 Neck bones | Inexpensive sections removed when creating St. Louis–style ribs or pork shoulder; lots of bone; sold cured and smoked. | Slow cooked; flavor agent for soups; greens; inexpensive riblets. | Varies | Varies |
| 420 Pigs feet | Sold in varying lengths; front and back available. | Flavor agent; can be hollow boned and stuffed as Zampone. | Bulk packaged | |

inside of the carcass and is used for shortening in baking recipes. The pork neck bones are sold fresh and smoked and used as a flavor agent.

Offals include the liver, intestines, caul fat, and kidneys. A classic use for pork liver is the French paté provençal or a country-style paté. Caul fat is used to wrap and bard other meat items. The intestines are used for sausage casings or could be sold as chitterlings.

## LAMB

### LAMB CARCASS BREAKDOWN

The lamb carcass is divided similar to that of veal. It is not split or sectioned at the time of slaughter; therefore, it is sold in saddles. This implies that most cuts are sold as pairs. When purchasing the rack and loin sections, it is typical to order them split by the purveyor.

Lamb is about 10 times smaller than beef, so there are not as many options when purchasing; for example, the processors won't divide the leg of lamb into each of its tiny subprimals. There are no marketed cuts such as brisket, skirt steak, and eye round, even though they all exist; they are just too small to market.

### Primal Cuts

- Leg
- Loin
- Hotel rack
- Chuck or shoulder square cut

### Minor Primals

- Breast
- Foreshank
- Leg

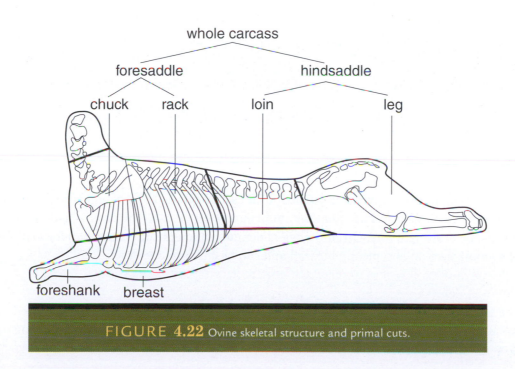

FIGURE **4.22** Ovine skeletal structure and primal cuts.

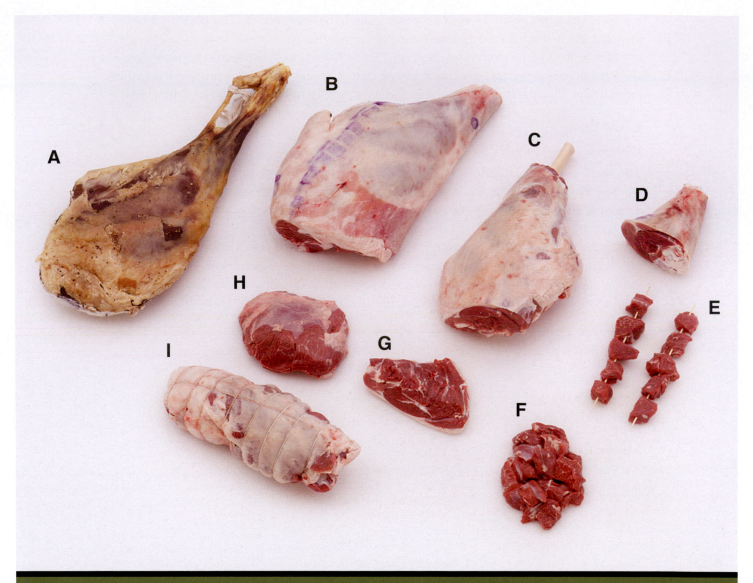

FIGURE **4.23** a. Dry-cured lamb prosciutto; b. leg of lamb; c. leg of lamb steamship, frenched; d. lamb shank; e. lamb leg kebabs; f. lamb shank cubes; g. lamb sirloin; h. lamb top round; and i. leg of lamb BRT.

Boning a leg of lamb

## LEG

The leg of lamb is often roasted whole, but it can be fabricated into manageable semi-boneless or boneless roasts. Smaller subprimals can be used for mini roasts, steaks, cutlets, or broiling items. Often the leg is denuded and cut into the kebab for grilling. The shank section is typically braised and can be cut osso buco style.

## LOIN

The loin can be purchased whole, split, boneless, or potion cut. Most chefs sell the loin cut as chops. Chops from the loin resemble small t-bones or porterhouses. Cutting an even chop may require the use of a band saw.

| TABLE 4-15 LAMB LEG HRI CUTS | | | | |
|---|---|---|---|---|
| **ITEM AND NAMP NUMBER** | **DESCRIPTION OR FABRICATION** | **SUGGESTED COOKING METHOD, OR APPLICATION** | **AVERAGE SUGGESTED WEIGHT IN POUNDS** | **TYPICAL PACKAGE SPECS** |
| 233 Lamb legs 233a Lamb leg, trotter off | Full primal leg, typically sold with trotter bone cut off, can be sold in pairs, requires trimming and possible boning. | Roasting, divided into smaller roasts. | 9 to 13 | 1 per bag, 6 per box |
| 233c Lamb leg, semi-boneless 233e Lamb leg, Frenched, sirloin off (steamship) | Semiboneless leg is easier to carve; may require trimming and frenching of shank bone. | Roast whole for carving; quality presentation at carving station. | 6 to 10 | 1 per bag, 6 per box |
| 234 Lamb leg, boneless 234a Lamb leg, boneless, shank off | Typically sold netted, shank off is higher quality, can be reformed and further trimmed, butterflied, sectioned. | Roast whole, butterfly and grill-like steak, divide into small subprimal roasts, cut as cubes for kebab. | 6 to 8 | 1 per bag, 8 per box |
| 233f Lamb hind shank | Sold whole; small, single portion. | Braise slow, can be frenched for presentation. | 1 to 2 | 2 per bag, 12 bags per box |
| 234d Lamb leg, outside 234f Sirloin tip (knuckle) 234g Sirloin | Trimmed bottom round, knuckle, sirloin sections of leg, may require minor trimming. | Small roast, cut for small butterflied leg or kebab. | 1 to 3 | 1 per bag, 12 per box |
| 234e Lamb leg, inside | Trimmed top round section, solid, high quality. | Small roast, cut for small butterflied leg, kebab, steaks, cutlets. | 1 to 2 | 1 per bag, 12 per box |
| 295a Lamb kebab | Ready to cook. | For skewers. | Specify size | Varies |

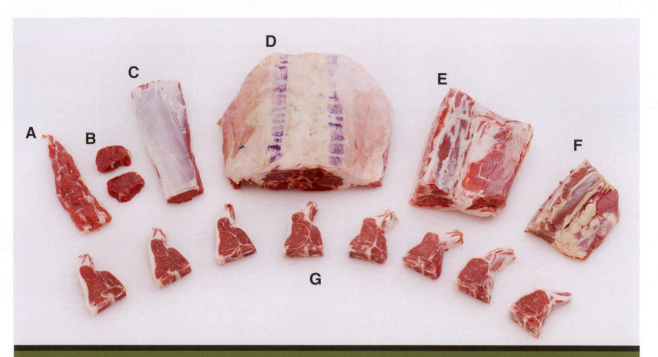

FIGURE **4.24** a. lamb tenderloin; b. lamb loin medallions (noisette); c. lamb loin boneless; lamb loin trimmed (saddle); e. lamb loin split; f. New Zealand lamb loin; g. lamb loin chops.

| ITEM AND NAMP NUMBER | DESCRIPTION OR FABRICATION | SUGGESTED COOKING METHOD, OR APPLICATION | AVERAGE SUGGESTED WEIGHT IN POUNDS | TYPICAL PACKAGE SPECS |
|---|---|---|---|---|
| TABLE 4-16 LAMB LOIN HRI CUTS | | | | |
| 231 Lamb loins 232 Lamb loins, trimmed | Full primal loins; require trimming, splitting, and band saw to cut into chops; can be boned. | Cut for chops, bone or notch for roast. | 8 to 12; be sure to specify yield grade! | 1 per bag, 6 per box |
| 232a Lamb loins, trimmed and split | Cut into chops with band saw or hand cut with cleaver. | Cut for chops, notch for roast, bone out for roast. | 2 to 3 | 1 per bag, 12 per box |
| 232b Lamb loin boneless, single or double | Can be purchased with or without exterior fat, may require trimming. | Roast whole, cut into medallions or noisette, cut thin for carpaccio. | 1 to 1.5 | 2 per bag, 6 per box |
| 246 Lamb tenderloin | Very small, may need some trimming. | Grill, broil, sauté, mini medallions, appetizers. | 3 to 8 ounces | Varies |
| 1232a Lamb loin chops | Small, t-bone style chop, may need some exterior fat or tail trimmed. | Grill, broil, pan-sear, sauté. | Specify size | Varies |

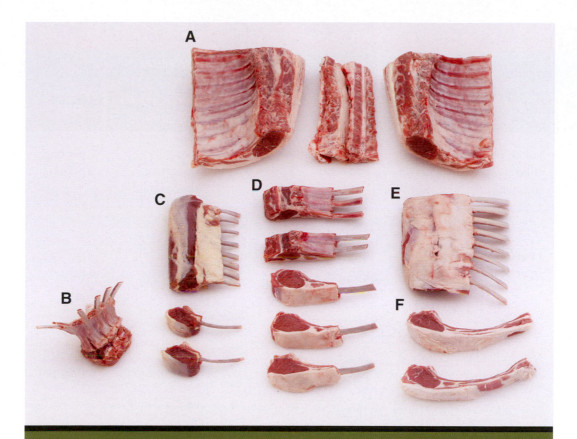

FIGURE 4.25 a. Lamb rack split and chined; b. mini crown roast; c. New Zealand lamb rack and chops; d. various lamb rack chops, frenched; e. U.S. lamb rack, frenched; and f. lamb rack chops, untrimmed.

## HOTEL RACK

The rack of lamb is traditionally sold unsplit but is not common today. The rack is sold basically fabricated to a variety of trim levels, the least of which would be "split and chined." It can also be purchased frenched with the rib bones exposed or boneless. When purchasing pre-frenched, it may be necessary to specify the length of the "lip" of fat left on the eye.

If purchasing portion cut chops, be sure to specify trim levels.

## SQUARE CUT CHUCK OR SHOULDER

The lamb shoulder can be purchased whole as a bone-in item or boneless as a BRT item. The shoulder can be cut into portion chops or cut into stew. Boning the shoulder in-house could be considered difficult.

## BREAST AND FORESHANK

The lamb breast is similar to pork spare ribs with plenty of meat between. Lamb ribs can be purchased as "Denver"-style ribs that are trimmed and prepped for grilling. Lamb ribs can have a fair amount of excess fat and may need to be parcooked to reduce flare-up on a char-grill. An alternative method for lamb ribs is to cut a pocket lengthwise and stuff the breast similar to the veal breast.

The foreshank is typically purchased whole for braising or can be cut into an osso buco.

Frenching a rack of lamb

Cutting lamb chops, double chops, and tying a crown roast

**TABLE 4-17 HOTEL RACK HRI CUTS**

| ITEM AND NAMP NUMBER | DESCRIPTION OR FABRICATION | SUGGESTED COOKING METHOD, OR APPLICATION | AVERAGE SUGGESTED WEIGHT IN POUNDS | TYPICAL PACKAGE SPECS |
|---|---|---|---|---|
| 204 Lamb rack | Full primal, requires splitting with saw and trimming. | Roast, grill, broil, sauté, pan-sear. | 7 to 9; be sure to specify yield grade | 1 per bag, 6 per box |
| 204a Lamb rack, split and chined | Requires trimming, can be frenched. | Roast, grill, broil, sauté, pan-sear. | 7 to 9; be sure to specify yield grade | 1 per bag, 6 per box |
| 204c Lamb rack, Frenched 204d | May require extra cleaning of bones. | Roast, grill, broil, sauté, pan-sear. | 2 to 3 | 1 per bag, 12 per box |
| 204e Lamb rack, boneless | Ready to cook, very expensive item. | Roast, grill, broil, sauté, pan-sear. | 1 to 1.5 | 2 per bag, 12 per box |
| 1204b Lamb rack chops | May require extra trimming; sold as single-, double-, or triple-bone chops. | Grill, broil, sauté, pan-sear. | Specify size | Varies |
| 1204c / d Lamb rack chops/ frenched | Trim levels can vary; sold as single-, double-, or triple-bone chops; lollipop chops are trimmed to the eye muscle. | Grill, broil, sauté, pan-sear, lollipop chop served as appetizer. | Specify size | Varies |

| TABLE 4-18 LAMB SQUARE CUT CHUCK OR SHOULDER HRI CUTS | | | | |
|---|---|---|---|---|
| ITEM AND NAMP NUMBER | DESCRIPTION OR FABRICATION | SUGGESTED COOKING METHOD, OR APPLICATION | AVERAGE SUGGESTED WEIGHT IN POUNDS | TYPICAL PACKAGE SPECS |
| 207 Lamb shoulder/ chuck, square cut | Full primal bone in lamb shoulder, may require boning, trimming. | Roast whole, slow braise, stew. | 6 to 8 | 1 per bag, 6 per box |
| 208 Lamb shoulder, boneless | Sold BRT (boned, rolled, and tied), may require some extra trimming. | Roast whole, slow braise, stew. | 3 to 4 | 1 per bag, 6 per box |
| 209b Lamb short ribs | Cut from the shoulder. | Braise, slow roast, very flavorful. | 2 to 3 | 1 per bag, 12 per box |
| 1207 Lamb shoulder chops, arm chops, blade chops | May require fat trimming and partial bone removal. | Broil, grill, sauté, pan-sear, braise. | 6 to 8 oz each | Varies |
| 210 Lamb foreshank | Sold whole or blocked. | Braise whole or cut as osso buco. | 1 to 2 | 2 per bag, 12 per box |
| Lamb neck | May be split. | Slow braise, pulling meat, stew. | 1 to 2 | Varies |
| 209 Lamb breast | Requires trimming, can be cut with pocket for stuffing, inexpensive. | Braising, grilling, slow roasting. | 2 to 3 | 2 per bag, 6 per box |
| 209a Lamb Denver ribs | Trimmed, ready to grill. | Braising, grilling, slow roasting. | 1 to 2 | 2 per bag |
| 295 Lamb stew | Cut from leg or shoulder. | Stewing. | Varies | Varies |
| 296 Ground lamb | Ready to cook. | Burgers, ingredient in other dishes, flavor agent. | Varies | Varies |

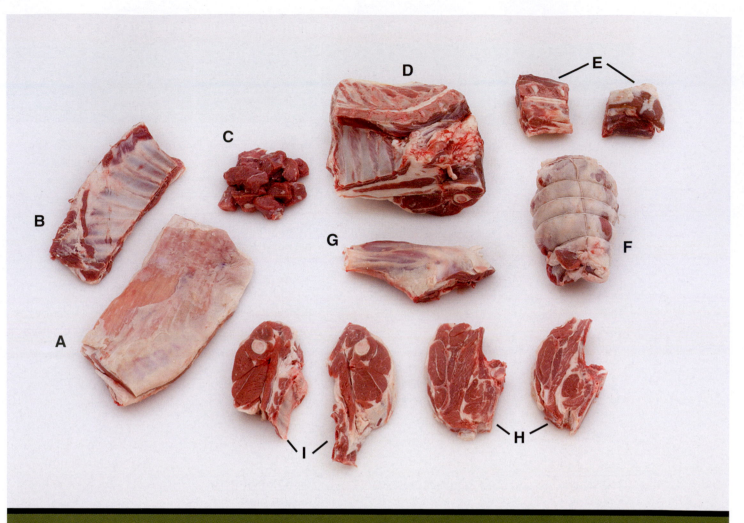

**FIGURE 4.26** a. Lamb breast; b. lamb Denver ribs; c. lamb shoulder cubes; d. lamb square cut shoulder; e. lamb neck; f. lamb shoulder BRT; g. lamb foreshank; h. blade shoulder chops; and i. arm shoulder chops

## GAME

The basic definition of game meats comprises those animals that are traditionally hunted. Humans have been hunting and gathering for thousands of years, and the type of game varies from region to region. Chefs have often turned to creating game dishes to showcase different flavors and to highlight their skills. Game presents challenges that other meats may not. Stronger flavors, extra-lean cuts, possible toughness, and customer acceptance are part of the challenge. Another idea is that game offers seasonality to menus. Fall being a traditional hunting time explains certain game dishes being more appealing in these months. That is not to say that game isn't appealing year-round. Many chefs choose to place game prominently on the menu through the entire calendar year.

Today we find "game" that are farm raised and fed similar to their domestic cousins. So what makes them game? The game we find commercially raised has typically not been altered out of its natural breed; therefore, it can require different fabrications and cooking techniques. Often feeding practices are not that much different than what we may find in the wilds. Some possible grain feeding and mineral supplements added to ensure health and quality may be part of the process but not to the extent that we find in domestic animal feeding.

Processing is typically done by smaller operators, and each has its own style of cutting and packaging. Game is not regulated the same as other meats and may not require USDA inspection. Be sure to purchase from reputable distributors. There are some distributors that specialize in game and fancy unique meats. Heirloom breeds of various meats may not be considered game but may be part of this type of purveyor's product list. Heirloom breeds are those not in popular use in modern meat production. They tend to have unique and sometimes game-like flavors. Be prepared to pay much higher prices for game and heirloom items. Consider using underutilized cuts such as those from the chuck area to minimize costs.

## GAME MEATS

Although there are thousands of game animals worldwide, we choose to focus on those that are typically available from vendors.

- Bison or American buffalo
- Rabbit
- Wild boar
- Venison
- Antelope
- Elk

## BISON OR BUFFALO

Meat from bison resembles beef and is sometimes described as "beefier than beef" due to its high iron count and rich, robust flavor. Bison is typically range fed and may be finished on some grain, but it tends to be leaner than beef. Most bison processors use the same cutting techniques as beef, and vendors typically use the same NAMP numbers and descriptions as beef. Typical purchases are the bison striploin, rib eye, and tenderloin peeled with the side muscle on (PSMO). Short ribs for barbeque are another popular item. Many casual dining establishments use bison burger. Use the same specs for beef when purchasing bison.

## RABBIT

Meat is sold typically as a whole carcass divided by weight ranges and also as parts such as the loin, front legs, or back legs. Whole rabbits are categorized as fryers or roasting rabbits in the United States. Fryers weigh up to 3.5 lbs and are about 12 weeks old, and roasters weigh up to 4 lbs and can be up 6 months old, making the roaster much tougher.

Rabbits are fabricated similar to poultry but have a bone structure similar to that of any other mammal. Basic fabrication is to divide the carcass into front and back legs and the loin section. Rabbits are also sold with "giblets," meaning that a small bag of offals is included.

## WILD BOAR

Modern wild boar is meat from feral swine or hogs that are allowed free range of territory to find food. Being in the wild, the pigs' diet is highly varied and diverse

| TABLE 4-19 NAMP HRI CUTS FOR BISON | | | | |
|---|---|---|---|---|
| **ITEM AND NAMP NUMBER** | **DESCRIPTION OR FABRICATION** | **SUGGESTED COOKING METHOD, OR APPLICATION** | **AVERAGE SUGGESTED WEIGHT IN POUNDS** | **TYPICAL PACKAGE SPECS** |
| Bison has a small round and very large chuck; the rib eye is larger than the striploin. | | | | |
| Top round, bottom round flat, eye round, knuckle | Sold whole, typically well trimmed or divided as tied roasts. | Roasts, steaks, very lean, can be dry. Best marinated and tenderized. | Varies with cut 10 to 15 pounds each | 1 item per bag |
| Shortloin 174 | Sold with tail trimmed to 2 × 3, 1 × 1, minimal fat coverage. | Fabricated as porterhouse, t-bone, and shell steaks; slightly smaller than beef. | 17 to 20 | 1 per bag |
| Striploin bone in/ Boneless 175/180 | 2 × 3, 1 × 1, 0 × 1 trim, minimal fat cover. | Cut for striploin or shell steaks, roasted whole, split for medallions. | 8 to 10 if well trimmed | 1 per bag |
| Tenderloin PSMO 189a | Peeled, side muscle on (PSMO). Requires trimming and removal of silverskin. | Steaks, medallions, filet mignon, roast whole. | 4 to 6 | 1 per bag |
| Flank steak, Skirt steak, Hanger steak | May need exterior membranes peeled. | Grill as steak, fajita, marinate, or tenderize (can be tough but very flavorful). | 1 to 2 | 2-4 per bag |
| Rib, export style 109 d | Rib bones in, fat lip trimmed to two inches (trim level can vary). | Bone in rib eye steak, cowboy steak, roast whole as bison "prime rib." | 12 to 16 | 1 per bag (sometimes sold split in half) |
| Rib eye, boneless lip on 112a | Rib eye with two-inch lip of fat. | Boneless rib eye steak, Delmonico steak. | 8 to 12 | 1 per bag |

*(continues)*

| TABLE 4-19 NAMP HRI CUTS FOR BISON (Continued) | | | | |
|---|---|---|---|---|
| **ITEM AND NAMP NUMBER** | **DESCRIPTION OR FABRICATION** | **SUGGESTED COOKING METHOD, OR APPLICATION** | **AVERAGE SUGGESTED WEIGHT IN POUNDS** | **TYPICAL PACKAGE SPECS** |
| Short ribs | Cut short, "flanken," or "Korean" style. | Braise, slow cook, barbecue. | 2 to 3 each; size can vary with processor | 4 per bag |
| Chuck/Shoulder/ Hump | Various chuck sections, roasts; bison has a larger chuck section, including a "hump." | Braise, slow cook, stew, grind. | 3 to 7 | 1 per bag |
| Brisket | Sold trimmed, fresh, or corned. | Braise, slow cooked, as barbecue. | 4 to 8 | 1 per bag |
| Portion Cuts | | | | |
| Porterhouse steak, T-bone steak, Bone-in or boneless rib eye, Sirloin steak, Filet mignon medallions | Portion cut to specs. | Dry cook, grill, broil, sauté, pan sear. | Varies | Most items packaged individually or as pairs but can vary with processor. |
| Stew, from chuck or trim pieces. | 1- to 2-inch pieces. | Stew, braise, chili. | Customer specified | Typical five pounds per bag, can vary |
| Ground bison | Bulk or formed as burgers. | Very lean, best not well done if used as burger. | Varies | Varies |
| Bison products: jerky, sausages, hot dogs, marinated or cured products | None. | Ready to eat. | Varies | Varies; be sure products include proper ingredients |

| | TABLE 4-20 NAMP HRI CUTS FOR RABBIT | | | |
|---|---|---|---|---|
| ITEM AND NAMP NUMBER | DESCRIPTION OR FABRICATION | SUGGESTED COOKING METHOD, OR APPLICATION | AVERAGE SUGGESTED WEIGHT IN POUNDS | TYPICAL PACKAGE SPECS |
| Whole broiler/ fryer | Sold whole with giblets, can be cut into parts. | Roast, grill, braise, stew. | 2 to 4 | 1 per bag |
| Legs, hind/fore | May require partial boning, remove back bones. | Roast, grill, braise, stew, pulled meats. | 2 per pack | 4 legs per pack |
| Loin section w/ ribs | Can be boney, may need partial boning. | Grill, broil, sauté. | 2 per pack | 2 pieces per pack |

consisting of root vegetables, berries, nuts, plants, bugs, and even small rodents. This diet ensures a stronger flavor and darker color. The wild boar is typically about half the size of commercial pork, and the meat is much leaner. The fat on a feral swine is darker in color, yellowish, and softer than that of commercial pork. Depending on diet, the fat can have a higher level of Omega 3 fatty acid and can spoil faster than typical pork.

Wild boar can be any number of different breeds. The wild domestic boars found in the United States are related to Spanish Iberico swine. Many game and hunting clubs have introduced Eurasian and Russian boar. These are typically sold as wild boar commercially. There are also large domestic feral swine that have escaped captivity that could be related to a variety of domestic breeds.

Although related to hogs, the wild boar is much smaller. Often processors do not follow hog schematics when breaking down the carcass. The loin is often divided into rack and shortloin sections. The ham includes all of the sirloin. Belly and bacon sections are about half the size of those of normal pigs. The shoulders are often sold as BRT roasts and not as typical Boston butts and picnics. Be sure to examine a vendor's spec sheet carefully before ordering. Boar meat can be very expensive, and the purchaser must be ready to conduct further fabrication on certain items. For example, frenched boar racks often arrive with a fair amount of debris on the bones that must be cleaned.

## VENISON, ANTELOPE, AND ELK

Venison is the meat from a variety of deer breeds that are raised commercially. It is common to find venison from small producers throughout the United States and also New Zealand, which is the world's largest processor. Venison is fabricated similar to lamb or veal. The carcass is not split down the spine, so there are saddles and pairs available. The carcass is divided into legs, loin, rack, and chuck. The loin and rack can be sold as one large piece known as a saddle. It is often purchased split, as is

| TABLE 4-21 NAMP HRI CUTS FOR WILD BOAR | | | | |
|---|---|---|---|---|
| ITEM AND NAMP NUMBER | DESCRIPTION OR FABRICATION | SUGGESTED COOKING METHOD, OR APPLICATION | AVERAGE SUGGESTED WEIGHT IN POUNDS | TYPICAL PACKAGE SPECS |
| Leg or ham bone in or boned, rolled, tied | Sold skin off, may require trimming; also sold cured and smoked. | Roast, cut for portions. | 8 to 10 | 1 per bag |
| Short loin | Cut for chops, t-bone style. | Grill, broil, sauté, pan sear. | 3 to 4 | 2 per bag; varies with processor |
| Boneless loin | Cut for medallions, cutlets. | Roast, grill, broil, sauté, pan sear. | 4 to 5 | 2 per bag, varies |
| Boar rack, 8 bones | Usually sold frenched; typically requires further fabrication and cleaning of bones. | Roast, grill, broil, sauté, pan sear. | 2 to 3 | 2 per bag |
| Shoulder whole/ boneless rolled and tied | Entire shoulder sold skin off and tied or netted. | Slow roast, braise, pulled meat, barbecue. | 3 to 5 | 1 per bag |
| Spare ribs | Small compared to regular pork, may need to remove sternum bone. | Slow roast, barbecue. | 1 to 2 | 2 per bag |
| Belly/bacon | Sold fresh or cured as smoked bacon | Roast or braise fresh belly, cook as strips for bacon. | 2 to 3; varies with processor | Varies |

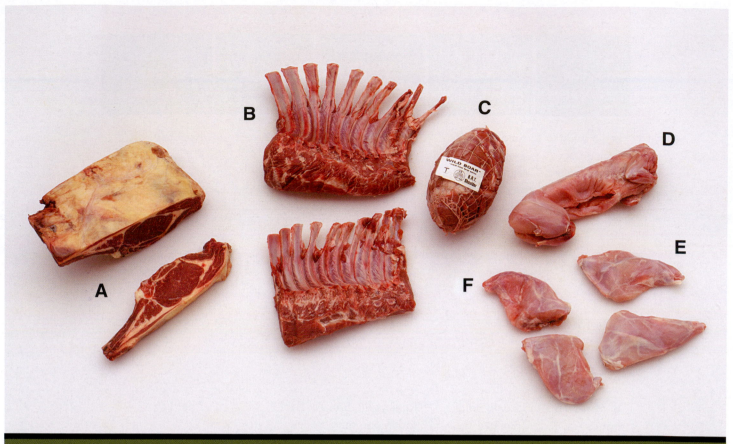

FIGURE 4.27 Assorted game: a. bison rib eye; b. wild boar racks; c. wild boar shoulder; d. fryer rabbit; e. rabbit leg, hind; and f. rabbit shoulder and leg.

lamb. The leg is sold whole or divided into subprimals like veal. The boneless denuded venison leg sold without the shank is referred to as a "Denver leg" from some distributors.

Antelope is related to venison, but they are larger than most deer, averaging around 280 lbs live. Antelope meat is mild, very lean, and dark red, similar to venison, and is high in iron, making it a very nutritious meat. Being slightly milder than deer meat, Antelope can be appealing as a grill or sauté item without heavy masking spices. Antelope is sold in the same format as venison, similar to lamb or veal. Racks, loins, saddles, legs, and shoulders are typical cuts.

Elk is also in the "deer" family but is larger still. It is typically sold split due to its size. The chops from elk are about the size of small pork chops. The leg is often divided into subprimals and used for cutlets or steaks.

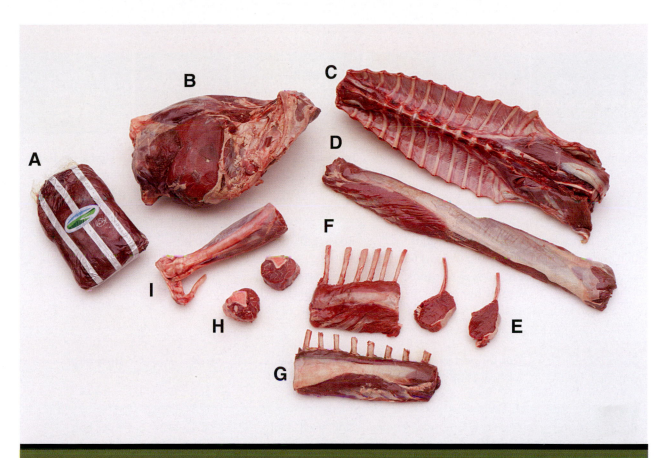

FIGURE **4.28** Venison cuts: a. venison Denver leg; b. venison leg, shank off; c. full venison saddle; d. boneless venison loin; e. venison rack chops; f. venison rack, long bone and frenched; g. venison rack, short bone and frenched; h. venison osso buco; and f. venison shank.

| TABLE 4-22  NAMP AND HRI CUTS FOR VENISON AND ANTELOPE | | | | |
|---|---|---|---|---|
| ITEM AND NAMP NUMBER | DESCRIPTION OR FABRICATION | SUGGESTED COOKING METHOD, OR APPLICATION | AVERAGE SUGGESTED WEIGHT IN POUNDS | TYPICAL PACKAGE SPECS |
| Leg, whole (similar to veal leg) | Entire bone in leg, lean; requires fabrication, boning, removal of silver skin, dividing into subprimals. | Roasts, portion cut steaks, cutlets, medallions, (stew, grind from trim). | 18 to 22 | 1 per bag |
| Leg, Denver style | Leg divided into subprimals, denuded, shank and trim excluded, very good yield. | Roasts, portion cuts, medallions. | 10 to 12 | Subprimals packaged separately |

*(continues)*

TABLE 4-22 NAMP AND HRI CUTS FOR VENISON AND ANTELOPE (Continued)

| ITEM AND NAMP NUMBER | DESCRIPTION OR FABRICATION | SUGGESTED COOKING METHOD, OR APPLICATION | AVERAGE SUGGESTED WEIGHT IN POUNDS | TYPICAL PACKAGE SPECS |
|---|---|---|---|---|
| Shank, osso buco | Sold as whole shank or portion cut as osso buco. | Braise, stew. | 2 to 3 | 1 shank per bag, portion cuts, package varies |
| Saddle, contains loin and rack section | Sold whole, unsplit; requires band saw to cut bone in portions; can be boned to create medallions or steaks. | Roast, grill, broil, pan sear, sauté; very lean, may require added lipids, such as butter, fat, or oil. | 18 to 20 | 1 per bag |
| Short loin, trimmed, split | Cut for porterhouse, t-bone, chops. | Grill, broil, sauté, pan sear. | 3 to 4 | 1 per bag |
| Rack, 8–10 bones; Sold as split rack, often Frenched | Cut for chops, may require removal of silverskin. | Grill, broil, sauté, pan sear. | 3 to 4 | 1 per bag |
| Chuck / Shoulder Boneless | Cut as roasts or stew, grind, remove heavy silverskin. | Braise, stew, slow cook. | 10 to 15 | 1 per bag |
| Breast, ribs/ short ribs | Peel silverskin, membranes. | Braise, slow cook, barbecue. | 2 to 3 | Varies |
| Portion cuts chops, cutlets, medallions | May require minor trimming. | Grill, broil, sauté, pan sear. | Varies, customer specified | Varies |

# POULTRY

## CHICKEN

### Purchasing Specifications

When purchasing chicken items, it is important to establish proper specifications with the vendor. Understanding average weights and requesting logical sizes ensure a consistent portion. Attached are typical package sizes and counts per bag and box.

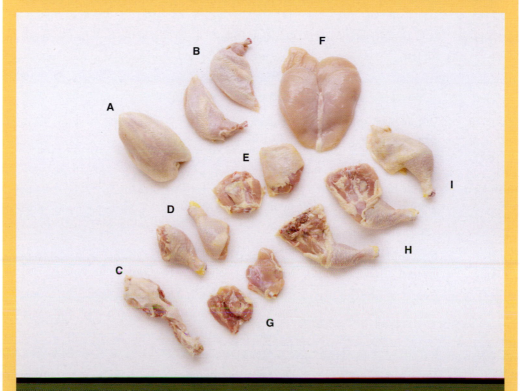

| TABLE 4-23 CHICKEN PURCHASING AND USAGE SPECIFICATIONS | | | | |
|---|---|---|---|---|
| ITEM AND NAMP NUMBER | DESCRIPTION OR FABRICATION | SUGGESTED COOKING METHOD, OR APPLICATION | AVERAGE SUGGESTED WEIGHT IN POUNDS | TYPICAL PACKAGE SPECS |
| Broiler/Fryer P1000 | Whole bird, sold with giblets, typically cut into parts. | Dry cook, broil, grill, roast, pan sear, fry. | Sold from 2.5 to 4.5 lbs in 1/4 or 1/2 lb increments | 10 per case or 16 per case, bulk package or individually wrapped |
| Broiler/ Fryer P1002 | Whole bird, without giblets (WOG). | Same as above. | Same as above | Same as above |
| Roaster P1100 | Whole bird, with giblets, can be cut as large parts. | Roasting whole, dry cook parts. | 5–9 lbs | 6 per case, individually wrapped |
| Capon P1200 | Whole bird, sold with giblets. | Roasting whole, carving. | 6–9lbs | 6 per case |
| Fowl/ Stewing Hen P1300 | Whole bird, sold with giblets. | Stewing, slow cooking, soup, pulled meat. | 5–8 lbs | 6 per case, bulk packaged or individually wrapped |
| Poussin P1400 | Whole bird, sold with giblets. | Roasting whole. | 1–1.5 lbs | 12 per case |
| Rock Cornish Hen P1500 | Whole bird, sold with giblets. | Roasting whole, semiboneless. | 1–2 lbs | 24 per case, individually wrapped |
| Broiler, 8 pc. (2 breast, 2 wings, 2 drumsticks, 2 thighs) P1005 | Cut, sold without giblets. | Dry cook, fry, barbecue, broil. | 3–3.5 lbs | 16 per case, bulk |
| Broiler, 10 pc. Same as 8 pc but breast cut in half P1007 | Cut, sold without giblets | Dry cook, fry, barbecue, broil. | 3–3.5 lbs | 16 per case, bulk |

| TABLE 4-23 CHICKEN PURCHASING AND USAGE SPECIFICATIONS (Continued) | | | | |
|---|---|---|---|---|
| ITEM AND NAMP NUMBER | DESCRIPTION OR FABRICATION | SUGGESTED COOKING METHOD, OR APPLICATION | AVERAGE SUGGESTED WEIGHT IN POUNDS | TYPICAL PACKAGE SPECS |
| Broiler halves P1008 | Split, sold without giblets. | Dry cook, broil, barbecue. | 3–4 lbs | 12 or 16 per case, bulk |
| Broiler quarters P1009 | Legs and breast, sold without giblets. | Dry cook, broil, barbecue, fry. | 3–4 lbs | 12 or 16 per case, bulk |
| Broiler Breast, bone in with ribs or without ribs P1012, P1013 | Whole unsplit breast, with wishbone. | Dry cook. | 1.5–2 lbs each (P1013 has a better yield) | 24 per case |
| Broiler Airline Breast P1016 | Boneless except for drumette wing portion. | Dry cook, broil, sauté, grill. | 6–9 oz each pc | Four 10-lb bags per case |
| Broiler breast, skin-on, with rib meat | Unsplit boneless breast with a small amount of extra rib meat. | Dry cook, broil, sauté, grill. | 12–18 oz each double breast | Four 10-lb bags per case |
| Broiler breast, skin-less, with rib meat | Unsplit boneless breast with a small amount of extra rib meat. | Dry cook, broil, sauté, grill. | 10–16 oz each double breast | Four 10-lb bags per case or individual portion tray packs |
| Roaster breast | Unsplit boneless breast with a small amount of extra rib meat. | Dry cook, broil, sauté, grill. | 16–24 oz each double breast | Four 10-lb bags per case |
| Broiler Cutlets | Split and trimmed breast with "tender" taken out. | Dry cook, sauté, grill, broil, breaded. | 4–6 oz each | Four 10-lb bags per case |

*(continues)*

TABLE 4-23  CHICKEN PURCHASING AND USAGE SPECIFICATIONS (Continued)

| ITEM AND NAMP NUMBER | DESCRIPTION OR FABRICATION | SUGGESTED COOKING METHOD, OR APPLICATION | AVERAGE SUGGESTED WEIGHT IN POUNDS | TYPICAL PACKAGE SPECS |
|---|---|---|---|---|
| Broiler tender | Small center section of breast. | Dry cook, breaded, grill, sauté. | 2 oz each | Four 10-lb bags per case |
| Broiler leg quarters with back bone P1030 | Thigh and drumstick attached. | Dry cook, moist cook. | 8–10 oz each | Bulk 20 or 40 lb case |
| Broiler leg, back bone removed P1031 | Thigh and drumstick attached. | Dry cook, moist cook. | 6–8 oz each | Bulk 20 or 40 lb case |
| Broiler thigh (bone in skin on or boneless skinless) | Thigh section. | Dry or moist cook | 4–6 oz each | Four 10-lb bags per case |
| Broiler Drumstick, bone in only P1035 | Shank section. | Dry or moist cook. | 4–6 oz each | 40 lb bulk |
| Broiler wings P1036 P1037, P1038 (larger roaster wings available as well) | Sold as whole wing or as drumette, flat only. | Dry cook, moist cook, deep-fat fry. | 2 oz each | Four 10-lb bags per case |
| Livers P1045 | — | Sauté, paté, mousse, flavor agent. | 1–2 oz each | 5 lb tubs |
| Necks P1042 | — | Soup, stock, barbecue. | 3–4 oz each | 40 lb bulk |
| Gizzards P1044 | — | Soup, stock, sauces. | 2 oz each | 5 lb tubs |

These are general specs for fresh chicken and can change from processor to processor. Every processor has some items they choose to package differently.

There are multitudes of processed chicken products that are not included in this list due to the massive amounts available.

The North American Meat Processor's *Meat Buyer's Guide* has established a standard number code system for meat purchasing.

Processed chicken products can be categorized into raw and precooked products. Raw products may be water added, preseasoned, vegetable protein added, breaded, or coated. Various chicken sausages are also available. All of these items need to be cooked before serving. Items can be sold fresh or frozen.

Precooked products are basically heat and serve. Examples are precooked seasoned portion cut breasts, pulled or cubed cooked chicken meat, and smoke-roasted or barbecue whole or cut birds.

Cutting an eight-piece chicken

Cutting a supreme and deboning a leg quarter

## DUCK

In the culinary world, the duck plays a very important and prominent role. Its meat is flavorful and rich. It is often slow roasted to achieve a tender poultry that reminds many of holidays and special occasions. Its fat is considered a valuable by-product used as a cooking agent. The roast duck and its fat renderings supply many memorable dining occasions.

Contrary to the traditional slow roast, duck breast can be grilled or seared to a medium rare like a fine steak. Cooking a boneless duck breast in this fashion has transformed it from a carving item on holiday dinner tables to a "cook-to-order" item found in many restaurants.

Cooked duck was preserved before the invention of refrigeration by cooking it slowly in its own rendered fat, known in France as *confit* or simply translated as preserves.

Beyond the fat and meat is the liver. The fattened liver, or foie gras, is a highly prized ingredient revered by many chefs and culinarians. Duck is not found hidden on the menu; it is often front and center, a culinary star item with a devoted following.

Boning a duck breast and scoring

Foie gras fabrication

### Purchasing Specifications

Ducks are purchased fresh or frozen. If fresh, they have a shelf life of about 4 or 5 days. If frozen, they are typically blast frozen at the plant and should remain at 0°F to −20°F. Freezing duck does not adversely affect the quality if it is stored and handled correctly.

Typically ducks are individually bagged if sold whole. They can also be purchased in a large variety of portion cut configurations such as quarters and boneless parts. The boneless breast from a Moulard duck is known as a *magret*.

The following guide gives packaging specifics. Not all duck producers follow a standard packaging count or size, so be sure to ask your purveyor for specifics when purchasing.

| ITEM AND NAMP NUMBER | DESCRIPTION OR FABRICATION | SUGGESTED COOKING METHOD, OR APPLICATION | AVERAGE SUGGESTED WEIGHT IN POUNDS | TYPICAL PACKAGE SPECS |
|---|---|---|---|---|
| Duckling<br>P3000<br>P3001 w/giblets<br>P3002 w/o giblets | Whole bird, usually sold with giblets. | Dry cook, roast whole or half, cut for parts. | 3–6 lbs | 6 per case individually wrapped or 12 per case iced |
| Duckling<br>Buddhist style | Whole bird, with head and feet attached. | Cooked whole for Peking-style duck. | 4–7 lbs | 6 per case |
| Roasting Duck<br>P3100 | Whole bird, sold with giblets. | Slow-roast whole or half, large parts. | 5–8 lbs | 6 per case |
| Mature Duck<br>P3200 | Sold whole, low quality, high in flavor. | Processed, braising, slow cooking, sausage. | 6–8 lbs | varies |
| Moulard Duck, Foie Gras Duck | Sold whole or as large parts. | Roast, grill breast as *magret*, confit, legs. | 6–9 lbs | varies |
| Duckling Quarters<br>P3009 | Two breast halves and two legs with all back and rib bones. | Dry cook, roast, broil, grill. | 3–6 lbs | varies |
| Duckling breast, bone in<br>P3012 | Bone in, unsplit. | Roast whole or fabricate into boneless breast. | 1.5 lbs each | 12 per case |
| Duckling Breast, Boneless<br>P3013 | Boneless, skin on or off. | Pan sear, broil, grill, cut skin to release fat. | 3/4 lb each full breast | 2 breast per pack, 6 packs per case |
| Moulard Breast, Boneless (Magret) | Large, skin on. | Pan sear, broil, grill, cure for "proscuitto." | 1.5 lbs each | 1 full breast per bag, sold by the lb. individually |

*(continues)*

| TABLE 4-24 DUCK PURCHASING AND USAGE SPECIFICATIONS (Continued) | | | | |
|---|---|---|---|---|
| ITEM AND NAMP NUMBER | DESCRIPTION OR FABRICATION | SUGGESTED COOKING METHOD, OR APPLICATION | AVERAGE SUGGESTED WEIGHT IN POUNDS | TYPICAL PACKAGE SPECS |
| Duckling Legs P3031 P3032 Also, drumstick and thigh sold separately | Bone-in or semiboneless (both have back bones removed). | Roast, grill, stuff, pulled meat, confit. | 1/2 lb each | 36–40 pc per case, 17+ lbs each case |
| Moulard Duck Legs | Bone-in, back bones removed. | Roast, grill, stuff, confit. | 3/4 lb each | 6 per bag |
| Duck wings P3036 | Wing tips removed. | Slow cook, barbecue, glaze. | 1–2 oz each | Sold in bulk |
| Duck liver P3045 | Dark red color, sold in bulk, may require removal of sinews. | Pâté, terrines, mousse, sausages. | 1–2 oz each | 5 lb tubs |
| Foie Gras Liver (French or NY style) P3046 | Fattened liver from a Moulard duck. | Sear whole, grill, terrines, mousse, paté, torchon. | 1–2 lbs each | 1 per pack |
| Foie Gras Butter | Pieces of liver that are too small for grading. | Mousse, grinds, sauce, spreads, forcemeats, custard. | Loose pieces | varies |
| Duck Paws (Feet) P3048 | Feet with webbing. | Stock, sauces, dim sum. | Loose pieces | Sold in bulk 25 lbs, weights vary |
| Duck Tongue P3050 | Small individual tongues. | Used for soup, slow cooked. | Loose pieces | Sold in bulk, varies |
| Duck Fat, fresh or rendered | Fresh needs to be cooked slowly to remove impurities. | Frying, sauté, flavor agent, confit. | Bulk pack | Rendered: 5 lb tubs; fresh: 10 lb box |

FIGURE **4.30a** a. Moulard; b. white pekin; and c. Buddhist style.

FIGURE **4.30b** a. bone-in pekin breast; b. white pekin breast; c. moulard breast; and d. smoked duck breast.

FIGURE **4.30c** Top to bottom: raw fat, rendered fat.

FIGURE **4.30d** French foie gras (bottom left) compared to New York foie gras.

## GOOSE

Similar to duck, goose is an all-dark-meat bird with a rich and valuable fat. It is often purchased frozen but can be found fresh seasonally, typically in the fall to early winter. They are flash frozen, giving the skin a whitish color. A fresh goose will have a somewhat tan color. Once thawed, a goose will last about three or four days.

## TABLE 4-25 GOOSE PURCHASING AND USAGE SPECIFICATIONS

| ITEM AND NAMP NUMBER | DESCRIPTION OR FABRICATION | SUGGESTED COOKING METHOD, OR APPLICATION | AVERAGE SUGGESTED WEIGHT IN POUNDS | TYPICAL PACKAGE SPECS |
|---|---|---|---|---|
| Young Goose P4000 Young goose w/giblets P4001 Mature goose P4100 | Whole bird, usually sold with giblets. | Dry cook, roast whole or half, cut for parts. | 8–16 lbs | 4 per case individually packaged, typically frozen |
| Young goose, Confucius style | Whole bird, with head and feet attached. | Cooked whole for Asian style. | 10–17 lbs | 4 per case |
| Goose breast, bone in P4012 | Whole unsplit breast. | Roasted whole, carved. | 5–8 lbs | 8 per case |
| Goose breast, boneless, skin on or off P4013 | Whole unsplit breast. | Grill, broil, roast. | 1.5–3.5 lbs each pack | 12 packs per case |
| Smoked goose breast | Whole or half. | Ready to eat, slice like ham, served warm or cold. | 1/2 lb each | 12 per case |
| Goose leg quarters P4030 | Includes thigh and drumstick. | Roast, confit, slow cook, braise, stew. | 3/4–1 lb each leg | 4 legs per pack, 8 packs per case |
| Goose wing P4036 | Consists of two sections excluding the tip. | Slow cook, slow roast. | 1/4 lb each | 4 lb packs, 10 packs per case |
| Giblets P4043 | Includes neck, heart, gizzard, liver. | Sauces, stock. | varies | varies |
| Goose livers | Dark purplish red color, sold in bulk, may require some cleaning and deveining. | Paté, terrines, sausages, sauces. | Sold in bulk | 2 lb, 5 lb, 10 lb packs |
| Goose liver, foie gras | Light beige, firm, fatty. | Paté, terrines, seared. | 1–2 lbs each | 1 per bag |

FIGURE **4.31a** Whole goose.

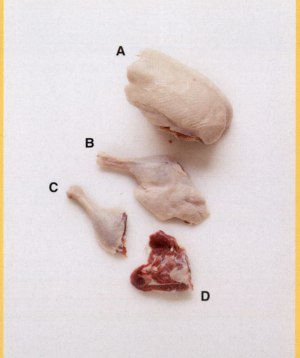

FIGURE **4.31b** a. Bone-in goose breast; b. goose leg; c. goose drumstick; and d. goose thigh, bone in.

FIGURE **4.31c** Top to bottom: goose foie gras liver, regular goose liver.

FIGURE **4.31d** Top to bottom: raw goose fat, tendered goose fat.

The goose is larger than duck or chicken, implying that the parts will create multiple portions. A whole goose breast will serve 4–6 people depending on its size. However, much of the goose is covered with fat, which can make portioning deceiving.

## TURKEY

### Purchasing Specifics

Turkey is sold typically around holiday seasons but is available year-round as a whole bird. It is sold in increments of two pounds. Turkey is also sold as parts and as many processed items. By processing the turkey, it can be marketed as numerous products such as slicing meats, sausages, turkey bacon, and ground meat.

Trussing a turkey and trussing a stuffed turkey

Raw turkey is sold fresh or frozen. Fresh turkey can be slightly frozen, chilled rapidly to 25°F but not frozen all the way through. Frozen turkey is brought down below 0°F very quickly in large blast freezers. This procedure ensures small ice crystals and minimizes the damage caused by freezing. There is a slight quality difference between fresh and frozen. Fresh is considered a higher quality, but if the frozen is thawed correctly, slowly at 35°F to 40°F, there is little difference between the two.

Carving a turkey

There are a variety of enhanced turkey products available. Enhanced products are pumped with a moisture-increasing agent or agents. The two basic categories of enhanced products are "basted" and "marinated." Basted products are primarily moisture enhanced without flavorings added. Marinated products have a variety of flavorings added as well as moisture. Salt and water are typically part of the mix, but many other ingredients are often added. Natural ingredients such as turkey stock or broth may be added to keep the term "natural" on the label. Sodium phosphate is often added to force moisture retention. Other ingredients include sugar, hydrolyzed vegetable protein, isolated soy proteins, sodium lactate, lactic, acid, artificial and natural flavorings, a large variety of spices, and smoke or smoke flavorings. Enhanced products will be more moist and tender, but the buyer will be paying for added water weight. Typically enhanced products will add an extra 10–15% water. Some products are enhanced with up to 25% added product. Be sure to ask the purveyor if product is enhanced and by how much.

Commercially raised turkey, like chicken, has a high incidence of bacterial contamination, especially salmonella. Be sure turkey is fresh or used within a day of thawing. Listeria is another contaminant that is associated with cooked and processed meat items. Again, use caution and be sure to use only fresh products.

### Processed Cooked Turkey Products

There are numerous processed turkey products that vary greatly in flavor and quality. The breast can be sold as a whole muscle precooked seasoned and ready to eat. There are also many turkey products that are made by tumbling the meat in a vacuum to loosen proteins, enabling the meat to be seasoned, formed, and shaped and then cooked. Many of these items are used as cold cuts for slicing. Turkey breast, turkey roll, and chopped and formed turkey are slicing items that vary greatly in quality.

There are many ground or emulsified turkey products such as hot dogs, bologna, salami, and seasoned patties.

| TABLE 4-26 TURKEY PURCHASING AND USAGE SPECIFICATIONS | | | | |
|---|---|---|---|---|
| ITEM AND NAMP NUMBER | DESCRIPTION OR FABRICATION | SUGGESTED COOKING METHOD, OR APPLICATION | AVERAGE SUGGESTED WEIGHT IN POUNDS | TYPICAL PACKAGE SPECS |
| Whole young turkey, sold fresh or frozen NAMP P2001 | Whole bird, usually sold with giblets. Sold with or without enhancement ingredients. | Roast whole. | 8–24 lbs | Individually packaged, sold 2 or 4 per box |
| Young hen turkey | Whole bird, sold with giblets. | Roast whole. | 8–16 lbs | Individually packaged, sold 2 or 4 per box |
| Young tom turkey | Whole bird, sold with giblets. | Roast whole. | 16–24 lbs | Individually packaged, sold 2 per box |
| Mature tom turkey | Whole bird, sold with giblets. | Roast whole. | 24–35 lbs | Individually packaged, sold 1 per box |
| Young turkey, front half NAMP P2003 | Full breast with back and wings attached, also known as "hotel breast." | Roast whole. | 6–20 lbs | Individually packaged, 4 or 6 per bag |
| Whole turkey breast with ribs NAMP P2012, P2014 | Full breast, unsplit or split. | Roast whole, bone out, and carve. | 4–18 lbs | Individually packaged, sold 4 or 6 per box |
| Boneless Turkey Breast | Full breast with skin on or off, with or without extra rib meat, whole or half. | Roast whole, slicing meat, cutlets. | 2–8 lbs | Varies, 4–6 per case |
| Breast cutlets, slices, tenderloins, cubes | A variety of precut portions, cut from the breast. | Sauté, grilling, breading. | Varies | Varies |

| TABLE 4-26 TURKEY PURCHASING AND USAGE SPECIFICATIONS (Continued) | | | | |
|---|---|---|---|---|
| **ITEM AND NAMP NUMBER** | **DESCRIPTION OR FABRICATION** | **SUGGESTED COOKING METHOD, OR APPLICATION** | **AVERAGE SUGGESTED WEIGHT IN POUNDS** | **TYPICAL PACKAGE SPECS** |
| Young turkey leg NAMP 2031 or 2030 | Full leg sold with or without back bone attached. | Roast, stew, soup. | 2–6 lbs per pair | Varies, can be sold in small packs or large bulk |
| Young turkey drumstick NAMP 2035 | Bottom half of leg cut a stifle joint. | Roast, stew, osso buco. | 1–2 lbs each | Varies, sold in small packs or bulk |
| Young turkey thigh NAMP 2033 | Thigh sold bone in or boneless. | Roast, stew, grind for forcemeats, turkey "ham." | 1–2 lbs each | Varies, sold in small packs or bulk |
| Ground turkey | Sold as bulk, patties, sausage, seasoned with other ingredients added. | Meat sauces, sausages, meat balls, forcemeats. | Bulk | Varied packaging bulk |
| Young turkey wings NAMP 2036 | Sold as whole wing or sectioned into flap or drumette. | Roast whole, barbeque, hot wings, braised, stew. | 1/4 to 1/2 lb each | Varies, sold in small packs or bulk |
| Turkey giblets | Gizzard, liver, heart. | Sauces, gravy. | Bulk, varies | Bulk, varies |
| Turkey neck | Typically frozen, 5–6 inches long. | Sauces, gravy, stock. | Bulk, varies | Bulk, varies, 20 lb box |

Turkey is often found cured and smoked. The entire bird, breast, legs, drumsticks, thighs, and wings are all found brined and smoked to give the meat a ham-like flavor. Turkey bacon has a flavor that is similar to pork and can be used as a substitute.

Lower quality turkey products are made from mechanically separated meat which is extracted from bones and then formed. These can be made from light or dark meat or a combination of both.

FIGURE **4.32a** Top to bottom, whole tom turkey; and whole hen turkey.

FIGURE **4.32b** a. Whole turkey wing; b. wing flap; c. drumette; d. whole turkey breast, bone-in with rib meat; and e. boneless turkey breast.

## GAME BIRDS

Birds typically sold as game today vary in definition. Commercially available birds are either raised similar to domestic poultry, including some that are raised indoors or are raised in fenced preserves for true game flavor properties. Some birds have been domesticated for many years but are unique in the marketplace, and therefore they are grouped and sold as game birds. There are also breeds of long-domesticated birds such as turkey and duck that are sold as game because they are raised as wild birds, having typically a smaller breast and a somewhat wild or foraged diet giving the meat a wild flavor. Due to their uniqueness, ratites such as ostrich and emu are often included with game birds.

Game birds tend to have a more robust flavor and are leaner and smaller than their domestic counterparts. Traditionally, cooking game birds presented challenges in that they can be slightly dry and somewhat tougher. Today the quality of the raw bird will dictate how the bird is cooked. If it is raised similar to most modern poultry and fed a grain diet, it will be more tender and moist. If it is raised as a foraged bird and allowed a lot of freedom, it can be tougher and drier but have a much more intense flavor. When choosing game birds it is important to have some knowledge of the farming technique and also how to identify quality features.

The NAMP *Buyer's Guide* does have numbers for a variety of game birds, but there are no USDA grades or specifications.

| TABLE 4-27 PHEASANT PURCHASING AND USAGE SPECIFICATIONS | | | | |
|---|---|---|---|---|
| ITEM AND NAMP NUMBER | DESCRIPTION OR FABRICATION | SUGGESTED COOKING METHOD, OR APPLICATION | AVERAGE SUGGESTED WEIGHT IN POUNDS | TYPICAL PACKAGE SPECS |
| Pheasant NAMP 7200 | Whole bird, usually sold with giblets. | Dry or moist cook, roast whole or half, cut for parts. | 2–4 lbs | Individual bags, 5–12 birds per case depending on size |
| Pheasant Breast, Airline, Skin on NAMP P7316 | Double lobes of breast sold attached with first wing portion. | Sauté, pan sear, served with sauce. | 6–8 oz each lobe. | 2 breast (4 portions) per tray pack, 11–16 trays per case depending on size. |
| Pheasant Breast, Boneless, skin on | Double lobes of breast. | Sauté, pan sear with sauce. | 4–6 oz each lobe | 2 breast (4 portions) per tray pack, 12–16 trays per case depending on size |

*(continues)*

**TABLE 4-27 PHEASANT PURCHASING AND USAGE SPECIFICATIONS (Continued)**

| ITEM AND NAMP NUMBER | DESCRIPTION OR FABRICATION | SUGGESTED COOKING METHOD, OR APPLICATION | AVERAGE SUGGESTED WEIGHT IN POUNDS | TYPICAL PACKAGE SPECS |
|---|---|---|---|---|
| Pheasant legs | Whole with skin on. | Slow cook, braise. | 4–6 oz each | 4 legs per tray |
| Pheasant backs | Whole | Used for stock. | Weight varies | Bagged |
| Smoked Pheasant, whole | Whole bird smoked, ready to eat. | Serve as is or heat. | 2–3 lbs each | 1 per bag, 10–12 bags per case |
| Smoked Pheasant Breast | Whole breast folded into "football" shape. | Serve as is or heat. | 8–12 oz each | 1 per bag |

**TABLE 4-28 GUINEA FOWL PURCHASING AND USAGE SPECIFICATIONS**

| ITEM AND NAMP NUMBER | DESCRIPTION OR FABRICATION | SUGGESTED COOKING METHOD, OR APPLICATION | AVERAGE SUGGESTED WEIGHT IN POUNDS | TYPICAL PACKAGE SPECS |
|---|---|---|---|---|
| Guinea Fowl NAMP P5000 | Whole bird | Roast whole or disjoint into parts. | 2 1/2 to 4 lbs each | 1 per bag, (12 per case, weight varies) |
| Guinea Fowl Airline Breast NAMP P5016 | Single or double lobes with section of wing | Sauté or pan sear, grill. | 7–10 oz each breast | 2 per pack, varies |
| Guinea Fowl Boneless Breast | Single or double lobe, sold skin on | Sauté, pan sear, grill. | 6–7 oz each | 2 per pack, varies |
| Guinea Fowl Leg Quarters NAMP P5030 | Whole legs | Broil, grill, braise, stuff. | 4–6 oz each leg | 4 per pack |

## TABLE 4-29 PIGEON AND SQUAB PURCHASING AND USAGE SPECIFICATIONS

| ITEM AND NAMP NUMBER | DESCRIPTION OR FABRICATION | SUGGESTED COOKING METHOD, OR APPLICATION | AVERAGE SUGGESTED WEIGHT IN POUNDS | TYPICAL PACKAGE SPECS |
|---|---|---|---|---|
| Pigeon/Squab NAMP P6000 | Whole bird, can be sold with head and feet on | Roast whole | 1 lb each | 1 per bag, (12–24 per case, varies) |

## TABLE 4-30 QUAIL PURCHASING AND USAGE SPECIFICATIONS

| ITEM AND NAMP NUMBER | DESCRIPTION OR FABRICATION | SUGGESTED COOKING METHOD, OR APPLICATION | AVERAGE SUGGESTED WEIGHT IN POUNDS | TYPICAL PACKAGE SPECS |
|---|---|---|---|---|
| Quail NAMP P7000 | Whole bird, can be purchased split, typically without giblets | Roast whole, grill, broil. | 4–5 oz each; Jumbo 5–7 oz | 4 or 6 per pack depending on producer |
| Semiboneless quail "Euro-quail" | Whole bird glove boned with legs and wings still intact | Roast whole, stuff, grill, broil. | 3 oz | 4 or 6 per pack |
| Boneless Breast | Very small, used for stuffing | Grill, broil, pan sear. | 1.5–2 oz | Varies |
| Semiboneless legs | Small, femur bone removed | Grill, roast, pan sear, braise. | 1.5–2 oz each | Varies, bulk pack |
| Partridge, whole | | | | |
| NAMP P7400 | Whole bird, typically without giblets | Roast, grill whole, split | 3–5 oz each | Individual pack, 12 per case |
| Scottish Grouse | Whole bird | Roast whole | 4–5 oz each | Individual pack |

## TABLE 4-31 OSTRICH PURCHASING AND USAGE SPECIFICATIONS

| ITEM AND NAMP NUMBER | DESCRIPTION OR FABRICATION | SUGGESTED COOKING METHOD, OR APPLICATION | AVERAGE SUGGESTED WEIGHT IN POUNDS | TYPICAL PACKAGE SPECS |
|---|---|---|---|---|
| Ostrich Fan Filet | 2–3-inch thick, denuded section free of fat | Very tender, best cut for steaks, cutlets, roast. | 2.5–3.5 lbs | 1 per pack, sold as individual pieces |
| Back tenderloin | Oval, very tender, denuded | Very tender piece similar to beef tenderloin. | 1–3 lbs | 1 per pack, sold as individual pieces |
| Inside strip | Small, tender cut | Tender, used for steaks, medallions. | 1/2 to 1 lb each | Varies, 1–2 per pack |
| Outside strip | Small, medallion size pieces | Moderately tender, steaks, roast. | 3/4 to 1 1/2 lb each | Varies, 1–2 per pack |
| Ground Ostrich | Very lean | Can cook out dry if overcooked. | Varies | Varies |

## FRESH FISH AND SEAFOOD

Depending on the choices, volume, and variety utilized by a food service operation, the selection, purchase, and proper storage of fresh fish can be one of the most challenging inventories that a chef-buyer will have to cope with. The purchase of fresh seafood can also be one of the most controversial, with much debate over what species are sustainable versus those being badly overfished, the ecological impact of various methods of aquaculture (farm-raising fish, shellfish, or shrimp), and the environmental impact of the methods utilized in the catch or harvesting of fish. The global location of the source of the purchased fish can also raise much discussion, especially in terms of the standards maintained by some farming operations and the carbon footprint incurred from sourcing fish from all over the planet. There are various organizations, such as the Monterey Bay Aquarium and Blue Oceans Institute, which regularly monitor the biomass of various species as well as the environmental impact of both the catch and aqua-farming methods, and then make ratings or judgments as to the sustainability of purchasing each species of fish. Unfortunately, many of the findings of these organizations and various government organizations contradict each other. These factors challenge buyers and their management in determining what species of fish they should feature on their menus.

Many species of fish also have a season, much like produce, which will determine the times of year when these fish will be in the best condition, not spawning, most readily available, and at the best dollar value. Other species have quotas placed upon them that will limit when and/or how much of that species can be caught or how many days each year they can be fished. With seafood consumption rising yearly, it is important to understand the complexities of the products we purchase and serve. The harvesting and purchase of fish should be done correctly, using modern regulated techniques that are sustainable. Knowledge and education regarding seasonality, aquaculture, nutrition, safety, and sanitation are essential. Buyers, chefs, restaurateurs, and home cooks all need a better awareness of the complexities involved in our consumption of the sea's bounty.

Another consideration is the form in which each species is purchased. Most species of fish will require the correct fabrication to scale, clean, and portion them for production. The proper yield from this process will mean the difference between profit and loss, and badly cut product could make for an unsatisfied customer. Buyers must be sure their staff has the proper skills when opting for as-purchased (AP) or pre-cut fish. Proper receiving of fresh fish is also imperative. Fresh fish should not have a strong "fishy" odor; the gills should be brightly colored, the eyes bright and not sunken, and the flesh firm with the scales intact. If purchasing drawn fish, make sure the cavity is moist and bright with no indication of "belly burn," which happens when the fish is not gutted promptly and the digestive enzymes work on the flesh. Again, improper receiving will cause both financial loss and poor customer satisfaction.

When purchasing fish fillets, judging the freshness can be more difficult for receiving personnel. However, there are signs to check. Look for a briny clean aroma with no strong fishy smell. Dry, brittle fillets or excess moisture in the container can indicate the fish has been frozen and then thawed. The flesh should be evenly colored with no blood or any yellow or gray discoloration. Ensure skinned product has been thoroughly and carefully done; some species are best purchased skin-on in order to verify the species is as requested, and the skin also helps protect the flesh. The packaging should be intact, indicating the product was handled properly.

Whole books are written on all the various species and culinary applications for the various fish and shellfish in the market. For this chapter, we just touch upon the general families of fish and their best cooking applications. For more information about specific storage information for fish and shellfish, see page 206 in Chapter 5.

## SHELLFISH

Shellfish are available in a wide variety of species and market forms, such as fresh, frozen, canned, and pasteurized. Wide demand has both expanded the number of market forms they are sold in and increased the need for insuring the food safety of these products.

### Shrimp

Shrimp is sold both fresh and frozen, but frozen is much more readily available in the market. Store fresh or thawed shell-on shrimp in crushed ice, and be sure to

FIGURE **4.33** Shrimp should be received below 40°F/4°C. They should have a fresh, clean aroma, and not be discolored or slimy.

FIGURE **4.34** Shrimp sizes from left to right: 31/40; 31–35; 21–25; 16–20; U10.

| TABLE 4-32 UNDERSTANDING SHRIMP COUNTS | | |
|---|---|---|
| **SHRIMP SIZE** | **COUNT PER POUND, GREEN, HEAD OFF** | **COUNT IN A 5-LB/2.27 KG BOX** |
| Extra colossal | Under 10 | 40–49 |
| Colossal | Under 12 or under 15 | (U12) 50–59 (U15) 60–74 |
| Extra jumbo | 16/20 | 75–97 |
| Jumbo | 21/25 | 98–120 |
| Extra large | 26/30 | 121–145 |
| Large | 31/35 | 121–145 |
| Medium large | 36/40 | 174–190 |
| Medium | 41/50 | 191–249 |
| Small | 51/60 | 241–290 |
| Extra small | 61/70 | 291–340 |

utilize it within a few days. Shelled shrimp must be stored in sealed containers to protect the flesh and should be used quickly as they deteriorate rapidly. Shrimp should be below 40°F/4°C when received and have a clean briny odor; the shells should not be discolored, brittle, or slimy; and the flesh should be white with no yellowing. Frozen shrimp should not show any sign of freezer burn or be encrusted with excess ice.

Shrimp are available with the shell and head on, and these are desired for some cuisines. Lower market demands dictate close inspection for freshness when received. Raw, shell-on shrimp with the head removed (Green Headless) is the most common form of both fresh and frozen shrimp, and is available in a wide range of sizes. Green headless shrimp can also be commonly purchased peeled or peeled with the vein removed (P&D). Other market forms of shrimp can be precooked, breaded frozen, butterflied, and broken pieces. Frozen shrimp are available in IQF form, with each shrimp frozen and separate, or in block form, usually packed in 4 or 5 lb/1.81 to 2.27 kg units.

Peeling and deveining a shrimp

Generally, the larger shrimp go for a more premium price, so it behooves buyers to ensure they are receiving what they pay for. The following chart indicates the various sizes and counts.

## Mollusks

Mollusks such as clams, oysters, and mussels are best when purchased alive; their shells protect them and aid in their shelf life so they can be harvested, packed, and transported. Scallops are available in their shell with roe for a premium price but are most often sold shucked and packed in bags or tins for sale. Warm-water species such

| Address    New England Shellfish Co. | Certification # MA 1234 | |
|---|---|---|
| Original shipper's certificate # xxxxx | If different from above xxxxxxxx | |
| Harvest date: 1/10/2007 | Shipping date: | |
| Type of shellfish:   oysters _____    mussels _____    soft clams _____ | | |
| Quantity of shellfish:   bushel _____    pounds _____    count _____ | | |
| This tag must remain attached until container is empty and then kept on file for 90 days. | | |
| To: | Reshipping certification # | Date of reshipping |

FIGURE 4.35 Sample shellfish tag.

FIGURE **4.36** Before preparing, tap any open clams. If they are alive, they will immediately close. Those that do not close are dead and should be discarded.

Opening clams and oysters

as queen conch have a very short shelf life and should be either shucked and consumed or frozen immediately. Fresh mollusks should be sold in netted backs to prevent suffocation. The shells should be sealed tightly or, if gapping, move or close when tapped. Open mollusks are dead and should be discarded. Shellfish should be received cold with a clean briny aroma and come from a certified interstate source with an accompanying tag verifying that source.

Clams are available live in the shell and shucked fresh. They are also found chopped in cans, frozen in or out of the shell, and in breaded strips. Quahog clams come in a variety of sizes from the small littlenecks (about 10 per pound) up to topnecks, cherrystones, and large chowder clams. Other fresh live varieties include the soft shell or steamer clam and petite Manila clams (about 20 per pound).

Mussels, like clams, are available live in the shell year-round, but tend to be more fragile with a shorter shelf life. These will periodically gap, so be sure to tap the shells to see if they close before discarding. Live mussels are available from the wild or farmed on ropes. The farmed ones tend to be cleaner and have a higher meat-to-shell ratio. Mussels are also available frozen, canned, smoked, or marinated.

Oysters, like clams, are live in their shell and are found in a variety of sizes; they are generally marketed by the region that they come from and are graded by shell size and shape. Oysters are also frequently sold shucked according to size from smaller standards up to the larger extra selects. Oysters are sold from the wild and farmed. Other market forms are frozen on the half shell, breaded, and smoked.

Scallops, as previously noted, are available live in the shell, but these are expensive and have a very short shelf life. Scallops are most commonly found fresh shucked. They are preferably sold as "dry," or untreated, or "wet," which have been bathed in a solution containing sodium tripolyphosphate. This solution adds water and weight and preserves the color of the scallop. Unfortunately, this process also affects the flavor and makes it difficult to sear or brown the scallops, and their extra liquid releases during cooking. The dry scallop will carry a premium price, but the quality is substantially improved. Scallops are sold by size from the largest colossal U-10 size to 10–20 jumbo counts to large or 20–30 count size. Bay scallops are smaller, and the Calico is very small, running about 200 per pound. Other market forms available are broken sea scallops, frozen, breaded, and smoked.

## Crab

Crabs are available in some form year-round; the most common types of live crabs available in the United States are the blue crab, the Dungeness, and the Jonah crab. Of these, blue crabs are the most common and are sourced along the eastern and Gulf coasts. These are also available as soft shell crabs during the season when they molt; soft shells are marketed by size from the largest "whales" down to mediums. These crabs are highly desired in season, but are very fragile and quickly to begin get leathery as their hard shells grow back. These are a challenge for both buyer and chef, but the demand every May drives the need to offer them in many restaurants.

Blue crab meat is also sold in pound containers, either fresh or pasteurized. Crabmeat is graded as jumbo lump for the premium large chunks; lump; and backfin, which is the smallest flake. The claw and knuckle meat is also available. Jonah crabs are from Maine and Canada and sold live or as picked meat. Dungeness crabs are large and a west coast favorite. Again, the meat can be purchased as well as the live whole crabs. Frozen king and snow crab legs and stone crab claws are also available.

FIGURE **4.37** Store live oysters in the refrigerator covered with a damp cloth or seaweed. Cook or serve as soon after receiving as possible.

FIGURE **4.38** Scallops in the shell should be received in a mesh bag or sack with an identification tag, which should be kept on file for 90 days after consumption. They should arrive alive and move when touched. If the scallops are not alive, they should be received below 40°F/4°C and smell sweet and briny.

FIGURE **4.39** Store live crabs in the refrigerator covered with a damp cloth or seaweed. Cook them as soon after receiving as possible.

Crab fabrication

Lobster fabrication

Cleaning squid

### Lobster

Of the many types of lobsters available around the world, the most common are the spiny lobster and the American or Maine lobster. Maine lobsters were once so common that these were often used as prison fare and even for fertilizer. Today, these are considered high-end fare. Lobsters must be alive when cooked, so buyers and chefs need to only buy as needed and receive them carefully. Live lobsters are stored in tanks in restaurants that use a significant volume. They can also be held briefly under refrigeration covered with damp newspaper and seaweed. Lobster tail meat or claw and knuckle meat are available canned and frozen. The quality of the frozen meat has improved dramatically in the last few years.

Spiny lobsters lack the large claws of the American lobster and are available from various places around the world. The tails are the most common form in many U.S. markets, sold as either warm or cold water depending on where they are sourced from. The cold-water tail is considered preferable and carries a higher price. These are sold frozen and by size.

### SQUID

Fresh squid is available from many parts of the world, although buying it cleaned is the most common practice. Fresh squid should have fresh briny aroma with no off or strong fishy scent. The flesh will be of varying shades of gray. If purchasing fresh whole squid, buyers need to make sure it is cleaned thoroughly and quickly after receipt. Squid freezes well and can be purchased that way in a variety of packaged forms; it is also available canned, dried, and smoked.

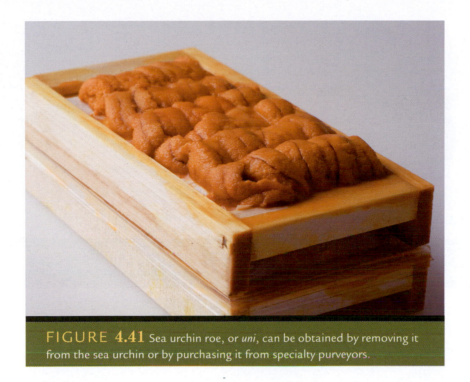

FIGURE **4.41** Sea urchin roe, or *uni*, can be obtained by removing it from the sea urchin or by purchasing it from specialty purveyors.

## SEA URCHIN

Sea urchin is available in season and is desired for the roe or gonads, commonly known as *uni*. The best quality *uni* will be yellow-gold in color and firm in texture. Urchins have a short shelf life and should be used within 48 hours. The *uni* is also available fresh in season or frozen in small trays.

## FIN FISH

With all fish, assuring freshness upon receipt is the most import part of the purchasing process. It is crucial to have a good monger that you can trust and that does a good volume of business so you know they are turning over their inventory quickly. However, careful inspection at your dock will remain critical to ensure the product will always meet your standards. Be sure there is no stronger fishy smell; the fish should smell like the sea. The fishes' eyes should be full and clear, their gills should be maroon to bright red, and the scales should adhere tightly to the skin. The flesh of the fish should be firm with no sponginess; check the cavities of drawn fish to insure there is no "belly burn" from not having been eviscerated quickly and properly.

### Anchovy

Found fresh throughout the Atlantic and Mediterranean, these small beautiful fish are prized fresh in many cultures but are most commonly found canned, ground to a paste, or smoked in the United States. These can be baked, grilled, broiled, or fried.

### Arctic Char

This delicious relative to salmon and trout is found in the wild and is extensively farmed. The coloring can vary somewhat, especially those caught in the wild. The fish

Scaling and gutting a round fish

Flat fish fabrication (quarter fillet)

Flat fish fabrication (full fillet)

Filleting a large round fish

Filleting a small round fish (up and over)

has a mild flavor and fatty texture, making it a good choice to prepare by a wide range of methods, from poached to sautéed, baked, broiled, or smoked.

### Barramundi

This species of bass come from the rivers and estuaries of Australia, but is now widely farm raised. In the wild, this fish can grow quite large, but the farm-raised fish are usually harvested at around 3 pounds. This fish is firm, mild, and sustainably raised; it can be baked, broiled, poached, sautéed, or fried.

### Chilean Seabass (Patagonian Toothfish)

Mostly caught around the southern regions of South America and Africa, this fish is very popular and the catch sadly often exceeds the allowed quotas. These are typically sold head off and have a good yield. Light in flavor and buttery in texture, this fish is good cooked in many ways, but buyers should insist on properly sourced product.

### Hybrid Bass

A farm-raised cross between wild striped bass and white bass, this fast-growing fish has a good yield; its size is good for a preparation that serves the whole fish. The flavor is mild, although some describe it as muddy. This fish is good prepared by almost all methods, and the skin is delicious when crisped.

### Branzino, Loup de Mer

This is a European bass that is found along the Atlantic coast, in the Mediterranean, and is now farm raised. The shipping costs to the United States raise its cost, but many chefs still favor the quality of this fish. The delicate and lean flesh benefits from the addition of fat or moisture in the cooking process, but is delicious cooked by almost any method.

### Black Sea Bass

This delicious fish is found all along the eastern U.S. sea coast, but the catch is controlled by a quota system. The beautiful black skin is often deliciously crisped and visually appealing on the plate. As with the other bass family members, this fish is tasty when cooked in almost any fashion.

FIGURE **4.43** Striped bass.

## Striped Bass

Available all along the eastern American shoreline, this wonderful fish was almost fished out a short while back, but an aggressive quota system has returned it to sustainability. These fish can be found from 5 to 50 lb in weight, but the smaller to mid-range will have a finer texture. The meat is white, mild, and delicious and can be prepared baked, broiled, grilled, sautéed, poached, or steamed. This fish is also excellent raw as a crudo.

## Tautog, Blackfish

This fish weighs in around 3 pounds and is more prized by sports fisherman than in the food service. This fish can be fried, baked, or broiled and works well in stew or chowder.

## Bluefish

This Atlantic species is very oily and lacks the popularity it once had. That oily flesh should be consumed very shortly after landing and served aggressively flavored to complement its oily flavor. Broil, bake, sauté, grill, or smoke this fish.

## Bream, Daurade

This porgy family member comes out of the Mediterranean or is farm raised and generally a couple of pounds in size. The flesh is off-white to reddish in color, mild, and sweet, and it is best cooked using a moist heat method; small fish are best cooked whole.

## Catfish

This was once thought of as a muddy-tasting bottom feeder but is now a well-received, fast-growing farm-raised fish, most commonly sold in fillet form. The flesh is white, moist, and sweet. Properly raised, this fish is delicious cooked by baking, broiling, grilled, sautéed, or, of course, deep frying.

## Cod Family

This family of fish is found in the Atlantic and Pacific; the species include true and Pacific cod, hake, haddock, pollock, whiting, and cusk. This was once the major food crop in the oceans, but overfishing has decimated the biomass in many areas, while

FIGURE **4.44** Catfish.

excellent management has helped the population rebound in others. Cod has wonderful texture and excellent mild flavor. There is some argument over which species is preferred, but the Atlantic cod has long been the most commercially important. Any small (under 2 lb/907 g) codfish, haddock, or pollock can be referred to as a scrod. This fish is excellent cooked in a variety of ways and responds well to a variety of ethnic flavors. This fish is available drawn, head off, in fillet form, and smoked. The Pacific cod is not as abundant or commercially important as its Atlantic cousin, but is considered more sustainably managed.

### Flounder

Flounders are a flat fish that are bottom dwellers and have a white and dark side with both their eyes on one side of their head. This fish is found in many parts of the world and usually ranges from 1 to 4 lb/454 g to 1.81 kg. There are a variety of species in this family, including witch flounder, plaice, and yellowtail; these fish are best sautéed or poached but can also be baked and fried.

### Grouper

This member of the sea bass family inhabits the Caribbean and the coast of Florida. These can grow quite large but are generally found between 5 to 20 lb/2.27 to 9.07 kg in the commercial market. There are two species: the red grouper, which will be from red to light brown in color, and the black grouper, which is actually dark brown in color. The flesh of these fish is white, mild, and a bit sweet with a large flake. Like all bass, this fish can be cooked in a variety of methods.

### Halibut

This is the largest of the flatfish; it is found in both the Atlantic and Pacific and is now farm raised. Pacific halibut is seasonally available from March to November. The farmed and Atlantic varieties are available year-round but can be quite expensive. The flesh is dense and white and is good cooked most ways. The cheeks are also delicious, and the bones are prized for stock.

FIGURE **4.45** Flounder.

FIGURE **4.46** Grouper.

FIGURE **4.47** Halibut.

### John Dory

Found in the Atlantic and Mediterranean, this fish runs from 3 to 5 lb/1.36 to 2.27 kg in size, but its large head makes for a poor yield and thus a poor food cost. The meat is delicate and handled much like flounder.

### Lingcod

This fish is found in the Pacific from Mexico on to the north and, despite its name, is not truly a member of the cod family. The fish looks pale green when raw but cooks up firm and white and has a very mild flavor. This fish can be baked, broiled, fried, or poached.

### Mackerel

This fish is found in the mid- to North Atlantic and in Europe down to North Africa and into the Mediterranean. Most often, the market size is 2 to 3 lb/907 g to 1.36 kg, and the flesh is oily but not terribly strong. This is especially true of the Spanish variety, which can be a bit larger and milder. The flavor of this fish lends itself to baking, grilling, and broiling. This fish can also be salted or smoked.

### Mahi-mahi

This beautiful fish is also called dorado or dolphin fish, although it is not related to that mammal. These fish are usually sold as "bullets" with the head, tail, and fins removed. They market around 15 to 25/6.8 to 11.34 kg with an excellent yield. This fish is best grilled and broiled, but can also be baked and stir fried.

### Monkfish

This fish is mostly sold head off, as the head is huge and very ugly and ruins the yield of the product. When receiving head on, do not fail to enjoy the cheeks. The flesh is dense, white, and sweet and can be prepared in almost all cooking methods.

### Mullet, Rouget

There are many species of this fish, but the red Mediterranean or rouget species are the most prized. The flesh is firm, rich in flavor, and oily. That oil content means a short shelf life, so use this fish quickly upon receipt. This fish is best prepared by grilling but can also be sautéed, broiled, deep-fried, or smoked.

FIGURE 4.48 Mackerel.

FIGURE **4.49** Monkfish.

## Opah

This large beautiful fish can be at found well over 100 pounds, and is known as the Hawaiian species, but it can be found in any temperate waters. The large size and odd body shape mean that the meat will vary in color from orange to red to pale pink or white and vary in texture and flavor. Due to the size, this fish is usually sold as fillets or loins. The flesh can be cooked by baking, broiling, frying, or steaming, or it can be smoked.

## Orange Roughy

Slow growing and overfished for many years, this fish does not have the market presence it once had. Generally sold in fillet form, the flesh is white and mild. Also be sure the skin and blood line are completely removed.

## Ocean Perch

This is a variety that comes from the North Atlantic and is known as a red fish, but it is not to be confused with the Gulf redfish. This fish is inexpensive and has a small, mild-flavored flesh. This fish can be baked, broiled, fried, sautéed, or poached.

## Pompano

This pan-sized fish is native to the U.S. Atlantic coast south from Virginia and the Gulf of Mexico. This has been a highly valued fish by many chefs and can command a high price. The flesh is firm, white, and mild in flavor with a small flake. This fish works with almost any cooking method but poaching.

## Porgy

There are a number of species of this fish that inhabit the Atlantic and Mediterranean. This is a good eating fish but is not well utilized. The fish has flesh similar in texture and flavor to snapper and is ideal when cooked whole on the grill. Porgys can also be baked, sautéed, broiled, fried, or used in soups and stews.

FIGURE **4.50** Porgy.

## Red Drum

More commonly referred to as channel bass or redfish, this fish is available along the Atlantic coast and into the Gulf, where it is most prized. Commercial fishing of this fish had to be banned for a time due to the extensive overfishing done to meet the huge demand. Fishing has once again begun, but under a strict quota system. The huge popularity of blackened redfish is what drove that demand, but this fish is also good poached, grilled, fried, baked, and sautéed.

## Sablefish, Black Cod

Native to the cold waters of the Pacific Northwest, this fish is prized for its rich buttery flesh. The high oil content of the flesh makes for a very short shelf life, but it also allows the fish to freeze well, which is how it is often marketed. That oily flesh is excellent for smoking, but this delicious fish is also excellent sautéed, grilled, baked, or broiled. Fresh fish is more likely available in the winter months.

## Salmon

### Atlantic Salmon

Today almost every Atlantic salmon is farm raised as the wild variety has been brought to near extinction. This is still an extremely popular and commonly utilized fish. How this fish is farmed is quite controversial, as some farms can be quite damaging to the environment; concerned buyers should do their homework as to how their salmon is farmed and fed. These fish range widely in size, but 8 to 10/3.63 to 4.54 kg is the most popular. These fish have firm, moist, oily flesh that is very popular smoked and cured, but almost any cooking method will work with this fish. The flavor lacks the subtlety and distinct flavor of the Pacific wild salmon, but is still very popular.

### Coho, Silver Salmon

This wild Pacific variety looks very much like an Atlantic salmon but is differentiated by having a gray tongue and an anal fin with 13 or more bones. The flesh of the Coho is softer and a bit oilier than other Pacific varieties and is excellent smoked or cured. This

FIGURE **4.51** Atlantic salmon.

fish is now being farmed in Asia and South America. The flesh is pink to red and has a medium flake. Availability fresh is limited to the late summer months.

### Sockeye

This Pacific breed of salmon is considered by some to be the best textured and flavored, and the fishery is well regulated. The fish runs a little smaller than others, typically 6 to 10 lb/2.72 to 4.54 kg, and they can command a strong price. The flesh is firm, dark, and high in fat. This fish is enjoyed raw and smoked, but is also excellent broiled, baked, steamed, poached, or grilled. This will be available fresh from May into late summer, depending on the size of the catch.

### Chinook, King Salmon

This Pacific species is the largest of all the salmon and the most highly sought after. Overfishing and environmental issues have greatly limited the number of fish and the areas where it may be fished; it is highly regulated. This fish has firm, richly flavored, oily red flesh, usually dark red in hue, but there is also a variety with ivory-colored flesh. This salmon can be prepared by almost any cooking method, smoked, or eaten raw. This fish is in season from early summer into fall depending on

FIGURE **4.52** Sockeye salmon.

the catch. Some small areas may open for fishing at other times, but supply would be limited and expensive.

### Sardines

This small fish is in the herring family and most popular fresh in Mediterranean and European markets, although they are growing in acceptance in the United States. These are most commonly found canned in oil or a sauce, but are good grilled or smoked when fresh.

### Skate

This fish is a ray and found on both sides of the Atlantic. The wing portion is eaten, and larger sizes are often preferred. This fish is best eaten a day or two after landing and also has a short shelf life. This fish will have a thick slimy skin, which is normally removed before service. The flesh has a string-like or corduroy-like appearance but is sweet and tender; this flesh works well poached or sautéed.

### Snapper

These fish come in many varieties and are found in warm-water areas around the globe. The meat is prized by chefs in many cultures for its firm texture and mild flavor. Efforts are being made now to limit the catch as its popularity is causing overfishing. In the United States, the red snapper is the most popular variety, but demand can lead mongers to market other varieties as true reds. Only purchase skin-on fillets to ensure proper identification. The meat will be a pale brown, contain a blood line, and

FIGURE **4.53** Skate.

FIGURE **4.54** Snapper.

FIGURE **4.55** Sole.

turn white when cooked. The firm texture allows this fish to be grilled, poached, fried, or baked stuffed, and the flavors complement the flavors found in warm climates such as hot peppers, mangos, lime, and coconut.

## Sole

The fish are similar to flounder, and often flounder are sold as sole. They have small eyes and an oval body shape with a rounder head and mouth. Of the six types in North American waters, few have any commercial viability. The west coast Petrale sole is actually a quality Pacific flounder, and lemon sole is the common name for a winter flounder caught in the northern Atlantic.

Dover sole is caught along the European coast and referred to as true sole; it is priced accordingly. Only purchase this fish whole to assure identification; this expensive fish is usually served one per person and is classically prepared at tableside in high-end restaurants. Other than sautéed, this fish can be poached or stuffed and baked. Dover sole freezes well, and this is a bit more affordable than fresh.

## Sturgeon

Most commonly found farm-raised today, white sturgeon is the preferred variety. The farmed fish run smaller than the wild variety and are usually sold as "bullets" with the head, tail, and fins off. The meat is firm and dense and is excellent smoked; it can also be prepared baked, broiled, grilled, or sautéed.

### Swordfish

This fish is available at times all over the world. Many areas now have catch restrictions to prevent the continued overfishing of this popular fish, and it is now much better managed. The price this fish can bring has also lessened the world demand. The flesh can range in color from orange (pumpkin) to pink and white and will cook up off-white. The flesh is dense and sweet, and is excellent grilled and served with simple additions that will not mask its flavor.

### Tilapia

This fish is widely farmed throughout the world and generally found between 1 and 3 lb/454 g to .36 kg in size. The flesh is white to pink with a blood line between the flesh and skin, and is fairly light in flavor and firm. This fish can be baked, broiled, fried, or sautéed.

### Tilefish

This beautiful fish is not as common in the market as it once was. The flesh cooks up white and is sweet and firm. This fish cooks by most methods and works well in sashimi.

### Trout

Trout, usually rainbow, is widely farmed in the United States and normally sold between 8 and 16 oz/227 to 454 g. These fish are usually sold in the round, dressed, or butter-flied. The fillets are delicate in flavor and texture, and are best served with butter, citrus, herbs, or nuts. Ideal sautéed, this fish is also excellent baked, poached, and smoked.

### Tuna

These large powerful fish travel the Atlantic and Pacific oceans and into the Mediterranean. The demand for these fish and modern technology in fishing techniques have devastated several species of this fine fish. Bluefin tuna is dramatically overfished, but attempts to develop and enforce a worldwide moratorium on harvesting this fish have been unsuccessful. There quite a few types of tuna from two major families: albacore and big eye.

FIGURE **4.56** Trout.

### Albacore

This fish has a light- to pale-colored flesh, which cooks white and is most commonly canned as white meat tuna.

### Bigeye

This fish is found around the world except in the Mediterranean. It is prized for its mild flavor and fatty flesh. These can grow very large and are sometimes referred to as ahi. This fish is quite similar to that of the yellowfin tuna.

### Blackfin

This is a small species with a pale flesh and a mild flavor; it is not often utilized.

### Bluefin

This is the largest and highest prized member of the species, and, as noted, its popularity has devastated the population. Expensive when available, this quality fish is highly popular.

### Yellowfin

Also marketed as ahi in the United States, this excellent tuna has become the market standard and may soon face the same overfishing issues as the bluefin.

### Bonito

This tuna has a dark, strongly flavored flesh and is of little value in the foodservice industry, except when dried and flaked and added to kelp and water to make dashi.

## Turbot

This is a large flat fish; the European variety is highly prized by chefs. This fish is found wild in the Norwegian Sea, around the United Kingdom, and through the Mediterranean. Turbot is also farm raised in Europe and Chile. The flesh of this species is white and firm and like dover sole; this fish should only be purchased whole to assure identification. Prepare turbot simply as to not mask its delicate flavor; this can be poached, steamed, baked, broiled, or sautéed.

FIGURE 1.57 Turbot.

## Wolf Fish

Despite being underutilized in the United States, the wolf fish is prized in Europe and this North Atlantic species has been disappearing from the ocean. When available, this has firm, sweet white flesh that will work with almost any cooking technique; the cheek muscles are especially delicious.

# INVENTORY MANAGEMENT AND THE STOREROOM

Everything purchased and received, then stored and inventoried, and then issued in a foodservice operation comes in and out of the receiving and storeroom department of that organization and is handled by those employed in that department. Therefore, the ability of this department to exercise all the proper controls will dramatically affect both the quality of the product purchased and the profitability of the establishment. In a business where success and profit are measured as a small percentage of total sales, the expertise and controls exhibited in this area are essential to that success.

## THE STOREROOM FUNCTION

The storeroom of any foodservice operation is the control center for everything utilized within that facility. Everything flowing in and out of these areas will determine the ability of the cooking and service teams to perform and will affect the quality of what they serve.

Any breakdown from when an order is placed to how the product is received, stored, and then issued will place a dramatically negative effect on the quality and cost of whatever is served (or wasted). These products are company assets and must be protected. Therefore, the proper function, layout, and performance of the storeroom are critical in any foodservice operation's success. If products are not available when needed and must be sourced from less than optimal sources, or are not available for sale, revenue and possibly customer satisfaction are lost. Product received out of code, out of specification, in the wrong pack or weight, or in poor condition will also cost the organization money. Product received or issued without the proper paperwork can cost the establishment money, making life difficult for those in accounting, and possibly adding administrative costs. Therefore bringing in the necessary products on time and properly storing them for the production team's use with the required paper trail is essential for any operation, big or small.

The size and formality of an operation's storeroom will depend on the sophistication, finances, and available space the given operation has. However, proper controls must always be exhibited in each delivery's receipt, storage, and issue or utilization. If not, the facility's proper fiscal and quality standards will not be upheld. Obviously, the more formalized and secure the storage facility, the better the control, but in all cases, steps should be taken to safeguard the product purchased and maintain its value.

## STOREROOM OPERATIONS

The function of a storeroom typically serves a dual purpose; it serves as the purchasing arm as all needed products are procured from outside vendors and received and stored by the storeroom team. The storeroom also serves as a vendor in that it distributes all the products to the company's internal customers. The chef/buyer or purchasing agent must have the ability to procure needed products in a timely fashion to insure the op-

FIGURE 5.1 Basic storeroom organization.

eration has the raw ingredients necessary to meet customer demand. The buyer also serves as the liaison between the realities and trends of the market and the internal end users. This means working with the operation's chefs to insure they understand what is available and in season and know what desired items may need to be reconsidered. Ideally buyers should be part of the menu-planning process along with the chef's production team in order to ensure all desired items are available in the required quality before the menu has final approval. However, the buyer must perform these duties in a financially astute manner in order to meet the needs of the business' management. All these roles must be successfully executed to insure the success of the venture.

Storeroom staffing is also contingent on the size and sophistication of the operation. In a small operation, purchasing is generally managed by the chef, and receiving and storage are handled by designated members of the kitchen staff. Larger operations may have a purchasing agent or steward, and still larger operations will likely have a team of individuals to manage all purchasing and storage duties. The owners of the business will have final authority in determining how much purchasing staff is fiscally warranted, and a buyer or chef will need to justify the cost of additional employees against the financial controls and level of controls required. If employing a full dedicated staff, these are the typical positions created:

- Storeroom Manager: Coordinates all functions of the department, including scheduling staff, purchasing, receiving, product specification and rotation, issue, setting par levels, inventories, verifying food costs, and ensuring that all the needs of the operation are being met.
- Buyer: Works directly with the purveyors, insuring proper product specification, bid comparisons, blind cuttings, and so on. This person may represent the business at food shows and exhibitions as well. May also work with management in purchasing services and leasing needs. This person usually forms the personal relationship between vendor and client.
- Receiving Clerk: Responsible for the proper receipt of all incoming deliveries. Insures the received product's invoice and purchase order match, specifications and quality standards are met, debit and/or credit memos are issued, and all products are properly stored and rotated.
- Stock clerk: Maintains cleanliness and order of storage areas, works with receiving clerk in properly storing and rotating goods, fills in-house customer needs or requisitions, and advises buyer if inventory levels suddenly change or par stock levels need adjustment.

# STOREROOM AND RECEIVING FACILITY LAYOUT

Ideally, the storeroom of a foodservice operation should be separate from the production areas, secure, sanitary, safe to work in, and well lit, and should allow for an efficient flow of people and goods. The storage area is often where management feels it can limit the allotted space, the feeling being that with the high price per square foot of space, it is best to utilize as much as possible for seating for paying customers. This is an understandable idea, and surely with square footage so dear, space should not be wasted. However, if buyers lack sufficient space to buy well, work safely, and maintain the integrity and quality of the ingredients, then dollars and efficiency will surely be squandered. The ability to balance the organization's needs is essential.

There are several formulas that have been developed to determine how much square footage is appropriate for storage; most of these formulas multiply a fixed amount of space by the number of seats by the number of meals served per day. However, the range and type of cuisine served and the ratio of refrigeration to dry storage space also need to be evaluated based on the type of menu involved. A typical rule of thumb is to designate 10% to 12% of the total allotted usable business space for storage, half as dry and half as refrigerated. Again, the type of foodservice and style of menu will determine an operation's exact needs.

In planning the storeroom layout, one also needs to learn the local health, sanitation, and insurance codes. Generally food needs to be stored 6 in/15.24 cm off the floor and 18 in/45.72 cm below the sprinkler heads. The aisles must be wide enough so employees can bend and turn safely, usually at least 30 in/76.2 cm wide. Both doors and aisles should be wide enough to accommodate the width of carts if not pallets as well. Sufficient lighting is also important. There should be room for sufficient air flow, and

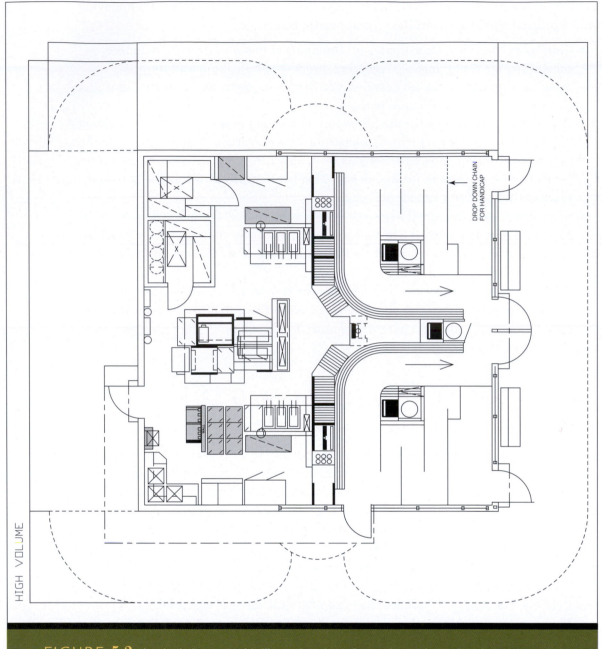

FIGURE **5.2** The shaded areas in this illustration show the total area devoted to the storeroom in relation to kitchen and retail space in a high-volume, quick foodservice restaurant.

good temperature control is essential. Shelving units should be labeled on the aisle end to alert everyone to what is stored in that unit. This speeds the fill rate, and these labels should not be changed more than is absolutely necessary so employees are not wasting work time hunting for ingredients.

There should also be an area nearby to accommodate step ladders or stools if needed, storage bins or lugs, carts, and hand trucks. This type of equipment is essential for the safe and efficient movement of the product in and out of the facility. Therefore, these all need to be stored in close proximity to the work that needs to be done without blocking essential aisles, doors, or utility panels.

Receiving space is often given a lower priority by owners and management than even the allotted storage space. Also, in many cramped urban settings, the amount of space that can be utilized for receiving is even less as the only access may be a doorway on the sidewalk or a tight alleyway. However, if funds and space allow, it makes sense to make the needed investment in a proper receiving area. This is where the controls exist to insure that what is received matches the orders placed and the chef's specifications. Lack of space and equipment to fully exercise these controls will certainly cost the operator in dollars and possibly customer satisfaction. A proper receiving area can also help prevent costly employee injuries as well. Bringing in deliveries through doorways and carrying cases up or down narrow stairways into kitchens or storage areas can be dangerous, but this happens all too often.

If an operation does have ample space for a loading dock, the typical height from street level is usually about 4 to 5 ft/1.22 to 1.52 m, but the height of delivery vehicles can vary a great deal more than that. Therefore, it is essential to provide a ramp that can bridge the gap and height variance. Some docks will have hydraulic ramps built into the dock floor, but most are simply heavy metal plates that are put into position as needed. Even with these ramps, be sure the slope is not so severe as to make the delivery slide too fast or tip over. Safety is always essential in this area.

| EXAMPLES OF MEAT RECEIVING SPECIFICATIONS FOR A VARIETY OF CUTS | | | |
|---|---|---|---|
| ITEM DESCRIPTION | SKU # | SPECIFICATION | UNIT OR SIZE |
| Beef, loin, Full loin trimmed | 3 8090 | MBG# 172, Choice, yield 2–3, no excess internal fat, maximum fat cover of 1" at any point (see above). Requires fabrication! | 60–70 lbs |
| Beef Bones | 3 8020 | Frozen, 3" cut cross section. Minimum of 50% neck or vertebrae. No sour smell or gray meat. | 50 lb case |
| Beef Bones Marrow | 3 8021 | Cut from shank bones 2– 3" wide, no ends. | 10 lb bags |
| Beef Brisket, Corned | 3 8015 | Raw, somewhat trimmed, in Cryovac. | 10 lb avg. |
| Beef Brisket, fresh | 3 8018 | Deckle off, choice yield grade 2–3. MBG #120, in Cryovac. Trimmed well, almost free of exterior fat. | 10–12 lb avg. |
| Beef Cheeks | 3 8024 | Well trimmed. Frozen. Bright Red in color. | 65 lb cs |
| Beef Flank Steak | 3 8084 | Packed in cryovac. MBG #193. No tackiness, yellowing fat or sour smell. USDA choice or higher. | 6 per bag 1.5–2.0 lb avg. piece |
| Beef, Ground 85% lean | 3 8034 | Ground from meat room trimmings and/ or beef gooseneck rounds, fine ground 2 x (standard hamburger grind ) | 5 lb bag or as ordered |
| Beef, Ground Shank Meat | 3 8082 | Ground from well trimmed beef shanks, coarse ground 1x for consume' | 5 lb bag or as ordered |
| Beef Hanger Steak | 3 8023 | Whole, untrimmed hangers, choice grade | 4 per bag |
| Beef Knuckle | 3 8040 | Skinned, MBG #167A Packed in cryovac, fresh, no excess purge or brown blood. Joint removed. USDA choice or higher. | 9–10 avg. |
| Beef Oxtails | 3 8056 | Steer, frozen, 2" cut | 15 lb cs. |

FIGURE **5.3** Example of proper receiving specifications.

In addition to a leveling ramp, there are other pieces of equipment that are desirable for the loading dock if space and budget allow. An ice machine for seafood is critical in maintaining the necessary temperature and quality of the fish. A hand sink is important for sanitation. Scales of an appropriate size for the type of product purchased are essential to verify delivered weights, and good lighting is mandatory to allow visual inspection. A hot-water hose and squeegee are desirable for maintaining cleanliness. Many operators prefer to move accepted meats and produce directly out of the delivery boxes and into bins or storage lugs to insure any insects in the folds of the boxes are not brought into the facility. These operations would require an ample supply of these containers and space to store them that is in close proximity to where they will be used. These containers may share space with the aforementioned hand trucks or carts used to move deliveries without them needing to be left in traffic aisles.

There should also be a receiving office on or within very close proximity to the loading dock. This office would provide a desk for staff to use, a PC, phones and a directory, and ample filing space for requisitions, invoices, and other billing information, as well as credit or debit forms, specification sheets, company catalogs or product listings, and inventory sheets for both ordering and fiscal controls.

**FIGURE 5.4** It is important to have an easy way to transport food from the receiving area to where it will be stored, such as this hydraulic ramp.

## REFRIGERATION

Ideally in a restaurant or any foodservice operation, there will be separate coolers to accommodate the various inventory lines at the correct temperature. The variances may seem slight, but the closer a food item is stored to its ideal temperature, the longer that item will maintain its integrity. However, such ideal conditions typically only exist in large, well-funded operations or highly successful restaurants. When only a single walk-in cooler is feasible, the temperature should be maintained at approximately 34°F to 38°F/1°C to 2°C. Product is then arranged in these coolers so that items needing to be held at colder temperatures are near or under the compressor and those that hold better at slightly warmer temperatures are stored near the door. This is not ideal, but in many cases this is how it needs to be done. Freezers should maintain a temperature of −10°F to 0°F/−23°C to −18°C.

## MEAT AND POULTRY

Traditionally, meats were transported as whole or split carcasses. Train or tractor trailer loads were delivered to meat processors close to their final destination. In the 1960s, the invention of vacuum packaging allowed for meat to be stored for much longer with minimal loss. Fabrication could be done much farther from the customer and in plants that were much closer to the farms. Plastic packaging made from polymers originally had some problems with leaking. Today this process has been improved to securely package meats—even those with bone in—with minimal leakage. Meats should be inspected upon arrival for loose bags where air has entered. "Blown" bags or "leakers" should be returned, especially if there is discoloration and odor present.

Poultry items, such as broiler chickens, are often packaged in modified atmospheric packaging (MAP). This package is loose around the item and is filled with a $CO_2$ mixture to slow bacterial growth. Upon opening, there should be no strong sulfur odors, and poultry should not be slimy.

FIGURE **5.5a** Poultry is received and stored in one area of a refrigerator, elevated off the floor, to reduce chances of cross contamination.

FIGURE **5.5b** Beef is hung to dry age in its own area of a refrigerator.

## FISH AND SEAFOOD

### Round and Flat Fish

Fish should be received packed in crushed or flaked ice. After checking for freshness, immediately place all seafood under refrigeration. The best way to store round fish is to pack their cavities with ice, place the fish in the swimming position, and surround the entire body with more ice. Proper drainage is very important as is the need for more ice as necessary, since melting will occur. Flat fish are best stored with their thicker, dark side down, at a slight angle, and packed in ice. This is critical to preserving freshness and maintaining quality.

### Shellfish

All shellfish should be received from a clean, cold delivery truck and are best stored between 34°F to 38°F/1°C to 3°C. Live shellfish should have a mild clean aroma and acceptable appearance. Shucked shellfish or mussels, clams, or oyster meats should smell briny, have clear liquor with an acceptable meat-to-liquid ratio, and be devoid of shells or sand. A FIFO (first in, first out) system should be practiced with all highly perishable foods based on quality characteristics and date of receipt.

### Shrimp

With a shelf life of only a few days, fresh shrimp must be used immediately and kept as cold as possible. Store shell-on shrimp buried in drainable crushed ice or in a covered container in the coldest part of the refrigerator. Avoid storing shell-off fresh shrimp in ice because it may burn the delicate flesh; instead store them in a covered container in the refrigerator and use immediately.

### Lobster

Lobsters should always be purchased live, cooked, or frozen. Store live lobsters in aerated saltwater holding tanks or in the refrigerator covered with damp newspaper or seaweed for as little time as possible. Do not pack live lobsters in ice, and do not submerge them in fresh water; this will kill them. Monitor live lobsters for lethargic signs, and cook them as soon after receiving as possible.

FIGURE **5.6a** Drawn fish should be gently packed in crushed or flaked ice.

FIGURE **5.6b** Drawn fish should be stored with their cavities full of ice and not in contact with other fish.

FIGURE **5.6c** Flat fish should be stored in crushed ice at angles, and never stacked.

FIGURE **5.7** A fish cooler should have large, deep bins that can hold fish and seafood packed in crushed ice. A drain in the center of the floor is ideal for easy cleanup.

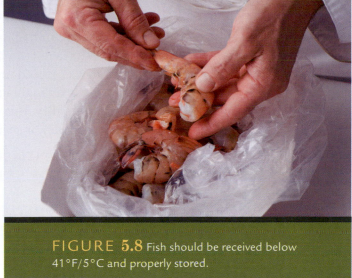

FIGURE **5.8** Fish should be received below 41°F/5°C and properly stored.

## PRODUCE

With the exception of tomatoes, unripe avocados, potatoes, bananas, and dry onions, all of your produce items will likely require refrigeration. There is an ideal temperature range for each type of produce, generally starting at about 33°F/1.5°C and then going upward to 45°F/7°C. If at all possible, you would have separate fruit and vegetable walk-ins, but such is not always the case. If one walk-in cooler is all that is available, careful arrangement of your produce from the warmer area near the door to the coldest area, which may be near the blower, may have to suffice. The relative humidity should also be high, around 80% to 90%, to reduce dehydration.

Produce that is stored under refrigeration should be kept as dry as possible to lessen the spoilage rate. Avoid washing produce prior to storage or placing produce with an ice pack over other product. Produce often has its own outer wrapping to preserve freshness. Do not peel vegetables or remove the outer leaves from lettuce or cabbage until ready to use. However, the leafy tops of items such as carrots, radishes, and beets should be removed as they continue to absorb the moisture and nutrition from the vegetable.

Some fruits such as stone fruits and pears should be held at room temperature until fully ripened. They can be refrigerated at that point but should be quickly utilized to maintain quality. Fruits and vegetables that emit a great amount of ethylene gas such as melons, bananas, and apples can actually promote the ripening of underripe produce, but just as quickly promote the spoilage of already ripe produce. Obviously these items should never be stored near anything that is fully ripe. Vegetables with powerful odors such as onions can also taint the flavor of other refrigerated items (e.g., dairy products and absorbent fruits). Using caution when storing these items is always prudent.

## DAIRY AND CHEESE

Dairy products such as milk and eggs should be stored at specific temperatures. Dairy should be stored at 35°F to 39°F/1.5°C to 4°C, and eggs should be stored around 40°F to 45°F/4°F to 7°C. Cheese needs to be treated differently, however. As a preservation method for milk, different types of cheese evolved in different places, and the best storage conditions for each type are available in the homelands of those cheeses. Whatever the type of cheese, if it was created before the advent of refrigeration, it was stored under available natural conditions.

If only one storage area is available for all of your cheeses, it is best to stay at or near 50°F/10°C and 80% humidity. But following are some more specific conditions that are best for certain categories of cheese.

Natural rinds: 49°F to 51°F/9°C to 10°C, 88% to 90% humidity
Washed (smear-ripened) cheese: 52°F to 54°F/11°C to 12°C, 94% to 96% humidity
Bloomy and goat cheeses: 48°F to 50°F/9°C to 10°C, 88% to 90% humidity
Large cheeses (Gruyère, Emmenthaler, Parmigiano-Reggiano): 48°F to 52°F/9°C to 11°C, 88% humidity.

In general, blue cheeses should be kept separate from other cheeses, especially bloomy rinds (to avoid turning everything blue), and at a colder temperature to keep the interior mold from spreading too much. A good base temperature would be 38°F to 40°F/3°C to 4°C with 64% to 66% humidity. These are also good conditions for other cheeses that you don't want to ripen any further.

Cheeses should be left whole for as long as possible, because once they're cut, they begin to lose moisture. With large whole cheeses, you should only cut out (or off) the amount that is going to be used for service and the rest should be wrapped lightly to preserve moisture. You should never wrap cheese tightly in plastic wrap, as it should be allowed limited access to air. This is because many cheeses, especially those made with raw milk, are "living," developing things and need to breathe. So, parchment paper, waxed paper, and semipermeable cheese paper are all viable wrapping stock. Younger cheeses, presumably with higher moisture content, should be turned over every other day or so to maintain the consistency of their paste, because fat is lighter than water.

## COOLER SHELVING AND ORGANIZATION

Cooler doors should have plastic strip curtains inside to lessen the fluctuation of temperature when staff is entering and leaving these areas throughout the day. Clear curtains also allow a person to view if others are entering, leaving, or working near these cooler doors, which could prevent an accident. Again, if space allows, walk-in coolers should also have a work table and scale for clerks or cooks to work on without the need to run in and out of the refrigerated space. Walk-in coolers are generally erected near the proper storage area or in a pre-preparation area, and are easily accessible to the receiving area. Reach-in or low-boy boxes are utilized on or near the cooking line. Reach-in coolers are also frequently used to store items that require a more specific humidity or constant holding temperature such as cheeses or nuts.

Proper shelving for refrigerated areas should be laid out in a manner that best utilizes all available space while still allowing for traffic and the safe and efficient loading and removal of stored merchandise. Shelving must have an open grid and be laid out in a way that allows for continuous air flow around stored goods. Units should be modular, so the configuration can be changed as needed, and of standard sizes and construction. Wood shelving is unsuitable for the damp conditions in coolers and cannot be properly cleaned. Metal or wire shelving is often used, but high-density plastic is most commonly used today because it is cheaper and lasts longer. Some products are treated to be antibacterial, which is a good food safety precaution.

Shelving is usually 18 to 24 in/45.72 to 60.96 cm wide, and shelves are spaced 18 in/45.72 in apart to allow for boxes to be easily opened and for sufficient air flow. Some shelves have modular sections that can be removed for easy cleaning without the need to empty the entire unit. Shelving units can be freestanding or hung from the walls.

Dunnage racks are low flat racks with heavier bars instead of shelves; they are used for holding stacks of heavy items such as bags of flour or potatoes that are purchased in higher quantities but not palletized.

Products with an ice pack, such as broccoli or fish, should be stored below other product so as not to drip water into the other items. Floors in these coolers should have floor drains so dripping water does not pool and create a safety hazard. Iced fish and meat products should be held above drip pans or in drainage boards that can be easily cleaned.

Space allowing, other items that are helpful inside a walk-in cooler to lessen traffic flow in and out are scales of an appropriate size to the product stored there, a work station or table for cutting cheeses and the like, and a hand sink. Coolers should also be alarmed to alert staff if temperatures rise or fall outside of a preset range.

FIGURE **5.9** Items with an ice pack should be stored below other products.

## DRY STORAGE

Dry storage areas should be secure, well lit, and maintained for cleanliness and to prevent pest infestation. In order to maintain optimal product integrity, these areas should also be temperature controlled to remain between 60°F to 70°F/16°C to 21°C. There should also be caged or secure areas to properly house and maintain items that may be subject to the temptation of pilferage, such as liquor, wine, and small high-ticket items such as saffron or truffles.

The floor plan of the dry storage area should be carefully evaluated to ensure the optimal use of all available space and to allow efficient traffic flow of people and materials in and out of the area. Shelving should be spaced to allow employees to bend and turn when adding product to the shelves or taking it away. There are also racks that hang from runners suspended from the ceiling that allow more shelving to fit in cramped quarters; however, there is a loss of speed and mobility when product is stored and issued in this way. Shelving is usually tiered in rows down the length of the storage area and anchored to the wall or floor for stability. The contents of each unit should be marked on the aisle side to expedite location when staff is looking for needed product.

FIGURE **5.10** Products such as the dunnage rack are utilized in storage areas to keep heavier items off the floor without the loss of excess space.

Health regulations usually require the bottom shelf of each unit to be 6 in/15.24 cm from the floor and 18 in/45.72 cm below the sprinkler heads in the ceiling. Fragile ingredients are best stored closer to the floor to minimize breakage if they should fall, and heavy items are best stored on the center shelves to lessen bending with or lifting up such items. If heavy and bulky items are used and stored in volume, a dunnage rack is the best option. Storage or bin locations should remain consistent to help facilitate locating items and conducting inventories expediently.

## SPECIAL NEEDS STORAGE

There are other items that are sometimes stored in or near the storeroom that deserve special consideration. For financial and regulatory reasons, many beverage bottles now need to be returned for refund. These bottles need to be held in bins that may have to be separated by type or by vendor. These bottles need to be at least rinsed or washed to prevent strong odors and pest infestation. Chemicals such as those utilized in ware washing can be quite potent and poisonous. These should all be received packed in strong containers that won't leak, but for safety's sake should be stored well away from food products.

White tablecloth–style restaurants will require clean, separate dry storage for clean tablecloths and napkins as well as storage bins for soiled product. These dirty items not only will stink but also can attract pests; an appropriate area will need to be provided for these items. Employee uniforms, aprons, and side towels will also require a staging area for clean product and hampers or bins for soiled garments if there is no separate designated locker room for staff.

# SANITATION

Good sanitation is essential in the proper storage of food and goods; it protects the operation's assets (the products purchased) and helps protect the operation against liabilities. After proper receiving, good sanitation is essential as a control point in preventing contamination and food-borne illness. Contamination of food products while they are held in storage can come from chemicals used on the premises, pest infiltration, improper holding temperatures, foreign objects, and cross contamination from raw meat, poultry, or fish dripping onto other food items. In the kitchen, contamination is frequently caused by dirty hands, uncovered wounds, contagiously ill employees, and dirty knives and work surfaces. These same things can cause contamination in the storage area if management does not take the required precautions. Buyers need to maintain an ample supply of plastic cutting boards, sanitizing solution, disposable gloves, and hats and hair nets, and keep them in close proximity to both production and storage facilities.

For food safety, buyers must always remain alert to signs of deterioration of the food products stored there and insure all holding temperatures meet regulatory standards. The buyer should also be conscious of strong or "off" odors or a change in the proper appearance of foodstuffs such as wilting, dark spots, or other discoloration. The texture should also be monitored for soft spots, shriveling, leaching fluids, and slime. Such signs can be severe and require taking immediate action or catching them at very early stages, alerting the buyer or chef that these items need to be utilized immediately. In all instances, it is wise to err on the side of caution; it is much cheaper to replace lost product than face litigation.

## HAZARD ANALYSIS CRITICAL CONTROL POINTS (HACCP)

Hazard Analysis Critical Control Points is a scientific food safety program which takes a systematic and preventative approach to the conditions that are responsible for most food-borne illnesses. Anticipating how food safety problems are most likely to occur and taking steps to prevent them from occurring are the purposes of a HACCP plan. The HACCP system has been adopted by both food processors and restaurants, as well as by the FDA and USDA, but it is not yet a requirement in all foodservice establishments. However, instituting such a plan may prove advantageous on a variety of levels, most of all in assuring the safety of everyone served in that establishment. The heart of HACCP is contained in the following seven principles:

1. **Assess the hazards.** The first step in an HACCP program begins with a hazard analysis of the menu item or recipe. The types of hazards of concern are biological, chemical, and physical conditions. The biological hazards are typically microbiological, which include bacteria, viruses, and parasites. The plan is to flow chart each step in that recipe from when the raw ingredients are received until the item is served to the customer.

2. **Identify the critical control points.** Once a flow diagram is determined, the potential hazards are established in order to identify the critical control points (CCPs). A critical control point is the place in the utilization of the food where you have the ability to prevent, eliminate, or reduce an existing hazard or to prevent or minimize the likelihood that a hazard will occur. It is important to only identify those areas where you exercise some control in the process. To quote the 1999 FDA Food Code, a critical control point is "a point or procedure in a specific food system where loss of control may result in an unacceptable health risk."

3. **Establish critical limits and control measures.** Many critical limits have already been established by local health departments and are the standards used for measurement at each critical control point. For example, an established critical limit for the cooking step in preparing chicken is a 165°F/74°C final internal temperature. In order to hold this chicken on the line before actual service, a temperature of 140°F/60°C would have to be maintained to prevent pathogenic microbes. Holding is the critical step in this process. Control measures are planned in advance to facilitate the achievement of your critical limit.

4. **Establish procedures for monitoring CCPs.** Critical control points have to be monitored to meet the critical limits at each step. How the CCP will be monitored and who will do it must be determined and adhered to. Monitoring improves the systems by allowing for the identification of problems or faults at particular points in the process and puts more control or improvement in the system.

5. **Establish corrective action plans.** A plan of action must be identified. If a deviation or substandard level occurs for a step in the process, specific corrective actions must then be determined for each CCP, as each food item and its preparation will vary greatly from one kitchen to the next.

6. **Set up a record-keeping system.** Documentation must be maintained to demonstrate whether the system is working or not. Recording events at CCPs ensures that critical limits are met and

Purchasing

Receiving

Storing

Preparation

Cooking

Holding

Cooling

Reheating

Serving

**FIGURE 5.11**
HACCP flow chart.

monitoring is done. Documentation typically is done by recording time and temperature logs and by keeping checklists and forms.

7. **Develop a verification system.** This step establishes that the HACCP procedures are working correctly. If procedures are not being followed, you must determine what modifications need to be made.

### HACCP FOR MEAT AND POULTRY

The HACCP program, designed to reduce pathogens, is used by meat processors to identify the most critical areas where pathogens can present problems, and to set up systems to monitor all those critical areas. The program, which is now recognized worldwide, allows for sharing the responsibility of inspection, rather than having a government agency in total control of all inspections. It is a system where the plant design, equipment, day-to-day production, packaging, storage, and everything to do with food safety are examined by the USDA and then monitored by the processors. The USDA inspects the systems in place as well as the actual production. This encourages the processors to be innovative in maintaining higher levels of food safety, because they are involved in the process. If deciding to sell meat on a wholesale level, you should become accustomed to HACCP plans and designs. The USDA website has examples of HACCP plans and tips to create your own plan for a variety of plant operations: See www.usda.gov.

When deciding on a purveyor, it makes sense to tour the warehouse and cutting facilities. Be sure that the facility is inspected and proper HACCP plans are in place and followed. A high-volume meat purveyor is normally USDA inspected, and the inspector is typically on-site during production times.

The critical part of any style or size storeroom allotted for the foodservice operator is to ensure the receiving, inventory, and issuing methods used there will protect the financial well-being of that operation. The facility needs to be clean with proper temperature controls to avoid contamination and laid out in a way to protect the employees functioning there. Each of the products needs to be stored in its own proper way to protect these assets from quickly deteriorating and losing palatability and with enough controls to protect the operation against theft or loss.

# INVENTORY MANAGEMENT

Proper inventory management is integral to any successful business venture that purchases raw ingredients to be resold or converted into a finished product for sale. Good inventory controls and management are required for accurate forecasting and ordering needs, for determining exact costs, and as a control in identifying waste or theft. A foodservice establishment's bottom line is tied directly to inventory control; food cost is second only to labor expenses in most foodservice operations. In any size and stage of an operation, proper inventory management is critical in understanding costs and maintaining controls.

Food is a greater inventory challenge than most other products, such as small equipment and china, or those used in a manufacturing plant. Issues relevant to seasonality, availability due to weather conditions, the high perishability of many produce

# INSPECTION FOR MEATS

The purpose of this study is to understand the importance of inspection laws for meat and meat products. In this time, when the trend is to find local farm connections for the restaurant, it is very important to make sure that all meats are inspected and passed before considering using them.

The Stratmore Inn is an exclusive country estate resort that features award-winning dining, elegant suites, and wonderful grounds with a short but challenging nine-hole golf course, tennis courts, hiking trails, and a large lake for swimming and boating. The kitchen is run by Chef Henri Benoit, a certified executive chef and winner of the recent New England Chef of the Year award. Chef Benoit's philosophy of cooking includes using as many local, seasonal ingredients as possible. The resort has its own garden system with seasonal vegetables on the menu, and they source local fruits and additional vegetables from farmers that Chef Benoit has developed a relationship with at the local farmer's market. At the farmer's market, there is also a grass-fed beef cattle grower, Jerry Granderson of Greener Pastures Beef, who sells a variety of pre-portioned frozen cuts to

customers every Saturday. These cuts are cut and packaged by the farmer's son, who has a small, sanitary setup in a building on the farm. Farmer Granderson sells only to end-user customers for their freezer or personal use.

The Stratmore menu, although it features local produce, does not have much in the way of local meat items. They use naturally raised beef from a distributor, but it arrives in vacuum packaging and not as whole carcass. Chef Benoit has some butchery knowledge, and his sous chef worked for a butcher a few years back, so they decided they would try to purchase a whole, locally raised beef carcass and fabricate it in house, aging some of the primal cuts for steaks and roasts, utilizing the bones for stock, and grinding the trimmings for an upscale lunch burger.

One weekend, Chef Benoit was at the market and spoke with Granderson about using local meat on the Stratmore menu. Benoit explained that he would love to put the Greener Pastures name on the menu, which indicates to his customers that the Stratmore supports local produce growers, and pasture-raised beef would be a perfect fit. Jerry was excited to hear this, gave Chef Benoit a price for a full carcass, and told him he could deliver it the next Tuesday morning. The price was negotiated and fair, payment was to be on delivery, and the deal was sealed with

**Beef skeletal structure**

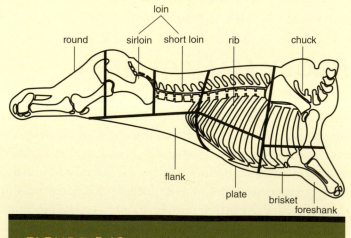

FIGURE **5.12** Beef was traditionally transported in split carcasses; it can now be purchased in smaller fabricated pieces or even as split carcasses from a local farmer.

a handshake. Chef Benoit returned to his kitchen with the good news and told his menu planner to write in some specials for the upcoming week featuring the local beef.

On the following Tuesday, farmer Granderson showed up with a refrigerated truck with the large primal cuts of beef. They were loaded into the walk-in cooler and allowed to hang on some hooks that the sous chef had designed. Chef Benoit gave the farmer a check for the total, they enjoyed a cup of coffee, and then the farmer was on his way.

Later that day, the sous chef began breaking down some of the beef and noticed a stamp on the side of the beef that stated, "NOT FOR SALE." There were no other USDA inspection stamps or markings that may have indicated state inspection. The sous chef brought this to the attention of Chef Benoit and asked what it meant. The chef decided to call the state agricultural office and ask. He discovered that farmers have the right to sell meats they have slaughtered without inspection under exemption permits. They can sell it to an end user such as a home cook or family, but any establishment that is going to resell the meat cannot purchase it, hence the "NOT FOR SALE" stamp. The agent at the agricultural office stated there could be heavy fines and penalties for selling the meat in a restaurant.

Unfortunately, Chef Benoit had to call the farmer and ask if he could take back the meat. Granderson said he would but that it was a great inconvenience, so he would need some compensation for all of his trouble. Chef agreed to give him a hundred dollars. The Stratmore also had to scramble to redo its menu; customers who were staying there were disappointed after having read the upcoming choices the night before.

There are two people at fault here. First, the farmer knew the rules and had stamped the meat accordingly, so he knew the chef could not resell the meat. He knew the chef was not buying it for his own use and therefore could have been fined for making the delivery. The chef also was at fault for not understanding the laws dealing with meat purchasing and inspection. A proper inspection stamp is vital when purchasing most meat products, no matter how clean or properly handled the meat is. State and federal guidelines are clearly explained on either the USDA's or your state agriculture department's website.

and seafood items, and the yield factors of primal meat cuts and fin fish all complicate the ability to maintain an accurate inventory management system. Also, in most food-service operations, each product could likely be handled by a number of people and not always held in a secure environment. A typical restaurant is liable to have an inventory consisting of many small, desirable, edible, and often expensive items which will increase the likelihood of "tastings" and pilferage, and thus a greater need for tight controls.

The combinations of loss due to spoilage, poor portion controls, mishandling delicate product, theft, tracking, employee consumption, and giving favored customers free products (comps) without managerial approval can all serve to damage an operation's profitability. "Comped" food items for special customers are something that management may opt to do in order to encourage loyalty or show appreciation. However, these items should only be done at management's discretion and accounted for appropriately. Employees need to know that unauthorized gifts constitute thievery and are cause for dismissal. With most foodservice operations already operating on very tight profit margins, losing a few percentage points in food cost may seem minor, but can actually be a serious issue.

Many foodservice operators fear running out of crucial items and thus disappointing paying customers. This fear can drive chefs and buyers to hold more inventory in stock than necessary. A critical aspect of controlling cost is to handle only as much inventory as necessary. Ideally, product should only come in as existing inventory is depleted but before new demand cannot be fulfilled. In manufacturing, this is referred to as just-in-time (JIT) purchasing. However, demand in the foodservice industry, particularly restaurants, can be fickle, so product needs can be difficult to gauge with that level of precision. Given that, however, tying inventory levels as close as possible to forecasted needs without holding far too much product is preferred. Forecasting needs is done through an assessment of determined bookings such as a function or reservations, historic data from past business volume, a review of upcoming holidays, and the weather forecast, and following typical usage based on inventory par levels. Unless an operation has a "captive" audience and predetermined menus, forecasting needs is a skill that requires experience as customer preferences change daily; it takes a practiced eye to assess past usage and projected bookings and then order correctly. Obviously, the flip side to overordering product is to work so tight as to create frequent product outages and shorts. This creates the need for emergency purchases and/or disappoints customers, and neither is good for the bottom line. Balance and common sense are imperative in striking the best inventory levels.

Tighter inventory levels help management control theft and portion size simply by the message they give employees. An inventory bloated with too many items in too large a quantity is more difficult to monitor closely, and hence it is easier to pilfer and allow increased portion sizes from it. Produce will lose water weight to evaporation as it sits, and meat products will purge liquid over time; these ounces of loss quickly turn into many dollars' worth of lost inventory. If inventory levels are closely attuned to need, then management will be more acutely and quickly aware if inventory appears to be moving out quicker than known business levels would indicate. Another way that tight inventory control contributes to business results is in customer satisfaction; higher turnover of inventory means fresher product, which in turn means happier diners.

Inventory management is an essential tool in the proper management of a food-service operation. Inventories are used to determine need and drive the purchase of essential raw ingredients used to fabricate finished goods. Holding inventory represents a huge outlay of business dollars that can most likely be better served than by sitting on the shelf and losing quality. Good inventories can assure a buyer that all appropriate cost levels are being maintained and bring attention to a problem when they are not; good inventory management will help assure your customers are happy with what they are served. Executed properly, with common sense, this is an essential tool in good purchasing.

## INVENTORY TYPES

As noted, inventories are taken to determine the purchasing quantities of needed items, monitor security, and control costs. Product inventories used to determine purchasing needs are usually divided into the various product lines (dairy, meat, dry goods, etc.) or by a specific vendor. The frequency in conducting these various inventories will depend on the product perishability, the available storage space, and the frequency of available deliveries.

Highly perishable items such as fresh produce, fresh seafood, and meat will often be counted and ordered daily or several times a week to insure a fresh product. Dry goods can usually be counted weekly, if storage space allows, with a secondary cursory walkthrough later in the week to identify items that are moving faster than anticipated or are missed. Your location and the available delivery schedule of your chosen vendor will factor into your frequency of ordering, but try to only purchase enough product to take you from one delivery to the next.

Many types of foodservice operations today will have computer-driven inventory systems that will automatically add incoming merchandise to inventory as it is received and subtract items out as they are sold. This allows for more precise and immediate knowledge of the current inventory levels. Many items can also be given a preset low point of inventory, or order point, that when reached will cause the system to either flag the needs or process an order to bring on-hand inventory back up to a determined maximum storage level. These are excellent tools providing the data are correct and the reordering flags afford the buyer time to replenish the inventory in time. The size of the operation may also be a factor in determining the program's cost effectiveness.

The complexity and depth of these systems vary. Some simple software programs that cost a few hundred dollars can manage the purchasing needs for small eateries and bakeries where the ingredient list, vendor file, and operational needs are quite simple. Then there are much more complex and customizable systems used in large hotels, casinos, and schools that can cost hundreds of thousands of dollars to purchase and implement. Besides the hard dollars involved in the purchase of these platforms, there is also a huge expense in time and effort in ensuring the system will do all that is required, implementing said system into an ongoing operation, and thoroughly training all those employees that will need to make use of the system. There can also be periodic "upgrades" to the system that can add to

the expense of these systems. Management must analyze the amount of risk and controls required to control those risks and determine the appropriate ROI to determine the level of complexity and expense required to meet their needs. There is no "one-size-fits-all" approach to these systems, and care must be used in determining what will both meet operational needs and do it for a cost that makes sense for the volume of dollars involved. For example, if a system can save an operation 5% in annual food cost that does $2 million in business, savings of $100,000 may be projected and weighed against the total cost of the system to determine the return on the initial investment.

The e-procurement programs can also void the need to do full, wall-to-wall inventories on a monthly basis. These are the time-consuming but important full inventories used to determine the costs of goods sold, which are used as controls by an operation's financial department. Such inventories supply the data needed to measure the dollar amount of product consumed in that time frame against the dollar amount of sales to ascertain if an operation's percentage of costs is in line with the predetermined food cost percentages the menu prices were based on. A significant variance will identify problems with overportioning, inaccurate pricing, or theft to management.

With the modern computer-based systems, it is possible to cycle count small portions of the inventory each day to verify that the amount of product on hand matches the figure the systems show should be in stock. Cycle counts do not need to be done on the last day of a financial cycle and can be divided by a product line, a section of the storeroom, or the volume of product sold. Some high-ticket items may be counted frequently, and other lower-cost or slow-volume items could be counted less often. These are done to facilitate ordering and control, but are not used as an accounting tool to determine total food costs. The frequency of cycle counting an item can be adjusted if the volume used or price changes radically or if there are often shortage or availability issues. Often the entire inventory is simply divided into sections that are counted in rotation throughout the month.

Whatever method is selected in order to successfully track inventory for financial controls, there are a number of factors required to assure a consistent ability to achieve and maintain accuracy. The ability to determine that proper food costs are met, product is maintained in stock and not going out the door, and inventories are held at the appropriate levels depends on such consistently accurate reporting.

# THE CULINARY INSTITUTE OF AMERICA

Asian Inventory as of _____

Harry Wils #37604
Welcome Oriental Mkt #20078
Krishna Mkt #16546
Bangkok Mkt #12083

| ITEM | PACK | VENDOR | CODE | DATE | | | | |
|---|---|---|---|---|---|---|---|---|
| Spice Anardana Powder | bg | K | 6267 | | | | | |
| Spice Musk Seed Black | 6/20oz jr | HW | 5524 | | | | | |
| Rice Paper 8" | 50/12oz | HW | 6191 | | | | | |
| Rice Paper 12" | 50/12oz | HW | 6189 | | | | | |
| Wrapper Bean Sheet 16oz | 24/16oz | HW | 3035 | | | | | |
| Starch Tapioca 1# | 1#/ ea | HW/WO | 6271 | | | | | |
| Starch Wheat 14oz | 50/14oz | WO | 5803 | | | | | |
| Flour Rice (Red) 1# | 24/1# | HW/WO | 6076 | | | | | |
| Flour Rice Glutinous Green | 24/1# | HW/WO | 6076 | | | | | |
| Flour Steam Bun  16oz | 16oz/bg | WO | 6085 | | | | | |
| Green Tea | cn | WO | 5836 | | | | | |
| Tea Jasmine 1# tin | 1# tin | WO | 6280 | | | | | |
| Water Chestnut Powder 1# | 1# bx | WO | 6309 | | | | | |
| Skewers 10" 100ct | 16/100ct | HW | 7210 | | | | | |
| Skewers 6" 100ct | 12/24-100 | HW | 7212 | | | | | |
| | | | | | | | | |
| Spice Ajwain Seeds | 16-1oz bg | Krishna | 5033 | | | | | |
| Rose Petals Dried 1oz | 16-1oz bg | HW | 6194 | | | | | |
| Spice Cumin Seed Black | 16-1oz bg | Krishna | 5527 | | | | | |
| Spice Nigella Seed | 7oz bg | Krishna | 5525 | | | | | |
| Spice Fenugreek Seeds | 16-1oz bg | HW/K | 5195 | | | | | |
| Spice Pomegranate Seed | 4oz bg | HW | 5675 | | | | | |
| Spice Chili Powder Korean | 4oz pkg | WO | 6371 | | | | | |
| Pepper Chili Chinese Whole | 3.5oz bg | WO | 6040 | | | | | |
| Spice Pepper Szechwan (Hua Jiao) | 2oz pkg | WO | 6176 | | | | | |
| Spice Anise Star 3oz | 3oz pkg | WO | 6266 | | | | | |
| Lily Buds Dried 6oz | 6oz pkg | WO | 6082 | | | | | |
| Spice Five Spice Powder | 4oz pkg | WO | 6190 | | | | | |
| Seed Sesame Black 7oz | 7oz pkg | WO | 6155 | | | | | |
| Peppers Hot Pickled (R/G) | 1# jr | WO | 6171 | | | | | |
| Sauce Blk Bean Garlic 13oz | 13oz jr | WO | 6228 | | | | | |
| Lychee Nuts cn | 20oz cn | WO | 6010 | | | | | |
| Spice Asafoetida 1.75oz | 12/1.75oz | HW | 6193 | | | | | |

FIGURE **5.14a** Inventory can be tracked manually by the buyer. (Continues)

# THE CULINARY INSTITUTE OF AMERICA

Asian Inventory as of _____

Harry Wils #37604
Welcome Oriental Mkt #20078
Krishna Mkt #16546
Bangkok Mkt #12083

| ITEM | PACK | VENDOR | CODE | DATE | | | | |
|------|------|--------|------|------|---|---|---|---|
| Spice Togarashi .5oz | 10/.5oz jr | HW | 6265 | | | | | |
| Spice Sansho Pepper .5oz | 10/.5oz jr | HW | 6264 | | | | | |
| | | | | | | | | |
| Sauce Hoisin 15oz | 24/15oz jr | HW | 6227 | | | | | |
| Sauce Bean Koon Chun | 24/13oz jr | WO | 6218 | | | | | |
| Sauce Plum 15oz jr | 24/15oz | HW | 6230 | | | | | |
| Sauce Soy Thick Chinese | 24/1# | HW | 6236 | | | | | |
| Sauce Garlic Spicy 8oz | 12/8oz jr | WO | 6226 | | | | | |
| Paste Hot Bean Chin 16oz | 24/16oz jr | HW | 6149 | | | | | |
| Noodle Bean Thread 2oz | 400/2oz pkg | HW | 6012 | | | | | |
| Chopsticks Fancy | 10 pack | WO | 7213 | | | | | |
| | | | | | | | | |
| | | | | | | | | |
| Fish Anch Salt Dry 8oz | 6/8oz pkg | | 6258 | | | | | |
| | | | | | | | | |
| Chopstick 100ct | 10/100ct | HW | 6042 | | | | | |
| Sushi Mat 1ea | 100/cs | WO | 6287 | | | | | |
| Wasabi Powder 3.5oz cn | 48/3.5oz | HW | 6186 | | | | | |
| Water Chestnut 29oz cn | 24/29oz cn | HW | 6308 | | | | | |
| Bean Curd Season 10oz cn | 24/10oz cn | WO | 5361 | | | | | |
| | | | | | | | | |
| Coconut Milk 96oz | 6/96oz cn | HW | 5201 | | | | | |
| Coconut Milk 14oz | 24/14oz cn | HW | 5200 | | | | | |
| Sauce Soy Mush 21oz | 24/21oz | HW | 6233 | | | | | |
| Sauce Soy Tamari 10oz | 12/10oz | HW | 5796 | | | | | |
| Sauce Soy Tamari Lite 10oz | 12/10oz | HW | 6235 | | | | | |
| Oil Aromatic Peanut 96oz | 6/96oz cn | HW | 6138 | | | | | |
| Oil Sesame 56oz | 10/56oz | HW | 6144 | | | | | |
| Mushrooms Straw 15oz | 24/15oz cn | HW/WO | 6133 | | | | | |
| Bamboo Shoots 28oz cn | 24/28oz cn | HW | 6004 | | | | | |
| Nuts Ginko 14oz cn | 48/14oz cn | HW | 6107 | | | | | |
| Sauce Mirin 24oz btl | 12/24oz btl | HW | 6112 | | | | | |

FIGURE **5.14a** Inventory can be tracked manually by the buyer. (Continues)

# THE CULINARY INSTITUTE OF AMERICA

Asian Inventory as of _____

Harry Wils #37604
Welcome Oriental Mkt #20078
Krishna Mkt #16546
Bangkok Mkt #12083

| ITEM | PACK | VENDOR | CODE | DATE | | | | |
|------|------|--------|------|------|--|--|--|--|
| | | | | | | | | |
| | | | | | | | | |
| | | | | | | | | |
| | | | | | | | | |
| | | | | | | | | |
| Oil Mustard 16oz btl | 12/16oz btl | Krishna | 6140 | | | | | |
| | | | | | | | | |
| Paste Curry Green 4oz | 48/4oz cn | HW | 6151 | | | | | |
| Paste Curry Red 4oz | 48/4oz cn | HW | 6151 | | | | | |
| Paste Curry Massman 4oz | 48/4oz cn | HW | 6151 | | | | | |
| Paste Curry Yellow 4oz | 48/4oz cn | HW | 6151 | | | | | |
| | | | | | | | | |
| Juice Yuzu 5.29oz | 12/5oz jr | | 6011 | | | | | |
| Sauce Soy Ponzu 15oz | 12/15oz | HW | 6113 | | | | | |
| Mustard Chinese Hot 10oz | 24/10oz jr | WO | 5503 | | | | | |
| Sauce Kicap Manis 21oz | 12/21oz btl | WO | 6217 | | | | | |
| Lotus Rootlet 16oz jr | 24/16oz | HW/WO | 6156 | | | | | |
| Paste Korean Hot Pepper | 12/2.2# jr | WO | 6150 | | | | | |
| Paste Korean Soybean | 12/2.2# jr | WO | 6147 | | | | | |
| Sauce Fish Tiparos 24oz | 12/24oz btl | HW | 6232 | | | | | |
| Sauce Veg. Oyster | 12/18oz btl | HW/WO | 6237 | | | | | |
| Sauce Oyster 5# cn | 6/5# cn | HW | 6229 | | | | | |
| | | | | | | | | |
| Mush Shitake Dry 4oz | 5# bulk | WO/HW | 6126 | | | | | |
| Mush Woodear Dry 4oz | 1# bulk | WO/HW | 6116 | | | | | |
| Fish Bonito Flakes 100gm | 1#/500gm | HW | 6257 | | | | | |
| | | | | | | | | |
| Seaweed Nori Sheet 7oz | 60ct/10ea | HW | 6240 | | | | | |
| Seaweed Kombu Dry 4oz | 24/3/4oz | HW | 6242 | | | | | |
| Seaweed Arame/Hijiki 1oz | | HW | 6244 | | | | | |
| Seaweed Wakame 3oz | 24/3oz pk | HW | 6243 | | | | | |

FIGURE **5.14a** Inventory can be tracked manually by the buyer. (Continues)

(continued)

# THE CULINARY INSTITUTE OF AMERICA

Asian Inventory as of _____

Harry Wils #37604
Welcome Oriental Mkt #20078
Krishna Mkt #16546
Bangkok Mkt #12083

| ITEM | PACK | VENDOR | CODE | DATE | | | | |
|------|------|--------|------|------|---|---|---|---|
| Sauce Chili Sweet Thai | 12/32oz btl | HW/WO | 6224 | | | | | |
| Paste Chili Thai Nahmprik | 24/1# jr | HW/WO | 6154 | | | | | |
| Vinegar Coco Palm 32oz | 12/32oz btl | HW/WO | 6305 | | | | | |
| Vinegar Rice 24oz btl | 12/24oz btl | HW/WO | 6306 | | | | | |
| Vinegar Chinkiang Blk | 21oz btl | WO | 6304 | | | | | |
| Wine Rice Shao Xing | 12/21oz btl | HW/WO | 6187 | | | | | |
| Sauce Soy Kim Ve Wong gal | 4/1gal | HW/Gins | 6219 | | | | | |
| Vinegar Black Taiwan | 21oz btl | | 6307 | | | | | |
| | | | | | | | | |
| Noodle Sweet Potato 12oz | 24/12 oz | WO | 5243 | | | | | |
| Noodle Rice 1/4" Red | 30/1# | HW | 6209 | | | | | |
| Noodle Rice 1/8" Green | 30/1# | HW | 6208 | | | | | |
| Noodle Rice 1/16" Blue | 30/1# | HW | 6207 | | | | | |
| Noodle Rice Stick 1# | 48/1# | HW | 6206 | | | | | |
| Noodle Udon Dry | 30/1# | HW/WO | 5241 | | | | | |
| Noodle Soba 10.5oz pkg | 30/10.5oz | HW/WO | 5239 | | | | | |
| Noodle Rice 1/2" | 30/1# | HW | 5242 | | | | | |
| Noodle Somen | 24/1# | HW | 6211 | | | | | |
| | | | | | | | | |
| | | | | | | | | |
| | | | | | | | | |
| Sugar Jaggery 1# | 12/1# | K/WO | 6180 | | | | | |
| Sugar Cane 20oz cn | 24/20oz cn | HW | 6183 | | | | | |
| Sugar Palm 1# | 24/1# | HW/WO | 6184 | | | | | |
| Paste Tamarind 1# | 50/1# | HW | 6281 | | | | | |
| Dates Pitted Chinese 12oz | 12 oz bg | WO | 6310 | | | | | |
| Adzuki Beans 13oz | 50/13oz bg | HW | 6282 | | | | | |
| Shrimp Chips 8oz | 48/8oz bx | WO | 6238 | | | | | |
| Ginger Crystalized 4oz | 5# bulk | HW | 5365 | | | | | |
| Baby Corn 15oz | 24 /15oz | HW | 6050 | | | | | |
| Breadcrumb Panko 7oz | 36/7oz | HW | 6017 | | | | | |

FIGURE **5.14a** Inventory can be tracked manually by the buyer. (Continues)

# THE CULINARY INSTITUTE OF AMERICA

Asian Inventory as of _____

Harry Wils #37604
Welcome Oriental Mkt #20078
Krishna Mkt #16546
Bangkok Mkt #12083

| ITEM | PACK | VENDOR | CODE | DATE | | | | | |
|---|---|---|---|---|---|---|---|---|---|
| Braedcrumb Panko Bulk | 25 # | HW | 5463 | | | | | | |
| | | | | | | | | | |
| **BACKROOM GROCERY** | | | | | | | | | |
| Dal Channa 2# | 55# bulk | Krishna | 5043 | | | | | | |
| Dal Moong 2# | 55# bulk | Krishna | 5043 | | | | | | |
| Dal Toor 2# | 55# bulk | Krishna | 5043 | | | | | | |
| Dal Urad 2# | 55# bulk | Krishna | 5043 | | | | | | |
| | | | | | | | | | |
| Rice Long Grain 25# | 25# bg | HW/WO | 5738 | | | | | | |
| Rice Med Grain 20# | 20# bg | HW/WO | 5741 | | | | | | |
| Rice Sushi 20# | 20# bg | HW/WO | 5742 | | | | | | |
| Rice Sticky Long Grain 20# | 20# bg | WO/HW | 5736 | | | | | | |
| | | | | | | | | | |
| | | | | | | | | | |
| **Dairy Box** | | | | | | | | | |
| Flour Atta 10# bg | 10# bg | Krishna | 6083 | | | | | | |
| | | | | | | | | | |
| **Freezer Items** | | | | | | | | | |
| Wrapper Springroll (WeiChuan) | 40/11oz | WO | 3038 | | | | | | |
| Beans Soy in Pod | 24/1# | WO | 6247 | | | | | | |
| Beans Soy Peeled | 24/1# | HW/WO | 6248 | | | | | | |
| Coconut Frzn (Grated)1# | 24/1# | WO | 3031 | | | | | | |
| Fish Surimi | 12/cs | WO | 3054 | | | | | | |
| Wrapper Wonton | 48/1# | HW/WO | 3158 | | | | | | |
| **Outside Freezer** | | | | | | | | | |
| Wrapper Dumpling Shang | 48/1# | HW | 3157 | | | | | | |
| Wrapper Mu Shu Pancake | pkg | WO | 3034 | | | | | | |
| Wrapper Shoa Mai | 48/1# | HW | 3160 | | | | | | |
| Noodle Lo Mein 1# | 16/1# | HW | 3036 | | | | | | |

FIGURE **5.14a** Inventory can be tracked manually by the buyer. (Continues)

(continued)

# THE CULINARY INSTITUTE OF AMERICA

Asian Inventory as of _____

Harry Wils #37604
Welcome Oriental Mkt #20078
Krishna Mkt #16546
Bangkok Mkt #12083

| ITEM | PACK | VENDOR | CODE | DATE | | | | |
|------|------|--------|------|------|---|---|---|---|
| **Refrig. Items** | | | | | | | | |
| Beancurd Brine Soft 1# | 12/1# | HW/WO | 1041 | | | | | |
| Beancurd Silk Firm 1# | 24/1# | HW/WO | 1042 | | | | | |
| Beancurd Smoked 12oz | 12 pkg | WO | 3009 | | | | | |
| | | | | | | | | |
| | | | | | | | | |
| Sauce Siracha 17oz | 12/17oz | HW | 6221 | | | | | |
| Bean Ferment Black 8oz | 8oz pkg | WO | 6203 | | | | | |
| Fish Shrimp Dried 7oz | 7oz pkg | WO | 6256 | | | | | |
| Ginger Pickled 12oz | 12/12oz | HW/WO | 1133 | | | | | |
| Sauce Chili Garlic Viet 16oz | 12/16oz | HW/WO | 6225 | | | | | |
| Kim Chee 1qt | 1 qt jr | WO | 6098 | | | | | |
| Meat Saus Chinese 1# | 24/1# | WO | 6222 | | | | | |
| Sauce Chili Sambal Oelek 18oz | 12/16oz | HW | 6231 | | | | | |
| Miso Red 500gm | 8/cs | WO | 6114 | | | | | |
| Miso Sweet 500gm | 12/cs | WO | 6117 | | | | | |
| Miso White 500gm | 8/cs | WO | 6115 | | | | | |
| Diakon Radish Pickled | ea | WO | 6202 | | | | | |
| Oil Coconut 16oz | 12/16oz | Krishna | 6139 | | | | | |
| Paste Shrimp Thai Trassi | 3.5oz | WO | 6197 | | | | | |
| | | | | | | | | |
| | | | | | | | | |
| | | | | | | | | |
| | | | | | | | | |
| | | | | | | | | |
| | | | | | | | | |
| | | | | | | | | |
| | | | | | | | | |
| | | | | | | | | |

FIGURE **5.14a** Inventory can be tracked manually by the buyer.

# PHYSICAL INVENTORY SHEET
## *by Package*
### CIA–Hyde Park–Culinary Institute of America

Location: _____     Date of Physical Count: _____

Package:  xDry Room Inventory for Physical Inventory        Counted By: _____

| NUMBER | ITEM | TRANS UN (PACKSIZE) | BASE UN | REMARK |
|--------|------|---------------------|---------|--------|
| 5183 | Sauce Chili 12oz | JR  *(1.0000 JR)* | *(SAME)* | |
| 5779 | Sauce Hot Franks 12oz | BT  *(1.0000 BT)* | *(SAME)* | |
| 5787 | Sauce Hot Franks (Gallon) | GL  *(1.0000 GL)* | *(SAME)* | |
| 5928 | Sauce Worchestershire | BT  *(1.0000 BT)* | *(SAME)* | |
| 5790 | Sauce Tabasco Green | BT  *(1.0000 BT)* | *(SAME)* | |
| 5786 | Sauce Tabasco Chipotle | BT  *(1.0000 BT)* | *(SAME)* | |
| 5785 | Sauce Tabasco 12oz | BT  *(1.0000 BT)* | *(SAME)* | |
| 5791 | Sauce Hot Crystal 12oz | BT  *(1.0000 BT)* | *(SAME)* | |
| 5506 | Mustard Dijon | JR  *(1.0000 JR)* | *(SAME)* | |
| 5520 | Mustard Gulden's | GL  *(1.0000 GL)* | *(SAME)* | |
| 5504 | Mustard Creole | JR  *(1.0000 JR)* | *(SAME)* | |
| 5486A | Mostarda Pear | JR  *(1.0000 JR)* | *(SAME)* | |
| 5486B | Mostarda Crab Apple | JR  *(1.0000 JR)* | *(SAME)* | |
| 5507 | Mustard Dijon Seyval 16oz [8oz x 2] | JR  *(1.0000 JR)* | *(SAME)* | |
| 5508 | Mustard Dijon Bulk | CN  *(1.0000 CN)* | *(SAME)* | |
| 5518 | Mustard Pommery | JR  *(1.0000 JR)* | *(SAME)* | |
| 5868 | Vinegar Balsamic 7oz | BT  *(1.0000 BT)* | *(SAME)* | |
| 5868A | Vinegar Balsamic 17oz | BT  *(1.0000 BT)* | *(SAME)* | |
| 5869 | Vinegar Champagne | BT  *(1.0000 BT)* | *(SAME)* | |
| 5436 | Ketchup Bottles | JR  *(1.0000 JR)* | *(SAME)* | |
| 5874 | Vinegar Malt | BT  *(1.0000 BT)* | *(SAME)* | |
| 5866 | Vinegar Manodori Balsamic | BT  *(1.0000 BT)* | *(SAME)* | |
| 5886 | Vinegar White Wine | BT  *(1.0000 BT)* | *(SAME)* | |
| 5880 | Vinegar Sherry Wine | BT  *(1.0000 BT)* | *(SAME)* | |
| 5872 | Vinegar La Saba Balsamic | BT  *(1.0000 BT)* | *(SAME)* | |
| 5555B | Verjus Fusion White | BT  *(1.0000 BT)* | *(SAME)* | |
| 5555A | Verjus Fusion Red | BT  *(1.0000 BT)* | *(SAME)* | |
| 5557 | Oil Olive Spanish Unfiltered | BT  *(1.0000 BT)* | *(SAME)* | |
| 5529 | Oil Olive Spanish Puesole | BT  *(1.0000 BT)* | *(SAME)* | |
| 5542A | Oil Olive Extra Virgin Ravida | LT  *(1.0000 LT)* | *(SAME)* | |
| 5531A | Oil Limonolio | BT  *(1.0000 BT)* | *(SAME)* | |
| 5871 | Vinegar Balsamic Bulk Pack | EA  *(1.0000 EA)* | *(SAME)* | |

**FIGURE 5.14b** Inventory can also be tracked automatically using a computer tracking program. (Continues)

(continued)

# PHYSICAL INVENTORY SHEET
### by Package
### CIA–Hyde Park–Culinary Institute of America

Location: _____     Date of Physical Count: _____

Package: xDry Room Inventory for Physical Inventory     Counted By: _____

| NUMBER | ITEM | TRANS UN (PACKSIZE) | BASE UN | REMARK |
|---|---|---|---|---|
| 5890 | Vinegar Red Wine | BT *(1.0000 BT)* | *(SAME)* | |
| 5549 | Oil Olive Extra Virgin California Arbequina | TU *(1.0000 TU)* | *(SAME)* | |
| 5562 | Oil Olive French Extra Virgin | CN *(1.0000 CN)* | *(SAME)* | |
| 5542E | Oil Olive Liguria XV | BT *(1.0000 BT)* | *(SAME)* | |
| 5889 | Vinegar Sweet Aged White | BT *(1.0000 BT)* | *(SAME)* | |
| 5531 | Oil Pepperolio | BT *(1.0000 BT)* | *(SAME)* | |
| 5542 | Oil Olive Extra Virgin Colonna | LT *(1.0000 LT)* | *(SAME)* | |
| 5542B | Oil Olive Extra Virgin Coltibuonno | LT *(1.0000 LT)* | *(SAME)* | |
| 5542C | Oil Olive Extra Virgin Numero Uno | LT *(1.0000 LT)* | *(SAME)* | |
| 5639 | Pasta Penne | LB *(1.0000 LB)* | *(SAME)* | |
| 5625 | Pasta Gemelli | LB *(1.0000 LB)* | *(SAME)* | |
| 5600 | Pasta Papardelle | BX *(1.0000 BX)* | *(SAME)* | |
| 5612 | Pasta Elbows | LB *(1.0000 LB)* | *(SAME)* | |
| 5598 | Pasta Tubetti | LB *(1.0000 LB)* | *(SAME)* | |
| 5622 | Pasta Bowties | LB *(1.0000 LB)* | *(SAME)* | |
| 5642 | Pasta Rigatoni | LB *(1.0000 LB)* | *(SAME)* | |
| 5632 | Pasta Spinach Nests | LB *(1.0000 LB)* | *(SAME)* | |
| 5640 | Pasta Penne Plus | LB *(1.0000 LB)* | *(SAME)* | |
| 5620 | Pasta Lasagne | LB *(1.0000 LB)* | *(SAME)* | |
| 6056 | Fregola | PK *(1.0000 PK)* | *(SAME)* | |
| 5606 | Pasta Egg Fettucine Nests | BX *(1.0000 BX)* | *(SAME)* | |
| 5614 | Pasta Fettucine | LB *(1.0000 LB)* | *(SAME)* | |
| 5596 | Pasta Capellini | LB *(1.0000 LB)* | *(SAME)* | |
| 5624 | Pasta Linguine | LB *(1.0000 LB)* | *(SAME)* | |
| 5630 | Pasta Spaghetti | LB *(1.0000 LB)* | *(SAME)* | |
| 5595 | Pasta Bucatini | LB *(1.0000 LB)* | *(SAME)* | |
| 5626 | Pasta Orzo | LB *(1.0000 LB)* | *(SAME)* | |
| 5621 | Pasta Fussili | LB *(1.0000 LB)* | *(SAME)* | |
| 5597 | Pasta Orecchiette | LB *(1.0000 LB)* | *(SAME)* | |
| 5737 | Rice Jasmine | LB *(1.0000 LB)* | *(SAME)* | |
| 5733 | Rice Basmati | LB *(1.0000 LB)* | *(SAME)* | |
| 5734 | Rice Carolina | LB *(1.0000 LB)* | *(SAME)* | |

**FIGURE 5.14b** Inventory can also be tracked automatically using a computer tracking program. (Continues)

# PHYSICAL INVENTORY SHEET

*by Package*

**CIA–Hyde Park–Culinary Institute of America**

Location: _____     Date of Physical Count: _____

Package: xDry Room Inventory for Physical Inventory     Counted By: _____

| NUMBER | ITEM | TRANS UN (PACKSIZE) | BASE UN | REMARK |
|--------|------|---------------------|---------|--------|
| 5746 | Rice Converted | BG *(1.0000 PK)* | PK | |
| 5631 | Pasta Spaghetti Plus | LB *(1.0000 LB)* | *(SAME)* | |
| 5748 | Rice Wild | LB *(1.0000 LB)* | *(SAME)* | |
| 5736 | Rice Sticky Long Grain | LB *(1.0000 LB)* | *(SAME)* | |
| 5152 | Base Beef Economy | EA *(1.0000 EA)* | *(SAME)* | |
| 5153 | Base Beef Ultimate | EA *(1.0000 EA)* | *(SAME)* | |
| 5156 | Base Chicken Economy | EA *(1.0000 EA)* | *(SAME)* | |
| 5157 | Base Chicken Ultimate | EA *(1.0000 EA)* | *(SAME)* | |
| 5155 | Demi Glace | EA *(1.0000 EA)* | *(SAME)* | |
| 1113 | Corn Husk | PK *(1.0000 PK)* | *(SAME)* | |
| 5232 | Corn Meal White 5# | BG *(5.0000 LB)* | LB | |
| 5344 | Flour Bread 10# | BG *(10.0000 LB)* | LB | |
| 4134 | Flour Pastry 50# | BG *(50.0000 LB)* | LB | |
| 3131 | Juice Carrot | EA *(1.0000 EA)* | *(SAME)* | |
| 5757 | Spice TCM 2# | TU *(1.0000 TU)* | *(SAME)* | |
| 1171 | Herb Epazote | LB *(1.0000 LB)* | *(SAME)* | |
| 5281 | Spice Dextrose | TU *(1.0000 TU)* | *(SAME)* | |
| 6078 | Flour Semolina | LB *(1.0000 LB)* | *(SAME)* | |
| 5234 | Corn Meal Yellow | LB *(1.0000 LB)* | *(SAME)* | |
| 4143 | Flour High Gluten Organic 50# | BG *(1.0000 BG)* | *(SAME)* | |
| 4145 | Flour Rye Medium White Organic | BG *(1.0000 BG)* | *(SAME)* | |
| 4138 | Flour Soy 25# | BG *(1.0000 LB)* | LB | |
| 4136 | Flour Rice Brown S/O | EA *(1.0000 EA)* | *(SAME)* | |
| 5805 | Potato Starch 50# Bulk S/O | EA *(1.0000 EA)* | *(SAME)* | |
| 4135 | Nine Grain Cereal 50# S/O | CS *(1.0000 CS)* | *(SAME)* | |
| 6069 | Polenta Buckwheat | PK *(1.0000 PK)* | *(SAME)* | |
| 5149 | Avocado Leaves 4oz | PK *(1.0000 PK)* | *(SAME)* | |
| 4123 | Flour Cake | LB *(1.0000 LB)* | *(SAME)* | |
| 6073 | Flour Durum | LB *(1.0000 LB)* | *(SAME)* | |
| 5732 | Rice Brown | LB *(1.0000 LB)* | *(SAME)* | |
| 5742 | Rice Sushi | LB *(1.0000 LB)* | *(SAME)* | |
| 5744 | Rice Brown Basmati | LB *(1.0000 LB)* | *(SAME)* | |

**FIGURE 5.14b** Inventory can also be tracked automatically using a computer tracking program. (Continues)

(continued)

# PHYSICAL INVENTORY SHEET
## *by Package*
### CIA–Hyde Park–Culinary Institute of America

Location: _____          Date of Physical Count: _____

Package: xDry Room Inventory for Physical Inventory          Counted By: _____

| NUMBER | ITEM | TRANS UN (PACKSIZE) | BASE UN | REMARK |
|---|---|---|---|---|
| 5735 | Rice Carnaroli | KG  (1.0000 KG) | (SAME) | |
| 5738 | Rice Long Grain | LB  (1.0000 LB) | (SAME) | |
| 5747 | Rice Spanish | KG  (1.0000 KG) | (SAME) | |
| 5741 | Rice Medium Grain | LB  (1.0000 LB) | (SAME) | |
| 5006 | Spice Allspice Whole | JR  (1.0000 JR) | (SAME) | |
| 5037 | Spice Cinnamon Mexican | LB  (1.0000 LB) | (SAME) | |
| 5677 | Spice Zahtar | JR  (1.0000 JR) | (SAME) | |
| 5676 | Spice Sumac Ground | JR  (1.0000 JR) | (SAME) | |
| 5004 | Spice Allspice Ground | JR  (1.0000 JR) | (SAME) | |
| 5008 | Spice Anise Seed | JR  (1.0000 JR) | (SAME) | |
| 5034 | Spice Arrowroot Flour | JR  (1.0000 JR) | (SAME) | |
| 5074 | Spice Basil Leaf | JR  (1.0000 JR) | (SAME) | |
| 5078 | Spice Bay Leaves | JR  (1.0000 JR) | (SAME) | |
| 5147 | Spice Cardamom Ground | JR  (1.0000 JR) | (SAME) | |
| 5158 | Spice Cayenne Ground | JR  (1.0000 JR) | (SAME) | |
| 5161 | Spice Celery Seed Ground | JR  (1.0000 JR) | (SAME) | |
| 5165 | Spice Celery Seed Whole | JR  (1.0000 JR) | (SAME) | |
| 5262 | Cream of Tartar | JR  (1.0000 JR) | (SAME) | |
| 5176 | Spice Red Pepper Crushed | JR  (1.0000 JR) | (SAME) | |
| 6001A | Spice Achiote Paste 2.2# | PK  (1.0000 PK) | (SAME) | |
| 5197 | Spice Cinnamon Sticks | JR  (1.0000 JR) | (SAME) | |
| 5222 | Spice Coriander Ground | JR  (1.0000 JR) | (SAME) | |
| 5079 | Spice Bay Leaves Ground S/O | PK  (1.0000 PK) | (SAME) | |
| 5190 | Spice Cinnamon Ground | JR  (1.0000 JR) | (SAME) | |
| 5192 | Spice Cloves Ground | JR  (1.0000 JR) | (SAME) | |
| 5194 | Spice Cloves Whole | JR  (1.0000 JR) | (SAME) | |
| 5178 | Spice Chili Powder | JR  (1.0000 JR) | (SAME) | |
| 5223 | Spice Coriander Whole | JR  (1.0000 JR) | (SAME) | |
| 5269 | Spice Cumin Ground | JR  (1.0000 JR) | (SAME) | |
| 5268 | Spice Cumin Seed Whole | JR  (1.0000 JR) | (SAME) | |
| 5274 | Spice Curry Powder | CN  (1.0000 CN) | (SAME) | |
| 5282 | Spice Dill Weed | JR  (1.0000 JR) | (SAME) | |

FIGURE 5.14b Inventory can also be tracked automatically using a computer tracking program. (Continues)

# PHYSICAL INVENTORY SHEET
## by Package
### CIA–Hyde Park–Culinary Institute of America

Location: _____          Date of Physical Count: _____

Package:  xDry Room Inventory for Physical Inventory          Counted By: _____

| NUMBER | ITEM | TRANS UN (PACKSIZE) | BASE UN | REMARK |
|--------|------|---------------------|---------|--------|
| 5300 | Spice Fennel Seed Whole | JR  (1.0000 JR) | (SAME) | |
| 5350 | Garlic Powder | JR  (1.0000 JR) | (SAME) | |
| 5362 | Spice Ginger Ground | JR  (1.0000 JR) | (SAME) | |
| 5108 | Spice Poultry Seasoning | CN  (1.0000 CN) | (SAME) | |
| 5469 | Spice Lavender Flower Dry S/O | JR  (1.0000 JR) | (SAME) | |
| 5480 | Spice Marjoram Leaves | JR  (1.0000 JR) | (SAME) | |
| 5560 | Spice Old Bay Seasoning | CN  (1.0000 CN) | (SAME) | |
| 5512 | Spice Mustard Dry Coleman | CN  (1.0000 CN) | (SAME) | |
| 5470 | Spice Mace Ground | JR  (1.0000 JR) | (SAME) | |
| 5825A | Sugar Splenda Packets | CS  (1.0000 CS) | (SAME) | |
| 5230 | Pickle Cornichons 12oz | JR  (1.0000 JR) | (SAME) | |
| 5683 | Spice Mint Leaves | JR  (1.0000 JR) | (SAME) | |
| 5521 | Spice Mustard Seed Whole | JR  (1.0000 JR) | (SAME) | |
| 5146 | Spice Caraway Seed Whole | JR  (1.0000 JR) | (SAME) | |
| 5526 | Spice Nutmeg Ground | JR  (1.0000 JR) | (SAME) | |
| 5576 | Spice Onion Powder | JR  (1.0000 JR) | (SAME) | |
| 6173 | Spice Peppercorns Mixed | JR  (1.0000 JR) | (SAME) | |
| 5590 | Spice Paprika Spanish | JR  (1.0000 JR) | (SAME) | |
| 5587 | Spice Paprika Hungarian Hot | CN  (1.0000 CN) | (SAME) | |
| 5588 | Spice Paprika Hungarian Sweet | CN  (1.0000 CN) | (SAME) | |
| 5674 | Spice Pepper Black Whole | JR  (1.0000 JR) | (SAME) | |
| 5670 | Spice Pepper Coarse Ground | JR  (1.0000 JR) | (SAME) | |
| 5672 | Spice Pepper Black Ground | JR  (1.0000 JR) | (SAME) | |
| 5694 | Spice Pepper White Whole | JR  (1.0000 JR) | (SAME) | |
| 5692 | Spice Pepper White Ground | JR  (1.0000 JR) | (SAME) | |
| 6172 | Spice Peppercorn Green in Brine | CN  (1.0000 CN) | (SAME) | |
| 5706 | Spice Pickling | JR  (1.0000 JR) | (SAME) | |
| 5722 | Spice Poppy Seed Whole | JR  (1.0000 JR) | (SAME) | |
| 5752 | Spice Rosemary Leaves | JR  (1.0000 JR) | (SAME) | |
| 5675 | Spice Herbs de Provence | EA  (1.0000 EA) | (SAME) | |
| 5792 | Spice Sesame Seeds Hulled | JR  (1.0000 JR) | (SAME) | |
| 5830 | Spice Tarragon | JR  (1.0000 JR) | (SAME) | |

FIGURE **5.14b** Inventory can also be tracked automatically using a computer tracking program. (Continues)

(continued)

# PHYSICAL INVENTORY SHEET
## *by Package*
### CIA–Hyde Park–Culinary Institute of America

Location: _____     Date of Physical Count: _____

Package: xDry Room Inventory for Physical Inventory     Counted By: _____

| NUMBER | ITEM | TRANS UN (PACKSIZE) | BASE UN | REMARK |
|--------|------|---------------------|---------|--------|
| 5843 | Spice Thyme Ground | JR  (1.0000 JR) | (SAME) | |
| 5842 | Spice Thyme Leaves | JR  (1.0000 JR) | (SAME) | |
| 5860 | Spice Tumeric Ground | JR  (1.0000 JR) | (SAME) | |
| 5673A | Spice Pimenton Sweet | CN  (1.0000 CN) | (SAME) | |
| 5673B | Spice Pimenton Bittersweet | CN  (1.0000 CN) | (SAME) | |
| 5673 | Spice Pimenton Hot | CN  (1.0000 CN) | (SAME) | |
| 6092 | Spice Juniper Berries (OZ) | OZ  (1.0000 OZ) | (SAME) | |
| 5007 | Spice Annato Seed | PK  (1.0000 PK) | (SAME) | |
| 5372 | Spice Gumbo File | BT  (1.0000 BT) | (SAME) | |
| 5578 | Spice Onion Salt | JR  (1.0000 JR) | (SAME) | |
| 5148 | Spice Cardamom Pods | PK  (1.0000 PK) | (SAME) | |
| 5584 | Spice Oregano Leaves | JR  (1.0000 JR) | (SAME) | |
| 5528 | Spice Nutmeg Whole | OZ  (1.0000 OZ) | (SAME) | |
| 5693 | Spice Peppercorns Pink | OZ  (1.0000 OZ) | (SAME) | |
| 5762 | Salt Iodized | BX  (1.0000 BX) | (SAME) | |
| 5776 | Salt Sea Baleine | CN  (1.0000 CN) | (SAME) | |
| 5777 | Salt Fleur de Sel | EA  (1.0000 EA) | (SAME) | |
| 5775 | Salt Sea Coarse Grey | LB  (1.0000 LB) | (SAME) | |
| 5564 | Olives Black Ripe | CN  (1.0000 CN) | (SAME) | |
| 5850 | Olive Paste | JR  (1.0000 JR) | (SAME) | |
| 5570 | Olives Green Stuffed | JR  (1.0000 JR) | (SAME) | |
| 5571 | Olives Picholine | JR  (1.0000 JR) | (SAME) | |
| 5572 | Olives Nicoise | JR  (1.0000 JR) | (SAME) | |
| 5575 | Olives Mixed Pitted | TU  (1.0000 TU) | (SAME) | |
| 5567 | Olives Mixed Whole | BX  (1.0000 BX) | (SAME) | |
| 5574 | Olives Pitted Calamata | TU  (1.0000 TU) | (SAME) | |
| 5573 | Olives Calamata in Brine | TU  (1.0000 TU) | (SAME) | |
| 5585 | Spice Oregano Mexican | OZ  (1.0000 OZ) | (SAME) | |
| 5569 | Olives Green Queen Stuffed (Gallon) | GL  (1.0000 GL) | (SAME) | |
| 5035 | Spice Epazote Dried | OZ  (1.0000 OZ) | (SAME) | |
| 5586 | Spice Oregano Sicily | PK  (1.0000 PK) | (SAME) | |
| 6045 | Huitlacoche | CN  (1.0000 CN) | (SAME) | |

**FIGURE 5.14b** Inventory can also be tracked automatically using a computer tracking program. (Continues)

# PHYSICAL INVENTORY SHEET

*by Package*

**CIA–Hyde Park–Culinary Institute of America**

Location: _____          Date of Physical Count: _____

Package: xDry Room Inventory for Physical Inventory          Counted By: _____

| NUMBER | ITEM | TRANS UN (PACKSIZE) | BASE UN | REMARK |
|--------|------|---------------------|---------|--------|
| 6001 | Spice Achiote Paste | **PK** *(1.0000 PK)* | *(SAME)* | |
| 5749I | Relish Whup Asp Asparagus | **JR** *(1.0000 JR)* | *(SAME)* | |
| 5749G | Relish Sweet Potato Butter | **JR** *(1.0000 JR)* | *(SAME)* | |
| 5040 | Callaloo | **CN** *(1.0000 CN)* | *(SAME)* | |
| 5749C | Relish GT 1000s Tomato Cond. | **JR** *(1.0000 JR)* | *(SAME)* | |
| 5749D | Relish Mean Beans Beans | **JR** *(1.0000 JR)* | *(SAME)* | |
| 5749 | Relish Bee and Beez Pickles | **JR** *(1.0000 JR)* | *(SAME)* | |
| 5749B | Relish Corn | **JR** *(1.0000 JR)* | *(SAME)* | |
| 5749A | Relish Chow Chow | **JR** *(1.0000 JR)* | *(SAME)* | |
| 5749H | Relish Watermelon Rind Pickle | **JR** *(1.0000 JR)* | *(SAME)* | |
| 5749F | Relish Smokra Okra | **JR** *(1.0000 JR)* | *(SAME)* | |
| 5189 | Beans Lupini | **EA** *(1.0000 EA)* | *(SAME)* | |
| 5749L | Relish Mushrooms Marinated | **JR** *(1.0000 JR)* | *(SAME)* | |
| 5749K | Relish Garden Medley | **JR** *(1.0000 JR)* | *(SAME)* | |
| 5749M | Relish Olives Jalapeno Stuffed | **JR** *(1.0000 JR)* | *(SAME)* | |
| 5749J | Relish Apple Butter | **JR** *(1.0000 JR)* | *(SAME)* | |
| 5749E | Relish Peach Butter | **JR** *(1.0000 JR)* | *(SAME)* | |
| 5306 | Guava Paste | **CN** *(1.0000 CN)* | *(SAME)* | |
| 6067 | Cancha Corn Snack | **LB** *(1.0000 LB)* | *(SAME)* | |
| 3189 | Hibiscus Flowers | **PK** *(1.0000 PK)* | *(SAME)* | |
| 6044 | Chutney | **JR** *(1.0000 JR)* | *(SAME)* | |
| 5708 | Peppers Pimentos Sweet 14oz | **CN** *(1.0000 CN)* | *(SAME)* | |
| 6148 | Paste Panca Red | **JR** *(1.0000 JR)* | *(SAME)* | |
| 6090 | Harissa | **CN** *(1.0000 CN)* | *(SAME)* | |
| 6168 | Peppers Malagueta | **BT** *(1.0000 BT)* | *(SAME)* | |
| 5141 | Caperberries | **JR** *(1.0000 JR)* | *(SAME)* | |
| 6302 | Grape Leaves | **JR** *(1.0000 JR)* | *(SAME)* | |
| 5142 | Capers Salted | **KG** *(1.0000 KG)* | *(SAME)* | |
| 5143 | Capers Small Non-Pareil | **JR** *(1.0000 JR)* | *(SAME)* | |
| 6167 | Peppers Chipotle Adobo | **CN** *(1.0000 CN)* | *(SAME)* | |
| 6163 | Peppers Spanish Piquillo | **CN** *(1.0000 CN)* | *(SAME)* | |
| 5543 | Oil Dende | **EA** *(1.0000 EA)* | *(SAME)* | |

**FIGURE 5.14b** Inventory can also be tracked automatically using a computer tracking program. (Continues)

(continued)

# PHYSICAL INVENTORY SHEET
## by Package
### CIA–Hyde Park–Culinary Institute of America

Location: _____     Date of Physical Count: _____

Package: xDry Room Inventory for Physical Inventory     Counted By: _____

| NUMBER | ITEM | TRANS UN (PACKSIZE) | BASE UN | REMARK |
|--------|------|---------------------|---------|--------|
| 6250 | Sesame Tahini | CN (1.0000 CN) | (SAME) | |
| 6169A | Peppers Jalapeno Pickled 26oz | CN (1.0000 CN) | (SAME) | |
| 5731 | Pickle Relish | GL (1.0000 GL) | (SAME) | |
| 6146 | Hearts of Palm | CN (1.0000 CN) | (SAME) | |
| 5687 | Peppers Hot Cherry | GL (1.0000 GL) | (SAME) | |
| 5038 | Artichoke Hearts #10 | EA (1.0000 EA) | (SAME) | |
| 5688 | Pepperoncini | GL (1.0000 GL) | (SAME) | |
| 5477 | Syrup Maple HG | EA (1.0000 EA) | (SAME) | |
| 5479 | Syrup Maple B Grade (Gallon) | GL (1.0000 GL) | (SAME) | |
| 5826 | Syrup Pancake | GL (1.0000 GL) | (SAME) | |
| 5858 | Tomato Sundried | PK (1.0000 PK) | (SAME) | |
| 5859 | Tomato Sundried in Oil | GL (1.0000 GL) | (SAME) | |
| 6084 | Flour Manioc Coarse | LB (1.0000 LB) | (SAME) | |
| 6054 | Couscous Israeli | LB (1.0000 LB) | (SAME) | |
| 6055 | Couscous Whole Wheat | LB (1.0000 LB) | (SAME) | |
| 6094 | Grain Kasha | LB (1.0000 LB) | (SAME) | |
| 6079 | Wheat Berry Red | LB (1.0000 LB) | (SAME) | |
| 6052 | Couscous | LB (1.0000 LB) | (SAME) | |
| 4132 | Grain Spelt | LB (1.0000 LB) | (SAME) | |
| 5739 | Grain Quinoa | LB (1.0000 LB) | (SAME) | |
| 5236 | Corn Dried Field Blue | LB (1.0000 LB) | (SAME) | |
| 5235 | Corn Dried Field White | LB (1.0000 LB) | (SAME) | |
| 6074 | Grain Bulgar | LB (1.0000 LB) | (SAME) | |
| 6123 | Mushroom Black Trumpet Dried | LB (16.0000 OZ) | OZ | |
| 6132 | Mushroom Morel Dried | OZ (1.0000 OZ) | (SAME) | |
| 6120 | Mushroom Cepes Dried | OZ (1.0000 OZ) | (SAME) | |
| 6124 | Mushroom Chanterelle Dried | OZ (1.0000 OZ) | (SAME) | |
| 5862 | Matzo Meal | LB (1.0000 LB) | (SAME) | |
| 6072 | Flour Buckwheat | LB (1.0000 LB) | (SAME) | |
| 5343 | Flour Garbanzo Chick Pea | LB (1.0000 LB) | (SAME) | |
| 6095 | Grain Farro | LB (1.0000 LB) | (SAME) | |
| 4144 | Flour Whole Wheat Organic | LB (1.0000 LB) | (SAME) | |

FIGURE 5.14b Inventory can also be tracked automatically using a computer tracking program. (Continues)

# PHYSICAL INVENTORY SHEET
### by Package
### CIA–Hyde Park–Culinary Institute of America

Location: _____     Date of Physical Count: _____

Package: xDry Room Inventory for Physical Inventory          Counted By: _____

| NUMBER | ITEM | TRANS UN (PACKSIZE) | BASE UN | REMARK |
|--------|------|---------------------|---------|--------|
| 5346 | Oats Steel Cut | LB  (1.0000 LB) | (SAME) | |
| 5349 | Flour Wondra | LB  (1.0000 LB) | (SAME) | |
| 5099A | Beans Dried Local Navy | LB  (1.0000 LB) | (SAME) | |
| 5099 | Beans Dried Local Black | LB  (1.0000 LB) | (SAME) | |
| 5099C | Beans Dried Local Red | LB  (1.0000 LB) | (SAME) | |
| 6097 | Grain Local Tritacale | LB  (1.0000 LB) | (SAME) | |
| 5099B | Beans Dried Local Pinto | LB  (1.0000 LB) | (SAME) | |
| 6096 | Grain Local Spelt | LB  (1.0000 LB) | (SAME) | |
| 6068 | Corn Meal Local Polenta Coarse | LB  (1.0000 LB) | (SAME) | |
| 6068A | Corn Meal Local Polenta Fine | LB  (1.0000 LB) | (SAME) | |
| 4027 | Cherries In Brandy | EA  (1.0000 EA) | (SAME) | |
| 5452 | Lingonberries Wild | JR  (1.0000 JR) | (SAME) | |
| 5806 | Jam Raspberry | JR  (1.0000 JR) | (SAME) | |
| 5388 | Jelly Grape | JR  (1.0000 JR) | (SAME) | |
| 5386 | Jelly Currant | JR  (1.0000 JR) | (SAME) | |
| 5031 | Apricot Preserves | JR  (1.0000 JR) | (SAME) | |
| 5018 | Jelly Apple | JR  (1.0000 JR) | (SAME) | |
| 5582 | Marmalade Orange | JR  (1.0000 JR) | (SAME) | |
| 5801 | Jam Strawberry | JR  (1.0000 JR) | (SAME) | |
| 5024 | Apricots Dried | PK  (1.0000 PK) | (SAME) | |
| 5016 | Apples Dried | PK  (1.0000 PK) | (SAME) | |
| 5302 | Figs Dried | PK  (1.0000 PK) | (SAME) | |
| 5172 | Pears Dried | LB  (1.0000 LB) | (SAME) | |
| 6272 | Tapioca Pearls Large | LB  (1.0000 LB) | (SAME) | |
| 6270 | Tapioca Small | LB  (1.0000 LB) | (SAME) | |
| 5535 | Oil Almond | BT  (1.0000 BT) | (SAME) | |
| 5550 | Oil Peanut Roasted | BT  (1.0000 BT) | (SAME) | |
| 5356 | Gelatin Knox | CN  (1.0000 CN) | (SAME) | |
| 5541 | Oil Pumpkin Seed | BT  (1.0000 BT) | (SAME) | |
| 5533 | Oil Hazelnut | CN  (1.0000 CN) | (SAME) | |
| 5539 | Oil Safflower LT | BT  (1.0000 BT) | (SAME) | |
| 5556 | Oil Walnut | CN  (1.0000 CN) | (SAME) | |

FIGURE **5.14b** Inventory can also be tracked automatically using a computer tracking program. (Continues)

(continued)

# PHYSICAL INVENTORY SHEET
## by Package
### CIA–Hyde Park–Culinary Institute of America

Location: _____     Date of Physical Count: _____

Package: xDry Room Inventory for Physical Inventory     Counted By: _____

| NUMBER | ITEM | TRANS UN (PACKSIZE) | BASE UN | REMARK |
|---|---|---|---|---|
| 5537 | Oil Sunflower | BT (1.0000 BT) | (SAME) | |
| 5499 | Milk Evaporated Fat Free | CN (1.0000 CN) | (SAME) | |
| 5498 | Milk Evaporated | CN (1.0000 CN) | (SAME) | |
| 5494 | Milk Condensed 14oz | CN (1.0000 CN) | (SAME) | |
| 5496 | Milk Dried Non Fat | BX (1.0000 BX) | (SAME) | |
| 5308 | Anchovy Paste | EA (1.0000 EA) | (SAME) | |
| 5340 | Fish Tuna White | CN (1.0000 CN) | (SAME) | |
| 5341 | Fish Tuna in Oil | CN (1.0000 CN) | (SAME) | |
| 5342 | Fish Tuna Fillet in Oil 4oz | JR (1.0000 JR) | (SAME) | |
| 5339 | Fish Tuna Tongol | CN (1.0000 CN) | (SAME) | |
| 5316 | Fish Clam Juice | CN (1.0000 CN) | (SAME) | |
| 5314 | Fish Clams Chopped Canned S/O | CN (1.0000 CN) | (SAME) | |
| 5292 | Escargot | CN (1.0000 CN) | (SAME) | |
| 5532 | Oatmeal Old Fashioned | EA (1.0000 EA) | (SAME) | |
| 5258 | Cream of Coconut | CN (1.0000 CN) | (SAME) | |
| 5536 | Oatmeal Quick Oats | BX (1.0000 BX) | (SAME) | |
| 5370 | Grits Quick | PK (1.0000 PK) | (SAME) | |
| 5266 | Shortening Crisco 3# | CN (1.0000 CN) | (SAME) | |
| 5534 | Nuts Walnut Canned | 10 (1.0000 10) | (SAME) | |
| 5644 | Peanut Butter | JR (1.0000 JR) | (SAME) | |
| 5768 | Salt Kosher | BX (1.0000 BX) | (SAME) | |
| 6018 | Bread Crumb Panko Bulk | CS (1.0000 CS) | (SAME) | |
| 6017 | Bread Crumb Panko | PK (1.0000 PK) | (SAME) | |
| 5264 | Cereal Cream of Wheat | BX (1.0000 BX) | (SAME) | |
| 5260 | Cereal Cream of Rice | BX (1.0000 BX) | (SAME) | |
| 5898 | Wheat Germ | JR (1.0000 JR) | (SAME) | |
| 6002 | Amaretto Crumbs | CS (1.0000 CS) | (SAME) | |
| 5240 | Crackers Carr's Water | BX (1.0000 BX) | (SAME) | |
| 5250 | Crackers Assorted Cheese | BX (1.0000 BX) | (SAME) | |
| 5364 | Ginger Snaps | BX (1.0000 BX) | (SAME) | |
| 4159 | Ladyfingers | PK (1.0000 PK) | (SAME) | |
| 6003 | Amaretto Cookies | PK (1.0000 PK) | (SAME) | |

**FIGURE 5.14b** Inventory can also be tracked automatically using a computer tracking program. (Continues)

# PHYSICAL INVENTORY SHEET

*by Package*

CIA–Hyde Park–Culinary Institute of America

Location: _____       Date of Physical Count: _____

Package: xDry Room Inventory for Physical Inventory       Counted By: _____

| NUMBER | ITEM | TRANS UN (PACKSIZE) | BASE UN | REMARK |
|--------|------|---------------------|---------|--------|
| 6005 | Wafers Chocolate | BX  (1.0000 BX) | (SAME) | |
| 5804 | Starch Potato 1# | BX  (1.0000 BX) | (SAME) | |
| 5802 | Starch Corn | BX  (1.0000 BX) | (SAME) | |
| 5301 | Cereal Farina | BX  (1.0000 BX) | (SAME) | |
| 5366 | Graham Cracker Crumbs | PK  (1.0000 PK) | (SAME) | |
| 5817 | Sugar Domino Dots | LB  (1.0000 LB) | (SAME) | |
| 5814 | Sugar Bar | BX  (1.0000 BX) | (SAME) | |
| 5812 | Sugar 10x | BX  (1.0000 BX) | (SAME) | |
| 5303 | Pancake Mix | PK  (1.0000 PK) | (SAME) | |
| 5310 | Pancake Buckwheat Mix | PK  (1.0000 PK) | (SAME) | |
| 5816 | Sugar Brown Dark 1# | LB  (1.0000 LB) | (SAME) | |
| 5818 | Sugar Brown Light 1# | LB  (1.0000 LB) | (SAME) | |
| 5815 | Sugar Piloncilla | EA  (1.0000 EA) | (SAME) | |
| 5811 | Sugar Turbinado | BX  (1.0000 BX) | (SAME) | |
| 5813 | Sugar Maple | LB  (1.0000 LB) | (SAME) | |
| 5810 | Sugar 5# | PK  (1.0000 PK) | (SAME) | |
| 5454 | Lentils Casteluccio | PK  (1.0000 PK) | (SAME) | |
| 5451 | Lentils Red | LB  (1.0000 LB) | (SAME) | |
| 5085 | Lentils French Green | LB  (1.0000 LB) | (SAME) | |
| 5450 | Lentils | LB  (1.0000 LB) | (SAME) | |
| 5179 | Beans Black Dried | PK  (1.0000 PK) | (SAME) | |
| 5193 | Beans Pinto Dried | LB  (1.0000 LB) | (SAME) | |
| 5185 | Beans Cranberry Dried | LB  (1.0000 LB) | (SAME) | |
| 5196 | Beans Kidney Red Dried | LB  (1.0000 LB) | (SAME) | |
| 5180 | Beans Blackeye Dried | PK  (1.0000 PK) | (SAME) | |
| 5186 | Beans Great Northern Dried | LB  (1.0000 LB) | (SAME) | |
| 5664 | Peas Split Green | LB  (1.0000 LB) | (SAME) | |
| 5182 | Beans Giant Peruvian | CS  (1.0000 CS) | (SAME) | |
| 5660 | Beans Garbanzo Chick Pea Dried | LB  (1.0000 LB) | (SAME) | |
| 5151 | Barley Medium | LB  (1.0000 LB) | (SAME) | |
| 5188 | Beans Navy Dried | LB  (1.0000 LB) | (SAME) | |
| 5184 | Beans Fava Dried | LB  (1.0000 LB) | (SAME) | |
| 5187 | Beans Lima Dried | LB  (1.0000 LB) | (SAME) | |

**FIGURE 5.14b** Inventory can also be tracked automatically using a computer tracking program. (Continues)

(continued)

## PHYSICAL INVENTORY SHEET
### by Package
**CIA–Hyde Park–Culinary Institute of America**

Location: _____          Date of Physical Count: _____

Package: xDry Room Inventory for Physical Inventory          Counted By: _____

| NUMBER | ITEM | TRANS UN (PACKSIZE) | BASE UN | REMARK |
|--------|------|---------------------|---------|--------|
| 5547 | Oil Grapeseed | **GL** *(1.0000 GL)* | *(SAME)* | |
| 5484 | Mayonnaise | **GL** *(1.0000 GL)* | *(SAME)* | |
| 5892 | Vinegar Red Wine (Gallon) | **GL** *(1.0000 GL)* | *(SAME)* | |
| 5870 | Vinegar Apple Cider | **GL** *(1.0000 GL)* | *(SAME)* | |
| 5888 | Vinegar White Distilled (Gallon) | **GL** *(1.0000 GL)* | *(SAME)* | |
| 5882 | Vinegar Tarragon (Gallon) | **GL** *(1.0000 GL)* | *(SAME)* | |
| 6282 | Beans Adzuki | **LB** *(1.0000 LB)* | *(SAME)* | |
| 5083 | Beans Flagelot | **LB** *(1.0000 LB)* | *(SAME)* | |
| 5095 | Beans Cannellini | **LB** *(1.0000 LB)* | *(SAME)* | |
| 5135 | Bread Crumbs | **PK** *(1.0000 PK)* | *(SAME)* | |
| 2161 | ZZMilk Heavy Cream Ronnybrook S/O | **BT** *(1.0000 BT)* | *(SAME)* | |

**FIGURE 5.14b** Inventory can also be tracked automatically using a computer tracking program.

## MANAGERIAL SUPPORT AND COMMITMENT

Nothing else will have as significant an impact on maintaining good inventory control as managerial focus and support in achieving the desired results. This starts by management's ability to implement the required systems that will guarantee accurate results. The size and/or current economic position of the organization will likely have an impact of how technologically sophisticated the implemented systems are, but in any case good systems need be implemented and enforced. Such systems need to be assessed periodically to ensure they remain up to date and provide effective information and controls.

### ASSIGNMENT OF DUTIES

Having reliable data and accurate inventory management requires putting the right people in the correct task and insuring as little conflict of interest as possible. Whenever possible there should be a segregation of duties, meaning the person purchasing and otherwise responsible for a product line should not be the same person conducting a financial audit. In general, the same person should also not be responsible for the purchase, receipt, and issue of an inventory line. There is a lack of control and potential conflict of interest in combining these duties. This can occur if there is no check to insure what was purchased is actually in inventory or was utilized with the proper controls. This is prevented with a "blind count" wherein the person counting an area has no connection to its purchase or the inventory control system and works objectively. Counters do need to understand the nature of the product that they count, however. Alternatively, an inventory taken for the purpose of developing an order for purchase should be done by or for the person doing the purchase of that item.

Sometimes the size of an operation and its staff can make some of these guidelines difficult to manage, but the better the segregation, the more optimal the fiscal controls. Many large operations may employ outside financial audit teams that are separate in their duties from the purchasing and preparation personnel, but this is generally not a fiscally viable option for most foodservice operations. The size and scope of each individual operation must determine what level of controls is justifiable.

Counts should always be done in teams when conducting a full financial inventory. One person should count the items assigned to the team, and the other should monitor what is counted and record the information. Management should be responsible for determining assignments to assure each team is well suited and qualified for the job and supervising how that team performs. The team members should be chosen by the capabilities and relevant knowledge of the available staff to assure that the most qualified people are assigned to each area or station. (Once again, management should seek to avoid any conflict of interest.) Audits should be performed by a team other than the one performing the original count. Obviously, team performance should be monitored to ascertain if more training is needed or if teams should be staffed differently. Team members must be cognizant of the fact that each member's performance will affect how his or her team partner will be evaluated.

Management then needs to make sure all relevant employees involved in taking and controlling inventory are fully trained. No system will provide accurate data if those employing that system are ill prepared or lacking in the skills to properly execute them, and do not fully grasp why this accurate information is crucial. Second, management should tie employee performance reviews to achieving accurate inventory results and the ability to effect positive improvements from the data these inventories provide. Employees should realize that their ability to affect the bottom line in a positive or negative manner may also affect their personal bottom line.

The information gained from wall-to-wall physical inventories should also be communicated to the staff. Chefs need to know that the desired cost percentages are, or are not, being met and where controls are lacking. Staff members should understand the fiscal impact of proper and improper management. Timely and accurate inventory counts done for ordering purposes will also track usage and show when usage does not match sales. Understanding the dollars represented by product passing through a foodservice establishment helps maintain awareness amongst the staff of the importance of portion control and minimizing waste. Management attention to accurate inventories and a determination to resolve all discrepancies will also make employees much less willing to risk pilferage or condone it in others.

All of this must be seen by management as a daily practice that is analyzed and improved by consistent vigilance. Merely writing good guidelines without reinforcement will not be effective. The following guidelines will all be useful in assuring accurate inventory management.

## ACCOUNTABILITY

There should be a required level of accuracy in inventory performance. Food and beverage costs need to be maintained within a slim margin of accuracy. Monthly physical counts should have a discrepancy tolerance of around 95% to 98%. Mistakes, poor yields, and other forms of waste may account for some undetermined loss, but any greater variance should require an acceptable explanation and that a solution be found to stop the losses.

The employees responsible for each aspect of an inventory must be held responsible for the proper execution of those assigned duties. Timelines must be adhered to, counts must be accurate and designated to a specific employee(s), food cost percentages need to be met, and discrepancies need to be resolved and accounted for. Audits of each count should also be taken by different teams to ensure that accurate counts are being made. In small operations, all counts may need to be performed by only one or two employees. In this case, a manager or accounting person should conduct a thorough audit to verify the results. Also, over time, monthly results should be analyzed to identify trends and seek ways to identify and resolve variances. The key is to continuously look for ways to improve the processes and tighten controls. As noted, these results should be tied to the relevant employee's evaluation process.

## ESTABLISHED WRITTEN POLICIES

An organization's inventory policy should be documented in writing and given to each relevant new hire as part of that person's orientation process. These employees should not only be familiar with these policies but also well trained in how to follow them. Employees failing to properly execute these procedures should be made to review and be reminded of their importance. Said policies should be evaluated periodically to seek ways to improve them, especially if desired results are not always gained.

A written policy should outline all required steps, including:

- The inventory's objective
- The method of counting to be done
- The required timing of each phase
- The required preparation of the area being counted
- The separation of duties (one person counting, and one verifying and writing or entering the data)
- The proper forms and format for the information
- Tracking of any purchased inventory held off-site

---

## MONTHLY STOREROOM INVENTORY POLICY

- Always work in teams of two; lead person writes and observes second person's count for accuracy. Care should be given to properly differentiate similar items with the correct name or code number (e.g., flat vs. sparkling Pellegrino water).
- Inventory must start at the designated time, and nothing may be received or issued once the count has begun.
- Work from shelf to sheet to insure nothing is missed; work from top to bottom and from left to right. Confirm nothing is missed before moving to the next shelf unit or storage area. Check for additional product stored between units if need dictates.
- Record count by issue unit as indicated on the inventory sheets (#, ea., can, etc.). Indicate how many cases and units make up the count (e.g., 12 cases x 24 cns = 288).
- Make sure all written work is legible, and initial each completed sheet. Turn all completed work into the manager for auditing when assigned area(s) is completed.
- Once all designated areas are completed, management will reissue the completed inventory counts to auditing teams to verify the counts.
- Management will indicate which items should be audited.
- Auditors must initial each sheet upon conclusion. No area should be inventoried and audited by the same employee.

FIGURE **5.15** Sample written inventory policy.

- Proper review and accountability
- Required steps to attempt to reconcile discrepancies and document any adjustments
- Frequency and timing of each required count
- A summation of the policy and glossary of terms, if deemed appropriate

As noted, a written policy should not be seen as etched in stone; these guidelines should be periodically reviewed to ensure they remain current and yield the desired results. All changes made to the written policy must be immediately conveyed and explained to all relevant inventory personnel. The changes should be conveyed to the rest of the staff only if they affect the performance of their duties.

## FREQUENCY OF AND REASONS FOR SPECIFIC INVENTORY COUNTS

Inventories are conducted for purposes of financial control and accounting, and to determine purchasing needs for menu items and operating needs. Operational managers and financial management will determine the type and frequency of control inventories. Monthly and fiscal year-end full wall-to-wall inventories are still commonly conducted. However, modern ordering, receiving, and issuing technology can provide instant information as to what should be on hand, and ongoing cycle counts of specific areas of inventory to verify these numbers are now frequently done. Such inventories can be incorporated into daily operations easily and do not require a total cessation of business activities to accomplish or the usual accompanying payroll overtime. Specific intervals in which each area or type of inventory should be counted must be determined and adhered to. Such cycle counting is often combined with full counts that are done periodically such as quarterly or at the end of each fiscal year. Food cost is determined by taking a beginning inventory of product, adding all incoming deliveries during the specified time period, and then subtracting all product required for preparation and sale, or the product that had been issued from the storage area and transferred into production. That number should equal the amount of the subsequent inventory. The product cost utilized during that time period is factored into total sales to supply the food cost percentage. The dollar volume of the total inventory when measured against each daily food cost will also show how many days' worth of inventory are being held in stock. Some purchasers still determine their inventory volumes based on the dollar value held in stock being equal to roughly 2 weeks' usage or two turnovers in stock per month. Electronic systems today make it easier and more manageable to hold inventory based on vendor timing and forecasted need, rather than predetermined levels that are not consistent with actual usage.

Orders for product lines such as meat, fish, and produce are determined by comparing inventory on hand to the operation's forecasted needs. The business' chefs and/or buyers will determine how frequently it is necessary to inventory each product line to insure all needs are met. The operation's available storage space, volume of business, location, vendor ability and minimum deliveries, and style of business will help to determine that frequency. As a rule, however, perishables will be counted and purchased daily or multiple times per week. Dry goods and nonfood items can usually be done less frequently while still keeping inventory levels as low as possible without creating inefficiencies.

Modern e-procurement platforms can be set to determine high and low par inventory levels that will flag the need for more products when inventory levels reach the minimum or below and determine the required amount needed for purchase to return to the higher par number. When determining appropriate par levels for reference (in either manual or web-based systems), these numbers need to be adjusted as business demands and menu needs change. These systems will also not factor in variables like weather, large functions, holidays, and other circumstances that can dramatically affect an operation's needs and volume of business for that period of time. In such cases, the purchaser needs to adjust if menu items change for special occasion menus, or adjust the volume utilized for items directly related to a large function, such as rib roasts for a large wedding reception. Evaluation of historic data regarding the weather for a period of time in comparison to what is being currently forecast for that time period can also factor into accurate buying projections. Monthly discrepancies or shrinkage of inventory typical over a period of time should also be considered in determining correct purchase amounts. A knowledgeable purchasing agent or chef must continue to monitor the orders generated to insure they accurately reflect need and review stock levels on hand to insure that such preset par levels remain responsive to the needs of the business.

The value of these high-tech systems must be weighed against the size and scope of the operation. New cutting-edge technological systems are continuously coming to market and cost significant dollars to not only purchase but also implement. Management must be sure the needs of the business can justify the cost of whatever system looks appealing. In other words, the costs of a solution to maintain controls should not far exceed the risk to finance.

## SUPERVISION OF DUTIES

Once inventory teams are determined, there needs to be full supervision of all duties assigned. This starts prior to performance by assuring that each person is properly trained, both in technique and in the nature of the product being counted. This will include understanding what base unit is used for tallying each specific item; the base unit is the unit in which the item is issued (e.g., bottle, pound, ounce, box, or case). Supervisors make certain that these counts are done in a timely fashion and review the counts to verify that they are accurately taken and tabulated. The performance should be monitored as counts are taken as well and when results are confirmed or audited so that employees can be properly coached to insure their work is done correctly. Teams should perform in a focused professional manner with a current knowledge of the relevant area being counted.

## COMPLETE WALL-TO-WALL FINANCIAL COUNT CONTROLS

As noted, full inventory counts are done for the purposes of financial reporting and controls. Therefore, it is crucial to insure proper procedures are in place so that nothing is being brought in or issued out of the storage facility during the full inventory. Also, entrance to these areas should be limited only to employees participating in the inventory.

These counts also must be taken at the end of business on the final business day of that reporting period, such as the end of business on the last working day of the month. There are a number of controls necessary to implement for trustworthy accurate counts.

- Outside personnel must be informed of the timing of the inventory and barred from entry prior to beginning it.
- All incoming merchandise must be received and entered into the system prior to counting. All daily issues must also be charged out prior to the beginning.
- Precount preparation should be done to insure all inventory is located in its proper place and staged in plain view for efficient counts.
- Slow-moving inventory may sometimes be segregated and precounted prior to the full count. Such items may be used seasonally or held just for specific functions, or may be items held in inventory but not currently being utilized.
- Any inventory stored off-site or with the vendor must be accounted for. Occasionally inventory is purchased in a large quantity to leverage a better price or due to large minimums, such as is required for custom-printing jobs. In such cases, due to storage constraints, purchasers may negotiate with the vendor to hold this purchased product and then deliver it as needed within a predetermined period of time.
- Inventory tally sheets must be maintained in proper bin order, with correct product codes, and indicate proper base unit to be counted (pound, each, etc.).
- Counting and auditing teams must be identified and present as required.
- Insure that all teams are given any pertinent information about their assigned area prior to beginning inventory.
- Auditing teams confirm not only accurate counts but also that all information is given in the correct forms.
- Count discrepancies are flagged and proper count confirmed by management.
- Management must insure that all counts are time bound.

Cycle counts are easier to perform when financial management permits because it is easier to close small areas of inventory during hours of business operation than to time an entire wall-to-wall count with the required cessation of business. These smaller cycle counts also have less financial impact on payroll dollars as they require much less overtime to manage. Other controls relevant to access to the inventory area and limiting additions and subtractions remain essential. Typically, businesses operate today on a dual system, doing frequent cycle counts and annual or quarterly financially mandated full counts.

## PERFORMANCE AND RESULT EVALUATION

Taking an accurate and well-managed inventory is critical, but only in that it supplies buyers and management with good information; inventories must then be thoroughly reviewed and evaluated. The data gained will show if the desired food cost percentages are being met, and if product on hand is consistent with what was forecasted or within acceptable variances. If expectations are realized or improved upon, then management should convey and laud all relevant staff with this information but still examine results for areas where further improvement can be realized. Alternatively, if expectations fall short of the desired results, then management needs to delve into the causes and hold all relevant staff members accountable.

Variances can be measured by the percentage of the number of total units expended and counted, or as a dollar value of the product sold and in stock. With fresh food products, there will most certainly be some variance due to shrinkage from moisture loss, fabrication and trim loss, spillage, decay, and other factors that will affect expected yield to some degree, no matter how well documented. Such losses may typically account for only a few percentage points in variance. Variances above what management deems as an acceptable level need to be investigated, and a determination needs to be made as to the cause of the loss and how to prevent further loss in the same manner.

Variances should also be examined by the nature of the product; losses of very high-end products such as shrimp, truffles, or foie gras would likely result from much different and more dire reasons than a loss of a low-cost staple. The latter is more likely due to sloppy work, while variances in the former could mean theft.

Multiple variances in one specific area could indicate a problem with the skill set of the team doing the counting or how well prepared the area was for the inventory, if not pilferage. Sporadic problems across the entire inventory may indicate system reliability or tracking problems. Timing is usually critical in resolving and adjusting errors in the inventory results as management usually dictates a few, finite number of days before they need to close their books on the month. If discrepancies in an inventory can be accounted for and the appropriate charge or credit taken, then the rationale for those variances should be approved by management to insure corrections are not just being made to mask another issue. Significant or frequent discrepancies without prior managerial knowledge should be investigated as probable pilferage.

Accurate periodic counts can also help identify "dead" inventory, or stock that is no longer being used but remains on the shelf. Such unused assets should be identified and efforts made to utilize the product as it represents dollars just sitting idle or, worse, decaying. Detailed information on usage can also be gathered from these periodic counts and used by the buyer to leverage better pricing from a vendor if that volume can be shown to be significant.

Operations vary in how thoroughly they manage inventory information to drive their purchases and control costs. Some utilize an ad-hoc system wherein they simply generate orders based on perceived need with no effort given to evaluating purchases or product usage. Others may do more by taking counts and basically filling the gaps, much like restocking shelves in a grocery store. A third, higher level is practiced most frequently; this practice requires secure inventory that is counted periodically and charged out as required. This affords some controls but still lacks accurate forecasting to drive the purchases off the inventory numbers; it is better but can still result in losses and too much inventory cost.

It may make sense to conduct an inventory value assessment on a monthly or annual basis. Adding up all of the inventory value can help calculate the total worth of the business in case of an insurance claim or theft assessment. It can also help to track products that are not moving. For instance, an item might have been removed from the menu, but a certain amount of stock remains in storage, taking up space and capital. The establishment may decide to run a special to deplete the item or donate it where the value can be used as a tax write-off.

Calculating inventory turnover is another tool that purchasers use to help in ordering. Turnover of perishables is certainly an important figure, due to the possible degradation of the product. Turnover of nonperishable goods is important when deciding what the inventory volume should be. How much soap and paper towels are enough? Overpurchasing of this type of item can tie up capital, while not having enough inventory can result in expensive emergency purchases from retail stores. There is no perfect calculation for determining the amount of inventory to have on-site. It is a balance that is calculated over time by keeping good data and evaluating them over time.

Using a more technological approach entails an electronic system that can track current inventory levels and generate need-based reports on historical data using a high and reordering point par system. A reordering point is determined by factoring the current usage of each product and lead time until the next delivery, with a small safety margin, and the high level is the amount forecasted, again with a margin of safety built in, to safely last until the next scheduled delivery will come. This is a costlier but improved next step in a modern inventory control system. These systems have their use but still cannot always be trusted to accurately predict future needs from past data. Even more complex systems now exist that can be loaded with forecasts of future needs and plans that then factor in product on hand and on order to derive even more accurate purchasing needs. Even at this level, the results and information gained are only as accurate as the forecasted information that must be maintained in the system. These systems also are available with wireless scanners that read bar codes on inventoried items and input information into the system simply by punching in the count. Remember, the more sophisticated the system, the more costs associated with its purchase, implementation, and maintenance. The costs must be weighed against the risks and size of the business to insure an equitable value is gained.

Good buyers understand that inventory is an asset; it is the owner's money. Holding too much inventory costs money; perishables shrink, decay, and lose value; and overstocked dry goods tie up funds needlessly. Improperly managed inventory can go out the back door, diminished through overportioning and other waste, and disappear through pilferage. Properly utilizing and protecting the establishment's money are the most important functions of a purchasing professional's job, and a precise and well-managed inventory is an integral tool in doing that.

# SMALL AND LARGE EQUIPMENT PURCHASING

A foodservice buyer is often responsible for purchasing more than just food and dry goods; often they are assigned the task of purchasing equipment for the operation. Equipment purchasing requires another type of knowledge and possibly multiple suppliers. These items are necessary for the daily operation of the business but are not purchased on a regular basis.

Equipment can be divided into three separate categories: kitchen equipment, dining room and bar and service, and maintenance. Each has their special needs and requires knowledge of the job that needs to be done. Outfitting a foodservice operation from the start requires a long list of small equipment and careful planning to be sure that everything that is required for a smooth opening day is in place. Established restaurants often find that their equipment is worn or broken and needs replacing. The wear on equipment in a modern commercial kitchen is much more than that in a household or even a studio kitchen, and the buyer must have a good understanding of durability and function. Chefs may require new equipment for specific cooking techniques, and front-of-the-house managers might need equipment that is aesthetically pleasing to the customer. New maintenance and clean-up equipment can help reduce labor costs or cut down on the cost of cleaning products. The purchasing of all these products is crucial for the smooth operation of the business.

FIGURE **6.1** Maintenance equipment.

Buying equipment, though necessary, is a costly task, and the costs are often unplanned, making forecasting difficult. No one knows exactly when a coffee pot will break or a pan handle will fall off. So how can a buyer budget for these purchases? Most large-scale operations build a certain amount of equipment purchasing into their annual budget. Spending is often directed to the most essential equipment first and then outward to nonessentials that enhance the operation but might not be needed immediately. There is often competition for equipment dollars, and it is important to be sure all aspects of the operation get the upgrades they need to be successful. An example is purchasing new wine chillers and fancy flatware for the tables when the chef doesn't have enough sauté pans to keep up with the orders. Or the chef receives a new sous vide circulator while the clean-up crew is using a mop bucket with a broken wringer. There is a balance between what is needed for each area of the operation. A buyer must weigh what is most important and make purchases accordingly. Small equipment purchases need to be part of the total operating costs of each department. Large equipment purchases are more of an executive decision because these require a large amount of capital and possible bank loans. Large equipment requires much more research in price, functionality, serviceability, and feasibility. In this chapter, we will discuss buying both large and small equipment.

# SMALL EQUIPMENT

## SMALL EQUIPMENT INVENTORY

Buying small equipment first requires an idea of what is needed. A basic monthly inventory of equipment can help keep track of what is available and in what kind of shape it is. It also helps to identify theft and misplaced items. First, identify the equipment that is used, and determine the amount of equipment needed for operation. Not having enough equipment on hand can seriously affect the production or service capability of the restaurant. Having too much product can result in excess capital being tied up when it could be used for something else. Excess small equipment may also signal to staff that the operation is not managed well, and this can lead to pilferage. Each manager should keep a record of equipment and identify future needs and possible shortages. Listing all the equipment at the beginning of the month should involve the staff. This will help reduce the time of the task and give the staff a sense of ownership for it. For example, cooks will know they have 15 sauté pans, two with loose handles that may need replacing; wait staff may count 200 salad forks, but 6 are bent. Requests for equipment need to be part of staff meetings, and inclusion of the costs will help identify priority items and allow staff to understand those priorities.

Inventory of plates, cups, and flatware can be tedious work, however. Plates can be counted by stacking in a count of 20 and then simply stacking all the plates to that height. Silverware can be counted by 20 and then weighed to get a good estimate. Counting can also occur during the setup of place settings and then adding the overflow. The counts don't need to be perfect to get an idea of how much to purchase.

FIGURE **6.2** 20-quart mixer.

## SOURCING SMALL EQUIPMENT

Buyers may source small equipment from a variety of vendors. General broad-line foodservice vendors such as SYSCO have a large assortment of small equipment and are often comparably priced. Their catalogs have a variety of brand names in china, flatware, pots, pans, bar supplies, catering equipment, and much more. This type of vendor is very convenient in that the equipment can be delivered with the general food delivery. The sales staff may also have some information on how the product is used in other establishments or be able to answer questions about durability. Be sure to have equipment purchases accounted for separately from food purchases and approved in the budgeting process. The ease of purchasing can lead to excessive buying and overstocking of small equipment. Another drawback might be complacency when comparing prices. For example, if the food buyer also needs glassware, they may decide to simply buy them from the foodservice vendor rather than searching for the best price available.

| EQUIPMENT INVENTORY | | | |
|---|---|---|---|
| ITEM DESCRIPTION | PROJECTED AMOUNT | ACTUAL AMOUNT | DATE |
| Kitchen | | | |
| 8" sauté pans | 10 | | |
| 10" sauté pans | 10 | | |
| 12" sauté pans | 10 | | |
| 1 quart saucepan | 6 | | |
| 2 quart saucepan | 6 | | |
| 4 quart saucepan | 8 | | |
| Stockpots | 2 | | |
| Rondeaus | 4 | | |
| Rubber spatulas | 6 | | |
| Wooden spoons | 10 | | |
| Whisks | 6 | | |
| Slotted spoon | 8 | | |
| 2 ounce ladles | 4 | | |
| 4 ounce ladles | 6 | | |
| Scales | 3 | | |
| Thermometers | 5 | | |
| Quart measuring cups | 3 | | |
| Small mixing bowl | 6 | | |
| Medium mixing bowl | 6 | | |
| Large mixing bowl | 6 | | |
| Dining Room | | | |
| Dinner plates | 150 | | |
| Appetizer plates | 150 | | |
| Soup bowls | 150 | | |
| Dinner forks | 150 | | |
| Salad forks | 150 | | |
| Soup spoons | 150 | | |
| Dessert spoons | 150 | | |
| Dinner knives | 150 | | |
| Butter knives | 150 | | |
| Water glasses | 150 | | |
| Coffee cups | 150 | | |
| Saucers | 150 | | |

FIGURE **6.3** Equipment inventory list.

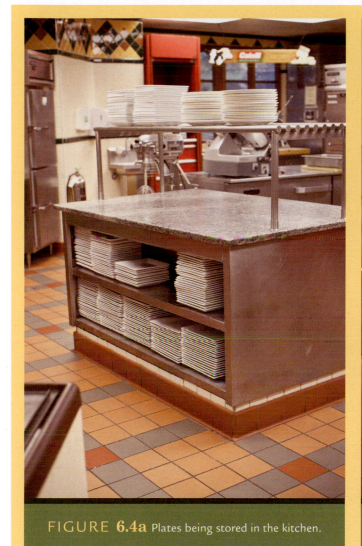

FIGURE **6.4a** Plates being stored in the kitchen.

FIGURE **6.4b** Plates and other service items being stored in the dining room.

Another type of vendor for equipment is a kitchen supply warehouse. This seller will be more of a specialist in the area and will have some expertise in the equipment, with their focus on commercial kitchen equipment only. They may have both small kitchen and dining room products and also large equipment such as ranges and refrigeration units. Such stores or warehouses may be local, and the buyer can view the equipment and may test out functionality. The foodservice establishment will often develop a relationship with this type of business, and such a business may be able to offer advice or showcase new innovations. Some also offer service or repairs. This is typical in a larger city, where there are thousands of potential customers available. Again, as with the foodservice vendor, prices need to be checked and comparisons made.

Other suppliers offer their products through catalogs or on the internet. Most companies today, even if they are local, will showcase products on their websites. Some offer forums that customers will use to discuss products. These operations may offer a larger selection and sometimes price advantages also, but the buyer must know the

FIGURE **6.5** Small equipment, such as plates and other service ware, can be purchased from foodservice vendors or kitchen supply warehouses.

exacting specifications of the products and be willing to pay shipping fees in addition to the price if purchasing from a distant distributor. Be sure to understand return policies such as restocking fees and warranty information.

## SMALL EQUIPMENT RENTAL

Small equipment may also be rented. The following describes specific items that may be rented and some aspects to consider when making the decision whether to rent or buy.

### LINENS

Many restaurants rent their linens and uniforms, which are provided by a specific linen company. This relationship can be important and expensive. Linens are a reflection of the quality of the restaurant. If the tablecloth has holes or stains or a napkin is unclean, it can be a very poor reflection on the restaurant. If a linen company is supplying uniforms that are damaged or stained, the wait staff or kitchen crew might look less than professional. A good linen company will be able to demonstrate week after week that they can provide consistent service and quality.

Another issue with linens is counts. It is very important to establish a proper inventory of linens so the establishment is not caught short during service. There is nothing worse than a banquet without enough tablecloths or napkins. Develop a checklist of linens to be ordered, including any special items. Many linen companies will charge for missing linens or uniforms. Inventory control is important; counting all linens is time consuming and unappealing but a necessary evil. Be sure to count all linens as they are received and spot check them for quality. Poor-quality items should be set aside for credit.

Often linen companies will require a contract and monthly payment. Be sure to have the contract viewed by either your lawyer or purchasing agent to be sure there are compensations for poor quality and the like. Some contracts can be binding over long periods of time, so read the fine print! Often large foodservice establishments will allow for a monthly or biannual bid for their linen business. This can help to insure the best price possible but also may lead to an inconsistency in product or quality. Be sure all bids are for similar-quality products.

Some restaurants will purchase linens and wash them. This requires a lot of time as well as specialized equipment. Washing, ironing, and folding can take many hours that might be better spent on other work. Some smaller owner-operator establishments will wash their own linens and save some significant money over time, while very large hotels will have a laundry department that can also do kitchen linens, but this is an option that should be analyzed carefully. How much does it really cost to wash each item? Things to consider when weighing this option include soap, labor, hot water, electricity, and machine parts. Figuring the cost of washing a napkin can be done, but it takes some commitment.

## OTHER SMALL EQUIPMENT RENTAL

Other small equipment may be rented, typically for special occasions and catering. There are rental stores that have china, flatware, glassware, and linens, all of which can be delivered to the catering site. As with any purchase, be sure to check in all equipment and count each item. These rental companies will require either a down payment upon the agreement and then the balance due after the event, or payment up front. A quality rental company can be a great asset to a catering company. Be sure to check the quality of the rentals beforehand so that they match the items at the event. Most rental companies have a large variety from which to choose. They may also rent other equipment such as holding ovens, chafing dishes, tents, tables, chairs, and more. The cost of these items needs to be calculated carefully into the overall cost of the party or function. Rental companies will also charge for broken, damaged, or missing equipment. Be sure the wait staff and kitchen crew understand the need for returning all equipment. There may be other charges for cleaning excessive debris off plates and glassware. Most rental companies don't require a thorough cleaning but do require a rinse and debris removal of place settings.

FIGURE **6.6** Kitchen suite.

# LARGE EQUIPMENT

## LEASING LARGE EQUIPMENT

There are two ways to equip a foodservice establishment. The first is to buy the equipment outright, and the second is to lease the property. Leasing should be considered for an establishment that has limited capital but expects a good cash flow when open. This frees up money for other uses. The leasing company will create a payment schedule that they design with the restaurant, and the contracts will dictate who is responsible for damage, warranty issues, repairs, and the like. Leasing often does not affect the restaurant's banking credit line, leaving that for other expenses. A lease might not be considered a liability on a balance sheet due to the fact that the restaurant does not actually "owe" for it and it can be returned. This can help to bolster a restaurant's credit. Many franchise restaurants lease their equipment and have service agreements to ensure continuous operation. Leasing requires an agreement for the length of time of the lease, and typically a 3-year lease is developed for a new operation. Large, expensive equipment such as ice machines or refrigeration units are commonly leased by high-volume restaurants that have a leased location also. For instance, the operator might see the restaurant as a 5-year plan and may not want to deal with liquidating all of the assets if the property lease is not renewed.

Some leases require the restaurant to purchase a product along with the lease; an example would be a coffee company creating a low-cost or free lease if that restaurant agrees to buy all of its coffee from that company. Soft drink companies will often provide coolers or bar equipment in exchange for featuring their product line. The restaurant would not be able to afford the very expensive machine on its own but now can offer fancy coffee without much capital expense. Various leases will include setup

FIGURE 6.7 In some cases, leasing equipment (like this espresso machine) can be the most cost-effective option.

and removal of the equipment, and, if the machine is in need of service, the leasing company will often provide their own service.

There are also "lease-to-own" programs. This becomes a sort of hybrid between a lease and a payment program to buy the equipment. This may make sense for start-up businesses that need capital in other places but then find they are successful and will be in business for the long term.

As with any contract, the lease should be read carefully so that all expenses and warranties are understood. Often there are substantial penalties for a restaurant attempting to end a lease early. Consulting a lawyer before entering into complicated leases is a good idea.

## PURCHASING LARGE EQUIPMENT

The outright purchase of large equipment requires much more focus and knowledge than the purchase of small equipment. The buying of a new range, a walk-in cooler, carpet, or a dish machine requires many hundreds or thousands of dollars. These are not purchases made on a whim, and they need to be included in the business plan of the operation. A large purchase requires some study of reliability, durability, and longevity of the product. The buyer should read nonpartisan reviews online to get an idea of the quality and price ranges of different products. Many sites are geared toward home kitchens, so be aware and find reviews written by foodservice operators, chefs, or managers. Internet reviews are valuable and provide sometimes unabashed

# LEASING

This case study is a lesson on leasing versus buying. Often, restaurants today will lease their equipment, and sometimes the lease will include a guarantee that all of the product used in that machine must be purchased from the lessee. The purchase of equipment can be another option, and warranty and reparability are important factors.

The Milan Café is located in a busy downtown office area and has been open for over 30 years. They serve a quality breakfast and lunch with fresh-baked goods, omelets, artisan sandwiches, salads, and a variety of coffees and teas. The business was started by Joseph and Maria Ligotti, who came to the city from Milan, Italy. The Ligottis take great pride in serving the best coffee, particularly espresso, cappuccino, and lattes. They use an old ornate coffee machine that they had imported 20 years ago. It was a beautiful copper-faced structure with valves and spouts that would make a signature sound when steaming the milk.

Joseph and Maria decided to sell their café to one of their wealthy patrons, John Monroe, who had been eating there for years and wanted to semiretire from his hectic software business. John wanted to keep the café just as it was, without changing the menu and atmosphere. He wasn't interested in making a huge profit but wanted a modest income and to continue to get his quality coffee. John hired a staff that trained with Joe and Maria; the cook and baker who were employed at the time of the sale decided to stay on. Everything seemed to be in order for the first month. Joe and Maria moved to a town near the ocean, and John was happy sitting in a booth and sipping his espresso. One morning, the old coffee machine began spewing steam into the air from a pipe in the back. John called Joe and asked what to do about it. Joe had worked the machine and knew every quirk it had. Joe explained that the machine was getting older and had been blowing gaskets, and some of the pipes were corroded. John asked who he used to repair it, but Joe simply said he had done all of the repairs himself, even rummaging for parts from a local salvage store.

John decided to call a coffee machine–leasing company to find out about replacing the old machine. The salesman told John that with his company's machine, John would basically get a quality, commercial-grade espresso machine for a very reasonable rental if John would buy all of his coffee from the company. The coffee was slightly less expensive than what he was buying and the machine would be guaranteed, with a replacement brought in one day if the machine broke. John was impressed by the figures and the service, and his business would certainly be able to afford it. He asked to taste the varieties of coffee the company offered. Unfortunately, he was disappointed with the flavor. Although it was good, it was not the same as the specialty Italian coffee the café had been buying for years. John asked the salesman how much the machine would be without the coffee contract, and the price was dramatically higher.

What is John's next move? Should he attempt to fix the old machine or acquiesce to the inferior coffee from the lease company? A new machine would be very expensive, and John was not willing to invest the amount needed. Another option was for John to purchase a machine from Rest-A-Ware, a used restaurant supply company. He drove to the large warehouse store, where a salesman showed him a few different machines. John and the salesman discussed the price and agreed on a machine that was about half the price of a new machine. It had been bought at an auction and was in fine shape. John then asked about the warranty. The salesman explained there was a 1-year warranty but also that this model was very dependable and repairable by the in-store repair department. John asked about other restaurants that had purchased one of the machines, and the salesman eagerly gave him the address of another restaurant that was using one. John went and talked to the manager of that restaurant to find that indeed it was a quality machine but had needed a repair. The repair was done by the Rest-A-Ware shop in a week, and the store also supplied a loaner for the days the machine was out.

John decided to go with the used machine and kept the old one as a decoration. He continued to use the Italian specialty coffee and was successful. The choice not to go with the lease company was not made on a purely monetary basis. The quality and flexibility of the outright ownership were very important in this case. When deciding to lease equipment, especially that which requires a specific product to be contracted with it, be sure the quality and price of the product are worth the overall effect on the business. The other lesson is that when buying used equipment, be sure there is some sort of guarantee or warranty, that the machine is dependable, and that there is a way to repair it if need be.

reviews. Often reviews may be contradictory, where one review claims the product is excellent while another condemns it. This usually is a sign that further information is needed.

## PURCHASING EQUIPMENT AND SUPPLIES

The purchase of commercial foodservice equipment and supplies to outfit a foodservice establishment is integral to your business plan. Whether the items are large, such as ranges, warewashers, or walk-ins, or small, such as kitchen tools, glassware, or serving platters, purchases require research. Questions to consider when evaluating equipment and supplies needs include:

- How will current and future menu ideas impact what you put in your kitchen?
- How will the equipment support these menu ideas?
- Does the equipment need to be multifunctional?
- What is the equipment footprint, i.e., will it fit in your kitchen?
- What is the equipment's reliability, durability, and expected life cycle under normal use?
- Is the product easy to use, clean, and train employees to use?

FIGURE **6.8** Oven.

- What support is available from the manufacturer?
- What is and what is not covered under warranty?
- Is the equipment's fuel source compatible with your kitchen?
- Is the equipment energy efficient?
- What is the annual and total cost of ownership?

Get to the bottom of these questions by networking with your peers, joining industry trade associations, attending trade shows, visiting manufacturer and industry Web sites, and collaborating with kitchen equipment specifiers/consultants, dealers, and manufacturers representatives. A wealth of information is available to assist you with your purchasing strategy; it is important to be thorough.

The North American Association of Food Equipment Manufacturers (NAFEM) is a trade organization of more than 550 manufacturers of products for food preparation, cooking, storage, and table service.

The biennial NAFEM trade show is the only show dedicated exclusively to showcasing equipment and supplies solutions for foodservice and restaurant kitchens worldwide. At the NAFEM Show, more than 800 products for a wide variety of foodservice

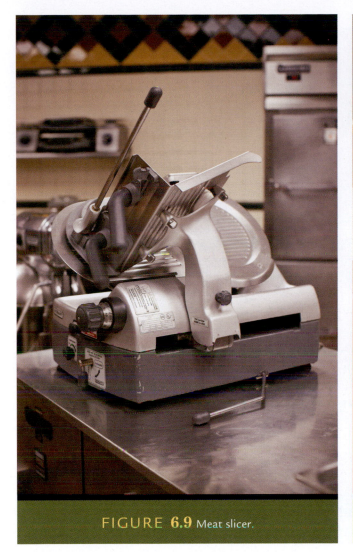

FIGURE **6.9** Meat slicer.

FIGURE **6.10** Lowboy refrigerator.

applications are on display. The show Web site, www.thenafemshow.org, is a great tool for researching products and innovations from today's manufacturers.

Additionally, NAFEM's general Web site, www.nafem.org, allows you to find manufacturers and products by manufacturer, brand name, and product type, and links you directly to the manufacturer's Web site and product specialists for additional information.

It might also make sense to scout out equipment by talking to other operators. Simply enjoying an appetizer and beverage at another establishment can lead to discussions with other operators about equipment. Many owners are members of restaurant associations that have regular meetings. These meetings are great places to network and discuss equipment. The National Restaurant Association is the largest in the United States, and they offer a huge "food show" every year that showcases the latest equipment and ideas for all types of operations. Often smaller state restaurant associations will host hotel and restaurant shows annually as well. Chef associations can also provide a venue for

NATIONAL
RESTAURANT
ASSOCIATION
RESTAURANT
HOTEL-MOTEL
S H O W

FIGURE **6.11**

FIGURE **6.12** Dishwasher.

networking, and often chefs are more than willing to offer opinions about kitchen equipment. These are great places to network with peers and discuss equipment. If you are looking for the latest equipment and information, it may make sense to attend a show. Networking at an equipment show is also valuable.

A repair or service company can provide feedback on equipment also. Who better to explain the qualities or shortcomings of certain brands than those who repair them on a regular basis? These are the experts who know the quality of the product from the inside out and can often tell you which products are defective in design and which are reliable. An operator may even offer a barter dinner in exchange for a consult by a repair professional. Be aware that some repair operations are also representatives of a company that sells equipment, and they may attempt to sway the buyer in the direction of a particular brand. Culinary schools use a variety of equipment, and many instructors will give an opinion on the products. This is another source of information. Maintenance crews can tell what products have needed repairs or some of the design flaws of a product.

Many foodservice operations close annually and are forced to liquidate their assets. Although this is sad for the owner, it creates a large amount of used equipment. A savvy buyer can find many of their equipment needs at prices that are much less than the prices of buying new. Used equipment can also be purchased from a number of different sources. Some dealers offer both new and used equipment. A dealer will often offer a short warranty on the used product. Other sources are ads on internet sites such as Craig's List or eBay. Purchasing certain equipment from these sources may be acceptable, and extremely good prices can be found. But buyer beware! Used equipment can be damaged or worn and may need repairs before it is functional. Some items may not be in the advertised condition or require parts that aren't available anymore. Contact the seller and ask why the item is being sold, what the condition is, and what the return policy is. Often distressed goods are sold only to be returned for refund, but the seller will charge a restocking or shipping fee, and that is how they make their profit. Shipping fees for large items can also sometimes exceed the purchase price.

Used equipment can be purchased at auctions. When a foodservice operation closes due to financial reasons, their equipment might be liquidated by their creditors. A live auction is often exciting, and real bargains can be found. Equipment is often grouped together into "lots" to speed things up. Be sure to arrive early to look over the lots. Ask questions about any mechanical equipment. Often the owner or staff is present, so ask about the age and serviceability of the products. Write down all of the lots you wish to bid on, and have a price cap in mind. It is sometimes easy to get caught up in a bidding war and lose sight of the value of the lot. Many dealers of used equipment will attend auctions. Some may be looking for a specific item but will freely offer advice about the other equipment they don't need. Most auctioneers will require cash payments, but today credit cards might be accepted. Many auctions have rules, and the buyer may need to remove the equipment on the day of the purchase; in this case, a crew and vehicle would be required to haul away the equipment. As with the internet auction, let the buyer beware. Any faulty equipment will be sold "as is," and there are typically no warranties for auction purchases.

The used restaurant equipment business is a unique phenomenon. Sellers can be deceptive about the condition and quality of equipment. Prices of used equipment are definitely negotiable! Remember, a used equipment dealer probably got the item at auction for a fraction of its original value. Treat the buying of used equipment like a used car purchase—know your specs and what you are looking for, understand the warranty if any, never buy impulsively, shop around, and think about the purchase over a couple of days.

Equipment purchasing or leasing is an essential part of operating a foodservice establishment. Anticipating equipment needs is very important when determining how much capital is required to run a restaurant. Take the time to research products and equipment, and buy cautiously. Salespeople and dealers are in business to sell, so being sure that you understand the purchase beforehand is very important. Impulse buying should never influence the purchase, and you should keep a balanced approach to buying so all of the needs throughout the restaurant are met.

# TRENDS IN THE INDUSTRY

There are some interesting changes afoot in the foodservice industry, and many of these trends actually hearken back to an earlier time when the world's food supply was less industrialized and globally marketed. There is no doubt that innovations in how the food supply is grown and marketed have greatly expanded our ability to feed the masses, especially in the United States, for a low cost. The boom in corporate factory farming after World War II, while highly effective, has proven to have had a largely negative effect on both the safety of the environment and the consumer. Many of these "new" trends are an attempt to find a balance between the need to feed everyone while looking to improve the quality of life we lead and quality of the food we consume, and do little harm to the environment while doing so. As with all changes that impact millions of people and big business, most of these changes come with a huge amount of debate as to what will work and what the priorities need to be.

What is clear is that the needs of all parties have relevance, and it is unlikely that a "one-size-fits-all" approach is the answer. There undoubtedly is a need for a less centralized, healthier, higher quality, environmentally safe method of raising food. Equally important is the ability to nutritiously feed an ever-growing population at prices they can afford. These trends will certainly continue to grow and adapt over time.

# BUYING LOCAL

Much has been made in recent years about the advantages and need to support the farms and businesses in the surrounding area near your place of business. There are both positive and negatives aspects to this philosophy, because there is some debate as to the definition of "local." Is local within 100 miles of the establishment, or one day's commute? Or is it viewed more broadly as regional (e.g., the Pacific Northwest) or domestic product only?

There is also some debate about how stringent one should be when buying local. Does this mean the business simply places a preference on what is grown and produced well locally, or is there a strict adherence to the local mantra no matter how limiting or what the quality of the product? If the establishment is located in the northern United States, would that eliminate citrus, avocados, and bananas from the menu? Consider beverages. Most establishments would have to forgo serving tea and coffee if they are grown in a faraway land or only serve wines bottled locally from local grapes. The list could go on and on.

If the owner of the foodservice operation wants to consider making an ecological and political statement and only source locally, there is something laudable in that. However, unless you are located in one of a very few ideal areas of the country, your menu options can be seriously limited. The challenge for the buyers at these sites is finding enough quality items within the designated local region to allow the cooks to create a compelling menu; and the challenge to the owner will be in building a sufficient customer base that not only approves of the philosophy but also is willing to support it.

This is not to say it is unwise or foolhardy to pursue a "buy local" agenda, but rather notes the challenges an extreme view will present and highlights the need to evaluate how rigid to be in determining those limitations. Consider whether only restaurants on a coastline should serve fish. Or would it be more prudent to serve a sustainable species that comes from whatever fishing area lies closest to your location at certain times of the year? For example, a restaurant in the Northeast might want to feature swordfish when they are swimming off of Block Island but avoid that species when the catch is coming from South America. American restaurants could consider wild-caught American shrimp but opt not to serve those that are farm-raised in Southeast Asia.

Fresh produce is another area that both drives the need to support quality, locally grown product but still raises the question of when to use items not grown in that operation's local region. This also raises the issue of produce seasonality, which is also addressed in this chapter. Clearly, buying produce from your local growers when in season should yield a superior product. When grown and managed properly, the quality and yield should be superior and the practice supports the agricultural culture in that area. However, some regions of the country only have a 4- to 6-month growing season; this limits what a locally focused foodservice establishment can feature the rest of the year. The desire to showcase local produce purchased in season is a major reason for the resurgence of canning and pickling product in recent years, both at home and in the foodservice industry. This is a cost-effective means of providing tasty produce year-round in different forms from how they were prepared in season. Many operations, sadly, lack the storage and skill set to take advantage of well-priced and superior-tasting produce in this way; striving to master and implement this skill could prove to be valuable to those establishments that wish to focus on local products and have the means to do so. Whatever the policy, when a buyer can obtain the necessary fresh product from a grower that picked it that morning, or anything that didn't need to be shipped thousands of miles to market and take days to do so, the buyer would be wise to take advantage of that quality.

## FARM-TO-FORK INITIATIVES

The move to source and utilize more products locally has spawned what is known as the Farm-to-Fork Initiative. This term was coined in the mid-1990s by Senator Hillary Clinton in New York State to bolster that state's agricultural community. On the West coast, Alice Waters has practiced and preached this philosophy for many years at her famous Chez Panisse restaurant in Berkeley, California, and it was put into practice at the Culinary Institute of America in Hyde Park, New York, 20 years ago. This movement is now composed of many farmers, businesspeople, government support, and other groups that wish to see more produce and animals raised on small local farms. That product then moves directly from the grower to the restaurant, school system, or other foodservice establishment utilizing it for a fair market value by eliminating the number of middlemen that diminish the value the growers can obtain for their labor.

This practice of buying from local producers also heightens the value of the product for the end user by ensuring that the produce purchased has been out of the field only for a day, and it allows them to show their community that they support their neighbors.

FIGURE 7.1 Many restaurants and establishments are sourcing local produce or even picking herbs and vegetables from their own restaurant gardens.

# LOCAVORE RESTAURANT

This study reflects the difficulties in subscribing without compromise to a philosophy that may make good sense from a political or environmental viewpoint, but will not be self-sustaining as a business model. The same concept in a warmer agricultural area may be easier to adhere to, but compromise on some level may always be necessary. The test for the buyer and chef in these styles of operation is to locate sources that closely adhere to the philosophy, and allow for an acceptable range in product choices for the menu and for a cost that can be sold at a profit.

Three young people with a variety skills and background in foodservice had come to an agreement to combine their talents and go into the restaurant business near their hometown of Saratoga in upstate New York. Ryan was a gifted young chef, his friend Torin had a background in managing the back of the house and the physical plant, and Zoe was a musician who also knew the bar and dining room aspects of the business. Taking their first initials, they named their soon-to-open bistro the Adirondack RiTZ.

These three entrepreneurs had the financial backing they required. They had a small but well-chosen location, and now needed a vision for the theme that their restaurant and menu would take. They determined to ride the wave of popular support of the Farm-to-Fork Initiative and work to minimize their carbon footprint by developing a concept that would use strictly local products available within 150 miles of their planned restaurant. This philosophy also meant they would be seasonally driven in their menu choices, thus keeping their evolving offerings creative for their patrons. The three had worked in area restaurants since high school and haunted local farmer's markets and stands every weekend. They knew that there was an abundance of local produce, cheese, meat, and dairy products available to them. They could use these to develop inventive menus and adapt to whatever products were best available that week or day.

However, when they began to develop their menu, they began to uncover a plethora of snags and issues not fully considered when going into the venture. They were lifelong residents of the area, so they fully understood how short the growing season was and how weather patterns changed from year to year that could further lessen the amount and variety of products grown for them. Ryan was a highly industrious and inventive chef, and he was certain he could develop interesting menus year-round, especially if his team pickled, preserved, or froze as much of the seasonal bounty as time, space, and funds would allow. However, when put in practice, it became clear how daunting it would be to assure that *every ingredient* would be local. Recipes called for acidulation from citrus such as limes and lemons, which are not grown in upstate New York. Chocolate certainly wasn't local, and neither were such basics as salt and pepper. Beer and soda were actually produced locally, but what about liquor, wine, coffee, and tea? Maybe they could develop a menu concept without many of these staples (maybe), but even if they could, would they be able to build a customer base sufficient to support their concept on a weekly basis year-round? They figured they could get an early rush from curious diners and possibly fare all right during the local growing season, which is also the local tourist season, but not enough to sustain three partners year-round. That was clear.

Their initial compromise eliminated the stipulation that they would locally source for all of the staples, such as spices and all grains, but they would be sure to use a local distributor and to work toward only one or two weekly deliveries in order to lessen their carbon footprint. With produce and center-of-the-plate protein items, they would remain true to their local credo, except for fish. For fish, they would try to limit their purchases to sustainable species fished off the North Atlantic coast when in their best season; otherwise, there would be virtually nothing from the sea to offer. Wines were chosen mostly from vineyards from upstate New York, and beers from local breweries. Coffee and teas were never going to be local, but in doing some informal questioning of friends and family in the area, it was quickly determined these could not be dropped from the menu. The compromise they made was to utilize a local roaster and serve only fair trade options.

Opening day finally came, and the menu was far from the idealized locavore menu the three partners had originally conceived of. It was, however, as close to that ideal as they felt they could go and assure their dream would remain sustainable . . . that is, by staying in business. After the RiTZ opened, the owners took great care to educate their customers so that they understood the motivations behind the owners' seasonal menu selections and their philosophy. They asked for opinions on not only the choices available but also the quality of the ingredients and how they worked in each dish. The customers' answers to these questions were considered, and adjustments were made accordingly in their menu development; at all times, they tried to balance their customers' wishes with the restaurant's vision and do so while utilizing good business sense.

Shrimp was difficult, as it was widely requested but nothing remotely local was available except for small sweet Maine pink shrimp that have a short season and more limited applications. Eventually, they opted to feature shrimp but only when wild-caught fresh shrimp from American waters could be procured. The customers also learned to adapt and appreciate the flavors of foods only purchased when at their seasonal best, instead of having anything flown or trucked in regardless of the source or time of the year. They also appreciated that Ryan adapted the menu constantly to what was found locally; Torin built many relationships with local growers and producers, whose products he purchased and featured on the menu. This practice built an excellent rapport with their community, who appreciated the support this restaurant gave to its neighbors. It was also good business as these same people chose to patronize the company that supported their efforts.

The Adirondack RiTZ has flourished for several years now. The three owners have succeeded by tempering idealism with realism and by consistently looking for what worked and what was not well received in each season. Their ability to augment their winter menus with delicious local products processed when in season, and purchased at reasonable prices and when at their seasonal best in quality, has improved steadily and is well appreciated by the bistro's patrons.

# ST. ANDREW'S CAFÉ
## MIDDAY MEAL

St. Andrew's Café embodies all that is good about the local, sustainable food movement. As much as possible, we draw our produce and meats from local farmers and purveyors and believe that we can dine well all year long by thoughtfully using the abundance of seasonal harvests.

· · ·

### Starters from the Kitchen Garden

**White Onion Soup** 5.00
with Rye and Bobolink Cheddar Croutons

**Purée of Asparagus and Spring Garlic** 5.00
House-made Pancetta and Feather Ridge Egg

**Purée of Mushroom and Celeriac Soup** 5.00

**Soup Sampler** 6.00
A tasting of our three soups

**Heirloom Tomato Sampler** 6.00
with a Panzanella-style Salad

**Local Greens Salad** 6.00
with Mushrooms, Cucumbers, Radishes,
and Brother Victor's Red Wine Vinaigrette

**Heirloom Tomato and Watermelon Salad** 6.00
with Brother Victor's Sherry Vinaigrette

**Braised Meiller Farm Pork and Sauerkraut
Pierogi** 8.00
with Bulich Farm Mushrooms and and Clab-
bered Cream

**Country-Style Terrine** 7.00
with Onion-Raisin Compote, Caraway
and Hennepin Mustard, and Pickled Vegetables

· · ·

### Entrées from Pasture and Sea

**Grilled Grass Fed Beef Hamburger** 10.00
Choice of Two Toppings: House-smoked Bacon,
Ewe's Blue,
Bobolink Cheddar, Grilled Onions, Roasted
Mushrooms

**Sautéed Soft Shell Crabs** 15.00
Fava Bean and Lemon Pesto with Baby Arugula

**Korean-Style Short Rib Tacos** 9.00
with Cucumber Kimchi, Asian Slaw, Chipotle,
Soy and Lime

**St. Andrew's Macaroni and Cheese** 12.00
Smoked Chicken, Oyster Mushrooms
and Rainbeau Ridge Goat Cheese

**Wood-Fired Oven Pizza of the Day** 9.00

**Meiller Farm Lamb** 14.00
Roasted Fingerling Potatoes and a Red Wine Jus

**Potato Dumplings** 12.00
with Wild Mushroom Ragoût, Fava Beans, Peas
and Basil Pesto Broth

· · ·

### Sides from the Field

**Taliaferro Farm Braised Summer Greens** 3.00

**Wild Hive Polenta Cakes** 4.00

**Farmer's Vegetable of the Day – Priced Daily**

**Sautéed Bulich Farm Mushrooms** 4.00
with Fresh Herbs and Shallots
**Fingerling Potato Salad** 3.00

FIGURE **7.2** St. Andrew's Café sources as much food as possible for their menu from local farms.

Proponents of the Farm-to-Fork measure are educating chefs and buyers on how to locate and negotiate with farmers as well as how to build their menus based on the season and current availability. The measure also entails teaching farmers how to interact directly with buyers and chefs in the food business by explaining about standardized pack sizes, growing to specification, being within easy reach of communication, and insuring timely delivery of product. The logistics of connecting farm to restaurant and assuring a profitable delivery of product has always been daunting. However, growers and producers are learning to align their needs and unify their efforts to find ways to function collaboratively to make this initiative work. Some farms are pooling their resources into consortiums or working with small firms to organize the pick-up and dispersal of their crops in order to reduce redundancy and leave them more time to be in their field rather than on the road.

The advantage to foodservice buyers is access to food grown by farmers they know are using methods they approve of and often food grown exactly to that chef's specifications; the food often arrives "still warm from the morning sun." Peaches, beans, corn, and even potatoes harvested within hours of delivery are far healthier and more delicious than product held in storage and transported for days or weeks. The advantage to farmers is a known appreciative outlet for their product, and assured marketability at a price that will afford them a living. The advantages do not stop there . . . the end user or consumer gets a more delicious and healthy meal at market value, and the local environment remains cultivated and green rather than paved or polluted.

Critics may claim this movement is elitist and expensive, but this is not necessarily so. Locally grown food from family farms will undoubtedly come with a higher price tag, but it also brings a much greater value. Better shelf life, higher yield, higher nutrition, better flavor, and greater enjoyment can make those dollars spent go considerably further in bringing health rather than merely caloric intake. From the foodservice perspective, the value of a longer shelf life with less trim and waste allows the chef to utilize better ingredients without a significant or possibly any increase in budgeted food cost percentages.

Many restaurants have made a huge point of marketing themselves as buying and sourcing as locally as possible and supporting farm-to-fork initiatives. This may be a relatively recent initiative, but it is already getting some negative press as being overhyped or boring in execution. Here is where purchasers and chefs need to

collaboratively work together to step up and do their due diligence in assuring that the product sought out not only is excellent in quality but also makes for a varied, vibrant, and colorful palate for the menu. Supporting local producers and growers is an excellent philosophy providing the quality matches the hype; merely being local does not automatically mean the product is of top quality. Buyers must ensure their local merchants provide the quality and selection their chefs require to fully express their talents. Restaurants essentially may market a particular philosophy, but they need to sell the consumer a quality and interesting product to remain successful. This is especially true when supporting that philosophy will likely come with a higher purchasing and selling point. Business owners want their word-of-mouth publicity to reflect enthusiasm for the food and ambiance, not recognition of a noble cause that yields a disappointing dining experience.

Many restaurants are taking the local initiatives even closer to home and raising many of their own ingredients. Some work within tight land and space constraints, but still manage to raise some herbs or greens.

Others are fortunate and ambitious enough to raise many of the vegetables as well as raise some poultry for meat and eggs, as well as other animals. Restaurants such as Primo in Rockland, Maine, and Blue Hill at Stone Barns in Pocantico Hills, New York, are well known for the quality of their food that is raised on their own land. Buyers still need to understand the needs of their chefs, factoring in this proprietary growth to assure all needs are met.

## SEASONALITY

Similar to the philosophy about local food, another trend that previously existed and is becoming new again is buying seasonally. When produce and many types of fish are in season, they are of the best quality and the most plentiful for the least cost. This is the very definition of value: only buying something when it is at its best and also for the best price. This also makes for interesting menus that evolve with the seasons, which can improve customer satisfaction and maintain the staff's interest.

Some operators may feel that their customer base will demand certain products all the time. Management may need to have the purchasing department continue to source these items, but having some focus on seasonality only makes sense. It is also important to remember that being in season is weather dependent, not strictly calendar driven. A long winter will delay much-sought-after harbingers of spring like morel mushrooms and ramps; likewise, a late frost will keep summer treats, such as corn, tomatoes, berries, and peaches, in the market longer. Menu options need to be driven by the quality and price as well as the common sense of the buyer and management.

As noted, many species of fish have a season. The availability of some species (e.g., wild salmon or wild striped bass) is controlled by regulations and quotas. Other species are just more plentiful and at better values at a specific time of the year. Equally, certain species, such as flounder and other ground fish in the spring, may be of poor quality due to spawning or in short supply at other times. Smart buyers and chefs will work with their fishmonger to determine what items have the best availability at each time of the year.

Seasonality can extend to some cheeses as well, especially with small artisanal sheep or goat cheese makers that only produce cheese according to the natural cycle of their animals. As when purchasing locally, working with a seasonal menu requires some thought and ability to adapt, but will generally yield better results.

## REDUCING CARBON FOOTPRINT

A product's carbon footprint is representative of the amount of fossil fuels expended to bring a product to market and then to its end use. The larger the footprint, the more these valuable and finite resources are diminished. Some estimates are frightening in that it is estimated that for each calorie of energy consumed by people, 11 calories are consumed bringing that food to market. Most food consumed in the United States travels an average of more than 1,500 miles before arriving in the consumer's kitchen.

With today's need for conservation and the ongoing desire to become more "green" in our practices, the concern over a product's carbon footprint has grown in both personal and professional expenditures. This concern has only heightened the initiatives to buy locally and have food move from farm to fork. It has also narrowed the price difference in supporting small local farms versus large corporate farms across the country as the cost of transporting these crops continues to rise. Depleting fewer resources when making purchasing decisions is in part making said purchases in a sustainable manner. Lowering the carbon footprint of purchased products not only can mean that a purchaser is better managing the world's natural resources but also can mean that good business decisions are being exercised. Buyers not only want to seek out vendors closer to their location and try to consolidate deliveries as much as possible, but also these buyers should be looking at how and from where their sources source.

# SUSTAINABILITY

The term sustainability is often debated due to how in-depth and fervent one's opinions are about the terms and principles relating to its practice. The safest definition is probably the simplest. A product or growing method is sustainable when it does no harm to people, animals, or the environment and ensures that the land can support both the grower and the crop into the future. Or it requires satisfying our needs now without risk to people or the environment in the future.

There can be many caveats that some parties include when defining this practice, such as in no way should a sustainable practice taint the soil or water supply from agricultural runoff or animal waste. Insuring the quality of living and working conditions of both growers and laborers is another common tenet in this thinking. Other definitions of sustainable agriculture will try to define exactly what, if any, artificial or chemical fertilizers can be utilized. This can be difficult as the type of crop and growing location can have a profound impact on what will work where.

Methods used to save the soil and limit chemical use include crop rotation to limit depletion of the soil; farmers will also alternate rows of crops such as wheat and corn in 50-foot-wide bands across hillsides to save the soil. They also must plow across the hillsides as plowing up and down can lead to much more erosion of the topsoil. Companion planting is done to draw pests away from the true crop, such as by growing summer savory along with bean crops as it repels the beetles that eat the beans. Catnip is also used as it repels a variety of beetles.

Floating row covers are also used for several reasons; they raise the temperature under the ground cover by a few degrees to speed growth early in the season and protect against frost at the end of each season. These covers also protect young plants from many pests. Farmers will also introduce beneficial insects, such as ladybugs and parasitic wasps, to their fields that feed on other insects but leave the crops alone. This method only works well if the insect population is relatively small and the farmer doesn't require immediate results. There are also pesticides approved for organic use, but care must be taken in their application. Such products are deemed safe for the environment but can be fatal to helpful insects such as honeybees, and toxic if ingested by humans. There also are products referred to as insecticidal soaps that are both safe and effective, but need to be applied directly on the unwanted pests to work properly.

Utilizing black plastic mulch with drip irrigation saves water and lessens the need for herbicides. The plastic serves as a weed barrier to the unwanted plants, thus reducing the need for chemicals. Water is saved as the dripped irrigating water evaporates, then condenses on the plastic as the day cools and drips back onto the ground. When herbicide is required, there are federally approved organic compounds that should have a less negative effect on the environment. There may be some disagreement regarding these claims, as some farmers believe them to be no less harmful than other potent chemicals.

## THE NEED FOR SUSTAINABILITY

There was a time, not very long ago, when the scale of doing business and the current technology meant that all food was basically raised in a sustainable manner. However, in the mid-20th century shortly after World War II, the way we approached agriculture, particularly in the United States, changed rapidly. The use of bigger machinery, stronger chemicals, much bigger farms, poultry factory farms and immense stockyards, and corporate ownership created a much higher output of food for significantly less money. This created an economy that allowed the consumer to purchase much more food for a significantly lesser portion of their income. Food became very big business, driven by everyone's need for its product and protected by government encouragement and subsidies.

However, all of this food for less brought with it a variety of significant issues that were not immediately and thoroughly recognized by a great deal of society. These ills include contaminated water, topsoil erosion, less product variety, fewer animal species, far fewer family farms, increased abuse of labor, the decline of rural communities, and a huge decline in the nutritional quality and safety of much of our food supply. Having a small percentage of our population producing our food and having it distributed by ever-fewer and larger consortiums make us very vulnerable if anything terrible were to impact that segment of our economy. A great many people depend on a very small percentage of the whole for our nutritional survival. Also, the shrinking planet and global food chain have made almost all fresh food products available

year-round and not just when in season locally. This constant availability has brought with it a serious decline in those foods' special flavor as well as a huge carbon footprint for the sake of continuous access.

These conditions have created the call for and rise of the sustainability movement, despite the willingness of most people to sacrifice health and quality for ease and price. This movement's purpose is to address the food culture's environmental and social concerns. In doing so, it has also given rise to improving standards in business, in government, and with consumers, and it has helped focus everyone on the long-term safety issues of the current system.

The goals of the sustainability movement are to improve the environmental impact of agriculture on the environment, improve the economic situation for small family farms and producers, and create more social and financial equality for those living and working within the industry. The idea is to create "stewardship" for both the land and the people that grow our food properly.

For agricultural products to be sustainable, the practice has to be supported all the way through the continuum from seed to consumer. The farmer cannot make sustainable product alone; the vendor, buyers, chefs, and final customer all have to believe in the system enough to support the product with a fair price. This is applicable to livestock as well as produce; in order to be sustainable, the animals raised must be treated humanely and in a nonpolluting manner and have a demand in the market.

Skeptics of the sustainability model do not question its merit, but rather its pragmatism. The issue is that very little is completely sustainable in that some depletion or harm to the environment will always occur. Also, can the world feed over 6 billion people without some form of large industrial food production? The answer may be that it is unlikely, but not supporting a sustainable marketplace on any level will only hasten the decline of our environment and lessen the quality of our food supply.

Sustainable practices have been dramatically effective in regard to some areas of the seafood industry. In areas where quotas have been set and limitations enforced on the size of the catch or number of fishing days allowed, the biomass and viability of these species have improved dramatically. The resurgence of the population of wild striped bass along the eastern seaboard in the United States is a great example of this, as is the increase in the biomass of haddock on the Georges Banks in the north Atlantic. Certain species that are highly prized and not regulated, such as the bluefin tuna, may soon become extinct.

There are several organizations that are trying to get the word out about the dangers of overfishing and advocating a ban on many fisheries until their populations can be restored to an appropriate biomass. These include the Monterey Bay Aquarium, the National Fisheries, the Marine Stewardship council, and a host of others all preaching the gospel of saving the ocean and its fish. There will always be some dispute amongst these groups, chefs, fishermen, and brokers as to what species are endangered, rebuilding, or safe for consumption. Each buyer must work with the chef and manager to develop menus based on their own research.

Each foodservice owner and the chef/buyers that support the owner's philosophy must try to make the market more sustainable. This includes supporting a more decentralized market model, continuing to seek out and support local growers and species, attempting to promote more seasonally focused menus, insisting that growers and laborers are adequately paid considering fair trade practices, and avoiding products and species that ravage the environment.

Food products are the most commonly discussed and debated portion of the sustainability movement, but buyers can surely find other avenues to lend support to this agenda. Owners and buyers can look for LEED certifications for construction, which is an internationally recognized certification system. LEED's aim is to insure construction is designed in a manner to reduce energy and water usage as well as $CO_2$ emissions. It also aims to ensure the safety of the environment inside these buildings and maintain a stewardship of natural resources. It provides management and their buyers with clear guidelines for new construction as well as retrofitting existing facilities.

Energy Star appliances should also be sourced by buyers wishing to conserve energy to both conserve resources and reduce their energy costs each month. Energy Star is a joint government initiative from both the U.S. Environmental Protection Agency (EPA) and Department of Energy to identify those appliances with approved levels of energy consumption. There may be some tax advantages as well for business owners utilizing these approved products. Management can also mandate the practice of recycling, purchase biodegradable take-out containers, drive alternative energy vehicles, or take other initiatives that may lead these businesses to apply for GRA certification (see below).

Being sustainable in business is insuring that your business practices social responsibility. The desire needs to be for your business to flourish in a responsible manner while supporting your local community and ecosystem. The end result is the survival of your business in the long run in a mutually advantageous manner without a strong negative impact on your community. As noted, many purchases and practices that can be employed to lessen a business' impact on the environment can also lessen that purchase's financial impact on the bottom line. This may require some compromise in order to succeed, but the philosophy should be to do as little damage as possible while continuing to further business.

# THE SLOW FOOD MOVEMENT

The Slow Food Movement has grown up in many ways around the need for our food system to become more sustainable. The Slow Food Movement is a grassroots effort that was founded in 1989 in order to promote the sustainability of our food system. This organization has grown to over 100,000 members in a dozen countries. The movement wishes to bring more attention to what we eat and its origins, and it was formed to try to counteract the effects of the fast-food lifestyle, such as obesity from excessive fats and sugars, poor flavor and damage to the environment, as well as the loss of local foods and their traditions. The Slow Food Movement advocates that the food we eat be good both for our bodies and for the ecosystem in which the produce is grown, as well as economically fair to those who grow it. The idea is simply that the food we raise and eat should be good for the planet and those eating it, or that pleasure and responsibility with regard to the food we eat need to be thought of as mutually dependent. The process should be economically fair to both grower and consumer, and this will supply food that simply tastes better and will continue to be grown in the future. Slow Food is also heavily involved in protecting biodiversity as each year many traditional species of plant and animal cease to exist. It may sound counterintuitive, but one way to insure a species will continue to exist is to raise it commercially, but responsibly.

Pig's Ear Chips

Pork Rillettes

Roasted Bone Marrow with Herb Salad

Pickled Kidneys on Toast

Black Pudding, Lima Beans, Thyme and a Poached Egg

Ox Heart with a Parsnip Puree and Fried Leeks

Guinea Fowl Liver Pate with Pickled Beets and Cherries


Calf's Liver and Onions, Garlic Mashed Potatoes,

and Swiss Chard

Pork Chops with Rutabaga Mash and Roasted Kale

Polenta with Asiago, Mustard Greens, and Wild Mushrooms

Crispy Roasted Pork Belly, Potato Cake, Green Beans

and Braised Red Cabbage

FIGURE 7.3 Example of a nose-to-tail menu.

# NOSE-TO-TAIL MENU CREATION

Another trend that combines supporting local growers, sustainability, a lower carbon footprint, and slow food cooking is being fostered in a small but growing number of quality restaurants. This trend is known as nose-to-tail cooking and is employed when developing a menu. For this philosophy, the buyer procures whole animals for the chefs to utilize completely in their menus instead of buying just the better known and higher priced cuts common in the food industry. In this manner, the chef is challenged to utilize every tasty morsel of the animal by being creative in the development and marketing of the dish. It supports the rancher by giving him a market for the whole carcass and not just the prime cuts, exposes the consumer to a whole new experience of good if adventurous eating, and allows the restaurateur to turn a profit from these lower priced, lesser known and appreciated cuts. The issue is finding the staff that has the skill set to fully butcher and make the most of each savory cut of meat. Some chefs will not just fully utilize all of the common and seldom-used cuts of meat, but also prepare and sell quality dishes using the heart, feet, brains, liver, testicles, and sweetbreads; even the ears, snout, and tail can be enjoyed. The blood can be made into a pudding or sausage, and the bones can be used for stock . . . or to feed the employees' pets.

This is a sustainable practice because more people can be fed from one animal than when only the prime cuts are utilized; consequently, there is less of an environmental impact for each pound of product consumed. In the United States, we consume 15% of all animals raised for food in the world with just 5% of the world's population. Getting more nutrition out of each animal slaughtered only makes sense.

Some restaurants employ a slightly different philosophy; this is called the head-to-tail as opposed to nose-to-tail style. In this style of restaurant, they also employ all the various organs and parts but will use them from a variety of species and not just from one whole carcass at a time. This is also a sustainable practice in some fashion as more parts of each animal are being utilized for nutritional benefit.

Clearly, this style of cooking will not suit every operation and palate, but the notion is growing in its appreciation, in the number of establishments doing it, and in the press. Buyers in these operations will need to contact farms and operations that can supply them with the necessary quality and specifications for these animals and have the ability to transport them to their locations and fabricate them. This may also require staff that has not only butchery but also charcuterie skills in order to utilize these parts in sausages, terrines, and salumis.

# ORGANIC PRODUCTS

The desire to procure and sell products raised in an organic manner probably isn't just a trend any longer as it moves from the small health-food store venue where it began back in the 1960s into the forefront of large American commercialism. Prior to the 1940s, pretty much all food was raised organically. Therefore, what was necessary then is new again; the demand now is for an ever-increasing supply of foodstuffs believed to be healthier and safer. This demand has made the organic moniker more commercially viable and profitable. The fact that the "big box" stores can profitably market products deemed "certified organic" testifies to the ever-growing segment of the population that believes being certified organic means that the food is healthier. How this demand for greater supplies of organic products at competitive prices will actually affect the quality and definition of what is considered to be raised organically remains to be seen. These organic products will certainly not be locally or domestically raised as these large corporations will source products worldwide to find the best price. This raises the fear that the standards used in the United States for organic certification may differ from those used elsewhere and be less reliable for nondomestic products in order to lower costs.

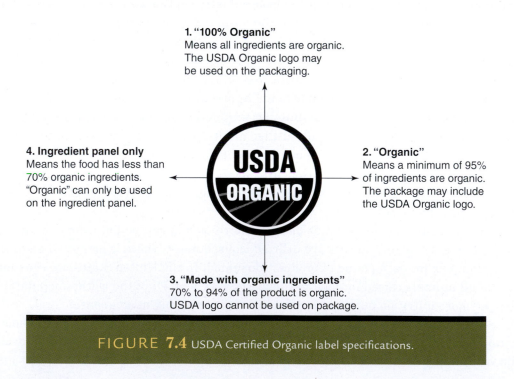

1. "100% Organic"
Means all ingredients are organic.
The USDA Organic logo may
be used on the packaging.

4. Ingredient panel only
Means the food has less than
70% organic ingredients.
"Organic" can only be used
on the ingredient panel.

2. "Organic"
Means a minimum of 95%
of ingredients are organic.
The package may include
the USDA Organic logo.

3. "Made with organic ingredients"
70% to 94% of the product is organic.
USDA logo cannot be used on package.

FIGURE **7.4** USDA Certified Organic label specifications.

The amount of regulation and paperwork required for small family farms to be certified organic has driven many of these farmers to stop pursuing that certification even though everything they raise is done in a healthy, safe, and sustainable manner. The ability of large corporate firms to begin to market food as certified organic, but raised anywhere in the world, because it is financially beneficial to do so, further hurts the small family farm's ability to remain tenable. Certification takes away much of their profit margin, and competing against the "big box" store diminishes their market share. It is recommended that chefs and buyers wanting to promote nutritious and healthy menus look toward small local farms that they can visit and know to be safe rather than simply write their order specifications to demand organic certification. This is not to say that there is no benefit for wanting foods raised organically; the fewer chemicals in our food supply, the better. However, knowing where your food comes from and how it was raised is always preferable if you are in a position to procure these products in that manner.

# THINKING GREENER

Many foodservice operators today recognize the need or the common sense in making their establishments as ecologically friendly or as "green" as possible. "Reduce, reuse, recycle" is rapidly becoming a necessary focus in today's world. This makes sense from environmental, health, and consumer relations standpoints. Buyers not only will need to stay abreast of this because equipment is constantly being developed that is more energy efficient, but also the world is changing and much of where this trend is taking the industry will likely soon be required by law.

The Green Restaurant Association (GRA) is a nonprofit organization with roughly 350 certified members that has spent the last 20 years working to educate operators, manufacturers, and purveyors about the need to develop and promote a greener method of operating in the foodservice industry, which is the number one energy-consuming segment of American business. The GRA provides consultation, information, assessment, and even certification to businesses in the foodservice trades. In order to obtain certification, a business must achieve a high level of green practices and purchases and then continue to grow in improving or expanding those traits up through four levels.

The following are areas on which restaurants and other operations are evaluated in order to earn points toward certification. Initial certification requires a minimum of 100 points, and more to climb up through the four tiers. Buyers working for a foodservice operation that is not opting certification would still benefit from having a good working knowledge of these points and the ability to factor them into their thinking when making purchasing decisions.

- Energy: Energy Star–rated heating and exhaust systems, windows, cooking equipment, ware-washing equipment, and refrigeration. High-efficiency hand dryers, programmable thermostats, ceiling fans, highly efficient air-conditioning systems or no air conditioning, reflective roofing, and window film. Hot-water system efficiency, wrapped tanks and pipes, and low-yield faucets are also assessed as well as the type of lighting, insulation rating, and weather stripping.
- Office equipment: Energy Star–rated cordless phones, PCs, monitors, copiers, fax machines, and scanners. Paper with a minimum of 30% recycled material.
- Renewable energy sources: Geothermal, solar, and wind.

- Waste: Recycling paper, plastic, aluminum, glass, cardboard, and grease (for biodiesel). Composting pre- and postconsumer waste, including food waste, and utilizing biodegradable or compostable disposable ware like take-out containers, flatware, and bags. Reducing waste by going paperless as much as possible, electronic billing, double-sided copiers, and reducing packaging and the use of bottled water.
- Chemicals: Moving away from toxic cleaners and ware-washing detergents, and utilizing ionized water for general cleaning and sanitizing. Avoiding all bleached paper products.
- Purchasing sustainable and local food products whenever feasible.

Obviously, moving in this direction will take research and time to implement. However, the GRA cites many possible benefits to those operators that move toward and ultimately obtain certification. These benefits include the following:

- You're simply doing the right thing.
- Good publicity can be garnered in your community.
- By cutting waste, you can cut expense.
- Many foodservice employees are concerned about the quality of their environment; it is good for morale.
- Public awareness can bring in new supportive customers and help ensure return business.
- Creates a healthier place for everyone to work.
- Legislation will likely move you in that direction . . . be ahead of the curve.

# ORGANIZATIONAL CONSULTANTS

Some larger hotels and foodservice operations are employing outside firms in order to help them purchase inventory. These establishments gain the assurance that they will be paying a very competitive price without the time-consuming process of comparing bids on hundreds of items on a daily, weekly, or monthly basis. This is done using a prime vendor system for each major inventory line such as meat, fish, produce, dry goods, and so forth. The consultant and buyers will work together to best determine what vendors both can capably meet the client's specifications and have the ability to buy correctly themselves so that they are also paying the correct price for what they sell. The consultant will then work with the vendor to assign a very tight margin of profit over their landed cost for each type of product they sell. The more each item needs to be fabricated, culled, hand selected, or handled in any way, the higher that margin will go. Buyers and their chefs need to get used to working largely with items that meet their specifications and not by brand name. Purchasing to satisfy the end users' loyalties and personal preferences goes out the window, and gaining acceptance for this method of purchasing can be trying. However, the benefit to the bottom line for high-volume operations is often seen as worth the hassle of implementation.

The gains to the client beyond price assurance are in soft dollars that are harder to measure but very real nevertheless. Working with a consultant in this type of program lessens or eliminates the payroll dollars spent comparing bids, and lessens receiving and administrative duties and costs by cutting down on the number of firms delivering and the associated paperwork. This system also lessens the time a buyer needs to spend talking to and negotiating with multiple vendors for each type of inventory purchased. In short, it greatly streamlines the process of procurement as well as cuts costs. The negative is in the limiting of options the buyers and end users have in their choice of product and vendor. However, even in a prime vendor system, the buyers are generally only required to purchase 80% of required purchases from the program vendor. That 20% gap should give the buyers enough room to satisfy their customers' demands for most specific needs. Often, the program vendors are also required to rebate a small percentage of their total sales back to the client after the consultant conducts his or her yearly audit. Once the heavy initial fees have been recouped, these rebates can often more than compensate for the consultant's annual fee.

The program's vendors gain from being assured a large share of the client's business each month and knowing they will make the same percentage over cost regardless of how the market tracks. Their downside is in the need to stock most of the items their customers demand even if the volume is low. A consultant will try to utilize the same vendor for a number of clients; this gives the company much more volume, and it gives the consultant a "bigger stick" if the firm doesn't meet their obligations. In addition to the negotiated "cost plus" percentage, the vendor must agree to specified days or numbers of deliveries, minimums, and caps on some high-priced items as well. Should the consultant's periodic audits confirm the vendor has undercharged a client, the company is assessed the difference. If it is found the vendor is overcharging the customer, the difference must be credited. Flagrant overcharging can result in fines or the vendor being removed from the program. It is the sheer volume of business that makes all this additional effort and tight margins worth it, which is why this trend is limited to foodservice operations that work on a large volume.

As this is written, these are among the more prominent trends in the foodservice business. As with all trends, some of these may simply fade away in the years to come and others will slowly become the norm in how business is practiced. Many of these trends are in direct response to what were the new trends 60 or more years ago. Those trends moved us away from the small farms and decentralized food distribution system to the huge conglomerates and factory-farming systems we now seek to correct.

The trends did what they set out to do, in that they gave us the capability to serve many people many calories and do it for a low cost; and it made a lot of large corporations rich. The negative impacts discussed in this chapter were not readily known when these trends evolved, and this is the impetus for many of today's trends. The question remains regarding the feasibility of feeding our ever-growing population if we revert to a locally focused, decentralized model. It is likely the trends for the future will have to be in melding these starkly different models into a form which will feed the world without destroying it. The challenge for the purchasing segment of the food-service industry will be in seeking out these trends and supporting them in a way that allows their business to continue and prosper.

# ORGANIZATIONAL CONSULTANT

In this scenario, the utilization of an organizational consultant was effective and warranted due to the high volume of annual food purchases and the wide range of inventory items involved. For this company, a savings of 7–10% in food cost plus the additional savings in soft dollars from handling fewer deliveries, bids, and sales calls are very significant. Plus, after the initial year's investment, annual fees are low in comparison to the program's rebates and continued savings. The savings and benefits are clearly significant.

The same consultant would not provide a similar benefit for a small operation for several reasons. First, vendors are willing to sell for a reduced margin of profit based on the ability to move a high volume of goods; there would be little advantage for them to do so for a small operation. Similarly, the consultant will base his fee on the total volume of purchases and the estimated savings, as a small firm would be unlikely to hit those minimums. For the client, while any savings is always desired, the size of the initial investment and annual fees, plus the trouble of implementation, would yield little to no advantage. Every firm will need to weigh the costs against the expected return to determine if such a consultant would be a good fit for that organization, and then interview potential firms to find the one that will best service their needs.

The Premier Restaurant Group corporation consists of five unique white tablecloth restaurants, an upscale bakery and coffee shop, one casual cafeteria, and an on-premise catering operation. Total food purchases for this group exceeded $7 million annually.

The Premier Group had an excellent reputation, and each individual operation had consistently performed well. Due to the unique concept and excellent performance of each unit, historically each chef had been allowed to determine the exact specifications and brands of the products used in their own operation. All of these units were located in close proximity to one another, and therefore Premier had built a central commissary with a dedicated purchasing staff to manage all these various needs. This freedom of choice for the chefs led to a large and often redundant inventory that had grown without any true examination over time. The buyers had been charged with first meeting the demands of the chef and then being as aggressive as possible in negotiating or bidding for the best possible price.

After years of continuing this type of approach, the company's CFO worried about the increasing need to maintain proper food cost; the mushrooming number of stock-keeping units (SKUs) on hand, especially those with a low turnover rate; and the administrative costs in managing so many items, deliveries, and vendors. He determined to hire an outside consultant to evaluate their buying practices. After taking several proposals and conducting several interviews, an organizational consultant, Panzer Associates, was retained.

Panzer met with Premier's buying team, carefully explained their business model, and frankly told them that the implementation process would be arduous and painful for many people, but over time the buyers that bought into the new model would be grateful for the efficiencies gained and see a substantial improvement in their food cost percentages. They also needed to understand that Panzer worked under a cost plus preferred vendor (for each major line of inventory) model. This would mean many current vendors would no longer be required, that Panzer may opt to bring in other vendors they already had a relationship with, and that whatever vendor was chosen for each product line would be required to meet the specification on almost every item the client required. Panzer also required that products be chosen by exact specification only; brand names would not be allowed unless that brand offered the most optimal cost to the client, and personal preferences were out.

Initially, the buyers were outraged, could not believe this outsider could do better than they could, worried about job security, wanted to stay loyal to those they had done business with for years, and worried about their relationships with in-house customers that would no longer be able to get any product they demanded. The chefs and bakers worried that the new vendors and products would not deliver the quality required and resented losing their freedom to choose. Unit management worried about staff morale and losing customers if the quality of the end product suffered. However, the executive management held firm, and all employees were directed to give this every opportunity to succeed. Also, Panzer was reminded that the quality of the end dish was essential, and no product could be mandated if it could not perform well in the dish.

As predicted, there was a great deal of stress, hard feelings, and bruised egos to placate, and a tremendous number of details to work out and products to be cut in order to implement the new system. Vendors were let go, new vendors were added, and relationships needed to be created and mended, but this was business and people eventually understood and worked into their new roles. Over time, the cooks stopped complaining about the new extra virgin olive oil or the lack of favored brands, and buyers enjoyed writing and receiving fewer orders . . . and loved not doing weekly and monthly bids. The test came at the end of the fiscal year, when the final audits were conducted and it was determined that Premier overall had purchased 82% of their product needs "in program" and lowered their food cost by 7%; not quite as much as Panzer had projected, but a substantial amount of money given the size of their annual purchases. Savings in soft dollars from improved administrative functions were also realized.

In the following year, Panzer assessed each program vendor a rebate to the Premier Group based on each company's annual sales ranging from 0.5% to 1.0%. These rebates alone saved the Premier Group over twice their annual fee to Panzer. Over the years, due to service or other issues, some companies fell out of the program and others were added, with each one more easily accepted by the client. The culture shock of implementing this consultant's program had been long and difficult, but after time all employees would wonder how they had managed before.

# READING AND RESOURCES LIST

Ainsworth, Mark. *The Kitchen Pro Series Guide to Fish and Seafood Identification, Fabrication, and Utilization.* Delmar Cengage Learning: Clifton Park, NY. 2009.

Cournoyer, Norman, and Karen Moreris. *Hotel Restaurant and Travel Law.* Delmar Cengage Learning: Clifton Park, NY. 2007.

Feinstein, Andrew Hale, and John M. Stefanelli. *Purchasing for Chefs.* John Wiley and Sons: Hoboken, NJ. 2007.

_____. *Purchasing: Selection and Procurement for the Hospitality Industry.* John Wiley and Sons: Hoboken, NJ. 2007.

Fischer, John. *The Kitchen Pro Series Guide to Cheese Identification, Classification, and Utilization.* Delmar Cengage Learning: Clifton Park, NY. 2010.

Garlough, Robert. *Modern Food Service Purchasing.* Delmar Cengage Learning: Clifton Park, NY. 2010.

Lynch, Francis T. *The Book of Yields: Accuracy in Food Costing and Purchasing.* New Jersey: Wiley, 2010.

Matthews, Brad, and Paul Wigsten. *The Kitchen Pro Series Guide to Produce Identification, Fabrication, and Utilization.* Delmar Cengage Learning: Clifton Park, NY. 2010.

Menzies, Gavin. *1421: The Year China Discovered America.* Harper Collins: New York. 2002.

NAMP North American Meat Processors Association. *The Meat Buyers Guide: Meat, Lamb, Veal, Pork and Poultry.* New Jersey: Wiley, 2010.

Nestle, Marion. *What to Eat.* North Point Press: New York. 2007.

Peddersen, Raymond B. *Foodservice and Hotel Purchasing.* CBI Publishing: Boston. 1981.

Provisioner's Price List. *The Southwestern Historical Quarterly.* October 1947.

Reed, Lewis. *Specs: The Foodservice and Purchasing Specification Manual.* John Wiley and Sons: Hoboken, NJ. 2006.

Rice, Kym S., for Fraunces Tavern Museum. *Early American Taverns: For the Entertainment of Friends and Strangers.* Regnery Gateway: Chicago. 1983.

Schneller, Thomas. *The Kitchen Pro Series Guide to Meat Identification, Fabrication, and Utilization.* Delmar Cengage Learning: Clifton Park, NY. 2009.

_____. *The Kitchen Pro Series Guide to Poultry Identification, Fabrication, and Utilization.* Delmar Cengage Learning: Clifton Park, NY. 2009.

Woog, Adam. *A Cultural History of the United States: The 1900s.* Lucent Books: Farmington Hills, MI. 1999.

## Websites

U.S. Government Accountability Office
www.GAO.gov

*Restaurant Startup and Growth Magazine*
www.restaurantowner.com

Planet Green
http://planetgreen.discovery.com

www.udsa.gov

## Photo Credits

### Ben Fink
Pg 30, 35, 44, 97, 107, 111, 116, 118, 122, 127, 129, 131, 133, 135, 138, 141, 143, 146, 148, 149, 152, 158, 159, 161, 168, 170, 174, 180 (fig 4.33), 184, 186, 187, 188, 189, 190, 191, 192, 193, 194, 195, 196, 197, 200, 204, 205, 207 (fig 5.7), 210, 246, 247, 249, 250, 251, 252, 253, 256, 257, 258

### Keith Ferris
Pg 39, 40, 61, 62, 63, 64, 65, 66, 67, 68, 69, 70, 74, 75, 76, 77, 78, 80, 81, 82, 83, 85, 86, 87, 88, 89, 180 (fig 4.32), 182, 183, 185, 206, 207 (fig 5.8), 209, 218, 267, 268 (bottom), 270, 272

We would like to thank Ginsberg for generously supplying the photo for Fig 2.3a. We would also like to thank Donald Bennett of The Bethel Journals for all of his help and for providing the photo for Fig 1.8.

# GLOSSARY

**Acceptance**—The agreement by one party of the contract to accept the offer put forth by the other.

**Affinage**—Period of aging or maturing during which cheese is ripened. Cheese becomes what it was meant to be by reaching optimal moisture content, texture, and flavor.

**Agora**—The activity centers found in ancient Greek city-states. Government buildings, markets, and religious temples were often located there.

**Allium genus**—This is the genus that contains onions and garlic. It is also related to the lily family.

**Anthocyanins**—The color compounds that look purple in produce. These compounds are believed to supply antioxidants that aid in cardiac and brain function as well as aid in cancer protection.

**Aquaculture**—The process of gathering fish in their natural habitat and raising them within controlled environments for cultivation and harvest purposes.

**Arbitration or mediation**—When a third party is appointed by the parties or a court to settle a dispute.

**Bacchus**—The ancient Greek god of wine.

**Beta-carotene**—A color pigment responsible for the orange color of carrots, for which it is named, and many other fruits and vegetables (for example, sweet potatoes, oranges, cantaloupes, and melons).

**Betalain**—A class of red and yellow indole-derived pigments that causes the red color in beets and chard.

**Bill of sale**—The invoice; represents the contract.

**Bob veal**—Very young beef animal, under 10 days old, small with underdeveloped flavor, inexpensive, used for processed veal items, prebreaded cutlets, and grind.

**Bolting**—The term that describes what happens if lettuce is not harvested in time; the stalk continues to grow through the head and may flower.

**Brassica**—A genus of plants in the mustard family including cabbages, broccoli, and cauliflower.

**Breach of contract**—When one or both parties of a contract do not keep the promises of the agreement.

**Broad-line distributors**—Suppliers that carry a full line of products including dry goods, frozen goods, equipment, flatware, china, and linens. Many broad liners also carry perishable items such as produce, meat, and dairy.

**Buyer**—Works directly with the purveyors, insuring proper product specification, bid comparisons, blind cuttings, and so on. This person may represent the business at food shows and exhibitions as well. May also work with management in purchasing services and leasing needs. This person usually forms the personal relationship between vendor and client.

**Cancellation and restitution**—When a contract is breached, the damaged party can cancel the contract and sue for "restitution." This is when a party has given something out in advance such as a deposit or goods and then the contract is not fulfilled, so the harmed party is given enough compensation to return them to their precontract financial condition and the contract is then voided, releasing all parties from future obligation.

**Capsicum**—A genus of plants from the nightshade family; this includes all peppers and chilis.

**Carbon footprint**—The amount of fossil fuels expended to bring a product to market and then to its end use. The larger the footprint, the more these valuable and finite resources are diminished.

*Caveat emptor*—Meaning "buyer beware," this implies that the burden of determining the quality, condition, and price of an item is on the purchaser, not on the seller.

**Clingstone**—In stone fruit, this means the pit or stone is more tightly adhered to the flesh of the fruit.

**C.O.D.**—Cash on delivery.

**Cod**—Found in areas where cold and warm waters converge, cod is an extremely versatile fish for cooking. It has brown spots speckling its brownish body that is lined with white stripes on either side. The majority of species live in the northern hemisphere, the most commercially important being Atlantic cod.

**Companion planting**—A method of planting used to limit chemical use by strategically planting crops to draw pests away from the true crop.

**Compensatory damages**—This compensation simply returns the harmed party to their financial situation before the act occurred or finishes the terms of the contract.

**Consideration**—The amount of money, property, services, or action that is transferred.

**Contract**—Written or oral agreements. Has four basic components that make it enforceable: *legality*, *offer*, *acceptance*, and *consideration*.

**Cost plus**—An agreement between vendor and buyer of a set percentage over actual cost; this assures the vendor the same level of profit regardless of how the market tracks.

**Crop rotation**—A planting method in which crops are moved from one location to another annually to promote soil health, disease resistance, and insect and pest control.

**Cycle count**—An inventory-managing process in which areas of inventory are counted on a regular basis throughout the year, which produces high accuracy in inventory purchasing.

**Dead inventory**—Stock that is no longer being used but remains on the shelf.

**Dunnage racks**—Low flat racks that have heavier bars instead of shelves and are used for holding stacks of heavy items, such as bags of flour or potatoes, that are purchased in higher quantities but not palletized. Keeps stored food raised off the floor without losing excess space.

**E-procurement**—A method of conducting business-to-business transactions electronically instead of in person or by phone. Buyers can source product and purchase from online catalogs or product listings and purchase directly.

**Equipment dollars**—The purchasing budget for equipment that most large-scale operations build into their annual budget. Spending is often directed to the most essential equipment first and then outward to nonessentials that enhance the operation but might not be needed immediately.

**Ethics**—Moral code that dictates that buyers are respectful of a purveyor's confidence and never share one company's pricing with another firm to drive down their bid price.

**Farm to Fork Initiative**—The move to source and utilize more locally grown and produced products. This term was coined in the mid-1990s by Senator Hillary Clinton in New York State to bolster that state's agricultural community.

**FIFO (first in, first out) system**— Practiced with all highly perishable foods based on quality characteristics and date of receipt.

**Fill rate**—The percentage rate of items ordered by a vendor that are filled on time without shortages or back orders out of each scheduled delivery. Fill rate is a service factor to consider in opting for a vendor to develop a business relationship.

**Floating row cover**—Ground covers used to raise the temperature under the cover by a few degrees to speed growth early in the season and protect against frost at the end of each season. These covers also protect young plants from many pests.

**Food cost**—Determined by taking a beginning inventory of product, adding all incoming deliveries during the specified time period, and then subtracting all product required for preparation and sale, or the product that had been issued from the storage area and transferred into production. That number should equal the amount of the subsequent inventory.

**Freestone**—In stone fruit, the seed or stone easily separates itself from the flesh.

**Fresh cheese**—Young cheeses that do not need to age at all, often high in moisture content and highly perishable. The main flavor profile is that of the milk they were made from, and thus they are sometimes considered bland.

**Garum**—A fermented fish sauce used as a flavor enhancer in ancient Roman times.

**Gill veils**—A veil is the thin covering underneath a mushroom's cap over its gills, which are plate-like structures arranged on the underside of a mushroom's cap.

**Green market**—Market at which to purchase seasonal and local produce directly from farmers.

**Green Restaurant Association (GRA)**— A nonprofit organization with roughly 350 certified members that has spent the last 20 years working to educate operators, manufacturers, and purveyors about the need to develop and promote a greener method of operating in the foodservice industry, which is the number one energy-consuming segment of American business.

**HACCP (Hazard Analysis Critical Control Points)**—A scientific food safety program which takes a systematic and preventative approach to the conditions that are responsible for most food-borne illnesses.

**Hanging meat**—Large carcass, primal, or subprimal cuts that are never stored in vacuum packaging, typical for dry aging. Be sure hanging meats are wrapped in paper or loose plastic when receiving. If aging hanging cuts, be sure allow for good air circulation.

**Heirloom tomato**—Open-pollinated tomato varieties that were introduced before 1940, or tomato varieties more than 50 years in circulation.

**Hydroponics**—A method of growing plants using mineral nutrient solutions, without soil.

**Implied warranty**—Where the seller at the time of contracting has reason to know any particular purpose for which the goods are required and the buyer is relying on the seller's skill or judgment to select or furnish suitable goods, there is, unless excluded or modified under the next section, an implied warranty that the goods shall be fit for that purpose.

**Institute for Supply Management (ISM)** — An organization of purchasing professionals that defines the specific abilities and assets that buyers should obtain or have in order to advance this management field.

**Inventory**—Everything purchased and received, then stored and inventoried, and then issued in a foodservice operation.

**Inventory management**—An essential tool in the proper management of a foodservice operation.

**Inventory policy**—An organization's inventory policy in written document form. Should not be seen as etched in stone; these guidelines should be periodically reviewed to ensure they remain current and yield the desired results. Employees should be familiar with policies and well trained in them.

**Inventory value assessment**—Adding up all of the inventory value to calculate the total worth of the business in case of an insurance claim or theft assessment. Also tracks products that are not moving. Performed on a monthly or annual basis.

**IQF (individually quick frozen)**—Rapidly frozen portion cut meat items.

**Just-in-time (JIT) purchasing**—The purchasing of inventory only as existing inventory is depleted, but before new demand cannot be fulfilled. A critical aspect of controlling cost.

**Kitchen supply warehouse**—A supplier that specializes in large and small commercial kitchen equipment.

**Lease to own**—A sort of hybrid between a lease and a payment program to buy equipment. This may make sense for start-up businesses that need capital in other places but then find they are successful and will be in business for the long term.

**Leasing**—The renting of equipment. Should be considered for an establishment that has limited capital but expects a good cash flow when open. This frees up money for other uses.

**LEED (Leadership in Energy and Environmental Design)**—An internationally recognized certification system; in stewardship of sustainable practices, owners and buyers can look for LEED certifications for construction. LEED's aim is to insure construction is designed in a manner to reduce energy and water usage as well as $CO_2$ emissions. It also aims to ensure the safety of the environment inside these buildings and maintain a stewardship of natural resources.

**Leveling ramp**—A ramp that bridges the gap between the loading dock and street level.

**Liquidated damages**—Damages that are specified in the language of the original contract and are a reasonable compensation in the case that the contract is breached. In other words, the contract tells both parties what the remedy is if one party defaults on the contract.

**Locally grown produce**—Produce that should show a pronounced gain in quality due to its freshness and short shipping distance. When purchasing, the chef has the ability to have some product grown to his or her exact specifications. There is a reduced carbon footprint in sourcing locally, improved yield because the product came out of the field that day and has not spent days or weeks in transit and cold storage before arriving at your door, and that amazing farm fresh flavor.

**MAP (modified atmospheric packaging) storage**—Similar to vacuum package but bag has modified air content rather than a tight seal. Typically $CO_2$ or NO is used to help preserve meat.

**Meat purveyor**—A vendor of meat products; may or may not process meat in house.

**Mercantile laws**—The body of rules applied to markets; derived from the practices of traders.

**Minimum order requirements**—Minimum dollar values for orders established by purveyors to guarantee that all deliveries will generate some margin of profit, or at least insure against loss.

**Multiple-vendor bidding**—A purchasing system used by purchasers involving a small group of approved vendors.

**National Restaurant Association (NRA)**—The largest restaurant association in the United States.

**Niche market meats**—Meat items that differ from the standard commercially produced meat items; may refer to breed, feeding style, cutting style, producer's size, locality, or any other factor that may be considered "niche." Typically implies small market item.

**Nominal damages**—A token damage paid to the nonbreaching party to state who won or lost. This is when no real financial harm came from the breach.

**North American Meat Processors (NAMP)**—An association of meat processors responsible for the *Meat Buyer's Guide*, which categorizes commercially produced meat cuts.

**Nose to tail**—A trend that combines supporting local growers, sustainability, a lower carbon footprint, and slow food. The buyer procures whole animals for the chefs to utilize completely in their menus instead of buying just the better known and higher priced cuts common in the food industry.

**Offers**—Where all product specs, prices, delivery times and places, and terms and responsibilities of all parties are discussed and negotiated.

**Operational or buying consultants**—Hired by an organization to act as liaisons or agents in determining what vendors to use while ensuring a mutually acceptable, but narrow, margin of profit. In such a relationship, the consultant generally represents a group of high-volume accounts, which allows the consultant to leverage a great deal of buying power to drive these agreed-upon narrow margins.

**Order point**—The point in an item's inventory level at which it needs restocking to come back up to a determined maximum storage level.

**Organic**—Foods that are grown without the use of chemicals.

**Organizational consultant**—Outside firms employed by larger hotels and foodservice operations in order to help them purchase inventory. These establishments gain the assurance that they will be paying a very competitive price without the time-consuming process of comparing bids on hundreds of items on a daily, weekly, or monthly basis. Same as a buying consultant.

**Par inventory level**—Points of low or high inventory levels. The need for more products when inventory levels reach the minimum or below and the required amount needed for purchase to return to the higher par number. When determining appropriate par levels for reference (in either manual or web-based systems), these numbers need to be adjusted as business demands and menu needs change.

**Point-of-sale system**—Touch screen meal-ordering systems invented in the mid-1990s.

**Portion control or portion cuts**—Individual, uniform, cut portions, ready to cook and requiring no fabrication.

**Poultry**—Domestic breeds of fowl used for meat or egg production including chicken, duck, goose, and turkey.

**Preservation methods**—Methods such as salting, fermenting, brining, curing, smoking, and drying that have been developed so food can be carried or stored for months.

**Primal cut**—First, major cuts of a carcass, untrimmed and requiring further fabrication.

**Prime**—Highest grade given to meat by the USDA.

**Procurement**—The exchange of payment for the goods desired.

**Product knowledge**—Essential to be able to write the required detailed specifications for products sought and to determine the best choices when developing a menu and purchasing to meet those needs.

**Product specifications**—Crucial to the buyer in guaranteeing the exact nature of the ingredients ordered and received. Specifications also assure that any bids received pertain to equivalent products, which provides an accurate comparison and notifies the vendor of the exact nature of what the customer needs.

**Punitive damages**—A lawyer may seek further compensation, beyond the simple remedy of the terms of the contract, to punish the defaulting party. This is not typical in contract law but may apply when there is a repeat offender.

**Purchaser-specified options (PSO)**—Refers to any number of available trim specs for items, including fat depth, length, and bone length.

**Purchasing agent**—The buyer.

**Quality grade**—The grade applied by the USDA that determines the palatability of a meat item; can assign value. Not a mandatory grade and is paid for by the purveyor.

**Receiving clerk**—Responsible for the proper receipt of all incoming deliveries. Insures the received product's invoice and purchase order match; specifications and quality standards are met, debit and/or credit memos are issued, and all products are properly stored and rotated.

**Rind**—Outside covering of some but not all cheeses. Rinds provide protection, texture, and flavor, and can even help with the identification of a cheese.

**Roaster**—Large mature broiler chicken ranging from 5 to 9 pounds.

**Seasonality**—The availability of meat, seafood, and produce items in certain seasons. Modern meat farming has eliminated most seasonality for these products, but there are some items that increase in quality at certain times of the year. Can also refer to the seasonal pricing of items.

**Shellfish tags**—Certain information about the product that is useful in dealing with potential food poisoning. Tags are kept on the fish until the entire package is emptied and then must be dated and kept for 90 days.

**Slow Food Movement**—A grassroots effort that was founded in 1989 in order to promote the sustainability of our food system. This organization has grown to over 100,000 members in a dozen countries. The movement wishes to bring more attention to what we eat and its origins, and it was formed to try to counteract the effects of the fast-food lifestyle, such as obesity from excessive fats and sugars, poor flavor, damage to the environment, as well as the loss of local foods and their traditions.

**Small purveyors**—Offer fresh, local products, but often operate in smaller quantities and have less flexible delivery hours.

**Specialty meat vendor**—A source for custom cuts, heritage breeds, grass-fed meat, specialty game, or extreme-quality meat products.

**Specific performance**—A remedy where the court will order a specific performance or action to be completed by the breaching party for remedy. This occurs when a remedy proposed by that party is considered inadequate. If a company states they will compensate with money but the injured party needed a specific task done that only the breaching party can do, then a specific performance may be ordered.

**Specification sheet**—The written detailed specification for products sought. Includes the product's name, a product code if relevant, the desired size or weight, the trim level, and the pack size for each ingredient. Also called a spec sheet.

**Specifications**—Detailed description of foods for purchase; also called specs.

**Stewardship**—Making responsible decisions regarding the care of the land in satisfying our needs now without risk to people or the environment in the future.

**Stock clerk**—Maintains cleanliness and order of storage areas, works with receiving clerk in properly storing and rotating goods, fills in-house customer needs or requisitions, and advises buyer if inventory levels suddenly change or par stock levels need adjustment.

**Storeroom**—The control center for everything utilized within that facility. Everything flowing in and out of these areas will determine the ability of the cooking and service teams to perform and will affect the quality of what they serve. The function of a storeroom typically serves a dual purpose; it serves as the purchasing arm as all needed products are procured from outside vendors and received and stored by the storeroom team, and it serves as a vendor in that it distributes all the products to the company's internal customers.

**Storeroom manager**—Coordinates all functions of the department, including scheduling staff, purchasing, receiving, product specification and rotation, issue, setting par levels, inventories, verifying food costs and insuring that all the needs of the operation are being met.

**Strip cropping**—A planting method used to limit depletion of the soil. Farmers will alternate rows of crops such as wheat and corn in 50-foot-wide bands across hillsides to save the soil. They also must plow across the hillsides as plowing up and down can lead to much more erosion of the topsoil.

**Subprimal**—Cuts created by dividing the primal; often sold as hotel, restaurant, and institution–style (HRI) cuts.

**Sustainability**—A product or growing method is sustainable when it does no harm to people, animals, or the environment and ensures that the land can support both the grower and the crop into the future. Alternately, it requires satisfying our needs now without risk to people or the environment in the future.

**Sustainable business relationship**—A business relationship in which vendors and buyers continue to work together in a manner beneficial to both.

**Tuna**—An extremely powerful and fast fish, there are many species available worldwide, each purchasable in cuts with unique flavors and textures. Fatty and very rich in flavor, it is often consumed raw as well as sold canned throughout the United States.

*Umami*—Describes a savory, meaty taste. Included as one of the basic tastes our tongue senses along with sour, sweet, salty, and bitter. Often associated with monosodium glutamate (MSG), mushrooms, Worcestershire and Thai fish sauce, and many cheeses.

**Uniform Commercial Code (UCC)** —The group of articles that insures uniformity and consistency throughout the states so contracts can be enforceable across state lines. Business contracts fall under the UCC, which gives certain protections to buyers and sellers.

**USDA**—United States Department of Agriculture, responsible for inspecting and grading meat.

**Vacuum packaged**—Tightly sealed heavy plastic bag that provides an anaerobic environment and increases shelf life; typical brand name is Cryovac packaged. Can be utilized for large subprimals or individual portion cuts. Most typical form of packaging meats sold to foodservice today.

**Vacuum-packaging system**—Implemented by the Iowa Beef Processors (IBP). Transformed the industry further by allowing meats to be processed and shipped with a much longer shelf life and no longer requiring the meats to be shipped as whole carcasses.

**Variance**—The range in which food cost percentages are acceptable. This is done through inventory data gained through review and evaluation. Can be measured by the percentage of the number of total units expended and counted, or as a dollar value of the product sold and in stock.

**Vendor**—Supplier of goods.

**Wall-to-wall inventory**—The full inventories used to determine the costs of goods sold, which are used as controls by an operation's financial department. Such inventories supply the data needed to measure the dollar amount of product consumed in that time frame against the dollar amount of sales to ascertain if an operation's percentage of costs is in line with the predetermined food cost percentages the menu prices were based on.

**Wild boar**—Reddish meat from feral swine, which are smaller than regular pork; has a stronger flavor than regular pork.

**Win-win relationship**—A business relationship when vendors and buyers work together to establish a working relationship that meets the needs of both parties in that the buyers get the quality and service they need for an appropriate cost and vendors gain a customer they can move merchandise with profitably.

**Yield grade**—Identifies the amount of salable meat or the cutability in a carcass.

Appendix A

## BUTCHER'S YIELD TEST

Butcher's Yield test on a _____ to a _____

1. AP Weight    x    AP Price per Pound   =   AP Cost
_____      _____      _____


2. Trim Weight      Trim Price Per Pound

Fat    ____     x     ____     =

Bones ____     x     ____     =

Usable ____     x     ____     =

3. Total Trim Weight _____      Total Trim Value _____

4. AP Weight  –  Total Trim Weight      = New Fabricated Weight
            (edible portion)

5. AP Cost  –  Total Trim Value      = New Fabricated Cost
            (edible portion cost)

6. New Fabricated Cost / New Fabricated Weight      = New Fabricated Cost per Pound
            (edible portion cost per lb.)

7. New Fabricated Price per pound / AP Price per pound  = Cost Factor

8. New Fabricated Weight / AP Weight      = Yield %

9. How many _____ oz. portions?
(convert new fabricated weight to oz. and divide by oz. portion size.)

10. Cost of _____ _____ oz portions.
(convert new fabricated price per pound to price per oz. and multiply by the total of oz. portions)

## BUTCHER'S YIELD TEST

**Beef Rib Eye, Lip On Fabricated to Portion Steaks**
**Difficulty level: Easy**
**Approximate Fabrication Time: 10 Min.**

### BUTCHER'S YIELD TEST

| AP Weight | 13 |
|---|---|
| AP Price per Pound | $5.90 |
| AP Cost | $76.70 |

| | Trim Weight | | x | Trim Price Per Pound | = | Trim Value |
|---|---|---|---|---|---|---|
| Fat | 2.9 | lbs | | $0.00 | | $0.00 |
| Bones | 0 | lbs | | $0.00 | | $0.00 |
| Useable Trim | 0 | lbs | | $0.00 | | $0.00 |
| Other | 0 | lbs | | $0.00 | | $0.00 |
| Total Trim Weight | 2.9 | lbs | | Total Trim Value | | $0.00 |

| | | |
|---|---|---|
| Fabricated Weight | 10.1 | lbs |
| Fabricated Cost | $76.70 | |
| Fabricated Cost per Pound | $7.59 | |
| Cost Factor | 1.29 | |
| Yield % | 78% | |
| How many portions in the fabricated weight? | 12 oz. | 13 |
| What is the cost of 1 12 oz. portions? | $5.70 | |

## BUTCHER'S YIELD TEST

Beef Tenderloin, Peeled with Side Muscle On (PSMO), Fabricated to Medallion
Difficulty level: Modest
Approximate Fabrication Time: 15 Min.

### BUTCHER'S YIELD TEST

| AP Weight | 6.3 |
|---|---|
| AP Price per Pound | $8.50 |
| AP Cost | $53.55 |

| | Trim Weight | | x | Trim Price Per Pound | = | Trim Value |
|---|---|---|---|---|---|---|
| Fat | 0.9 | lbs | | $0.00 | | $0.00 |
| Bones | 0 | lbs | | $0.50 | | $0.00 |
| Useable Trim | 1.3 | lbs | | $1.95 | | $2.54 |
| Other | 0 | lbs | | $0.00 | | $0.00 |
| Total Trim Weight | 2.2 | lbs | | Total Trim Value | | $2.54 |

| | | |
|---|---|---|
| Fabricated Weight | 4.1 | lbs |
| Fabricated Cost | $51.02 | |
| Fabricated Cost per Pound | $12.44 | |
| Cost Factor | 1.46 | |
| Yield % | 65% | |
| How many portions in the fabricated weight? | 6 oz. | 11 |
| What is the cost of 1 6 oz. portions? | $4.67 | |

## BUTCHER'S YIELD TEST

Veal Top Round, Cap Off, Fabricated to Cutlets
Difficulty level: Modest
Approximate Fabrication Time: 7 Min.

### BUTCHER'S YIELD TEST

| AP Weight | 8 |
|---|---|
| AP Price per Pound | $10.50 |
| AP Cost | $84.00 |

| | Trim Weight | | x | Trim Price Per Pound | = | Trim Value |
|---|---|---|---|---|---|---|
| Fat (can vary with yield) | 0 | lbs | | $0.00 | | $0.00 |
| Bones | 0 | lbs | | $0.00 | | $0.00 |
| Useable Trim | 0.7 | lbs | | $3.00 | | $2.10 |
| Other | 0 | lbs | | $0.00 | | $0.00 |
| Total Trim Weight | 0.7 | lbs | | Total Trim Value | | $2.10 |

| | | |
|---|---|---|
| Fabricated Weight | 7.3 | lbs |
| Fabricated Cost | $81.90 | |
| Fabricated Cost per Pound | $11.22 | |
| Cost Factor | 1.07 | |
| Yield % | 91% | |
| How many portions in the fabricated weight? | 6 oz. | 19 |
| What is the cost of 1 6 oz. portions? | $4.21 | |

## BUTCHER'S YIELD TEST

Leg of Lamb Fabricated to a Boned, Rolled, and Tied (BRT) Leg Roast
Difficulty level: Difficult
Approximate Fabrication Time: 15 Min. (may be longer depending on skill level)

### BUTCHER'S YIELD TEST

| | |
|---|---|
| AP Weight | 11.5 |
| AP Price per Pound | $3.25 |
| AP Cost | $37.38 |

| | Trim Weight | | x | Trim Price Per Pound | = | Trim Value |
|---|---|---|---|---|---|---|
| Fat | 1.7 | lbs | | $0.00 | | $0.00 |
| Bones | 1.8 | lbs | | $0.50 | | $0.90 |
| Useable Trim | 0.8 | lbs | | $2.50 | | $2.00 |
| Other | 0 | lbs | | $0.00 | | $0.00 |
| Total Trim Weight | 4.3 | lbs | | Total Trim Value | | $2.90 |

| | | |
|---|---|---|
| Fabricated Weight | 7.2 | lbs |
| Fabricated Cost | $34.48 | |
| Fabricated Cost per Pound | $4.79 | |
| Cost Factor | 1.47 | |
| Yield % | 63% | |
| How many portions in the fabricated weight? | 6 oz. | 19 |
| What is the cost of 1 6 oz. portions? | $1.80 | |

## BUTCHER'S YIELD TEST

**Leg of Veal Fabricated to Cutlets**
**Difficulty level: Expert**
**Approximate Fabrication Time: 1 Hour 20 Min.**

### BUTCHER'S YIELD TEST

| | |
|---|---|
| AP Weight | 49.5 |
| AP Price per Pound | $4.25 |
| AP Cost | $210.38 |

| | Trim Weight | | x | Trim Price Per Pound | = | Trim Value |
|---|---|---|---|---|---|---|
| Fat | 5.7 | lbs | | $0.00 | | $0.00 |
| Bones | 6.1 | lbs | | $0.85 | | $5.19 |
| Useable Trim | 6.75 | lbs | | $2.50 | | $16.88 |
| Other (Osso Buco) | 3 | lbs | | $7.50 | | $22.50 |
| Total Trim Weight | 21.55 | lbs | | Total Trim Value | | $44.56 |

| | | |
|---|---|---|
| Fabricated Weight | 27.95 | lbs |
| Fabricated Cost | $165.82 | |
| Fabricated Cost per Pound | $5.93 | |
| Cost Factor | 1.40 | |
| Yield % | 56% | |
| How many portions in the fabricated weight? | 6 oz. | 75 |
| What is the cost of 1 6 oz. portions? | $2.22 | |

# CENTER CUT PORK LOIN

## BUTCHER'S YIELD TEST

Kat Tomosky
Group 165

Center Cut Pork Loin Fabricated to a Boneless Roast
Difficulty level: Moderate, requires some boning skills
Approximate Fabrication Time: 10–12 Min.

### BUTCHER'S YIELD TEST

| AP Weight | 12.7 |
|---|---|
| AP Price per Pound | $1.95 |
| AP Cost | $24.77 |

| | Trim Weight | | x | Trim Price Per Pound | = | Trim Value |
|---|---|---|---|---|---|---|
| Fat | 0 | lbs | | $0.00 | | $0.00 |
| Bones | 1.2 | lbs | | $0.25 | | $0.30 |
| Useable Trim | 1.2 | lbs | | $1.20 | | $1.44 |
| Other | 1.2 | lbs | | $3.50 | | $4.20 |
| Total Trim Weight | 3.6 | lbs | | Total Trim Value | | $5.94 |

| | | |
|---|---|---|
| Fabricated Weight | 9.1 | lbs |
| Fabricated Cost | $18.83 | |
| Fabricated Cost per Pound | $2.07 | |
| Cost Factor | $1.06 | |
| Yield % | 72% | |
| How many portions in the fabricated weight? | 8 oz. | 18 |
| What is the cost of 1 8 oz. portions? | $1.03 | |

## BUTCHER'S YIELD TEST

**Kat Tomosky**
Group 165

Boneless Beef Striploin Fabricated to Portion Cut Steaks
Difficulty level: Easy/Moderate
Approximate Fabrication Time: 7–10 Min.

### BUTCHER'S YIELD TEST

| AP Weight | 11 |
|---|---|
| AP Price per Pound | $6.25 |
| AP Cost | $68.75 |

| | Trim Weight | | x | Trim Price Per Pound | = | Trim Value |
|---|---|---|---|---|---|---|
| Fat | 1.3 | lbs | | $0.00 | | $0.00 |
| Bones | 0 | lbs | | $0.00 | | $0.00 |
| Useable Trim (end steak) | 1.1 | lbs | | $2.75 | | $3.03 |
| Other | 0 | lbs | | $0.00 | | $0.00 |
| Total Trim Weight | 2.4 | lbs | | Total Trim Value | | $3.03 |

| | | |
|---|---|---|
| Fabricated Weight | 8.6 | lbs |
| Fabricated Cost | $65.73 | |
| Fabricated Cost per Pound | $7.64 | |
| Cost Factor | $1.22 | |
| Yield % | 78% | |
| How many portions in the fabricated weight? 10 oz. | 14 | |
| What is the cost of 1 10 oz. portions? | $4.78 | |

## BUTCHER'S YIELD TEST

Boneless Beef Top Sirloin Butt Fabricated to Portion Cut Steaks
Difficulty level: Easy/Moderate
Approximate Fabrication Time: 10–12 Min.

### BUTCHER'S YIELD TEST

| AP Weight | 13.8 |
|---|---|
| AP Price per Pound | $3.25 |
| AP Cost | $44.85 |

| | Trim Weight | | x | Trim Price Per Pound | = | Trim Value |
|---|---|---|---|---|---|---|
| Fat | 2.3 | lbs | | $0.00 | | $0.00 |
| Bones | 0 | lbs | | $0.00 | | $0.00 |
| Useable Trim (end steak) | 0.9 | lbs | | $2.75 | | $2.48 |
| Other | 0 | lbs | | $0.00 | | $0.00 |
| Total Trim Weight | 3.2 | lbs | | Total Trim Value | | $2.48 |

| | | |
|---|---|---|
| Fabricated Weight | 10.6 | lbs |
| Fabricated Cost | $42.38 | |
| Fabricated Cost per Pound | $4.00 | |
| Cost Factor | 1.23 | |
| Yield % | 77% | |
| How many portions in the fabricated weight? | 8 oz. | 21 |
| What is the cost of 1 8 oz. portions? | $2.00 | |

## FOOD COST FORM

**MENU ITEM**  Breakfast links 11 lbs yield        Date: _____ 01/14/2010

**Number of Portions >>>>**  1                       Size: _____

**Cost Per Portion:**  $14.48                        Selling Price: _____

                                                     Food Cost %: _____

| Ingredients: | RECIPE QUANTITY (EP) | | | | | COST | | | | |
| | Weight | Unit | Volume | Unit | Count | Unit | APC / Unit | | Yield % | EPC / Unit | Total Cost* |
|---|---|---|---|---|---|---|---|---|---|---|---|
| Pork Butt, B/O | 10 | # | | | | | $1.08 | # | 100% | $1.08 | $10.80 |
| Salt | 3 | oz | | | | | $0.03 | oz | 100% | $0.03 | $0.09 |
| White pepper | 0.33 | oz | | | | | $0.42 | oz | 100% | $0.42 | $0.14 |
| Bell's poultry seasoning | 0.33 | oz | | | | | $0.73 | oz | 100% | $0.73 | $0.25 |
| Sheep casing | 40 | ft | | | | | $0.08 | ft | 100% | $0.08 | $3.20 |
| Ice | 1 | lb | | | | | | | 100% | $0.00 | $0.00 |
| | | | | | | | | | 100% | $0.00 | $0.00 |
| | | | | | | | | | | #DIV/0! | $0.00 |
| | | | | | | | | | | #DIV/0! | $0.00 |
| | | | | | | | | | | #DIV/0! | $0.00 |
| | | | | | | | | | | #DIV/0! | $0.00 |
| | | | | | | | | | | #DIV/0! | $0.00 |
| | | | | | | | | | **Total Cost** | | **$14.48** |

Original menu price: _____

Actual Cost: _____

Final Menu price: _____

Final Food Cost %: _____

# FOOD COST FORM

**MENU ITEM**     Sweet Italian Links    11 lb yield     Date:    01/14/2010

Number of Portions >>>>    1      Size:

Cost Per Portion:    $13.19      Selling Price:     Food Cost %:

| Ingredients | RECIPE QUANTITY (EP) | | | | | COST | | | | TOTAL COST* |
| | Weight | Unit | Volume | Unit | Count | Unit | APC / Unit | Yield % | EPC / Unit | |
| --- | --- | --- | --- | --- | --- | --- | --- | --- | --- | --- |
| Pork Butt, B/O | 10 | # | | | | | $1.08 | 100% | $1.08 | $10.80 |
| Salt | 3 | oz | | | | | $0.03 | 100% | $0.03 | $0.09 |
| Black pepper | 0.75 | oz | | | | | $0.42 | 100% | $0.42 | $0.32 |
| Dextrose | 0.5 | oz | | | | | $0.04 | 100% | $0.04 | $0.02 |
| Fennel seed | 1 | oz | | | | | $0.46 | 100% | $0.46 | $0.46 |
| Paprika | 0.25 | oz | | | | | $0.39 | 100% | $0.39 | $0.10 |
| Casing, hog | 20 | ft | | | | | $0.07 | 100% | $0.07 | $1.40 |
| Ice | 1 | lb | | | | | $0.00 | 100% | $0.00 | $0.00 |
| | | | | | | | | | #DIV/0! | $0.00 |
| | | | | | | | | | #DIV/0! | $0.00 |
| | | | | | | | | | #DIV/0! | $0.00 |
| | | | | | | | | | #DIV/0! | $0.00 |
| | | | | | | | | | **Total Cost** | **$13.19** |

Original menu price:

Actual Cost:

Final Menu price:

Final Food Cost %:

# Appendix B

# TEMPERATURE, WEIGHT AND VOLUME CONVERSIONS

## TEMPERATURE CONVERSIONS

| | | |
|---|---|---|
| **32°F = 0°C** | 205°F = 96°C | 380°F = 193°C |
| 35°F = 2°C | 210°F = 99°C | 385°F = 196°C |
| 40°F = 4°C | **212°F = 100°C** | 390°F = 199°C |
| 45°F = 7°C | 215°F = 102°C | 395°F = 202°C |
| **50°F = 10°C** | 220°F = 104°C | **400°F = 204°C** |
| 55°F = 13°C | **225°F = 107°C** | 405°F = 207°C |
| 60°F = 16°C | 230°F = 110°C | 410°F = 210°C |
| 65°F = 18°C | 235°F = 113°C | 415°F = 213°C |
| 70°F = 21°C | 240°F = 116°C | 420°F = 216°C |
| **75°F = 24°C** | 245°F = 118°C | **425°F = 218°C** |
| [room temp] | **250°F = 121°C** | 430°F = 221°C |
| 80°F = 27°C | 255°F = 124°C | 435°F = 224°C |
| 85°F = 29°C | 260°F = 127°C | 440°F = 227°C |
| 90°F = 32°C | 265°F = 129°C | 445°F = 229°C |
| 95°F = 35°C | 270°F = 132°C | **450°F = 232°C** |
| **100°F = 38°C** | **275°F = 135°C** | 455°F = 235°C |
| 105°F = 41°C | 280°F = 138°C | 460°F = 238°C |
| 110°F = 43°C | 285°F = 141°C | 465°F = 241°C |
| 115°F = 46°C | 290°F = 144°C | 470°F = 243°C |
| 120°F = 49°C | 295°F = 146°C | **475°F = 246°C** |
| **125°F = 52°C** | **300°F = 149°C** | 480°F = 249°C |
| 130°F = 54°C | 305°F = 152°C | 485°F = 252°C |
| 135°F = 57°C | 310°F = 154°C | 490°F = 254°C |
| 140°F = 60°C | 315°F = 157°C | 495°F = 257°C |
| 145°F = 63°C | 320°F = 160°C | **500°F = 260°C** |
| **150°F = 66°C** | **325°F = 163°C** | 505°F = 263°C |
| 155°F = 68°C | 330°F = 166°C | 510°F = 266°C |
| 160°F = 71°C | 335°F = 168°C | 515°F = 268°C |
| 165°F = 74°C | 340°F = 171°C | 520°F = 271°C |
| 170°F = 77°C | 345°F = 174°C | **525°F = 274°C** |
| **175°F = 79°C** | **350°F = 177°C** | 530°F = 277°C |
| 180°F = 82°C | 355°F = 179°C | 535°F = 279°C |
| 185°F = 85°C | 360°F = 182°C | 540°F = 282°C |
| 190°F = 88°C | 365°F = 185°C | 545°F = 285°C |
| 195°F = 91°C | 370°F = 188°C | 550°F = 288°C |
| **200°F = 93°C** | **375°F = 191°C** | |

# WEIGHT CONVERSIONS

For weights less than 1/4 oz: use tsp/tbsp for U.S. measure with gram or mL equivalent
(see specific conversion tables).

**Formula to convert ounces to grams: number of oz $\times$ 28.35 = number of grams (round up for .50 and above)**

| |
|---|
| 1/4 ounce = 7 grams |
| 1/2 ounce = 14 grams |
| 1 ounce = 28.35 grams |
| 4 ounces = 113 grams |
| 8 ounces (1/2 pound) = 227 grams |
| 16 ounces (1 pound) = 454 grams |
| 32 ounces (2 pounds) = 907 grams |
| 40 ounces (2 1/2 pounds) = 1.134 kilograms |

# VOLUME CONVERSIONS

**Formula to convert fluid ounces to milliliters: number of fluid ounces $\times$ 30 = number of milliliters**

| | |
|---|---|
| 1/2 fl oz = 15 mL | 20 fl oz = 600 mL |
| 1 fl oz = 30 mL | 24 fl oz = 720 mL |
| 1 1/2 fl oz = 45 mL | 30 fl oz = 900 mL |
| 1 3/4 fl oz = 53 mL | **32 fl oz = 960 mL [1 qt]** |
| **2 fl oz = 60 mL** | 40 fl oz = 1.20 L |
| 2 1/2 fl oz = 75 mL | 44 fl oz = 1.32 L |
| 3 fl oz = 90 mL | **48 fl oz = 1.44 L [1 1/2 qt]** |
| 3 1/2 fl oz = 105 mL | 64 fl oz = 1.92 L [2 qt] |
| 4 fl oz = 120 mL | **72 fl oz = 2.16 L [2 1/2 qt]** |
| 5 fl oz = 150 mL | 80 fl oz = 2.4 L |
| 6 fl oz = 180 mL | 96 fl oz = 2.88 L [3 qt] |
| 7 fl oz = 210 mL | 128 fl oz = 3.84 L [1 gal] |
| **8 fl oz = 240 mL [1 cup]** | 1 1/8 gal = 4.32 L |
| 9 fl oz = 270 mL | 1 1/4 gal = 4.8 L |
| 10 fl oz = 300 mL | 1 1/2 gal = 5.76 L |
| 11 fl oz = 330 mL | **2 gal = 7.68 L [256 fl oz]** |
| 12 fl oz = 360 mL | 3 gal = 11.52 L |
| 13 fl oz = 390 mL | 4 gal = 15.36 L |
| 14 fl oz = 420 mL | 5 gal = 19.20 L |
| 15 fl oz = 450 mL | 10 gal = 38.40 L |
| **16 fl oz = 480 mL [1 pt]** | 20 gal = 76.80 L |
| 17 fl oz = 510 mL | 25 gal = 96 L |
| 18 fl oz = 540 mL | 50 gal = 192 L |
| 19 fl oz = 570 mL | |

# INDEX

## A

Accurate bidding, 42–43
Albacore, 197
Anchovy, 185
Antelope, 156–158
Apple Usage Chart, 79
Apples, 78–79
Arctic char, 185
Artificial rinds, and cheese, 87
Asia, 11–12
Asparagus, 67
Atlantic Salmon, 192

## B

Baby back ribs, 137
Barramundi, 186
Beans and pods, 69–73
Beef bottom and eye round, 109
Beef brisket, 120
Beef chuck, 118–120
   beef chuck roll, 120
   beef shoulder clod, 120
   NAMP HRI cuts for, 119
   subprimal cuts, 118
Beef chuck roll, 120
Beef classifications, 93–94
Beef flank, 115
Beef foreshank, 120
Beef hanger steaks, 120
Beef knuckle, 109
Beef loin, See Beef primal loin
Beef offals, 120–121
Beef plate, 120
Beef primal loin, 109–115
   beef flank, 115
   beef shortloin, 115
   beef sirloin tri-tip and flap, 115
   beef striploin, bone in or bone out, 110
   beef tenderloin, 110
   beef top sirloin butt, 115
   NAMP HRI cuts chart, 112–114
   subprimal cuts, 110
Beef purchasing specs, 105–121
Beef quality and yield grading, 96–97
Beef rib, 115–118
   NAMP HRI cuts for, 116–117
   rib eye, 115
   short ribs, 118
   subprimal cuts, 115
Beef rib eye, 115
Beef round, 106–109
   NAMP HRI chart for, 108
   subprimal cuts, 106
Beef round foodservice cuts, 109
   beef bottom and eye round, 109
   beef knuckle, 109
   beef shank, 109
   marrow bones, 109
   steamship round, 109
   top round, 109
Beef shank, 109
Beef short ribs, 118
Beef shortloin, 115

Beef shoulder clod, shoulder tender, top blade, 120
Beef sirloin tri-tip and flap, 115
Beef skeletal structure, 106
Beef skirt, 120
Beef striploin, bone in or bone out, 110
Beef tenderloin, 110
Beef top sirloin butt, 115
Berries, 80–82
Bigeye, 197
Bison or buffalo, 153–155
   HRI cuts for, 154–155
Black Mission Figs, 85
Black Sea Bass, 186
Blackfin, 197
Blood Orange, 80
Bloomy rinds, and cheese, 86
Bluefin, 197
Bluefish, 187
Bobolink Cheddar, 88
Bonito, 197
Boston butt, 137, 141
Braeburn Apple, 78
Branzino, Loup de Mer, 187
Bream, Daurade, 187
Brussels Sprouts, 65
Buddha's Hand, 80
Buying food, See Purchasing food
Buying local, 262–263

## C

Cabbage, 63–64
Canrales, 89
Carbon footprint, reducing, 270–271
Carnival Squash, 76
Case studies
   inspection for meats, 214–215
   leasing, 254–255
   Locavore restaurant, 264–265
   organizational consultants, 280–281
Catfish, 188
Cremini Mushrooms, 65
Cheese, 85–89
   categories of, 87–89
   types of rind, 86–87
Cheese aging room, 86
Cheese categories, 87–89
   fresh and young, 87
   medium–strength and nutty, 88–89
   mild aged, 87–88
   strong stinky, 89
Cheese rinds, 86–87
   artificial rinds, 87
   bloomy rinds, 86
   fresh cheese, 86
   natural rind, 86
   washed rinds, 86
Chicken, 160, 162–164
   purchasing specifications, 160, 162–164
Chilean Seabass (Patagonian Toothfish), 186
Chinook, King Salmon, 193
Citrus fruit, 79–80
Cod Family, 187–188
Coho, Silver Salmon, 192–193

Comice Pear, 78
Common dried legumes, 71–72
Cooking greens, 63
Confidentiality, and purchasing standards, 55
Conflicts of interest, and purchasing standards, 54
Crab, 183
Critical control points (CCPs), 212
Customer relationships, and purchasing, 54

D
Dairy and cheese refrigeration, 207–208
Dried legumes, 71–73
Dry goods specifications, 59
Dry storage, 210
Duck, 165–168
    purchasing specifications, 165, 166–167

E
Elk, 156–158
Equipment purchasing, 245–259
    evaluation questions for, 256–259
    large equipment, 252–259
    small equipment, 246–252
Establishing a vendor relationship, 31–35

F
Farm-to-fork initiatives, 263–269
Farmer, 105
Fin fish, 185–197
Fish
    purchasing specs, 179–197
    refrigeration of, 206
Flounder, 188
Food purchasing, skills for, See Purchasing food
Food purchasing, history of, 3–26
    Asia, 11–12
    Greece, 7–9
    Industrial Age, 18–21
    Mesopotamia, 5–6
    Middle Ages, 12–14
    and Modern Era, 23–27
    Neolithic era, 3–5
    the New World, 14–18
    North Africa, 6–7
    Rome, 9–11
    and transportation, 22–23
Fresh cheese, 86–87
Fresh fish and seafood, purchasing, 179–197
    fin fish, 185–197
    sea urchin, 185
    shellfish, 179–184
    squid, 184
Fresh produce, 00–85
    apples and pears, 78–79
    beans and pods, 69–73
    cabbage, 63–64
    citrus fruit, 79–80
    cooking greens, 63
    grapes and berries, 80–82
    greens, 62
    herbs, 77–78
    melons, 83–84
    mushrooms, 64–55
    onions, 66–69
    peppers, 75–76
    roots and tubers, 69
    squash, 76–77
    stalks and other vegetables, 66

stone fruit, 82–83
    tomatoes, 74–75
    tropical fruits, 84–85
Full carcass cuts, 101–102

G
Galangal, 69
Game
    birds, 175–178
    bison or buffalo, 153
    classifications, 95
    definition of, 151, 153
    meats, 153
    quality and yield grading, 99
    rabbit, 153
    venison, antelope, and elk, 156–157
    wild boar, 156, 158
Game birds, 175–178
    guinea fowl, 176
    ostrich, 179
    pheasant, 175–176
    pigeon, 177
    quail, 177
Game bison or buffalo, 153
    HRI cuts for, 154–155
Game meats, 153
Game rabbit, 153
    HRI cuts for, 156
Garrotxa cheese, 88
General foodservice purveyor, 104
Goose, 168–170
    purchasing and usage specifications, 169
Grano Padano, 89
Grapes and berries, 80–82
Green Restaurant Association (GRA), 279
Greens, 62–63
Greece, 7–9
Greener, thinking, 277–278
Greens, 62–63
Grouper, 188
Guinea fowl, 176

H
HACCP, See Hazard Analysis Critical Control
    Points plan
Halibut, 188
Ham, 134–135
Hazard Analysis Critical Control Points (HACCP)
    plan, 211–213
    for meat and poultry, 213
Heirloom dried legumes, 73
Herbs, 77–78
Hotel, Restaurant, and Institution style
    (HRI), 102
HRI cuts
    bison, 154–155
    Boston butt, 140
    lamb leg, 147
    lamb loin, 148
    lamb square cut chuck or shoulder, 151
    hotel rack, 150
    pork belly and spare ribs, 143–144
    pork loin, 138–139
    pork picnic, 140
    veal leg, 124–125
    veal loin, 128
    veal hotel rack, 130
    veal square cut shoulder, 132

HRI NAMP charts, *See* NAMP HRI charts
Humboldt Fog cheese, 87
Hybrid Bass, 186

I
Industrial Age, 18–21
Industry trends, 261–281
   buying local, 262–263
   farm-to-fork initiatives, 263–269
   nose-to-tail menu creating, 275–276
   organic products, 276–277
   reducing carbon footprint, 270–271
   seasonality, 269–271
   Slow Food Movement, 274–275
   sustainability, 271–275
   thinking greener, 277–278
Institute for Supply Management (ISM), 54–55
Internet, 105
Inventory counts, 239–240
Inventory management, 213–243
   frequency of specific counts, 239–240
   performance and result evaluation, 241–243
   supervision of duties, 240
   support and commitment, 236–239
   wall-to-wall controls, 240–241
Inventory types, 217–236
   automatically by computer, 225–236
   manually by the buyer, 219–224
Issues of influence, and purchasing
     standards, 54

J
John Dory, 190

K
Kale, 64

L
Lamb
   breast and foreshank, 149–150
   carcass breakdown, 145–146
   classifications, 94
   hotel rack, 149, 150
   leg, 146
   loin, 146, 148
   quality and yield grading, 99
   square cut chuck or shoulder, 149
Lamb breast and foreshank, 149
Lamb carcass breakdown, 145
   minor primals, 145
   primal cuts, 145
Lamb hotel rack, 149
   HRI cuts, 150
Lamb leg, 146
   HRI cuts, 147
Lamb loin, 146, 148
   HRI cuts, 148
Lamb square cut chuck or shoulder, 149
   HRI cuts, 151
Large equipment, 252–256
   purchasing, 253–256
   rental, 253–254
Leasing, 254–255
Legumes
   dried, 71–72
   heirloom, 73
Linens, 250–251
Lingcod, 190

Lobster, 185
Local businesses, supporting, 39–40

M
Mache, 64
Mackerel, 190
Mahi-mahi, 190
Managerial support and commitment, 236–239
   accountability, 238
   assignment of duties, 236–237
   established written policies, 238–239
   monthly storeroom inventory policy, 238
Market forms in meat purchasing, 101–103
   full carcass, 101–102
   Hotel, Restaurant, and Institution–style (HRI), 102
   portion cuts, 102–103
   primal cuts, 102
   subprimal cuts, 102
Marrow Bones, 109
Meat classifications, 93–95
Meat and poultry HACCP plan, 211
Meat and poultry purchasing, 92–178
   market forms, 101–103
   options in, 93–95
   purchasing specs, 105–179
   quality and yield grading, 96–101
   shipping and packaging, 101
   where to buy meat, 103–105
Meat and poultry refrigeration, 205
Meat purveyor, 104–105
Meat vendors, 103–105
   farmer, 105
   general foodservice purveyor, 104
   Internet, 105
   meat purveyor, 104
   retail discount store, 104–105
Medium-strength and nutty cheese, 88–89
Melons, 83–84
Menu planning, 57–58
   Mesopotamia, 5–6
Middle Ages, 12–14
Mild aged cheese, 87–88
Mimolette, 88
Modern Era, 23–27
Mollusks, 181–183
Monkfish, 190
Morel Mushrooms, 65
Mullet, Rouget, 190
Mushrooms, 64–55

N
NAMP HRI cuts chart
   beef chuck, 119
   beef loin, 112–114
   beef plate, brisket, and foreshank, 121
   beef rib, 116–117
   beef round, 108
   for bison, 154–155
   for fresh hams, 136
   for pork loin, 138–139
   for rabbit, 156
   for venison and antelope, 159–160
   for wild boar, 157
NAMP standards of purchasing practice, 54–55
   confidential and proprietary information, 55
   conflicts of interest, 54
   issues of influence, 54
   laws, regulations, and trade agreements, 55

perceived impropriety, 54
   professional competence, 55
   reciprocity, 55
   responsibilities to your employer, 54
   supplier and customer relationships, 54
   sustainability and social responsibility, 55
Natural rind, 86
Neolithic era, 3–5
New World, 14–18
North Africa, 6–7
Nose-to-tail menu creating, 275–276

**O**
Ocean Perch, 191
Onions, 66–69
Opah, 191
Operational consultants, 38
Orange Roughy, 191
Oregano, 77
Organic products, 277–278
Organizational consultants, 278–281
Ostrich, 178

**P**
Pears, 78–79
Peppers, 75–76
Perceived impropriety, and purchasing standards, 54
Performance and result evaluation, 241–243
Perishable food specifications, 59–60
Pheasant, 175–176
Pierre Robert cheese, 88
Pigeon, 177
Pods, 69–73
Pompano, 192
Porgy, 192
Pork
   belly and spare ribs, 140–142
   Boston butt, 137, 140
   classifications, 94
   ham, 134–136
   loin, 137
   market forms, 134
   market items, 142, 145
   offals, 142,145
   picnic, 140
   pork carcass breakdown, 133–134
   primal cuts, 134
   primal loin, 137
   quality and yield grading, 99
Pork baby back ribs, 137
Pork belly and spare ribs, 140–142
   HRI cuts, 143–144
Pork Boston butt, 137, 140
Pork carcass breakdown, 133–134
   market forms, 134
   primal cuts, 134
Pork chops, 137
Pork ham, 134–136
   NAMP HRI cuts for, 136
Pork loin, 135–139
   HRI cuts for pork loin, 138–139
Pork offals and market items, 142–143
Pork picnic, 140
   HRI cuts, 142
Pork primal loin, 137
   baby back ribs, 137
   pork chops, 137
Portion cuts, 102–103

Potatoes, 70
Poultry
   chicken, 160–164
   classifications, 95
   duck, 165–168
   goose, 168–171
   quality and yield grading, 97–98
   turkey, 171–174
Primal cuts, 102
Produce purchasing, 60–85
   *See* Fresh produce
Produce refrigeration, 207
Product specifications, 58–60
Professional competence, and purchasing standards, 55
Purchasing food
   buying local, 262–263
   cheese, 85–89
   fish, 179–197
   fresh produce, 60–85
   history of, 3–26
   meat and poultry, 92–179
   menu planning, 57–58
   product specifications, 58–60
   standards, 54–57
Purple Basil, 77

**Q**
Quail, 177
Quality and yield grading, 96–101
Queso Fresco, 87

**R**
Rabbit, 153
   HRI cuts for, 156
Reciprocity, and purchasing standards, 55
Red Chard, 64
Red Drum, 192
Red Leaf Lettuce, 63
Reducing carbon footprint, 270–271
Refrigeration, 204–209
   dairy and cheese, 207–208
   dry storage, 210
   fish and seafood, 206
   meat and poultry, 205
   produce, 207
   special needs storage, 210–211
Responsibilities to your employer, and purchasing, 54
Retail discount store, 104
Rhubarb, 66
Rinds, types of, 86–87
   artificial rinds, 87
   bloomy rinds, 86
   fresh cheese, 86
   natural rind, 86
   washed rinds, 86
Rome, 9–11
Roots, 69
Round Carrots, 69

**S**
Sablefish, Black Cod, 192
Salmon, 192–194
Sanitation, 211–213
Sardines, 194
Saturn Peaches, 82
Savoy Cabbage, 65
Scallions, 68
Sea urchin, 185

Seafood, purchasing specs, 178–197
Seasonality, 269–270
Shellfish, 179–185
   crab, 183
   lobster, 184
   mollusks, 181–183
   shrimp, 179–181
Shrimp, 179–181
Shrimp counts, 180
Skate, 194
Slow Food Movement, 274
Small equipment, 246–252
   inventory list, 248
   rental, 250–252
   sourcing, 247–250
Snapper, 194
Social responsibility, and purchasing, 55
Sockeye, 193
Sole, 195
Specialty product vendors, 33–35
Squash, 76–77
Squid, 184
Stalks and other vegetables, 66
Standards, 54–57
Steamship Round, 109
Stone fruit, 82–83
Storeroom function, 199–201
Storeroom operations, 200–201
Storeroom and receiving facility layout, 201–211
   basic floor plan, 202
   example of proper receiving specs, 203
   refrigeration, 204–209
Striped Bass, 187
Strong stinky cheese, 89
Sturgeon, 195
Subprimal cuts
   beef chuck, 118
   beef primal loin, 110
   beef rib, 115
   beef round, 107
   veal legs, 122
   veal loin, 126, 128
   veal square cut shoulder, 130
Supervision of duties, 240
Supplier relationships, and purchasing, 54
Sustainability, 271–274
   and purchasing, 55
Swordfish, 196

T
Tautog, Blackfish, 187
Thinking greener, 277–278
Tilapia, 196
Tilefish, 196
Tomatoes, 74–75
Top round, 109
Transportation, 22–23
Trends in the industry, *See* Industry trends
Tropical fruits, 84–85
Trout, 196
Tubers, 69
Tuna, 196
Turbot, 197
   Turkey, 171–174
   processed cooked turkey products, 171
   purchasing specifics, 171, 172–173

V
Veal, 121–133
   carcass breakdown, 121–122
   classifications, 94
   hotel rack, 127–129
   legs, 122–126
   loin, 126–127
   offals, 132–133
   quality and yield grading, 97–98
   square cut shoulder, 129–132
Veal boneless strip loin, 126
Veal bottom and eye round, knuckle, 126
Veal breast, 131
Veal carcass breakdown, 121–122
Veal fore shank, 131
Veal hotel rack, 127–129
   subprimals or HRI cuts, 128, 130
   veal rack, 128–129
Veal leg top round, 126
Veal legs, 122–126
   bottom and eye round, knuckle, 126
   leg top round, 126
   shank, 126
   subprimals or HRI cuts, 122, 124–125
Veal loin, 126–127
   subprimal/HRI cuts, 126, 128
   veal boneless strip loin, 126
   veal shortloin or loin chops, 126
   veal tenderloin, 127
Veal offals, 132–133
Veal rack, 128–129
Veal shank, 126
Veal shortloin or loin chops, 126
Veal shoulder clod, 131
Veal square cut shoulder, 129–132
   veal breast and veal fore shank, 131
   veal shoulder clod, 131
   subprimals or HRI cuts, 130, 132
Veal tenderloin, 127
Vendor evaluation form, 32
Vendor relationships, 29–51
   accurate bidding, 42–43
   establishing, 31–35
   evaluation form, 32
   financial considerations, 36–37
   service considerations, 35–36
   specialty product vendors, 33–35
   as viable, 41–43
   win-win philosophy, 37–41
Venison, 156–158
   NAMP HRI cuts for, 159–160

W
Washed rinds, 86
Wild boar, 153–156
   NAMP HRI cuts for, 157
Wall-to-wall financial count controls, 240–241
Win-win philosophy, 37–41
   competitive bidding, 40–41
   operational consultants, 38
   supporting local businesses, 39–40
Wolf fish, 197

Y
Yellowfin, 197